# GOD IN THE STADIUM

# GOD IN THE STADIUM

## Sports and Religion in America

Robert J. Higgs

THE UNIVERSITY PRESS OF KENTUCKY

Copyright © 1995 by The University Press of Kentucky

Scholarly publisher for the Commonwealth,
serving Bellarmine College, Berea College, Centre
College of Kentucky, Eastern Kentucky University,
The Filson Club, Georgetown College, Kentucky
Historical Society, Kentucky State University,
Morehead State University, Murray State University,
Northern Kentucky University, Transylvania University,
University of Kentucky, University of Louisville,
and Western Kentucky University

*Editorial and Sales Offices:* The University Press of Kentucky
663 South Limestone Street, Lexington, Kentucky 40508-4008

**Library of Congress Cataloging-in-Publication Data**

Higgs, Robert J., 1932–
    God in the stadium : sports and religion in America/Robert J. Higgs.
      p.     cm.
    Includes bibliographical references and index.
    ISBN 0–8131–1923–5 (alk. paper).–ISBN 0–1831–0853–5
    (pbk. : alk. paper)
      1. Sports–United States–Religious aspects–Christianity.
    2. College sports–United States–Religious aspects–Christianity.
    3. United States–Social life and customs.    I.  Title.
    GV706.42.H54   1995
    796'.01–dc20                     95–8999

This book is printed on acid-free recycled paper meeting
the requirements of the American National Standard
for Permanence of Paper for Printed Library Materials.

To

Reny,
Julia,
Laura,
Ed,
Beck,
Ray,
Kathy,
and Bob

"He [man] cannot even invent a religion and keep it intact;
circumstances are stronger than he and all his works.
Circumstances and conditions are always changing,
and they always compel him to modify his religions
to harmonize with the new situation."

*Mark Twain in Eruption 67*

# Contents

# Preface

The impetus for this book goes back to my boyhood in rural middle Tennessee in the late forties, when neighboring women chastised me and teammates for taking up baseball on Sunday afternoons. They also criticized my father, who on Sunday mornings sat silently in the congregation of Higgs Methodist Chapel in Anes Station (population twenty-one) and on Sunday afternoons gladly gave his pasture to baseball. He even tipped, illegally I suppose, the operator of the county road grader to scrape off a diamond for us, which we kept in beautiful shape by throwing the cow manure aside with corn scoops and dragging the diamond regularly with a crosstie pulled by a jeep. A former center for the University of Tennessee football team (1921), my father, listed as "Kelly" in pictures of that team, was determined that we would have a good place to play. He made a field for us, and people came.

The only sad part was the unending objection of some of the women, who accused the ball players and my father of breaking the Sabbath commandment. When I asked one of the women what she thought we should do on Sunday, she answered quickly, "Why, what you're supposed to do on Sunday afternoons: stay home, read the Bible, pray, and seek God's forgiveness. That's how you keep the Sabbath holy!" At the time I thought she was crazy; now, seeing the bizarre excesses in sports, I know she had a point. Over the years I have come to respect her more without loving my father less.

My father was not a pious man, but in his own ways he helped satisfy the diverse longings of the human soul. He was a Protestant in the backwoods of the Bible Belt practicing the ancient pagan and Catholic virtue of *eutrapelia*, "well-turningness" (see Rahner 100-102), without ever having heard the term, worshiping on Sunday morning and enjoying baseball in the afternoon. He was a Methodist practicing the Westminster Catechism: "The chief end of man is to glorify God and enjoy him forever." He and some of my neighbors knew, I believe, that worship was not play nor was play a form of worship. Unsophisticated as we were, we knew that there was a vast distinction between natural gifts and gifts of the spirit, between the fruits of talent and the fruits of the spirit; and in that isolated pocket of the world we would have been dumbfounded by efforts to equate them like those we see every day in our supposedly enlightened age.

In addition to my father I want to mention another wonderful individual, W.B. "B" Cooper, a dear friend of my father. As operator of the store in Anes Station, superintendent of the Sunday School, sponsor of our ball team, and even manager for a while, he too came under some criticism for his involvement in Sunday ball. He was also the uncle of Tom Hearn Jr., who used to spend part of his summers in our village. Now as president of Wake Forest University, Hearn has been a voice of sanity in efforts to reform college athletics (see Alexander). How much his attitudes toward sports were shaped by his Uncle "B" I don't know. I can only say that for myself those Sundays now seem almost Edenic, starting with church and Sunday School, Sunday dinner, baseball in the afternoon, a replay at "B's" store with cold drinks, and then a dip (and bath) in the blue hole. Like the rest of the world, our village had its problems, but in the relationship between sports and religion I've rarely seen such sanity, thanks to Bob, my father, and "B." There was never a word from them about the moral character of baseball or its relation to God and Country. Baseball was fun and that was sufficient. I have been pretty much stunned ever since by the other purposes that sports have been made to serve.

Our play came after our work. Thoreau writes in *Walden* that this is the proper time for it to occur: "A stereotyped but unconscious despair is concealed even under what are called the games and amusements of mankind. There is no play in them, for this comes after work. But it is a characteristic of wisdom not to do desperate things" *(Thoreau* 111). Rank amateurs or true lovers of the game, we were, I suspect, wiser than we knew. Today work and play often become indistinguishable, as in professional sports, without always exhibiting the baleful symptoms noted by Thoreau. If George Will wants to call baseball players "men at work," that is fine with me. I have no quarrel with this merging of work and play and even see happy possibilities in the result. I am less sanguine about the strange coalition that has emerged between organized sports and organized religion.

Shortly after becoming aware of a conflict between organized sports and organized religion, especially on Sunday—a conflict that now has all but vanished in the wake of "sportianity," as Frank Deford has called muscular Christianity—I learned of a schism in Christianity itself. At church my mother and May Turner would try to select and play hymns focusing on the softer, more reflective side of belief, such as "Take Time to be Holy" and "Savior, Like a Shepherd Lead Us." How different in meaning were these from "Onward Christian Soldiers," which the Naval Academy Band played regularly on Sunday mornings as I and other Protestant members of the Brigade of Midshipmen marched into chapel in uniform and white gloves before droves of smiling, taxpaying tourists. This is religion as theater, religion on parade. Later, reading Hans Kung, I came to understand that these different hymns and different forms of worship were manifestations of the two basic movements within Protestantism, the mystical and the prophetic (evangelical). While the meditative side of Protestantism has diminished, the energetic side has flourished, renewing in the electric age its questionable old ties with sports and conservative politics.

For many years now I have been wondering just what the relationship between sports and religion should be in our culture. There seem to be several options:

1. Sports are a form of adiaphora (things indifferent), a theological concept that would mean that sports have no effect on cultural values and deserve little consideration.
2. Sports belong entirely to what Howard Cosell called the Toy Department of life, not really a serious part of our lives but nevertheless with a value worth holding on to.
3. Sports, as Robert Frost proclaimed, lie near the soul of culture, displaying and even proving all that we hold dear.

The history of the relationships between religion, sports, and education leads me to suspect that the answer might be "all of the above," depending on the context; but others seem to believe that sports parallel or even join religion in significance. All this needs further study.

Looking back, I realize that this book, so long in the making, is nothing more nor less than the study of the sometimes contradictory influences upon my life: Christianity, sports, education, and the military. These have also been major influences, I have come to realize, upon Western civilization and American culture. The relationships among them at present, however—especially those between major sports and evangelical religion—are so skewed as to constitute a heresy.

Because of the nature of this book I wish to emphasize that the views expressed herein are my own and do not necessarily reflect those of institutions or friends who have assisted me in its preparation. In am in the debt of Fred Borchuck, director of the Charles Sherrod Library at East Tennessee State University, and of the library staff, especially David Parsley (Acquisitions), Dorothy Jones and Claudette York (Circulation), Carol Norris (Online Searching), Rollie Harwell (Periodicals), and Mark Ellis and Rita Sher (Reader Services). I could not have completed this project without the almost daily generous assistance of Beth Hogan (Interlibrary Loan) over a long period of time.

I wish to thank the Research Development Council of East Tennessee State University for the splendid services of research assistants Elaine Stephens and her successor, George Buck, during the academic year 1987–88. On his own time George also read the manuscript and made several suggestions. Later, at my request, he served as my personal editor and helped to sustain me in my effort by his skills, his extensive knowledge of literature and philosophy, and by his friendship. I am grateful to the Department of English for the services of Douglas Powell and John Perry.

I would like to thank other friends as well. My neighbor Charles Gunter was a steady source of bibliographic material on sports in general, and Don Johnson, editor of *Aethlon: The Journal of Sport Literature*, and Lyle Olsen, managing editor, enlightened me on several aspects of this subject. Drake Bush and Mick Davenport have often sent me articles on sports and related topics. Ron Giles and Bonny Stanley have frequently mentioned works of interest to me, and Styron Harris, chair of the Department of English, has provided numerous leads on English sports culture and muscular Christianity. Fred Norris of the Emmanuel School of Religion has generously responded to my request for commentary or interpretation on scriptural passages, and Ralph Turner has provided considerable insight into the nature of Nazi sport. Many thanks go to Dick Crepeau for his penetrating commentary. My mentor of many years, Neil Isaacs, as always, has cheered me on.

Portions of chapters of this book have appeared in *Tennessee Folklore Society Bulletin* and *The Transcendentalist Spirit: Proceedings of the Virginia Humanities Conference, 1991.* I am grateful for permission to reprint the material here.

As always I wish to thank Reny, my wife, for support in all manner of ways and to my daughters, Julia and Laura, too. I am grateful, too, to Ruth Tapp and the English office staff at East Tennessee State University for their endurance in helping to bring this project to a conclusion. In particular, I wish to pay special tribute to Deanna Bryant, who typed endless versions of the manuscript on the computer. I am eternally grateful for her unwavering help and encouragement.

# From Sabbath Bans to Super Sunday

Wherever we look in American society we see links between sports and religion and even the confusion of one with the other. These activities, which are at once social and individual and may be universal to all cultures, share a history in our own heritage. But they are not the same activities; they have different purposes and are carried out in different ways and usually at different times. At some points in our past they have seemed at odds, but recently, and increasingly, they have served one another and have become almost inseparable. This alliance has in the view of some been good for both. I will contend that sports and religion—I will mostly be thinking of Christianity—are in many ways incompatible. I would even argue that the ways in which modern sports have become entangled with religious practices constitute a (Christian) heresy, though this book will not focus on an argument for this judgment. Here attention will be given to the evolution in the United States of the general acceptance of sports as an appropriate partner to religion, to the history of their connection, and to the personalities and attitudes that led us to the present situation. Since educational institutions have been a primary setting for the development of what seems to me the religion of sports, some history of education must also be included. I am neither theologian nor historian and will not attempt a complete analysis or history. I can only hope that others will add to and correct my understanding. Yet I feel confident that we must seek to eliminate the confusion between sports and religion and confident also that additional study will only further verify my perception of the dangers of linking them as we now do.

On Christmas Day, 1621, Governor William Bradford of Plymouth rebuked the young men he found "in ye streets at play, openly; some pitching ye ball and some at stooleball, and such like sports." In the governor's view, there should not have been "any gameing or revelling in ye streets," nor, if we can judge from the notorious incident of the Maypole of Merry Mount, any reveling in the country either. "Had the leaders at Plymouth, Salem, and Boston been in Parliament in 1643, they would have voted with the majority that all copies of the *Book of Sports* be seized and burned" (Krout 10). This book, issued by James I of England on 29 May 1618, identified recreations that were permissible on "the Sabbath, after the end of 'Divine Services' " : these included dancing, archery, leaping, vaulting, and other "harmless recreation" but not bear- or bullbaiting (R.W. Henderson, *King's Book* 540)

From his pulpit in October 1987, Jerry Falwell, one of the strongest voices of religious conviction in the contemporary United States, praised Kelvin Edwards, a graduate of Falwell's Liberty University in Lynchburg, Virginia, for his play in the Cowboys' victory over the Eagles. Edwards expressed some surprise: "Dr. Falwell said that he announced my name in church and . . . everybody started cheering in church. I said, 'Wait a minute! People cheering for me in church?' " The Cowboys' coach, Tom Landry, didn't seem to mind the apparent incongruity. Told of Falwell's interest in his team, Landry said, "We'll take all the help we can get" ("Is Falwell a Cowboy Fan?" 37). For the spring 1988 graduation speaker at Liberty, Falwell chose former Annapolis boxer and Marine hero Oliver North. When asked why he chose an indicted man, Falwell made a comparison with the Divine: "We serve a savior who was indicted and convicted and crucified" ("North Address" 8). In September 1989 Falwell stated that his greatest challenge in sports is to make Liberty University to Baptists what

Notre Dame is to Catholics and Brigham Young is to Mormons (D. Becker 1C).

Clearly something has changed in the relationship between sports and religion in our society. As I will try to suggest, the seventeenth-century Puritans were already moving toward more recent attitudes, but they made distinctions between sports and religion that we have now almost forgotten. They recognized, for one thing, some of the differences between sports and play. It is not my purpose to disparage sports or mythologize play, but I do hope to begin to show that certain aspects of sports make them unsuitable for an alliance with religion. In this book, *sports* will mean athletic competition for an extrinsic cultural *prize*, in contrast to *play*, the indulgence in physical or mental activity for an intrinsic natural *gift* (not to be confused, at least in my mind, with what have been called spiritual gifts). It may be impossible to separate sports and play completely, but important differences exist between them, at least in the abstract. In sports we *compete* with nature and others (and on occasion with ourselves); in play we commune with nature and others (and possibly ourselves). To be sure, we may do all these in the same event, since sports and play seem invariably to overlap. Religion, at least in a formal sense, is *communion* with others and/or with a transcendent Being in acts of prayer, song, and worship. If we asked what *competition* with God would be, one answer, taken from the old language of belief, whose tradition I will at least partly assume, is "heresy." (Sin in the traditional definition is not competition with God's word or order but disobedience, recognized as such either before, during, or after the act.) I take the difference between competition and communion to be clear and significant: play seems to me more innocent and thus more Edenic.

The difference between sports and play has been studied before, though not in the ways I will try to do here. Closely associated with this difference is a contrast between two archetypes of religious response to the world. Western history in large measure can be viewed as the transformation of the ideal of the Good Shepherd into the Christian Knight, of a social and nature gospel emphasizing play and festival into a gospel of wealth and worldly success emphasizing competition and conquest. Rarely have swords been beaten into plowshares; the usual pattern has been the recruitment of peasants and plowboys into wars, usually directed at a foreign "other," started by ruling, self-appointed heroes exhibiting the invidious traits of a leisure class. The shepherd's purpose is to nurture and protect; the knight's is to dominate and, it must be admitted, also to protect—at least that is often the claim made. In practice, the knight spends his time pillaging and plundering in foreign lands, triggering combat with a set of knights of some other persuasion or belief, who in turn wish to conquer and loot. The transformation of shepherds into knights becomes the tactic and temptation of all sides.

One key aspect of a knightly vision is a definition of success that seems to emphasize accumulation of goods and recognition of excellence defined through established practices. Knights attempt to achieve distinction from (and power over) others by displays of skill and accomplishment, sometimes called victory. By such means knights hope, perhaps, to demonstrate and verify their beliefs and attitudes, as if their success proved the rightness and completeness of their understanding of the world. By contrast, success for shepherds is more local and limited, more attuned to maintaining community. In religious terms a Good Shepherd tends the flock with meekness and kindness aspiring to a wisdom that accepts its restrictions while yearning for the "peace that passeth understanding." Knights train constantly for conflict and competition. Shepherds can be heroes, of course, but such status is not sought, nor is it celebrated, as a confirmation of desert. Shepherds do not collect trophies. Shepherds can also be violent, but theirs is a violence in the service of defense and harmony.

The categories are not pure, and thus knights have always held to shepherd values in some measure, partly by claiming to have two hearts (or faces), an unpitying one for abroad and a compassionate one for home. The home or watchdog heart, of course, expects obedience and approval by the "sheep" it guards, or else it quickly hardens, turning against its own as if they were the other. The soft heart of the knight is often a ruse, a self-deception concealing a single vision of domination and control. It is worth noting that the word *violence* comes from the Latin word for strength. A Latin phrase, *mens sana in corpore sano* (usually translated as "a sound mind in a sound body"), will also be important for studying the evolution of our knightly and sporting religion, with its emphasis on the whole person who heroically combines reason and strength in a model of complete (and certain) health—a model that is essentially male/manly. The recently developed contrast by some feminists between an ethics of justice and an ethics of care has clear affinities to the knight-shepherd pair. It should be remembered, however, that even a culture that would seem to be ordered around an ethics of care and affiliation might still exploit and devalue women and might still develop a knightly class. While men are the primary subjects here and manliness is a major theme, I am not advancing the argument that the qualities of knight or shepherd, good or bad, belong exclusively to males. In the cult of the hero, however, where "winning is the only thing," there is little room for traditionally feminine virtues like humility, limitation, or moderation, and almost no room for pity or tenderness.

While the archetypes of knight and shepherd must remain idealizations that are rarely if ever fully embodied in any single individual or society, our history has traced a steady movement away from the virtues and values that I would associate with shepherds toward the structures of a knightly worldview. Characteristics of both can easily be found in the fragments and possibilities of real lives. Nevertheless, society has endorsed knighthood and has accepted its attitudes with little question, especially in the modern period. One might even claim that this movement defines modernity.

In American history this evolution is clear. In the land that became the United States, Christian manliness has been a dominant symbol in five distinct but overlapping phases. The first is the colonial or Reformation phase, in which new Protestant knighthood was transferred from the Old World to the New, as seen in the examples of John Smith and Miles Standish, friend of the Puritans, inaugurating a three-hundred-year conflict, often taking the form of war with native heathens or "savages." (Cortés, the old Catholic knight, directed his attention to Central and South America). The second phase is the revolutionary or national, justified by belief in divine decree and manifest destiny, in which American-born knights and athletic heroes such as Nathan Hale emerged as models of manly courage in the struggle to lift the yoke of "foreign" oppression. Next comes a Hellenic or classic period, lasting through the Civil War: in the name of that ancient formula for health and education–"sound mind, sound body"–drills, exercises, and athletics were established (and consecrated) in schools, colleges, and academies, especially West Point. The fourth might be called High Roman or imperial, lasting from the Spanish-American War through the war in Vietnam, a period in which Theodore Roosevelt first and Douglas MacArthur later used sports as the manly symbol for America's entry on the world stage as a major power. The fifth is the Low Roman or "bread and circuses" phase, in which sports simultaneously serve the purposes of entertainment, religious proselytism, pacification of the masses, and political propaganda, still under the banner of Christian knighthood, as seen in the stadium revivals of Billy Graham and the sporting enthusiasm of Presidents Nixon, Ford, Carter, Reagan, Bush, and Clinton, all noted fans. Sports and Christianity have followed similar paths. In the beginning they were nationalized, then Hellenized, Romanized, and in our own time televised.

Not one of these phases is without some virtue and value, but the warpings of each have been transferred to succeeding phases, so that our national orthodoxy has become tilted far toward the sword of honor and conquest and away from the staff of care and toleration. Just as evolving stages of knighthood tend perhaps toward a completion of the corruptions essential to its form, so individuals may demonstrate a wide range of involvements and a mixture of attitudes. Nevertheless, the vision that has come to dominate our culture is knightly. And the American shepherds, such as Henry David Thoreau and John Muir, who exemplified a gospel of stewardship, and Martin Luther King Jr., who emphasized a social gospel in the workplace far more than salvation in the stadium, remain for the most part marginalized if not forgotten. From the beginning of our nation until now, we have moved toward an almost universal neglect of an excellence of being, opting instead for an excellence of doing. Recent grand knights and heroes like Hitler and Stalin should have alerted us to the inherent dangers and malevolence of such a stance. Instead, we have tried to counter such knighthood with our own, striving always to be number one, to win at any cost, with sports and religion cheering us on.

Sports and play among the American colonists was a complex matter. They were neither as rigid nor as narrow in their attitudes as we have often made them appear. While "the passengers of the *Mayflower* anchored in Plymouth harbor lacked compensation of sports or fireside warmth" (Marble 3), they soon became adept in sport—hunting and fishing—not for purposes of leisure but out of necessity. Far more of our culture may have come from the Indians than we realize: from them the Pilgrims learned New World gardening, fishing, and hunting. Squanto showed the men how to plant herring as fertilizer and the boys and girls how to gather clams and mussels and how to "tread eels." "The friendly Indians assisted the men, as the seasons opened, in hunting wild turkeys, ducks, and an occasional deer" (ibid., 23). The Pilgrims and the later Puritans had little time for sports as amusement, whatever their inclinations. The sports they cultivated—wrestling and skill in the use of broadsword and quarterstaff—were, like gardening, fishing, and hunting, geared toward survival not recreation, as was the case with the ancient Israelites (in contrast to the Greeks, who engaged in sports for personal distinction). Martial sports were appreciated because of their obvious value in combat.

Among a wide range of Puritan opinions about play was a "detestation of idleness," which has come to be regarded as a major Puritan trait. H.L. Mencken characteristically described the stereotype when he defined Puritanism as "the haunting fear that someone sometime might be happy" (223). The same trenchant humor was reflected earlier in the celebrated remark of Macaulay that the Puritans stopped bearbaiting not because of cruelty to the bear but because of the pleasure it afforded spectators (Dulles 9). The repulsion that many Puritans felt toward bearbaiting seems to be quickly dismissed in order to make them look as repressive as possible.

The culprit behind the myth of total Puritan antipathy to recreation has been identified as Samuel Peters, author of *A General History of Connecticut* published in London in 1781. In 1774 Peters was forced to leave Connecticut because of his conservative political views. Like Twain's "man that corrupted Hadleyburg," he got his revenge not just upon a town but upon an entire colony and Puritans everywhere. "In 1656 Governor Eaton had compiled a list of the New Haven Colony laws which Peters then enlarged by a considerable number of falsified 'blue laws,' which—according to him—existed before 1656 but were never codified" (Wagner 141). Here are some of the more famous of the "blue laws" or "bloody laws" that were never published, according to Peters:

> No one shall run on the sabbath day, or walk in his garden or elsewhere, except reverently to and from meeting.
>
> No woman shall kiss her child on the Sabbath or fasting day.
>
> No one shall read Common-Prayer, keep Christmas or Saintsdays, make minced pies, dance, play cards, or play on any instrument of music, except the drum, trumpet, or jewsharp. [Peters 58-59]

At Yale College, according to Peters, students were allowed "two hours of play with foot-ball every day," but otherwise "cooped up for four years" so that "they understand books better than men or manners" (ibid., 157). The Reverend Timothy Dwight of Yale called Peters's book "a mass of folly and falsehood," understandably perhaps missing some of Peters's efforts at humor. Furthermore, no less an authority than Constance Rourke wryly observes that the book is "not quite historical" (153).

Stereotypes, it must be admitted, contain an element of truth, and the Puritans no doubt were in some instances guilty as charged by Mencken, Macaulay, and Peters. Historical records do reflect a suspicion of recreation that today strikes us as ludicrous. Indeed, when prevailing modern attitudes are considered along with those of the salad days of the country, the picture is one of almost total contrast. For the Puritans, sports had little, if any, connection with religion except indirectly as a means of training for defense of a theocracy, and sports on Sunday were generally unthinkable, especially among the clergy. Today sports and religion have been sanctified in a holy union that would have stunned not only the Puritans such as William Bradford and Cotton Mather but also rationalists of the eighteenth century such as Thomas Jefferson and Benjamin

Franklin. Indeed, our own excesses match their extremes, so that we often seem as comically off center as they themselves were in their narrowest frames of mind. Nothing better illustrates the dramatic changes in American culture than the full pendulum swing of attitudes over the centuries toward sports and play.

In America the colonists did what they could to control sports by bans to match those in England. In 1647 in Massachusetts Bay a court order was issued against shuffleboard, and in 1650 an injunction was extended against "bowling or any other play or games in or about houses of common entertainment" (Manchester 16). In 1693 in eastern Connecticut a man "was fined twelve shillings and sentenced to six hours in the stocks for playing ball on the Sabbath" (Twombly 18).

Interdicts were not confined to New England by any means. In Virginia in 1619 "the assembly decreed that any person found idle should be bound over to compulsory work; it prohibited gaming at dice or cards, strictly regulated drinking, provided penalties for excess in apparel and rigidly enforced Sabbath observance." Decrees against racing within the city limits of New Amsterdam were issued in 1657, and two years later Governor Peter Stuyvesant proclaimed a day of fasting on which would be forbidden "all exercise and games of tennis, ball-playing, hunting, fishing, plowing, and sowing, and moreover all unlawful practices such as dice, and drunkenness" (Manchester 17). Attitudes toward sports in early America strengthen the observation of Perry Miller that in about 90 percent of their culture and religion there was no difference between Puritans and their fellow Englishmen of the seventeenth century. The Puritans, though, became the representative figures of narrow-mindedness and intolerance.

The examples could be multiplied, but to do so would only reinforce a negative stereotype neither fair nor fruitful (see "In Detestation of Idleness," in Dulles). Here the concern is not merely the Puritans' suspicion of sports but also the sanctification of sports in our own age. Perhaps the best-known modern ministry with the largest following is led by Billy Graham, one of the one hundred most "influential" people of the twentieth century according to *Life Magazine*. His crusades are international, his acceptance of sports characteristic of the modern church. Thus on New Year's Day, 1971, Graham led the Rose Bowl Parade, justifying his action by a peculiar interpretation of Scripture on leisure: "The Bible says leisure and lying around are morally dangerous for us. . . . Sports keep us busy; athletes you notice don't take drugs." (No one could be so innocent about drugs today.) Graham went on to say that St. Paul was an avid sports fan because he used so many illustrations from the Olympics in his letters ("Are Sports Good for the Soul?" 51).

God's wisdom, as we all know, is hard to come by, but God's strength in the Church of Sports has been breaking out all over. Evangelist Michael Crain of Chattanooga, for example, practiced " 'Karate for Christ' by splitting 10 inches of concrete with his hand in a demonstration of 'God's power.' 'There is,' said Crain, 'Communist power, black power, white power, and red power. But the greatest is God's power' " (ibid.). Just as Crain broke concrete slabs for Christ, so Paul Anderson, once billed as the world's strongest man, engaged in "Lifting to the Lord." *Christian Century,* says Lester Kinsolving, is quite right when it warns: "Don't challenge him—you might end up with a 'Rupture for Religion' " (10). Carrying on in this mighty tradition is the Power Team, a group of seven bodybuilders headed by John Jacobs, an accomplished weight lifter. Speaking out against drugs, teen suicide, family abuse, and the occult, Jacobs and the Power Team back up their words by awesome displays of strength, Jacobs snapping forty baseball bats over his thighs to the accompaniment of Christian singer Carman's song "The Champion." Another member, Keith Davis, a former college linebacker, runs headlong into a wall of ice, shattering it over the stage. "There's nothing wrong with drama if it's honest," Jacobs says. "A lot of churches are trying to reach young people with little games when Motley Crüe is next door with a laser show" (Pellis 4C). Ironically, Jack Butler seems closer to the traditional scriptural method of aligning strength and wisdom in his sad but funny book entitled *Jujitsu for Christ.* Roger, the protagonist, felt that "jujitsu was closer to the heart of things than karate was. This feeling was based on what he perceived as the more meditative, less aggressive nature of jujitsu. It was more Christian" (52).

The sports-religion connection is not a one-way street of evangelists reaching out to the world of sports; just as often sport-loving politicians, actors, and musicians seek to bless the alliance with their own charisma and fame. Ronald Reagan wrote the foreword to *Norman Rockwell's Patriotic Time,* which reminds viewers that sports and religion remain pillars of patriotism. In a similar but more violent view, the champion in a Sylvester Stallone Rocky movie prays in the corner before knocking out the evil Russian. Hulk Hogan wears a gold cross and says before Wrestlemania events that he bows to no man except "the Dude who walked on water." The sporting dramatization of Christianity is also reflected in popular music, though not without some humor, as seen in Glen Campbell's "I Knew Jesus before He Was a Superstar," Bobby Bare's "Drop Kick Me Jesus through the Goal Posts of Life," Ray Stevens's "Would Jesus Wear a Rolex on His Television Show?" and Carman's "The Champion." In the last, in a tart response to a threat from Satan, Jesus quotes Clint Eastwood: "Go ahead, make my day." Just as Jesus quotes movie stars in our popular culture so Santa Claus on occasion becomes a rabid sports fan, showing his true colors. During the Christmas holiday season of 1994 a Santa in Florida, according to television reports, challenged the father of a little boy to a fight over the upcoming Florida-Florida State football game!

In her article "The Lord and the Locker Room" Jane Leavy says that sporting ministries are "a regular growth industry":

> There are ministries for drag racers, Brazilian soccer players, power lifters and rodeo clowns. Athletes for Life sends jocks to antiabortion rallies.... Christ-like Living Ministries ... publishes materials dealing with how Jesus would coach in various athletic situations. ...

> The International Sports Coalition, formed in 1986, is an umbrella group representing more than 50 ministries.... Coalition officials count more than 100 sports ministries worldwide and say they all haven't been identified yet.

> There are missionary ministries and publishing ministries. Watson Spoelstra, a former sportswriter who founded Baseball Chapel, publishes a monthly newsletter called "Closer Walk: A Christian Sports Insider." The Logo is a sneaker and a sandal connected by their laces. [D8]

Today a baseball clinic can be an opportunity for testifying. A church in Akron, Ohio, held an event at which members of the Cleveland Indians and Milwaukee Brewers provided instruction on hitting, fielding, and base running:

> Following the instructional segment of the program, the Little Leaguers assembled in the grandstand to hear some of the players—members of the Fellowship of Christian Athletes—speak about their personal religious beliefs. . . .
>
> When the players' personal testimonies were over, the Little Leaguers were invited to come down to the playing field—just like at a Billy Graham Crusade—to make their confession of faith, fill out a card and receive a free Bible. [Plagenz, "R-Rated" 9]

Although not everyone approves of this close association of religion and sports, as demonstrated by a father who objected to the baseball clinic and "to professional athletes who abuse their awesome influence on the young . . . using crowd psychology and coercion on them . . . sowing seeds of confusion and manipulating them" (ibid.), the relationship is strong and flourishing and usually taken for granted. No longer do stars just sign their autographs but often add a spiritual message as well: " 'I usually add Joshua 1:9 or PTL,' says pitcher Mike Moore. 'It means "praise the Lord" ' " (Swan B1).

As spiritual awakening becomes equated with worldly success, enlightenment with sliding effectively into second base, Jesus becomes more and more a model for athletic achievement. Says Brett Butler, "I believe if Jesus Christ was a baseball player, he'd go in hard to break up the double play and then pick up the guy and say, 'I love you.' " Sid Bream drew a finer distinction: "If a pitcher is taking a potshot at our batters, and I know he is, I would definitely do something about it. When Christ said to turn the other cheek, he wasn't talking about that" (ibid.). Dave Rowe, former all-pro defensive tackle and a devout Christian, would probably agree with Butler; in 1985 he suggested at the King College Super Bowl luncheon in Bristol, Tennessee, that "if Jesus Christ had been an athlete, he'd be the greatest ever" (Link). Jesus, as far as we know, was not an athlete, but Bill Heyen, as if he had read Rowe's remarks, wrote a poem called "Until Next Time":

If Jesus played football,
he'd be an end.
He'd lope out under the long, impossible passes,
cradle them in his arms,
or, if he had to, dive for them, his fingers
owning that space
between ball and ground.
On short routes, his sprints, feints
and precise cuts
would fake the defense out of their cleats;
on his feet, still running,
in a moment of communion
he'd knock off their helmets
with a stiff arm.
Once in for six,
he'd spike the old pigskin.
In that spot would sprout a rose.
By the time time ran out,
both end zones would bloom with roses
where we would wait for him.
After his shower, he'd appear to us
to pose with us for pictures by his side.
He'd ask us home for supper.
We'd glide from the stadium together,
until the next time—
happy, undefeated, unafraid—
if Jesus played football.
                [265]

Roy Blount Jr. claimed "that so many Christians had invaded big-time sports that when he set out to select an 'All-Religious Team' and an 'All-Heathen Team' to compete in an imaginary 'Christians vs. Lions Bowl' he couldn't find enough genuine heathens to field a squad" (Hoffman 67). In baseball Mike Royko was more successful in such an endeavor. Puzzled and perhaps even mildly offended by all the muscular ministry activity sweeping the nation, he along with Bill Veeck and George Vass put together an all-star team of "The Fellowship of Drinking, Brawling, Wenching and Gambling Athletes." For left field Royko chose the most famous of all, Babe Ruth (also, with Graham, one of *Life*'s hundred most influential people of the twentieth century). Royko, by the way, cautions young ballplayers about following the ways of his "impious team," saying they might wind up as sportswriters, but he also reminds them and us of a simple truth: "Religion or good have nothing to do with athletic excellence" (8A).

What easily gets lost in all the modern missionary hype is well summarized by Jack Saarela, former chairman of the Campus Ministry Cooperative at the University of Florida: "I have problems with ministries that parade winners up on a stage—athletes, entertainers. The implication is if you accept Christ, you can be a winner, too. It's not any more honest than Madison Avenue saying if you want to be a winning person, drink a certain beer. To me, Christianity is about a man who died on the cross. He was a loser. He appealed to the losers in society" (Leavy D8). The chair of a campus ministries cooperative is not apt to be taken too seriously by the public when he speaks of Jesus as a "loser" who appealed to "losers." Ted Turner, however, caused a furor in June 1990, when he made essentially the same remark. Baptists, especially, were outraged and demanded an apology, which Turner supplied on *Crossfire* and elsewhere, in effect admitting that Jesus was a real winner after all, just as victorious knights and athletes flying his banner had always believed. Winner/loser is a dichotomy that belongs principally to the world of Caesar, which Jesus made clear: "Not as the world giveth, give I unto you" (John 14:27, KJV).

Saarela, in describing Jesus as a loser, is speaking of the Man of Sorrows, but that is not the Jesus of Athletes in Action, the Fellowship of Christian Athletes, and other groups, whose Christ is the glorious, victorious resurrected God. Hence their message is optimistic and triumphant. Malcolm Boyd has observed, "Billy Graham says we should be selling Christ like soap. I don't think so. I think we should be trying to *act* like Christ. He never was a celebrity. Jesus Christ was the exact opposite of a superstar" (quoted in Deford 69).

Because success for organized Protestant religions is measured in numbers of souls saved or converts gained, the technique of conversion is no longer a simple matter of letting one's light shine before others but the subject of seminars on mass communications. Before the Olympics in 1988, the International Sports Coalition sponsored a World Congress on Sports to train pastors from participating nations. The courses included "How to Utilize Athletes as an

Effective Medium to Communicate the Gospel," "Practical Principles on How to Evangelize and Disciple Top Athletes," "How to Capitalize on the Opportunities the Media Provides for Sharing the Gospel," and "How to Minister in a Hostile Environment" (Leavy D8). In a later survey, James A. Mathisen pointed to the continuing growth of the movement, saying that "the press and public have struggled to make sense of the increasing number of elite athletes who proclaim their faith in Jesus." He added, "If [the April 1991] Annual Sports Outreach America conference on sports evangelism practitioners in Dallas is any indication of the strength of the movement, these athletes' activities and the publicity given them are not likely to decline soon" (11). As of Super Sunday 1995 the Sports Outreach program was moving along at flank speed (or perhaps flanker speed), distributing, in conjunction with Radio Bible Class, a twelve-minute video of religious testimony by NFL players shown on huge screens set up in churches for this purpose and for presentation of the game. Many "clergy across the country see Super Bowl Sunday as a super chance to score with non-believers. They also say it's a challenge to keep regulars from a one-week walkout" (Harvey).

One of the most extraordinary manifestations of the symbiotic relationship between sports and religion is the occasion and content of pregame prayers. It may be clear what Rocky is praying for, but this plethora of prayer only reveals the strangeness of the alliance, both public and private, Catholic and Protestant. Vince Lombardi, for example, was noted for prayers in the locker room. Perhaps Catholics are not as sedulous as Protestants in invoking divine blessings on games, but they seem more clever in the endeavor. The following invocation was delivered in the early 1970s:

> "Your Son is our quarterback and You are our coach," prayed Miami's Catholic Archbishop Coleman F. Carroll, while delivering the invocation for the Miami Dolphins–Atlanta Falcons football game.
>
> "We sometimes get blitzed by heavy sorrows or red-dogged by Satan," continued the Archbishop. "Teach us to run the right patterns in our life so that we will truly make a touchdown one

day through the heavenly gates, as the angels and saints cheer us on from the sidelines." [Kinsolving 10]

In reporting this notable invocation, the *National Catholic Reporter* added: "And when that final gun goes off, dear Lord, lead us out of the parking lot of life through the interchange of Purgatory, on the freeway of Heaven, with our fenders undented, our spirits undaunted and our metaphors untangled. Amen" (ibid., quoted).

In perhaps our most violent sport, boxing, prayer and religious symbolism have been part of the scene for years. "Floyd Patterson once credited the Lord with helping him to flatten Archie Moore to win the heavyweight championship. 'I could see his eyes go glassy as he fell back,' Patterson said, 'and I knew if he got up again it wouldn't do him any good. I just hit him again and the Lord did the rest' " (quoted in John Day, Hoffman 68). According to his manager, Gerry Cooney and he would recite the Lord's Prayer in unison before each fight after which the manager would say in "benedictory tones," " 'Let's go in there and get this man out of the way. Let's kick his butt' " (quoted in Michael Norman, ibid.). In an explanation of his miraculous comeback to knock out John Tate in the last round of the 1980 heavyweight championship fight, Mike Weaver "told reporters that he had been reciting the Twenty-third Psalm since the fourteenth round. Not only that, tucked inside his left shoe, apparently to cover all theological bases, was a star of David given to him by his pastor" (ibid.). In the view of Malcolm X, the 1964 heavyweight championship title bout between Sonny Liston and Muhammad Ali, then Cassius Clay, had special significance. " 'This fight is the truth,' Malcolm told Cassius. 'It's the Cross and the Crescent fighting in the prize ring—for the first time. It's a modern crusade—a Christian and a Muslim facing each other with television to beam it off Telstar for the whole world to see what happens' " (quoted in Schulberg 198). At present the heavyweight title belongs to a Christian minister, George Foreman. While Foreman's Christian faith may account for his irresistible good nature and sense of joy in living, like that of Ali, it would not seem to account for his secular victories any more than other religious beliefs of other champions account for theirs.

The religionizing of sport is not limited to the glare of our famous rings and arenas but widespread throughout the republic, as evident in football games in colleges and high schools as in boxing matches at "Caesar's Palace." More teams pray before competing than don't, according to William S. Flynn, athletic director at Boston College in 1985 (Monaghan 37). Obviously serious constitutional questions are raised, which is what happened at Marshall County High School in Lewisburg, Tennessee, where I graduated in 1949 and was captain of the football team in my senior year. At that time, pregame prayer either in the locker room or on the sidelines never entered anyone's head, though coaches and many players were church members. Yet in 1991 pregame prayers had become so commonplace that principal Roy Dukes had to issue a memorandum ordering them to be stopped in compliance with federal regulations. In response to the subsequent outcry, the Marshall County School Board ordered county principals to "use secularistic prayer or those which use 'in his name' rather than 'in Jesus' name.' " The *Lewisburg Tribune* carried an outraged opinion by editor Jamie Bone entitled "Stand Up for the Right to Pray." Said Bone, "The morally conscious citizens of this community must not idly sit by and allow immoral decisions by our government to be upheld." He added, "If you don't like what America stands for, leave it" (4). No mention was made of Matthew 6:6.

If the insistence on pregame prayer is a warping of the Gospel as well as the Constitution, which I believe to be the case, then there was in the controversy in Marshall County also a positive side easily overlooked. Roy Dukes, the principal, is black. If praying before a game was unthinkable in 1949, so was the idea of white students playing with or against blacks, much less having one for a teacher or principal. Two types of Christianity have operated in the United States, one that continually forces the issue of prayer in classrooms and at ballgames and the other that at least helped to provide Dukes the opportunity to become principal. One is a salvation gospel represented by the stadium crusade of Billy Graham, the other a social gospel represented by Martin Luther King Jr. The one seeks to bring prayer to the playing field for the purpose of proselytism, the other to bring justice to social space. The one likes to pray before the show of marching bands or the march of one team down the field against another. The other marches to bring attention to the need for civil rights. There is overlap in their purposes but differences between them. Heresy or warping occurs when the salvation gospel outweighs the need for the common good, when the knight triumphs over the shepherd. The law against pregame prayer is a universe away from the one that put blacks at the back of the bus.

This new alliance of sports and religion is changing the face of both so much that drawing a line between them is becoming increasingly difficult. Some of the thirteen remarkable parallels of Harry Edwards illustrate this:

> Sport also has its "saints"—those departed souls who in their lives exemplified and made manifest the prescriptions of the dogma of the sport.

> Sport also has its ruling patriarchs, a prestigious group of coaches, managers, and sportsmen who exercise controlling influence over national sports organizations.

> Sport has its "gods"—star and superstar athletes who, though powerless to alter their own situations, wield great influence and charisma over the masses of fans.

> Sport has its high councils, controlled or greatly influenced by patriarchs who make and interpret the rules of sports involvement.

> Sport has its scribes—the hundreds of sports reporters, sports telecasters, and sports broadcasters whose primary duties are to record the ongoing history of sports and to disseminate its dogma.

> Sport has its shrines—the national halls of fame and thousands of trophy rooms and cases gracing practically every sports organization's headquarters.

> Sport also has its own "houses of worship" spread across the land where millions congregate to bear witness to the manifestation of their faith.

> Sport has its "symbols of faith"—the trophies; game balls, the bats, gloves, baseballs, and so forth, that "won" this or that game; the clothing, shoes, headgear or socks of immortal personages of sports.

> Sport has its "seekers of the kingdom," its true believers, devotees and converts. [260–66]

Edwards is ironic and perhaps even satiric in the comparison he makes between sports and religion, but Charles S. Prebish, professor of religious studies at Pennsylvania State University, is entirely serious in his claim that sports and religion are one and the same: "For me, it is not just a parallel that is emerging between sport and religion, but rather a *complete identity. Sport is religion* for growing numbers of Americans, and this is no product of simply facile reasoning or wishful thinking. Further, for many, sport religion has become a more appropriate expression of personal religiosity than Christianity, Judaism, or any of the traditional religions" (25–26).

Michael Novak does not go so far, seeing sports as a natural religion with all the dignity previously accorded revealed religion. Sports, he argues, partake of the divine because they foster glorious abstractions: "*Being, beauty, truth, excellence, transcendence*–these words, grown in the soil of play, wither in the sand of work. Art, prayer, worship, love, civilization: These thrive in the field of play" (xii). Much depends upon definition, but such a statement is, I believe, heretical, though I am not recommending that Novak be excommunicated. I do recommend that he approach such topics as the "joy of sports" with at least some humor. Further, millions of people still find "being, beauty, truth, excellence, transcendence" in their work. Novak thus changes the old wisdom of "To labor is to pray" into "To play is to pray." (Jacques Sarano presents a sacramental view of work almost opposite to that of Novak.) While he himself obviously is a lover of sporting knights, especially those at Notre Dame, Novak should not be so quick to dismiss the old and sacred values of working shepherds, including urban shepherds such as Dorothy Day (see Diehl), Mitch Snyder, and Mother Teresa, who, I trust, found (or find) at least some love, truth, and transcendence in their "work."

In the solemnity with which he has elevated sports to sacramental status, Novak revealingly departs from the great literary tradition that through humor pointed to the gulf between natural and revealed religion rather than to their similarities. "Christian orthodoxy had, for centuries, presented its case for belief in a two-stage argument: natural religion, that which could be apprehended by natural human reason, and 'revealed religion,' that which could only be comprehended in divine terms. The great spokesmen for Christianity clearly recognized the distinction. Those who made use of humor in defense of Christian principles, like More, Erasmus, Swift, largely confined themselves to 'natural religion' because it was through such 'argument' that doubters could be swayed. 'Natural religion' was the prolegomenon to a recognition of the necessity of the revealed Word" (H.K. Miller 51). Whereas Novak has rhapsodized about "End Zones, Bases, Baskets, Balls, and the Consecration of the American Spirit," one can only wonder what Thomas More, Erasmus, and Jonathan Swift would have to say about this new "religion." Where is such playful genius now that we need it? Today the tone of those endorsing the Church of Sports is invariably pious and reverential. Only occasionally does a spoof on all this solemnity emerge, such as *The Non-Runner's Book* by Vic Ziegel and Lewis Grossberger. Like Calvin Coolidge, the authors "do not choose to run."

Prominent among the humorless champions of the natural, I-can-do-everything way have been George Leonard and George Sheehan, the subtitle of whose books (Leonard's *The Ultimate Athlete* and Sheehan's *On Running*) might be "Do You Have a Full-Length Mirror in Your Home?" In the old days Charles Atlas stopped trouble with muscles and the ability to defend himself on the beach against bullies, but modern body gurus extend self-help to cosmic proportions. In Leonard's view the ultimate athlete is an ultimate person. Why, though, must we choose the athlete as a cosmic symbol instead of the ultimate monk, nun, or scholar? For Prebish, too, *ultimate* is a key word, since he essentially defines religion as an "ultimate experience." One would have to wonder whether the seminude, tabletop dancing advertised by a local bar as "the ultimate" would also qualify as a variety of religious experience. Our age is showing its values in Leonard's title and in Prebish's theology. Sheehan states those values explicitly: "*Success* rests with having the courage and endurance and, above all, the will to become the person you are, *however peculiar that may be*. Then you will be able to say, 'I have found my hero and he is me' " (205; italics added). Grammatically, it should be "he is I," but in either case, the idea is also heretical on several fronts. Goodbye to the heroes of yesteryear, and hello me! Narcissus is having his finest hour, as is Apollo, god of games.

Clearly, then, we have come a long way in three centuries to Super Sunday and the Modern Olympiad, *Playboy* and *Penthouse,* Las Vegas and Atlantic City. Gambling and sexual explicitness in print and photography were relatively tardy in gaining public favor—though not yet, for the most part, ecclesiastical approbation. Sports or competition, however, has been another story entirely, singled out for special benediction. Even the Puritans' suspicion seems a brief interruption of the evolution of a closer connection. The relationship between the modern church and sports has become symbiotic, with the church offering blessings on sports and sports bringing welcomed attention to the church. The interfusing has now entered into social metastasis.

In spite of the prominence and praise rendered them as forms of religion in the age of the Super Bowl, sports and play are not inherently holy, despite the seriousness or even smugness with which their promoters state the cases and causes: Michael Novak and the evangelists for sports; David Miller and Robert Neale for theological play; George Leonard and George Sheehan for self-energization; Hugh Hefner and Dr. Ruth for recreational sex or self-play. Sports and play, I argue, are not even a natural religion but entirely different categories of human experience, beneficent in and of themselves if held in perspective. When they appear to take on the raiments of traditional religion, then heresy, we may conclude, is afoot in the land.

It must be remembered, though, that what was said about the age of the Puritans holds true for our own time—multiplication of examples hardly demonstrates universality. Not every prayer is a prayer for victory, not every game a service, not every celebration a proof. Yet just below the surface of routine piety lies a sense of human life and meaning that makes our religion so easily available to the forms and fanaticism of sports and our sports a model of faith. To understand what has happened to us it would be necessary to probe into Christian theology and pagan philosophy, American history and Western mythology. As in the case of Rome, our stadiums were not built in a day. In the ensuing chapters we will review one fundamental part of this constructive process: the formation of knighthood in the city on the hill.

# 2

# The Old Knight
# in the New World

The simplistic idea of the Puritans as humorless detesters of idleness is no longer acceptable to historians, especially sports historians. Several recent studies have shown the complexity and diversification of Puritan attitudes toward sports, exercise, and games. An analysis of the diaries, letters, and sermons of three Puritan leaders–Michael Wigglesworth (1653–57), Cotton Mather (1681–1724), and Samuel Sewell (1674–1729)–has disclosed that "there was no one prevailing attitude toward physical recreation. It could be accepted as a means of staying healthy, it could be allowed only under certain conditions; or it could be fully welcomed as not only a necessity, but a pleasure-yielding human activity as well" (Wagner 147). For Cotton Mather, religion did not stand in the way of recreation: "Men and Brethren, we be misunderstood as if we meant to insinuate, that a due pursuit of religion is inconsistent with all manners of *Diversion;* No, we suppose there are Diversions undoubtedly innocent, yea profitable and of use, to fit us for Service, by enlivening and fortifying our frail Nature, Invigorating the Armed Spirits, and brightening the Mind, when tied with a close application to Business" (ibid., 144, quoted). At the turn of the present century Max Weber confirmed this judgment:

> The Puritan aversion to sports, was by no means one of princi-
> ple. Sport was accepted if it served a rational purpose, that of
> recreation necessary for physical efficiency. But as a means of
> spontaneous expression of undisciplined impulses, it was under
> suspicion; and in so far as it became purely a means of enjoy-
> ment, or awakened pride, raw instincts or the irrational gam-
> bling instinct, it was of course strictly condemned. Impulsive
> enjoyment of life, which leads away both from work in a calling
> and from religion, was as such the enemy of rational asceticism,
> whether in the form of seigniorial sports, or the enjoyment of
> the dancehall or the public house of the common man. [167–68]

Important public figures took an active part in recreational life; one
colony, Rhode Island, even provided recreation by law (Wagner
144).

The Puritans did not use *recreation* or *sport* in the sense that we
do today, which is also true for the terms *physical education, play,* and
*amusement* (ibid.). In this chapter, I will use the term *martial sports* to
describe competitive activities such as swordsmanship and wrestling
that were also useful in war. By *idle play* I will indicate fun and games
for the sake of enjoyment only. The seriousness of modern American
sports, which makes them so close to religion, and perhaps even a
religion in themselves, derives from the tradition of knighthood that
was transported to the New World in full bloom and that did not wither
on American shores, merely changing coloration and spreading.

Neither in England nor in America did the Puritans ever object
to martial sports. Like the ancient Israelites, they practiced them on
a broad scale. These would come under those forms of "Diversions"
that "fit us for Service," in the words of Mather. The Puritans objected
to nonutilitarian play, but only when the play had exceeded what in
their view were proper limits, which were certainly more restrictive
than our limits today. Ralph Barton Perry says that the Puritan "did
not deny to natural and worldly pleasures, or to health or to family
affection, or to social welfare, or to beauty and the cultural arts, a
place in the hierarchy of goods, nor did he exclude them from his
life. But in his eagerness to subordinate them he unduly disparaged
them." Play was subordinate to salvation, "the supreme good" that
takes "preference over all other goods" (quoted in Eisen 235-36).

In addition to personal "salvation," which meant—to put it simply—going to heaven, the Puritan valued almost equally the idea of prosperity. Indeed, salvation and prosperity were almost inseparable. The Puritans were not perfectibilitarians thinking that they might create an ideal society, but they did believe in bringing God's kingdom to earth, what they meant in part by a "New Jerusalem." It can even be argued that the covenant carries with it more the idea of God's earthly blessings than it does heavenly reward, as suggested in John Winthrop's epic sermon, "A Modell of Christian Charity," delivered aboard the *Arbella* in 1630.

If the city upon a hill is to survive against "enemies," constant readiness is essential, and herein enters the relevance of those sports that prepare the body for service to the state. Wasting time in idle play is subversion of the state, which was more or less inseparable from the church. As Carlyle said two centuries later, a "Great Man" is "a son of Order, not of Disorder" and has a mission "to make what was disorderly . . . into a thing ruled, regular. He is the missionary of Order" (203). This was doubly true for the Pilgrims and Puritans in the strange and inhospitable land where they had taken refuge. Unless its purposes were clear, play could easily be conceived as disorder and hence disruptive to the sacred mission of the state, the defense of which rested upon the leadership of the soldier, priest, and statesman and a muscular, well-armed, highly disciplined citizenry, knights all, owing to the severity of their condition.

Like the Hebrews of the Old Testament, the Puritans embraced those sports essential to the defense of their colony and looked with a skeptical eye upon physical activity that lacked apparent purpose. Their "detestation of idleness" became more famous than the fact that they were exceptional warriors skilled in all the martial sports of the day. They felt chosen by God to push the Canaanites from the Promised Land. Also like their own kind in England, they frowned upon several forms of idleness, believing these led to idolatry. (Since their religion was rational and intellectual, they did not consider study and self-reflection to be idleness.) With Cromwell's victory in the English Civil War, the Puritans in England abolished Old Church festivals and sought an end to horse racing, cockfighting, bearbaiting, dancing, theatrical entertainment, gambling, and desecration of the

Sabbath. They also banned maypoles and the Dover's Cotswold Games, prohibited Sunday amusements, and zealously guarded public morality, much as Calvin had attempted to do in Geneva, where he and his followers banned about two hundred amusements and filled the stocks with public offenders (W.J. Baker 80, 74).

How did the situation in colonial Massachusetts compare? It was not Disney World to be sure, but neither does it seem to have been Calvin's Geneva or Cromwell's England. One of the best and probably most reliable depictions of the time, focused roughly on the 1640s, appears in *The Scarlet Letter* (1850) by Nathaniel Hawthorne. Though living in the nineteenth century, Hawthorne was a student of the lore of his ancestors and a member of a community that still held to many of the old beliefs. In the chapter "The New England Holiday" he describes a parade in honor of the inauguration of the new governor, the historical governor Richard Bellingham, who becomes a character in the novel. In the procession are the governor, the magistrates, the ministers, and "all the great people and good people with the music and the soldiers marching before them" (Hawthorne 220). The mood is everywhere festive, even if opportunities for enjoyment are lacking. Only two events are emphasized, the marching by of soldiers and administrators and competitive events showcasing skills useful to the state: wrestling, the quarterstaff duel, and the exhibition of the buckler and broadsword—on the pillory, no less.

With characteristic insight, Hawthorne distinguishes clearly between the amusements the Puritans prohibited and those requiring "courage and manliness" that could serve the colonies in time of need. Hawthorne's depiction of knightly sport in *The Scarlet Letter* forms a bond with English tradition but foreshadows as well the emerging American "manliness," growing from the need for physical prowess in the conquest of a new land (Messenger 31–32). By his use of the words *courage* and *manliness,* Hawthorne reflected a major preoccupation in America and in Victorian England. The ideal enjoyed currency until World War II (see Mangan and Walvin). As more than one critic has noted, "Manliness has staying power" (John Springhall, quoted in Mangan and Walvin 53). This is in contrast, one might add, to "womanliness," which never took a corresponding hold in the American imagination as a heroic ideal, remaining instead a sort of code word for helpmate. The implication is that knights are male (see Schweitzer 30).

In "The New England Holiday" Hawthorne reveals a knowledge of Joseph Strutt's *Sports and Pastimes of the People of England,* from which he borrows the epigraph for his story "The May-pole of Merry Mount." When he refers to "the different fashions" of wrestling of "Cornwall and Devonshire," Hawthorne is again showing use of Strutt, who had written, "The styles of Cornwall and Devon are usually reckoned together, though they differed in at least one important particular, namely, that the latter sanctioned kicking and tripping, whilst the former confined themselves almost entirely to hugging" (69). Strutt lists the forms of wrestling under "Games of Strength," and Hawthorne went to some pains to show that they were quite prevalent and popular in Puritan society even if dancing around the maypole was not. In other words, the country started off "strong" even if it did not exhibit wisdom—making adulterers wear a symbol of their sin, for instance. The "kicking and tripping" of the Devon wrestling style show that the Puritans in their religious righteousness were not above an Odyssean trick or two, as also seen in the guerrilla ambushes the Puritans used against the Indians. We have made the Puritans too prim and proper for too long. They were tough as nails, wily and wary, and on occasion as savage as Crusaders.

A word needs to be said here about wrestling in general. It and not boxing is *the* fundamental sport. The fist is not a natural weapon. The opposable thumb was not added by nature to make a fist but to provide a handhold. Wrestling puts the hand to its natural use of grabbing and holding. It tests every muscle in the body and requires the greatest coordination of mind and body. It solves questions of physical prowess without death to an opponent and, under proper conditions, without injury. Since the beginning of standing armies it has been regarded as standard training for the warrior, and it appears in practically every country in every time in one form or another. It is revealing to note that one of the fourteen boys under eighteen who came over on the *Mayflower* was named Wrestling Brewser, who had a brother named Love (Marble 24). Wrestling is primarily a plebeian sport. In its simplest forms it requires no money or equipment.

Horsemanship and swordsmanship, by contrast, require extensive training and costly equipment, depending on how much invidious distinction one wants to display. Governor Richard Bellingham wanted to display a great deal. The governor was first elected in 1641. He was a Renaissance prince and, of course, a knight, with a long tradition of war and administration behind him. Hawthorne describes the English "suit of mail" that "had been worn by the Governor on many a solemn muster and training field" as well as in war. The governor's breastplate figures in the meaning of the novel, since it reflects Pearl's "naughty merriment" with so much breadth and intensity of effect that Hester Prynne feels as if it could not be the image of her own child, but an imp who was seeking to mould itself into Pearl's shape (145–46). In a real sense the breastplate itself creates the impishness in Pearl, for it symbolizes the power and authority that decree her separation from other children in the community.

The knightly regime determines every aspect of community life, including the play of the children, which is not really play at all but training for knightly adventures. As Hester walks about the town with little Pearl, she sees "the children of the settlement on the grassy margins of the street, or at the domestic thresholds, disporting themselves in such grim fashion as the Puritan nurture would permit; playing a going to church, perchance; or at scourging Quakers; or taking scalps in a sham-fight with Indians; or scaring one another with freaks of imitative witchcraft" (85). In any event the Puritans, while transporting their own version of knighthood to the New World, left shepherd games and merriment in England and, in the words of Hawthorne, "so darkened the national visage with it, that all the subsequent years have not sufficed to clear it up. We have yet to learn again the forgotten art of gayety" (221–22).

Hawthorne says that Bellingham fought in the war against the Pequod, and we can be sure that he fought bravely and with the greatest certainty of his cause, that of divine retribution. Governor William Bradford in *Of Plymouth Plantation* wrote that those that scaped the fire were slain with the sword, some hewed to pieces, others run through with their rapiers, so as they were quickly dispatched and very few escaped. It was conceived they thus destroyed about 400 at this time. It was a fearful sight to see them thus frying in the fire and streams of blood quenching the same, and horrible was the stink and they gave the praise thereof to God, who had wrought so wonderfully for them, thus to enclose their enemies in their hands and give them so speedy a victory over so proud and insulting an enemy. [quoted in Blair et al. 1:38–39]

Self-righteousness was a distinguishing feature of knighthood that the Puritans raised to an art form. Note what Carlyle has to say about Cromwell, the arch-Puritan, in this regard: "All of his great enterprises were commenced in prayer. In dark inextricable-looking difficulties, his officers and he used to assemble, and pray alternately for hours, for days, till some definite resolution rose among them, some 'door of hope,' as they would name it, disclosed itself" (218).

Some may argue that the Puritan officer and divine was not a knight like the Cavalier, but he clearly belonged to the same tradition. Certainly the Puritan was a fighter and an adept at martial sports, and more than the Cavalier, he believed in prayer. While the Cavalier judged according to class, the Puritan did so according to belief. Bellingham, for example, was set against the Quakers. Statesman, soldier, and priest, he is a clear example of the early New England theocrat, versatile and dogmatic at once, a believer in both election and special privilege. Like knights for centuries, he was sure that there was always an evil enemy and hence a need for constant preparation for war.

More famous than Bellingham, though probably not as versatile, was another better-remembered Puritan, Miles Standish. As presented in Longfellow's poem, he embodied the traits of the Old World knight.

In the Old Colony days, in Plymouth the land of the Pilgrims,
To and fro in a room of his simple and primitive dwelling,
Clad in doublet and hose, and boots of Cordovan leather,
Strode, with a martial air, Miles Standish the Puritan Captain.
Buried in thought he seemed, with his hands behind him, and pausing
Ever and anon to behold his glittering weapons of warfare,

Hanging in shining array along the walls of the chamber,—
Cutlass and corselet of steel, and his trusty sword of Damascus,
Curved at the point and inscribed with its mystical Arabic sentence,
While underneath, in a corner, were fowling-piece, musket,
   and matchlock.
Short of stature he was, but strongly built and athletic,
Broad in the shoulders, deep-chested, with muscles and sinews
   of iron;
Brown as a nut was his face, but his russet beard was already
Flaked with patches of snow, as hedges sometimes in November.
                                 [Longfellow 165]

Longfellow was not merely letting his fancy run wild in his depiction of Standish. In Longellow's poem, the captain and John Alden form a familiar pair in American literature, the athlete and the scholar, one the manly embodiment of knightly heroism, the other manifesting what the knight imagines as the only alternative. While Standish is not such a scholar, he is a reader of *Bariffe's Artillery Guide* and the *Commentaries* of Caesar. "And, like Caesar, I know the names of each of my soldiers!" Longfellow is not making up names, for the books he mentions were indeed in Standish's library (see Porteus 166). Well that Standish might say to John Alden, "I am a maker of war, not a maker of phrases." As a maker of war Standish had remarkable success, increasing the colonists' odds of survival by establishing defenses and maintaining civil order, as well as supervising trade policies. Standish was not reluctant to encourage aggressive, even violent behavior in this regard. In all things Standish played the role of military commander (Erwin 9).

    Standish's action against the Indians was more dramatic than that of his compatriots. Threatened and insulted by the chief Wituwamut, who bragged about the number of English and French he had killed with his knife, Standish determined on revenge. At Wessagusset Standish ambushed Wituwamut and his sidekick Pecksuot, who unwisely had made repeated fun of Standish's short stature. Taking the head of Wituwamut back to Plymouth, Standish had it mounted on a pole as a gory reminder that no ill will toward either Plymouth or Standish would be tolerated (ibid., 10). Or short jokes either, apparently! In effect Standish had followed what today we would call a terrorist policy, which was not uncommon among knights, especially Crusaders, and was often advocated by the church. The pilgrim pastor at Leyden, Holland, wrote to William Bradford: "Punishment to a few and fear to many" (ibid., quoted). Though Standish never joined a Puritan church, he was one of them—their most famous Christian knight.

Like Bellingham and others, Standish had little appreciation of dissent, especially of the kind exemplified by Thomas Morton, who set up a colony at Merry Mount for all kinds of fun and games and who, like the Indians, made merry over Standish's stature, referring to the battle-scarred veteran who came to arrest him as "Captain Shrimpe." Morton was also selling arms to the Indians. Knowing Standish's temper, one can only conclude that Morton was lucky to make it back to England with his head on his shoulders.

What Miles Standish was to the survival of the Massachusetts colony, another captain, John Smith, was to the one in Virginia. Both form a link with the Knights Templars of the Middle Ages. Instead of routing out the Turk from the Holy Land, their task was to take territory from the "savages" for a New Jerusalem. Instead of Acre or Constantinople, their tours of duty were Jamestown and Plymouth.

While Philip Barbour has established without a doubt that "Smith was a veracious chronicler, ... the question of what the Captain thought he saw or endured remains" (Davis 1:128). That question has made Smith a controversial figure, "denounced for supreme egotism and mendacity and equally praised as the last knight errant or the first gallant southern gentleman" (1:168). Textbooks, while not ignoring the debate centering around him, still typically introduce him with a billing that Smith himself could have devised: "The pink of gallantry, the flower of chivalry, the founder of Virginia, and the pride of Southern Land." Smith, like Franklin later, invented himself but with even grander vision. Who else could have been "President of Virginia and Admiral of New England"? He is our first PR man and shill for sports, as seen in "A Description of New England." In this New World, he says,

> man, woman, and childe, with a small hooke and line, by angling, may take divers sorts of excellent fish, at their pleasure. . . . is it not a pretty sport, to pull up two pence, six pence, and twelve pence as fast as you can haule and veare a line? He is a very

bad Fisher [who] cannot kill in one day with his hooke and line, one, two, or three hundred Cods. [quoted in Blair et al. 1:47–48]

Fishing is for the common man, woman, and child. For gentlemen (and knights) the New World offers even more advantages: "For Gentlemen, what exercise should more delight them, than ranging dayly the unknowne parts, using fowling and fishing, for hunting and hawking?" (ibid.).

Smith also denounces the "excess of Idlenesse" that brought about the ruin, in his view, of the Chaldeans, Syrians, Greeks, and Romans. What made Rome great was "the adventures of her youth, not in riots at home, but in dangers abroad" (ibid., 45). This is the common equation of knighthood with foreign adventure, not the noble defense of one's homeland. If the knight is successful, of course, the foreign land becomes a new homeland.

Smith notably draws on models of foreign success from Greece and Rome, while the Puritans usually chose them from among the Hebrews. Smith talks about why Rome and Greece fell; the New England governors always kept an eye on the Holy Land. Smith cites histories, and William Bradford quotes Scripture. Though all three cultures—Greek, Hebrew, and Roman— influenced knighthood, that of Rome, with its emphasis upon discipline and conquest, came to dominate in the cases of Smith and Standish. Smith saw himself as an example of the type of person he called for. He was a reader of Machiavelli's *Art of War,* Vannoccio Biringucio's *Pirotechnia,* and Antonio de Guevara's *Dial of Princes; or, Book of Marcus Aurelius.* Smith was therefore well schooled in the ways of the knight, including the art of horsemanship. At twenty he hired "a swain to be his 'man' not only for hunting and companionship, but to help him play-act his envisioned future as a gentleman-adventurer with his squire" (Barbour 14). All of Smith's readings concerned not imitation of Christ but imitation of the powerful.

Smith's background and training, considering the barbarism of his age perpetuated in large measure by knights themselves, would stand him in good stead for his adventures in Europe and America. The America that Smith anticipated "was not for the lily fingered or the blue blooded but for the aggressive, resourceful, and courageous." Smith's credo, based on his own view of history, can be simplified as follows: "Expand or die," or, put another way, "Idleness kills." Laziness, he thought, "was a major cause of the first catastrophes of starvation and Indian attack at Jamestown," and that laziness, in the words of one historian, has been "a regional characteristic down to the twentieth century" (Davis 1:68). Thus two of the dominant themes of southern literature have their origin at Jamestown, for here in addition to idleness are sown the seeds of southern gallantry that reach through Light Horse Harry Lee to his son, Robert E. Lee, the hero as aristocrat, who had much in common with Cromwell, the hero as king. We have tended always to contrast the Cavalier and the Yankee, the Virginia gentleman and the New England Puritan, but we are reluctant to compare them. When we do, we find the common strain of chivalry and knighthood, the deep attention to religious form, skill in arms, a high sense of honor, readiness for combat, and a certainty that war or intimidating power is finally the only solution to conflict.

Like Miles Standish, Smith was an expert swordsman and not adverse to decapitation. On duty in Transylvania, Smith accepted a challenge to Christians by a Turkish *bashi* (captain) to combat with him for his head, "to delight the ladies, who did long to see some court-like pastime." So many wished to accept the challenge that lots were drawn, and Smith won this contest and two others as well. Thereafter he designed and had impressed upon his shield three Turks' heads in token of the feat (Barbour 45–47).

It must be pointed out that the idlers at Jamestown were not engaged in idle play. In contrast to the jolly crowd at Merry Mount, Jamestown loafers were into pure idleness as only southerners can know it, like that of the Lester family of *Tobacco Road*. They were not the ones who confused leisure with activity. Like Standish and knights everywhere, Smith had little respect for idle time of any sort. He claims that the lives of two hundred idlers were saved by the industry of thirty or forty others doing their duty. Here too is the beginning of the up-and-doing theme of *Poor Richard's Almanac*, though Smith was not a model for Richard Saunders. Smith intended to be remembered as a model of something other than a saver of pennies and a quoter of axioms, though he certainly had plenty of them to quote. No, he is instead "the man of action and decision, the ingenious and brave soldier, the persuasive orator and debater, the savior of a handful of men who are the founders of a future nation: In a word, the epic hero" (Davis 1:21). The goal of the epic struggle in all of Smith's writing is the establishment of a New Jerusalem on the shores of Virginia, a land in which useful sports and commerce will flourish, as in New England.

John Smith belongs to the tradition of knighthood, as do the Puritans. Whether historically accurate or not, the stories of Smith's exploits are both amazing and revealing of the ways of tournaments and our chivalric heritage. He was by admirers named "an English Gentleman," a Christian gentleman. He became the true renaissance man: gentleman, knight, merchant, and adventurer.

Though this study focuses upon North American sports and religion, we should note that the same pattern of events unfolded in Central and South America: the conquering knight imposing his faith by word or sword upon a brave but relatively hapless population. The atrocities of the conquistadors have been well documented, but relatively little has been said about the knightly tradition behind the bloodshed. The man in charge was Hernando Cortés, quintessentially the man of his age. He was "a knight-errant, in the literal sense of the word. Of all the band of adventurous cavaliers, whom Spain, in the sixteenth century, sent forth on the career of discovery and conquest, there was none more deeply filled with the spirit of romantic enterprise than Hernando Cortés" (Prescott 3:353). He was, at the time of the conquest, slender, "but his chest was deep, his shoulders broad, his frame muscular and well proportioned. It presented the union of agility and vigor which qualified him to excel in fencing, horsemanship, and other generous exercises of chivalry. . . . He wore few ornaments and usually the same; but those were of great price. His manner, frank and soldier-like, concealed a most cool and calculating spirit" (Prescott 1:258-59).

Like a good historian, Prescott bends over backward to be fair and to try to set events against the backdrop of the time. In this regard, he reminds us that the natives too had systems of knighthood not unlike those that brought destruction upon them. As if they too had read Caesar's *Commentaries, The Art of War,* and *Mirror of Princes,* the Aztec princes used the same incentives as their European counterparts, establishing honorary orders with their own insignia and consequent privileges. "There seems ... to have existed a sort of knighthood, of inferior degree. It was the cheapest reward of martial prowess, and whoever had not reached it was excluded from using ornaments on his arms or his person, and obliged to wear a coarse white stuff, made from the threads of aloe" (Prescott 1:45). The obvious implication of all this is that knighthood cannot be attributed to Western cultural history alone.

Everywhere the world over, those who could not fight or would not fight were considered "unmanly," which is why in the European nations the character of Jesus had to be transformed into a fighter and soldier in order to justify the lust for recognition and power. Prescott does not say that the Spaniards merely beat the Indians at their own game of conquest, nor does he excuse the Christian nations for, in their view, imitating the Muslim in adopting the sword, a course for which they have scant justification in Scripture.

> The sword was a good argument, when the tongue failed; and the spread of Mahometanism had shown that seeds sown by the hand of violence, far from perishing in the ground, would spring up and bear fruit to after time. If this were so in a bad cause, how much more would it be true in a good one? The Spanish cavalier felt he had a high mission to accomplish as a soldier of the Cross. . . . Whoever died in the faith, however immoral had been his life, might be said to die in the Lord. Such was the creed of the Castilian knight of that day, as imbibed from the preachings of the pulpit, from cloisters and colleges at home, from monks and missionaries abroad,–from all save one, whose devotion, kindled at a purer source, was not, alas! permitted to send forth its radiance far into the thick gloom by which he was encompassed. [1:269-70]

The "one" to whom Prescott refers was the good bishop Las Casas, "the protector General of the Indians" who had the errors of humanity but also its rare virtues, devoting his later life to ameliorating an almost unparalleled structure of oppression (1:378). (Some sources indicate a conversion experience similar to St. Paul's.) Like Ignatius Loyola, Francis Xavier, and Don Quixote, he said "goodbye to all that" and entered into another tradition with entirely different expectations than the mere glory of conquest for temporal wealth and worldly applause. He became, in other words, a shepherd.

Neither the Pilgrims nor the Anglicans wanted a New Eden but rather a New Jerusalem. A New Eden would have suggested ease and indolence, whereas a New Jerusalem meant struggle and conflict. No gentleman, knight, merchant, or other adventurer (Smith's terms) came to America to lie down in green pastures but to build a city in the wilderness or on a hill. The North-American pattern was reflective of that of Hernando Cortés, who told his soldiers at the time of conquest, "I hold out to you a glorious prize, but it is to be won by incessant toil. Great things are to be achieved by great exertions, and glory was never the reward of sloth" (Prescott 1:263). Play is Edenic, while sports are agonic and completely reflective of the purposes of settlement of the country. To this day only theologians such as Harvey Cox, David Miller, Jurgen Moltmann, and Robert Neale even speak of the possibilities of innocent play, but few listen to what they have to say. The grand achievers are our models yet, and the most vocal cheerleaders are the televangelists such as Jerry Falwell, Oral Roberts, and Billy Graham and the winning coaches they admire. One group points back toward the verdant field and fertile orchards of Eden; the other forward to the city of God with a gymnasium on every corner and a super stadium standing in the suburbs like a great temple.

Thus was our continent settled and founded by extraordinary fighters and athletes. Standish, Smith and Cortés all symbolized the transfer of the knightly tradition from the Old World to the New. Though of different faiths, all were Christian knights with all the dubious virtues the term implies. Each illustrates the same old problem that the Old World failed to solve and, thus far, the new one as well: how to live peacefully and how to share and enjoy creation.

# 3

# Revolutionary Heroes and Fighting Parsons

The connections in American history between sports, religion, war, and exclusive education were evident from the moment of the nation's birth. Knighthood was brought to our shores by John Smith and Miles Standish and by the Puritan fathers, by adventure and by religion. During the Revolution, the fighting spirit of patriots and the fighting spirit of those who were in theory less worldly were hardly distinguishable. Behind the merger of interests lay an almost absolute and unquestioned acceptance of the values of the old martial sports: wrestling, horsemanship, and swordsmanship.

It is hard to overemphasize the role of colleges in efforts to maintain or increase the authority of religion in the United States. Before the Civil War, says one historian, "the whole number of colleges in the United States not founded by religion can be counted on one hand." Each of the first colleges was meant to be "a nursery of ministers" and was considered "a child of the church" (Tewksbury 56, 55). This being the case, the historical roads taken in any consideration of the development of religion led inevitably to the sites of our three most famous schools: Harvard (1636), Yale (1701), and Princeton (1746). It is true that Harvard has been marked by an "absence of a missionary impulse." According to Robin Lester, "the Presbyterians, led by Princeton graduates, founded or helped to found over one hundred institutions of higher learning in the nine-teenth century" and "the Congregationalists, led by Yale graduates, averaged more than one new college founding each year from 1861–1875" ("Rise" 11).

The early history of American college sports generally follows the paths of the Congregationalists and Presbyterians, especially in the case of football—evolving from soccer—the sport most frequently linked with education and religion, and also war. Harvard, Yale, and Princeton became national leaders in establishing standards for educational instruction and scholarly attainment. The "best" colleges had to lead in all fields, athletic as well as academic and cultural. From the 1880s to the 1940s, the days of football's greatest popularity at the Big Three, it "competed successfully with education for the attention of many undergraduates and was the strongest tie binding alumni to their Alma Mater" (Synnott 188). In America football and higher education grew up together.

Attitudes of early New England educators toward sports were mixed, as was the case generally among the Puritans. They often frowned on sports, but they were not on any campaign to wipe out sports in college. Even from the earliest days some evidence exists of the presence on campus of combative sport. One history of Harvard claims that

> the only time that Harvard students had for outdoor sports was on Saturday afternoons, before sundown. Evidence here is also scanty. Edward Johnson wrote that "the spacious plain" of the College Yard was "more like a bowling green than a wilder-ness"; but there is no evidence of anyone's playing at bowls on it. Thomas Shepherd, in one of his sermons, alluded to Satan appearing "with a ball at his foot," and threatening "to carry all before him, and to kick and carry God's precious Sabbaths out of the world with him. . . ." Among the forty or fifty boys there must have been more or less "rassling," and the Reverend John Wise, who graduated in 1673, was reputed a "famous wrestler." [Morison, *Harvard* 1:117]

What was important, it seems, was keeping sports in perspec-tive, in accordance with custom and laws. Henry Dunster, during his presidency of Harvard (1650–54), favored outdoor sport: fishing, fowling, or hunting, as long as the hunter was "accountable for any Detriment he doth upon Cornfields" (ibid.). Increase Mather, Harvard president from 1685 to 1701, at least permitted sports, as suggested in a letter to a father of one student who was drowned in Fresh Pond while skating in 1696: "Although death found him using recreations (which *students* need for their Healths sake) they were lawful recreations" (ibid., quoted). Even Cotton Mather, Increase's redoubtable son, fished. "Samuel Sewell tells of a time when the stern old Puritan went out with line and tackle and fell into the water at Spy Pond, 'the boat being ticklish' " (Dulles 25). For those who have read Mather's prose, this is a rather pleasing image.

While lawful generally, sports in the Ivy league in the eighteenth century were unstructured, as much play as competition. "What athletics there were at Princeton were unorganized, the spontaneous effort of a group of boys seeking fun and exercise. Two or three young men might run a race around campus while their fellows stuck their heads out of the windows to shout encouragement. They might indulge in a game of quoits, or bounce balls against the gable-end of the President's house, or take a turn at bandy [field hockey], or even roll hoops in the basement hallway" (Wertenbaker 194). While association football may have been popular in the colleges throughout the eighteenth century, some evidence indicates that at Princeton there was "no football and no cricket." A group sport, however, was played on ice with a stick and a ball, possibly hockey. Though Canadians take credit for the founding of ice hockey in the mid–nineteenth century, there is evidence that the game was played at Princeton in 1805 (ibid., 194) and even as early as 1786 (R.W. Henderson 136). In November 1787 the Princeton faculty banned field hockey, also called shinny, as "low and unbecoming gentlemen and scholars." Bans occurred at other schools as well. "At King's College in New York City, one student was caught swimming or bathing off campus and was punished by being confined to his room, where he was commanded to translate Latin for a week. Cruel and unusual punishments were not uncommon in colonial America" (Smith 10).

At Yale, at least toward the end of the century, sports consisted of hiking, swimming, sailing, hunting, skating, sliding, and football

(Kelley 106). Charles Goodrich, who received a bachelor's degree in 1797, reported:

> The only sports or amusements which I remember, were foot races of ten rods and football. . . . But Foot-ball was our common sport, almost everyday in good weather and very often twice daily and I forget if more. We had three lines in front of the College buildings down to the road that crossed the Green by *two* meeting houses if I remember. Of the three lines the two outside were eight or ten rods apart. We would begin on the middle line and if the scholars were generally out on both sides, whenever the ball was driven over one of the outside lines, the party on that side were beaten, and the other party enjoyed the shouting. There was no delay of the game by choosing sides, the parties were divided by the buildings in which they severally roomed. [ibid. 106–7]

What is evident in the account of Goodrich is the familiar movement in any culture from "turbulence to rules," as Roger Caillois explains in his classic study, the movement from spontaneous play (*paideia*) to "gratuitous difficulty" (*ludus*), from disorder toward order and control (27ff.).

The spirit of competition advances hand in hand with the rise of organized sport, however unsophisticated the organization may be. By the time of the American Revolution the group sport of football/soccer was beginning to serve the cause of patriotism. Nathan Hale, "the hero" of Yale, was also an athletic hero, at least in the eyes of self-assured patriots. Hale's diary, written while on duty in the Boston area in the early months of 1776, was full of "references to his fine spirit and to his devotion." According to Anson Phelps Stokes in *Memorials of Eminent Yale Men* (1915), "wrestling, 'chequers,' and football were among his diversions, but his main work was improving the efficiency of his men" (324–25). Hale demonstrates the importance given to manliness and its direct connections to religion and sports, as well as the transformation of fact into the myths that serve to bind together an image of the winning character.

Whatever qualities Hale may have had in fact, they were magnified considerably in the inevitable eulogizing that took place after his dramatic death. Remembered by a friend as "the idol of all his acquaintances," Hale was mythologized as a splendid example of heroism "who walked through goodness as he walked through life" (ibid., 319). Christian, athlete, scholar, and soldier, he has become a legend whose athletic skills and all-around abilities get expanded into achievements of greatness even though "almost *everything* important we wish to know (or to believe) about Nathan Hale seems to be a matter of intense controversy among his biographers" (Monjo 121). In every account Hale was the Christian gentleman, a Christian athlete and gentle knight, "always quick to lend a helping hand to a being in distress, brute or human (Stokes 319). He was just what the colonies needed, Washington remarked (M.M. Brown 152). Much like Washington himself, Hale has staying power. "No graduate," says Stokes, "so symbolizes to the undergraduate of Today [1915] the highest manifestation of the Yale spirit as this able student and manly youth who gladly gave up his life in his country's service" (317).

During World War II Hale was still firmly established in our pantheon, as seen in the super patriotic song "There's a Star Spangled Banner Waving Somewhere." In that "distant land so many miles away," only Uncle Sam's great heroes are welcomed: "Washington, Lincoln, and Perry, Nathan Hale and Colin Kelly, too." This lyric, American-style, moves full circle in reference to heroic values, starting with Washington, "the Founder of West Point," to Kelly, a graduate, who, three days after Pearl Harbor, became famous for a daring bombing raid on a Japanese cruiser in the Philippines.

Another Ivy Leaguer that Washington needed and wanted was "Light Horse" Harry Lee (Princeton, 1773), the father of Robert E. Lee and the archetype of the southern cavalier. At twenty-three he had already acquired his nickname through his exploits in gathering intelligence close to British outposts, and he turned down a chance to serve on Washington's staff. "I am wedded to my sword," he told his commander-in-chief, "and my secondary object in this present war is military reputation" (Boyd 41).

The term *military reputation* is key to the consideration of American knighthood, for it engages a particular type of manliness. In contrast to the Puritan knight, characterized by an Old Testament seriousness, and the emerging image of a somewhat gentle hero like

Hale, the Virginian from the outset was identifiable by resplendent dress, gay insouciance, and readiness for action at a moment's notice. Hale is a citizen-soldier who answers his country's call; Lee appears more the professional knight, almost welcoming the opportunity of combat in order to advance his reputation. Knightly manliness is evolving toward its traditional heart of diamond and away from its heart of wax.

Compared with the likes of Miles Standish, Governor Bellingham, and Nathan Hale, Light Horse Harry seems in appearance like a dandy, with all the glorified trappings such as Roman plumes and French frills that seem to distinguish the cavalier. Like all his classmates at Princeton, Lee prayed and studied most of the day, yet the Calvinist tones of Princeton had little effect on his cavalier soul. On his trips home to Virginia before the war, he could be seen "with powdered head, velvet jacket, pulled linen and smooth silk stockings, dancing, flirting, and drinking at Mount Airy, Lee Hall, Nomini Hall, and Stratford" (Boyd 145). In such behavior is found the heritage of the gallant as well as the seeds of *Gone with the Wind*. This dandification of the knight was largely a Mediterranean influence—Roman, Muslim, and French rather than Greek and Hebraic—though exceptions exist and lines become blurred. In his manner and dress and obligation to be a gentleman as well as a professional killer, the southern knight, even Robert E. Lee, became something of a darling, a courtier, a distant cousin indeed of the epic heroes of Jews (David), Greeks (Achilles), and Anglo-Saxons (Beowulf).

If Light Horse Harry Lee was not much burdened by scriptural injunctions against vanity, neither was he a careful scholar, at least in Jefferson's eyes, nor was he very good at business, spending a year in 1808–9 in debtor's prison; but his bravery was unquestioned and his oratorical skills widely known. Appropriately, he was asked to deliver the funeral oration of Washington, rising to the occasion with at least one immortal line: "First in war, first in peace, and first in the hearts of his countrymen." He was himself, whatever his shortcomings, "a maker of speeches and a doer of deeds," as he had described Washington. Unlike Hale, who was somewhat closer to an image of the shepherd forced to fight by circumstances, Lee set out to become a hero, finding a challenge wherever he could.

At Harvard the patriotic fervor did not seem to abound on the same scale as it did at Yale and Princeton, but Harvard too had preserved that form of knightly idealism wherein, especially in times of crisis, the call to preach and pray and the call to arms each seemed the natural consequence of the other. Though not as celebrated as the military heroes, the parsons were also makers of speeches and doers of deeds, including Joseph Warren and Thomas Allen (A.B., 1762). Allen, "the fighting parson of Pittsfield, accompanied the men of his flock to Bennington, himself fired the first shot in the battle, and lived to play a decisive part in the events that led to the framing of the State Constitution of 1780" (Morison, *Three Centuries* 148).

There is no evidence that Warren and Allen were lovers of sports, but they were vigorous souls, ready and willing to go to the scene of battle with those who listened to them. Allen is remembered as a man of "great energy," "democratic spirit," and "remarkable power" (Baldwin 141, 160). Both he and Warren represent the widespread involvement of the ministry in the Revolution; behind this effort was the pervasive influence of Harvard and Yale.

Harvard and Yale were associated with the Congregational Church (Harvard later with the Unitarian), William and Mary (1693) with the Episcopal, and Princeton with the Presbyterian, the chief purpose of all being to provide ministers for a frontier society. If Thomas Allen typifies the fighting spirit of the Harvard minister during the Revolution, the Reverend Samuel Doak embodies the stern Calvinism of Princeton during the same time. Both ministers illustrate the growing alliance between education, religion, and the military solution. Sports did not figure directly in either man's life, but both exhibited the "manliness" that by the time of the Revolution was expected of anyone who would be a leader in the efforts to throw off the yoke of British domination or to civilize the vast American frontier.

Doak is the classic example of the Ivy League graduate who moved on all fronts, educating the common folk, defending against the Indians, and, like so many of his New England counterparts, inspiring soldiers in time of battle. Graduating from Princeton in 1775, Doak became the Apostle of Presbyterianism beyond the Alleghenies and the Father of Education in Tennessee, bringing sacks full of books five hundred miles on horseback from Philadelphia into the backwoods of Tennessee in order to preach and start a school. In 1795 he founded Martin Academy, which later became, not surprisingly, Washington College, one of the first schools west of the Appalachian Mountains, and in 1818 with his son he founded Tusculum Academy, which became Tusculum College. The latter was named for the residence of President John Witherspoon at Princeton, which in turn had been named for Cicero's villa north of Rome. The Latin connection in the name underscores the emphasis upon classical method that had been promulgated by John Knox in his native Scotland. Reading, spelling, arithmetic, and English grammar were taught in the lower grades. Higher mathematics, Latin, and Greek were added to the studies of the more advanced pupil. With surprising success, the Presbyterian preacher-teacher convinced the youth that "the salvation of their souls depended upon the memorizing of thousands of heroic lines or upon explaining to their masters the intricacies of languages that had not been spoken by any considerable number of people since the fall of Constantinople" (Posey, *Presbyterian Church* 50).

The Tennessee historian James G.M. Ramsey, who studied under Doak, disagreed sharply with such a view. The goal of the preacher was to save souls, but that of the teacher was something else: "The acquisition of knowledge—mere literary attainment—was not the sole or even the primary object of Dr. Doak's instruction—it was mental discipline—it was to train the intellect—to teach the young man how to think—to think accurately and profoundly—to think for himself, and to beget a spirit of *manly* reliance upon his own powers of independent investigation, and vigorous thought" (italics added). To the standard curriculum Doak also added Hebrew, and in 1815 the graduating class from Washington College "was examined upon that language publicly—before an admiring audience, the first class of that kind that ever did so in Tennessee" (Calhoun 15–16).

The demands of the spirit and the mind and the physical rigors of frontier life left little time for play or triviality for the early Presbyterian preacher-teacher. Nor is there any evidence that Doak or others brought with them from Princeton any form of athletics to the backcountry of Tennessee. Dr. Ramsey, however, seems to take pains to show that Doak, in spite of his emphasis upon studies and salvation, was thoroughly masculine: "The whole countenance expressed strong intellect, *manly* good sense, calm dignity and indomitable firmness. . . . Though naturally very social and friendly, he spent little of his time in conversation and none of it in conviviality" (ibid., 14; italics added).

Since Ramsey (1797–1884) uses the adjective *manly* twice in a short space in his description of Doak, one might suspect that he is falling prey to what was a convention or even a cult in England and America in the nineteenth century, so that "one might reasonably conclude that manliness was one of the cardinal Victorian virtues" (Newsome 195). It was, though, a term hard to define, ranging from maturity and cultivated powers of intelligence (the opposite of childishness)–as seen by Coleridge in *Aides to Reflection* (1825)–to robust energy and spiritual courage (the opposite of effeminacy)–as seen by Thomas Hughes in *The Manliness of Christ* (1879) (ibid., 195–97). In the portrayals of Hale and Doak, it is clear from their own words or those of their contemporaries that the idea was quite current in the eighteenth century, even in America, and that those employing the term *manly* for both men meant to suggest something of the qualities that the word came to connote in Victorian England: maturity, consciousness of "duties of manhood," power of intellect, spiritual courage, and physical vitality.

The emphasis upon muscularity and manliness in the picture of Doak, for instance, makes clear that he, like Nathan Hale and Light Horse Harry Lee, was capable of physical action should the need arise. On 26 September 1780 at Sycamore Shoals in east Tennessee, Doak delivered the sermon and prayer before the departure of the Overmountain Men for the battle of King's Mountain. With many of their wives and children in their midst, the "sturdy Scotch-Irish Presbyterians, leaning upon their long rifles, listened in an attitude of respectful attention" as Doak appealed to the strength of their manhood and invoked divine protection for their long and difficult mission. Making no bones whatever about the matter, he intoned at the end, "O, God of battle, arise in thy might. Avenge the slaughter of thy people. Confound those who plot for our destruction. Crown this mighty effort with victory, and smite those who exalt themselves against liberty and justice and truth. Help us as good soldiers to wield the SWORD OF the LORD and GIDEON." The mountain men shouted in patriotic acclaim, "The Sword of the Lord and of our Gideons!" (Calhoun 28). The fate of Colonel Patrick Ferguson and the Tories at King's Mountain was sealed (Fuhrmann 8). It was here, in the view of some, that Tennesseans first got the name Volunteers, with all men eligible for the company volunteering except two (W.A. Henderson 13).

According to Theodore Roosevelt, John Sevier and many who marched over the mountains to victory were engaged in sport and celebration at Sevier's home when the challenge of war came (8:477). The scene was obviously dear to Harvard man Roosevelt. In any case, the Tennesseans were certainly athletic and expert hunters or sportsmen. Though dressed not in uniform but in "picturesque costume, the hunting shirt" (Ramsey 247), the Volunteers or Over-mountain Men with "their hardy looks" and "their tall athletic forms" had much in common with knights of the Middle Ages. They received the blessing of the church and Scripture (especially since they were fighting invaders, as had the Maccabees) and had acquired skill in killing from the necessity of hunting.

Certainly the leader of the Tory opposition, Ferguson, was a knight in the traditional mold. Inventor of the breechloading rifle, "a more dangerous man ... never followed the Red Cross of St. George. He was a most expert swordsman and credibly alleged to be the best shot in the world" (W.A. Henderson 9–10). As in all ages, the powerful and cunning, in some ways the best and the brightest, lead us inevitably to the field of carnage in order to demonstrate their manliness, to prove their courage, to distinguish themselves as heroes, and to test and confirm their convictions.

For Doak and the Princeton Presbyterians of his time, the emphasis was not upon the alliance of sports and religion but rather upon rigorous learning and religion. "Court records of the time are full of instances of thievery, fighting, drunkenness, and gambling. Duelling among the leaders was not uncommon." In addition there was cockfighting, horse racing, and wrestling, all reflective of "a type of moral rebellion" (Pridgen 27). A preacher-teacher such as Doak had to be strong physically in order to deal with many of his own community, as well as to fight against the British, the Indians, and the dangerous environment; but there was no place for physical training in the curricula of his schools. Like the ancient Israelites with whom these frontier Calvinists were often compared, they knew the necessity of a citizenry that was physically rugged and adept at combat sports, but they were at the same time skeptical of what sports and amusements could become if not practiced with some restraint.

In the next generation a noticeable shift occurred in the focus of education. If Doak, with his emphasis upon classical languages, was the representative figure of the last decades of the eighteenth century and the first quarter of the nineteenth, another Princetonian, Philip Lindsley (1786–1855) represented the next quarter of a century.

The ideal of the union of *mens sana in corpore sano* and the Christian soldier, exemplified so brilliantly by Nathan Hale, did not exactly flourish after the Revolutionary War, but it did not die by any means. The thinking of Lindsley, who became vice president at Princeton in 1817, demonstrated this ideal. Though no one at Princeton seemed to take him seriously at the time, Lindsley was pointing the way toward the future with his ideas on reform of education and the introduction of physical education and even organized athletics into the curriculum.

Lindsley was an early advocate of what has come to be called the catharsis theory, the belief that participation in sports provides a healthy outlet for youthful energy. The colleges, Lindsley thought, should provide "complete employment of a proper kind for all the time of every individual. Keep your youth busy [giving off steam] and you keep them out of harm's way" (quoted in Wertenbaker 163). Though Lindsley did not state what form of athletics he advocated, "he obviously had in mind running, jumping, wrestling, and other sports practiced by the Greeks and Romans" (ibid.). Though youth are exhorted to exercise and allowed time for it, Lindsley argued, they are unfortunately left to their discretion. As a result they spend their time in "idle lounging, talking, smoking, sleeping." Often the time is spent in "sedentary games, which, whether in themselves lawful or unlawful, are always injurious to the student because he requires recreation of a different kind" (Lindsley, *Address* 25). Lindsley also advocated a program of student self-help that has since become a distinguishing feature of American education.

President Ashbel Green of Princeton did not think too highly of Lindsley's theories. Green's plan in order to restore an atmosphere of piety at unruly Nassau Hall was to organize Sunday schools, Bible societies, and tract societies. But in January 1817 there occurred one of the worst riots in the history of Nassau Hall, a "tornado" in the words of Green. The causes of these "enormities," Lindsley believed, were to be found "in the fixed, irreconcilable and deadly hostility . . . to the whole system established in this college by chartered legislators and guardians, a system of diligent study, of guarded moral conduct and of reasonable attention to religious duty. The more carefully such a system is administered, the more offensive it will be rendered to such youth." The storm of the riot, he hoped, had swept away "the concealed taint of moral pestilence" and left the school with "a purer atmosphere" (Wertenbaker 169). Score one, perhaps, for the catharsis theory.

The new atmosphere, though, still lacked the progressive ideas of Lindsley. Offered the presidency of the college in 1823, he declined and assumed the presidency of the University of Nashville, where he remained in office for twenty-six years. In the South, he wrote a colleague at Princeton, his ideas were accepted more readily than at his alma mater (ibid., 175). His inaugural address as president of the University of Nashville (later to become part of Vanderbilt University) remained in the Princeton library for more than a hundred years before its pages were cut (164).

Lindsley was not, however, enamored of the South. At times Nashville seemed to him "to swarm with vagrant fiddlers, fire eaters, jugglers, lecturers, as well as beggars of all sorts, and descriptions" (Thorp 164). On the other hand, one could also find in Nashville in 1825 "traveling artists, a theater of sorts, a museum of natural history, and a reading room maintained by popular subscription" (165). In the opinion of some observers Nashville as early as 1801 had been a hotbed of deism, a heritage that could not have been helpful to Lindsley, who, even though he came to educate rather than proselytize, still had been trained as a Presbyterian minister.

Lindsley did not set out to perfect Tennesseans, but he did try to change them in the ways that he could. His message was different from that of the first wave of Princetonians who came to the South both to preach the Gospel and to teach classical languages (see Come). To be sure, Lindsley stressed languages and learning as much as any of the older generation, and he set the model himself, in one year, 1847, reading 117 books. Lindsley, though, brought another classical element into the picture about which the older generation had been quiet. Even from the beginning, he repeatedly stressed physical education and heroic ideals. In his lengthy inauguration address in Nashville in January 1825, he said that the schools of the Greeks and Romans "were all theatres of active sports and games and military tactics. Inured to labour, to athletic exercises, to temperance, to study, to every species of bodily and mental effort from infancy, their youth entered upon the duties of manhood with every advantage, prepared to serve their country in the cabinet or in the field, in peace and in war, at home and abroad, in public and in private, with the strength of Hercules and the wisdom of Minerva" (Lindsley, *Address* 24).

While extolling classical values, Lindsley anchored his educational philosophy in scripture so that every teacher was in effect a preacher. "In every place of education the bible ought to be the daily companion of every individual; and no man ought to be suffered to teach at all who refused to teach the bible. 'Train up a child in the way he should go, and he will not depart from it' is the doctrine of revelation, of reason, and of experience" (ibid., 26).

The last sentence is the key to understanding the essence of Lindsley's view of education, farsighted for its time. He placed experience and reason on the same plane as revelation, for without reason and experience revelation brought on such problems as sectarianism, which Lindsley saw everywhere in Tennessee. "The principle cause of the multiplication and dwarfish dimensions of western colleges is, no doubt, the diversity of religious denominations among us. Almost every sect will have its college, generally one at least in every state" (quoted in Woolverton 11). Suspicious of religious zeal, Lindsley wanted to keep the University of Nashville nonsectarian, though some Baptists and Methodists were suspicious of his own Presbyterian efforts (ibid., 8).

Though a Presbyterian minister, Lindsley in some ways represented the Enlightenment. He wanted to develop among the population mechanical skills—conducting what we today would call vocational education—without de-emphasis on the classics. His optimistic approach to education was strenuous and demanding and anticipated the provisions of the Morrill Act by several decades. With his focus upon practical arts and physical training, he was a pioneer in Tennessee and the West, but he also followed a tradition that reached back through the Enlightenment to the Renaissance and to ancient Greece, where music and gymnastics were regarded as mates of the soul, as Socrates makes clear in his discussion of the relationship in Plato's *Republic*.

Luther, Milton, Montaigne, and others broadened education to include some type of physical education, but it was not until the Enlightenment that interest in the education of the body began to break "through the confines of an intellectual aristocracy." The Enlightenment accented the power of knowledge "and assumed man's essential goodness and potential improvement." Franklin made positive references to running, leaping, wrestling, and swimming for boys in his *Proposals Relating to the Education of Youth in Pennsylvania* (1794), and Jefferson in 1785 recommended two hours of daily exercise, including running, walking, and horseback riding. In a proposal for a federal university, Benjamin Rush approved all exercises "calculated to impart health, strength, and elegance to the human body," and in a "Sermon on Exercise" he encouraged mountain climbing, swimming, skating, bowling, playing quoits, jumping, and playing such games as golf and tennis (Betts, "Mind and Body" 787–89). Lindsley's eclectic approach to education was very much in the spirit of the Enlightenment. In his inaugural address in Nashville he recommended that American colleges "borrow some ideas from the New Swiss schools, something from the Greeks and Romans, something from our military academies at Norwich and West Point, something from the pages of Locke, Milton, and other writers—something from common sense, from old and existing institutions" (*Address* 31).

It is clear in retrospect that Lindsley is a major figure in the development of sports in the schools, though education did not immediately go in that direction. Still, he was one of the first educators of influence to admit the value of physical training and to connect that training with classical ideals. He read Kant, who advocated play for its health benefits. He was one of the first American educators to use the phrase *mens sana in corpore sano,* which he thought a binding principle. In 1837 Lindsley, in setting forth his idea of the "noble university," included physical education along with a list of subjects both extensive and impressive (Thorpe 166). It is little wonder that scholars rate him as one of the most influential educators of the nineteenth century.

But in one sense Lindsley was a brilliant failure. He brought to the backcountry the fire of classical training in body and mind combined with Christian revelation, but he did not have faith in that crucial democratic dictum that all could and should drink deep at the Pierian Spring. He represented a religious and military eastern establishment that was in some ways squarely set against the egalitarian spirit of the frontier. While both practical and heroic with progressive attitudes, Lindsley, in typical Calvinist fashion, believed that certain conditions were fixed by fate or God. He was against slavery, holding that the sin of slavery hurt whites more than blacks, yet he felt that "Negroes required some kind of subjugation." In weaker moments he made disparaging comments about blacks, as he did about others in Tennessee. While "bemoaning the awful cruelty of separation of slave families," he "succumbed to the notion that Slavery was recognized in the Decalogue" and that Negroes "would perish if set free" (Woolverton 9). In spite of his reading in Enlightenment literature, he did not share with Franklin the view that the potential learning ability of blacks was the same as that of whites or with Jefferson the idea that some day the slaves would "be free." He showed none of the zeal for educating slaves that, say, Gideon Blackburn had for Indians.

The irony of Linsley's failure, considering his fortress view of education and references to military training, is illustrated by an editorial in the *Republican Banner and Nashville Whig* on 28 September 1849, expressing opposition to the Yankee president:

> Select a president from the South or West, of sound active mind,
> a well balanced head which will give him common sense about

everything, a man of firmness, of urbanity and a dash of chivalry in his composition. One who understands well the subject of our domestic institution of slavery, because Southern States are the largest field of patronage. It is not necessary that he should be learned in books, nor a Professor of any of the different creeds of religion. . . . If you expect a university ever to flourish in this city composed of young men of Tennessee . . . you must put a general at the head of them. [quoted in ibid., 8]

A general was exactly what the University of Nashville got in the Civil War, several in fact–in Union Blue.

Though viewed by some locals as a Yankee intellectual, Lindsley had more in common with his critics than at first meets the eye. He may have lacked "a dash of chivalry," but he was a knight nevertheless, on of the Calvinist variety. For Lindsley, excellence and equality were not compatible. It is no accident that Old Lindsley Hall at Peabody Normal School looked exactly like the military fortress. Separated from democratic idealism, which calls for and needs the education of all the people, the aristocratic system failed (and still fails) both to foster a community of citizens capable of enlightened self-government and to educate the whole person no matter how much the classics were invoked and despite the fact that such education was the professed goal. The elitist educational system that Lindsley practiced degenerated into dogma and indoctrination. It could teach neither relatedness nor social responsibility, the shepherd's alternatives to conflict and control.

One result of Lindsley's "great model" approach to education has been methodology courses in teacher training that reached high art forms at the George S. Peabody College and spread over the school systems of the South in ever-widening circles of mediocrity. At the core of this educational philosophy is the military drill method of instruction, the seating-chart syndrome with every chair lined up in battalion formation and every mind taught not to question and track ideas, as Socrates taught, but to follow. Where would the nation have been had enough citizens asked harder questions in the 1850s instead of spouting martial and religious clichés? Only a few, like Walt Whitman, were able to overcome such a limitation.

It is no wonder that for so long and still today we confuse

education with training, the principal method of preparation for athletes and soldiers. It is a system that abhors philosophical thinking and champions the "division of labor" as seen in specialized preparation for teaching, ministry, law, the military, and athletics. In the view of James G.M. Ramsey, the quality of learning in Tennessee was higher at statehood (1796) than a century later. What caused the decline in quality was not opening up public education to more and more people but a change in method and a change in belief in the goals. In the beginning classics were for the training of the mind, even among, especially among, children in the backwoods of Tennessee, who proudly recited in Hebrew or Latin at their graduation from grammar school. Generally the classics or Princeton methods were abandoned in favor of vocationalism, the training of the person to fill roles in an increasingly complex society. The same problems haunt us today on an unparalleled scale. We continue to talk about *mens sana in corpore sano* as Philip Lindsley did, but we show no real conviction that the mind is as worthy of development as the body. In fact, we may be more afraid of the mind than ever. The proof lies in our treatment of the athlete, whom we ask to pray before the games but fail to educate in a meaningful way through the week. It is decidedly an undemocratic, un-Christian, and heretical practice reflective of the worst aspects of European knighthood, which, under the label of Christianity, took root not only in cavalier country but also in the Puritan soil of the Ivy League and gradually subverted our entire educational system, North and South, East and West, down to the present day.

# 4

# The Acrobatic Christianity of the Early Frontier

While sports were Christianized in the nineteenth century, under the influence initially of the eastern schools and colleges and later the YMCA, on the southern frontier Christianity was muscularized by sport. "Sporting," says Thomas D. Clark, "was the lifeblood of the frontier" (30). The people who settled there were not always the most gentle or sophisticated or successful. Into this wilderness Protestantism would push with all the forces at its command to do battle against sports in the effort to win souls. The result of the conflict was a truce of sorts, an alliance between sports and religion, that still defines the nature of both in the South and beyond. It can be said that the spread of muscular Christianity in the United States in the nineteenth century was like a pincer operation aimed at the heartland of America. One prong was northern, urban, academic, knightly, elitist, and, after the Civil War, church-sponsored, while the other, earlier one was southern, rural, anti-intellectual, populist, and in desperate need of clergy, according to Protestant churchmen. A contrast between political, rational control and a more emotional (irrational) display is suggested, the one neoclassic, the other romantic. The northern movement provided the dogma or form; the southern the spirit. The Irish figured in both wings of the movement, to a lesser degree in the North (the Irish Catholics or "Fighting Irish"). More significant, the southern Scotch-Irish Protestants were the primary target of the Great Revival (1797–1805) that invigorated American evangelism and gave it the strength to confront its opponents.

If the Irish were directly involved in the evolution of our sporting heritage, so, we can be sure, were the English. Indeed, the effort to evangelize, civilize, and transform American culture by eastern educators and seaboard evangelists is reminiscent of the age-old battle between the Anglo-Saxons and the Celts, between the powers of the centers of "civilization," the Rome-London axis, and those on the fringe: the wild highlanders of Scotland, the lowlanders who became the Ulstermen, the unruly Irish Catholics, and, in the New World, the frontiersmen on the one hand and the Indians on the other (see Cunningham xxi-ii). The war between "Western Christendom" and the "Celtic fringe" took many forms, and one of the ongoing campaigns was that between the postrevolutionary churches of the Eastern Seaboard, mainly the Presbyterian, Methodist, and Baptist, and the unconverted, fighting, drinking, horse-racing Scotch-Irish who had played major roles in defeating both the Indians and the British.

Sports in early settlement days did not require extensive practice or training, but participants often displayed considerable strength and skill. A variety of competitions took place, including leapfrog, foot races, wrestling, and the throwing of shoulder stones, tomahawks, knives, or long bullets. But "the more exciting sports were bearbaiting, dogfighting, and gander-pulling" (Clark 37). The most controversial of sporting displays was the "rough and tumble," a free-for-all with two contestants (usually male but occasionally female) in which anything and everything was permitted, including biting, pulling hair, and gouging out opponents' eyes with specially prepared nails. In Virginia laws were passed against maiming in 1748 and against gouging, biting, kicking, or stomping in 1772 (Fischer 737). Observers may have exaggerated their descriptions of such frontier activities for dramatic or political reasons, such as showing how uncivilized some frontier folk were, but for the most part impromptu boxing and wrestling matches seemed to end without permanent physical damage or even unkind feelings. After a brawl, "the two fighters would shake hands, go down to the river and wash up, and then empty a demijohn together" (Alderman 229). The profanation of the Sabbath became a symbol of the evil the early churches sought to confront, and frontier sports and rough amusements figured prominently in such profanation, along with drunkenness, which had reached epidemic proportions.

Settlers, of course, had many reasons for moving from established, more civilized eastern comforts into the untamed areas where hardships were a way of life. Peter Cartwright, the famous Methodist evangelist, was not exaggerating when he described Logan County, Kentucky, where his father had lived, as "Rogues' Harbor," for "refugees from all parts of the Union had fled there . . . to escape justice or punishment." Here "murderers, horse thieves, highway robbers, and counterfeiters . . . put all law at defiance." Sunday, Cartwright said, "was a day set apart for hunting, fishing, horseracing, cardplaying, balls, dances, and all kinds of jollity and mirth" (Nottingham 20–21). But thousands of those who went west were simply poor people who came from places like Ulster to start a new life in the American South, especially Appalachia.

These immigrants were predominantly "Scotch-Irish," who carried in their veins, according to Frederick Morgan Davenport's somewhat "racial" approach in *Primitive Traits in Religious Revivals* (1905), both "the intelligent purpose of the Teuton" and "the strong emotionalism of the Celt" (60). This perception of a dual heritage may not, of course, be entirely factual, but the Scotch-Irish have been encumbered with this somewhat negative characterization by the ruling order in both England and America, which thought of itself as less susceptible to the forces of primitive passions. One historian has suggested a juxtaposition of two traditions in our past, "the Great Tradition" and "the Little Tradition"; the former refers to classical learning and high culture, including highbrow theology, while the latter refers to folk heritage and popular culture and the outpouring of the spirit of the commoner (Redfield 70–71). The two strains are supposed always to coexist. Here the focus is upon the "peasant" tradition of frontier religion. In some measure many settlers of Tennessee and Kentucky called the Scotch-Irish were the target of social control of an essentially English institution, Protestant evangelism, which succeeded in organizing in America not only religion but sports as well, incorporating "Celtic" elements into an essentially bourgeois "Anglo-Saxon"culture, wherein violence, decried repeatedly on an individual level, is institutionalized in a military culture that prizes combative sports such as football.

Presbyterian ministers coming from Princeton and other seminaries generally distrusted "free outpourings of the spirit," but hardshell Baptists and circuit-riding Methodists often had a different attitude toward the "exercises," which took strange forms and meant to many that the participants had been touched by the Holy Spirit. Many ministers, in order to induce the "exercises," thus practiced a "muscular Christianity" or "acrobatic Christianity" or "active Christianity," emphasizing the "heart" as opposed to the "head," the spirit and power in the blood. It was a brand of Christianity often set against some sports such as horse racing and cockfighting, especially if these were conducted on the Sabbath, and the accompanying sins of drinking and gambling. " 'Rastlin' with Satan" was the common metaphor for the individual's own battle with sin and the church's campaign against depravity throughout the backwoods (for English parallels, see Phillips 290). This familiar story was reflected in the martial metaphors of the Church Fathers, but on the American frontier the conflict took on unique and remarkable features. In their contests with Satan, frontier ministers adopted a combative attitude and an athletic manner that conveniently merged with the Christian muscularity later promoted by the colleges. It is sometimes difficult to distinguish between a Christian athlete and a muscular minister.

The idealism of the eastern schools was essentially English in character, military and athletic in origin, traceable to Greco-Roman culture, specifically Greek *arete* and Roman *mens sana in corpore sano*, and of course to the tradition of knighthood. The spirit of frontier evangelism also came from England, with John Wesley. There were degrees of the manifestation of the spirit, however; while Wesley emphasized fervor, he deplored the vociferous singing and posturing and leaping of the Jumpers, a religious sect that arose in Wales in

1740. "They are honest," said Wesley, "but understand little of their own nature" (quoted in Davenport 142). All is relative. To the Oxford establishment of his time Wesley himself seemed too enthusiastic, considering the physical effects that the Methodist sermons wrought in some of his listeners. Still the goal in England and America was social control, both political and moral, generated not by armed might but by conversion of the population to a "new life."

The folks in the Tennessee-Kentucky country at the beginning of the nineteenth century were susceptible to the Methodist manner and message. Ministers expertly fanned the emotion of the backwoods settlers, both in order to save their souls and to make them live more virtuous lives, giving up drinking and fighting. In the East and later in the South after the 1820s, the effort at control also took a different form, in the military drills, physical exercises, gymnastics, and calisthenics promoted by such Ivy Leaguers as Sylvanus Thayer, the Father of West Point and of U.S. technology, and Harvard man George Bancroft, the founder of the U.S. Naval Academy and co-founder of the Round Hill School in Northampton, Massachusetts, where in 1823 physical education in the United States began. In the Old Southwest, however, the place of conversion of behavior was not so much the playing field and parade ground as the campground.

Though it might be said that the ministers of the Old Southwest prepared or neutralized the territory of the frontiers for the later bearers of a more systemized and socially sanctioned type of athletic culture, in the vast rural South the roots of muscular Christianity were not in the schools and colleges run by educated Yankees with classical ideals integrating arms and religion. Instead, in the campground, illiterate and semiliterate homegrown ministers, mainly Baptists and Methodists, 'rastled valiantly with Satan, depending not on brains but on the power of the Spirit to see them through their ordeals. To be sure, the roaring evangelists often softened the ground for the northern invasion of organized Christian athletics, but the northern prong of the pincer movement did not begin its closing motion in the South until late in the nineteenth century and early in the twentieth, when the college missionary work of YMCA stalwarts Dwight L. Moody, Amos Alonzo Stagg, and James Naismith began to take effect nationwide. The cult of knighthood, strong in the South since the arrival of John Smith in 1607, dovetailed with the philosophy of Lindsley. But knighthood was by no means the exclusive property of Anglicans and Southerners, as proved by the mighty work in the subjugation of Indians elsewhere in the New World by Hernando Cortés and by Miles Standish. In the Old Southwest, however, it is not the exalted tradition of knighthood or the highbrow learning of the Ivy league but the "Little Tradition" or "peasant" legacy that must be considered. The peasant tradition is not exactly the same as the yeoman tradition, but in any event the folk culture, with all its flaws and virtues, was eventually overwhelmed by the knightly tradition prized so highly by southern aristocracy and the Ivy League founders of West Point. Based on the evolution of sports and religion, there is much less difference between cavalier and Yankee, in spite of the Civil War, than between cavalier and yeoman. The yeoman is always the sacrificial victim on the glorious altar of chivalry (see Taylor; Watson).

The achievement of the Scotch-Irish pioneers is a matter of record and, in the view of Theodore Roosevelt, of national pride. Roosevelt paints a romantic picture of "the Watauga Folk" who "won the land" and made homes in the wilderness where "none but heroes can succeed wholly in the work" (8:157). More often commentators shared the view of Benjamin Franklin, who called them "violent, narrow-minded drunkards–'white savages' " (Ayers 22). In the Revolution, though, their martial talents became a national resource. "Almost to a man," says a British historian, they fought "on the side of the insurgents. They supplied some of the best soldiers of Washington" (William Edward Hartpole Lecky, quoted in Ford 208). Still, their overall image remained mixed, to say the least. Observers frequently noted a strain of violent behavior as part of the makeup of their character, which manifested itself in a certain bullheadedness, regarding as synonymous *opponent* and *enemy*, and responding violently to any perceived affront (Ayers 22).

Almost in rebuttal of Frederick Jackson Turner's famous thesis that the frontier captured and transformed the colonists into fighters, the Scotch-Irish brought their love of fighting with them from the Old World. Edward L. Parker writes, in his *History of Londonderry,*

Their diversions and scenes of social intercourse were of a character not the most refined and cultured; displaying physical rather than intellectual and moral powers, such as boxing matches, wrestling, foot races, and other athletic exercise. At all public gatherings, the "ring" would be usually formed; and the combatants, in the presence of neighbors, brothers, and even fathers, would encounter each other in close fight, or at arms length, as the prescribed form might be; thus giving and receiving the well directed blow, until the face, limbs, and body of each bore the marks of almost savage brutality. All this was done, not in anger, or from unkind feeling toward each other, but simply to test the superiority of strength and agility. [quoted in Ford 243]

This is not to say that only the Scotch-Irish engaged in boxing or such fights as here described, but almost identical descriptions can be found in accounts of frontier gatherings. The relatively purposeless "diversions" of the Scotch-Irish no doubt contributed to their image as a "pernicious or pugnacious" people in the minds of easterners in the United States. The fights described by Parker bring to mind the frontier "rough and tumble," which put no limit short of murder on what opponents might do to each other. Facial disfigurement—the biting off of ears and noses and gouging out of eyeballs—became the distinguishing feature. It may well have been the English, as Henry Adams claimed, who introduced this "sport" to America ("United States in 1800" 74). Arnold Toynbee also rejects the Turner thesis, at least in part. While the mark of Red Indian savagery was visible in the white victors, the violence of the settlers of Appalachia, he believed, could be linked to the violent heritage of a culture always residing at the fringe of civilization, and later on the American frontier ("Scotland" 387–88).

It may be that such violent, untamed behavior is not consistent with more organized sports. E. Norman Gardiner in *Athletics of the Ancient World* suggests that "the athletic spirit . . . is found only in physically vigorous and virile nations that put a high value on physical excellence; it arises naturally in those societies where the power is in the hands of an aristocracy which depends on military skill and physical strength to maintain itself" (2). The key word here is *aristocracy*. The Lowland Scots who became the ancestors of the

Scotch-Irish had been caught between two aristocracies, that of the English and that of the Highland Scots, both of whom depended on military skill and physical prowess "to maintain" themselves. The Scotch-Irish, often placed on the same level with "the lower-class English," also have a sporting spirit, but it has been manifested through the years not so much by organized games as by spontaneous, relatively unstructured play.

In literature, religion, and sports the Old Southwest and then the western frontier exhibited a general retreat from formalism, complexity, and sophistication that characterized Tidewater and English high society. Prized instead were the simple ways of folk culture. In literature there was the tall tale told in regional dialect, in religion the bare meetinghouse or campground, and, in sports, games in which ordinary people could engage without extensive practice. Some amusements were work turned into social play, such as corn shucking, flax pulling, logrolling, house-raising, and maple sugar boiling. These events were relatively harmless unless too much liquor was imbibed, but as a rule extreme violence, as well as wanton waste, characterized the frontier sports and games (see Clark 31). Everywhere one looks in the literature of the nineteenth century, both in fiction and in actual accounts, scenes of violence proliferate.

The churches in the postrevolutionary, trans-Allegheny frontier faced enormous challenges. Church organization was in shambles. In the East churches had been destroyed, leaders killed, and several denominations—Methodist, Episcopal, and Quaker—operated under a cloud of treason for having supported the British. In 1777, for instance, Wesley prayed "that God would restore the spirit of love and sound mind to the poor deluded rebels in America" (quoted in Sweet, *Religion* 30). A number of Methodist ministers were jailed in Annapolis, several beaten, and some tarred and feathered. Owing to Wesley's Toryism, English preachers generally withdrew from America, the most notable exception being Francis Asbury, who cast his lot with the Americans (ibid., 31).

The disestablishment of the Church of England in itself led to a de-emphasis on formal religion, and deism was widespread owing to the popularity of Tom Paine's *Age of Reason*. Some estimates claim that in 1800 half of Kentucky was deist. Hardened veterans of the

Revolution swore they would never allow the establishment of a Puritan Sabbath in the western settlements (C.A. Johnson 9–10). Such a vow went squarely against one of the cherished aims of ministers. In the end, though, a tradeoff would occur between the English establishment and the Scotch-Irish influences. The Scotch-Irish got to keep their love of religion and sports, and the English gained social control through the organizational structure of religion and games. Eventually it would look as if there had been from the beginning one concerted force from the British Isles, from which other groups, especially blacks, would have great difficulty in acquiring basic human rights.

The Protestant churches had all kinds of clever devices for enforcing rules like the restrictions on Sabbath activities among the poor and illiterate, especially slaves. The fixed fate of the Negro even on the eve of the Civil War is merely the most obvious example. Stuck in a condition of perpetual dependence and servitude, slaves on Sunday could neither work for themselves nor play. Two of Hardin E. Taliaferro's "Sketches" from 1859–"The Rail Splitting Negro" and "The Negro Fisherman"–demonstrate the cruelty of such rules (89–90, 100–101). The sentences for sporting violation of the Sabbath were always severe, often final, and not limited to punishment of Negroes (see Baughman 380–81).

The perceived problem was not atheism as an idea but godlessness as a daily practice. Said one Presbyterian minister, "Worldly mindedness, infidelity, and dissipation threatened to deluge the land and sweep away all vestiges of piety and morality" (quoted in C.A. Johnson 9). In some homes religious instruction was provided as a matter of course, but the general tenor of the time was enough to cause sober reflection among those most determined to bring about change. In March 1797 Bishop Asbury wrote: "When I consider where they came from, where they are, and how they are, and how they are called to go farther, their being unsettled with so many objects to take their attention, with the health and good air they enjoy, and when I reflect that not one in a hundred came here to get religion; but rather to get plenty of good land, I think it will be well if some or many do not eventually lose their souls" (quoted in Cleaveland 29).

The camp meeting became the primary method of attack of the evangelical movement from the more established East. It did not originate in America but was perfected here. The climate, the lack of buildings, and the distribution of a sparse population over a vast area made the camp meeting a natural means for spreading the Gospel in the early Southwest. And the heritage and temperament of the pioneers as well as various pressures associated with frontier life generated an atmosphere ripe for exploitation.

In England the camp meetings were by comparison well-scrubbed affairs, almost like "parish wakes" and "May Day celebrations" (Phillips 299). In the United States the meetings were not nearly so subdued, decorous, or formal. They started on Thursday or Friday and lasted until the following Tuesday. From as far as a hundred miles away the people would come, sometimes by the thousands, especially if vigorous preaching was in store. They would camp in covered wagons or under the trees on the grounds. Preaching and praying and singing and shouting could be heard at all hours of the day and night, except for a period of relief before dawn. Not all the activity, however, was religious:

> Adolescents were frequently among the affected [by the religious frenzy]; it was therefore necessary to post guards to prevent young couples from wandering into the woods. Women threw themselves on the ground in suggestive postures, tore open their clothes, hugged and kissed everyone within reach. Those who carried out the victims were filled sometimes with a passion not strictly religious. It has been suggested that at the camp meetings more souls were begotten than saved.

> The stalls and store which were set up around the grounds frequently sold whiskey. It found ready purchasers, not only among the scoffing rowdies, but even among the faithful. Friction occurred between the religious and nonreligious elements, sometimes ending in a free-for-all fight. The Westerner, even when religious, was not docile, and did not consider seriously the admonition to "turn the other cheek." [Leyburn 199]

The conjunction of fighting, drinking, and religion suggests to some a strong presence of the Scotch-Irish. It was a classic contest between the free, independent Celtic spirit and the stern puritanism that forbade drinking, fighting, gambling, and all sports on Sunday. The result was not a clear-cut victory for either side, as we shall see, but a merging of interests in which the church eventually dropped all opposition to Sunday amusements, even violent sports, in exchange for tribute from those who loved to play. In 1800 it was by no means clear what path American culture would take. Civilization itself seemed to hang in the balance, at least in the minds of those on the camp meeting circuit.

In *The Great Revival,* John B. Boles calls the meeting at Cane Ridge in Logan County, Kentucky, "the truly Brobdingnagian meeting of the entire southern revival." It was an event so awesome as to qualify for Rudolph Otto's classic definition of the holy: that before which "words recoil and understanding cannot penetrate." Nothing quite like it had ever been seen before or since, not at Woodstock or football victory celebrations in Pittsburgh, Knoxville, or Columbus. Drawing upon numerous firsthand accounts, Boles presents a composite picture of this unique and forgotten scene in our American past.

> The crowd began gathering early on Friday, August 8, 1801.... By Saturday the throng was variously estimated between twelve and twenty-five thousand—entirely possible for this region of Kentucky.... A cacophonous clamor of shouted sermons, chanted hymns, ecstatic hosannas, and mournful wailing filled the air with the smell of smoke, sweat, and excitement.... As many as eighteen Presbyterian ministers were counted and probably more Baptists and Methodist preachers were present.... Using every technique known to their profession, the ministers urged their listeners to consider the terrors of hell and then imagine the glories of heaven. God seemed evidently to be at hand.... Whenever a listener would fall, overcome by his emotions, large numbers of worshippers would crowd around him, praising God and singing hymns. All of this added to the clamor and confusion. [65–67]

James B. Finley, the celebrated Methodist circuit rider, considered himself a free thinker at the time but dated his conversion from what he saw at Cane Ridge.

> After some time I returned to the scene of excitement, the
> waves of which, if possible, had risen still higher. The same
> awfulness of feeling came over me. I stepped up to a log,
> where I could have a better view of the surging sea of
> humanity. The scene that then presented itself to me was
> indescribable. At one time I saw at least five hundred swept
> down in a moment as if a battery of a thousand guns had been
> opened upon them, and then immediately followed shrieks
> and shouts that rent the very heavens. . . . I fled for the woods
> a second time and wished I had staid at home. [quoted in
> C.A. Johnson 64–65]

Accounts of falling, jerking, and other "exercises" at such camp
meetings are so astonishing as to make one wonder if the Protestant
churches and educational system together have not been in conspir-
acy to keep them hidden from subsequent generations, for few
except historians have ever heard of these manifestations of the
Great Revival. Testimony recounts that those experiencing the falling were never injured, as if protected by a higher power, but those
who underwent the "holy jerks," in many ways the most extraordinary of the exercises, did not share the same immunity. So violent
was the shaking in some instances that necks were actually broken.
Even the experiences that did not prove fatal left a "trail of shattered
nerves over the West" (Leyburn 198). Originating in east Tennessee,
the jerks spread across the frontier camp meeting circuit like a holy
virus. Peter Cartwright claimed that he had seen as many as five
hundred people affected with the jerks at one time, and they were
so contagious that more than one minister was smitten in the act of
trying to stop them. There is evidence that even the highly educated
Samuel Doak was afflicted (see Shurter 147), and there is no doubt
that one of his pupils, Gideon Blackburn, celebrated missionary to
the Indians and president of Centre College, was regularly beset
(Queener 16). It was as if the individual, without any choice in the
matter, had become not a contestant in the battle with Satan but a
battleground, where cosmic forces contended for victory, or a football, possessed first by one side in the drama and then by the other.
Football, in fact, was the metaphor that Richard McNemar employed
in his description of the jerks in 1808:

He must necessarily go as he was stimulated, whether with a violent dash on the ground and bounce from place to place like a foot-ball, or hop around with head, limbs and trunk, twitching and jolting in every direction, as if they must inevitably fly asunder. . . . By this strange operation the human frame was commonly so transformed and disfigured as to lose every trace of its natural appearance. Some times the head would be twitched right and left to a half round with such velocity that not a feature would be discovered, but the face appear as much behind as before, and in the quick progressive jerk it would seem as if the person were transmuted into some other species of creature. [quoted in Cleaveland 99]

Other "exercises" on the frontier were the rolling exercise, the barking exercise, the dancing exercise, and the laughing and singing exercises. The rolling exercise was so named because communicants rolled around like logs, unable to control themselves and oblivious to anything that might be in their paths. Boles says that the barking was probably an exaggeration of the grunts elicited by the jerks, but barking seemed to have a style of its own, according to the vivid description of eyewitness accounts: "It was common to hear people barking like a flock of spaniels on their way to meeting. . . . There they would start up suddenly in a fit of barking, rush out, roam around, and in a short time come barking and foaming back. Down on all fours they sometimes went growling, snapping their teeth, and barking just like dogs" (Boles 101).

After bringing on the more violent exercises, ministers were then faced with the practical problem of what to do with the afflicted, often quoting to them words from Scripture: "Bodily exercise profiteth little" (1 Timothy 4:8). The "exercises" of the Protestants on the southern frontier were not the same kind Paul was talking about in his letter to Timothy, and certainly they are of a different order from the "spiritual exercises" of Ignatius Loyola, but a frightened seminary-trained Presbyterian minister seeing the "holy jerks," for the first time would no doubt reach for any passage that might even remotely apply and bring solace to the affected worshiper and restore order and reason to the proceedings. There was also holy dancing and a sanctified sound called "holy whining." Holy dancing in fact was encouraged as a way of warding off more disagreeable exercises (Cleaveland 101). Those undergoing the experience had perhaps a more mixed reaction, both a sense of danger and confusion and also a feeling of being chosen by powers beyond human control, perhaps a demonstration of spiritual excellence.

Just as a score or more of sermons might be heard at any one time at a camp meeting, so might a dozen hymns clash at once, "many of which were the crudest doggerel" (Sweet, *Revivalism* 144). One of the most popular was "Shout Old Satan's Kingdom Down," whose chorus shows both how close the camp meetings were to pep rallies and how little distance we have come in the composing of cheers:

> Shout, shout, we're gaining ground, *Hallelujah!*
> We'll shout old Satan's Kingdom down, *Hallelujah!*
> When Christians pray, the Devil runs, *Hallelujah!*
> And leaves the field to Zion's sons,
>   *O glory Hallelujah!*
>        [ibid.]

Another Methodist fight song is worthy of notice because of the light it sheds upon the nature of the enemy of the frontier ministry, which consisted of an unholy trinity identified in the first line as "the world, the devil and Tom Paine." The song insisted that "the Lord defends the Methodist. / They pray, they sing, they preach the best" (ibid., 144). "We're number one" may be a direct descendant of such competition.

While Presbyterians were divided over the issues of sudden conversion, education of the ministry, and decorum of the congregation during services, Methodists especially used the proven techniques of the campground with stunning success. Of the eighteen Presbyterian ministers exhorting at Cane Ridge, less than half continued to support the revivalist program. What gave them pause, and some Baptist clergy as well, was the drift toward Armenianism (Posey, *Frontier Mission* 28–29). The Armenian doctrine of free grace, free will, and individual responsibility was much more compatible with many settlers than the Calvinist belief in predestination, and straight talk was much more appealing to the unlettered than a fancy style learned in seminaries back east. In the years after Cane Ridge the more startling exercises such as rolling, barking, and jerking waned considerably, but the enthusiasm of the preachers remained high, and "spread-eagle oratory" remained much in vogue. Sometimes they consoled, and sometimes they thundered, the basic technique being to take heaven by storm. The language of the body remained as important as that of the tongue. The physical manner in which the message was conveyed was summarized succinctly by Abraham Lincoln: "When I see a man preach I like to see him act as if he were fighting bees" (C.A. Johnson 188). This undoubtedly was what the campground preacher was doing in "the little one-horse town" in *Huckleberry Finn.* Huck says "he begun to preach . . . with his arms and his body going all the time, and shouting his words out with all his might" (Twain, *Huckleberry* 127). In these short lines by Lincoln and the "Lincoln of our literature" we glimpse the physical gyrations of acrobatic Christianity. Both Hardin E. Taliaferro and George Washington Harris offer further examples in their stories. Humor was not alien, of course, to ministers (see C.A. Johnson 129–30).

So taken were frontiersmen with competition that any preacher displaying a sporting spirit was apt to be warmly received. Once when Andrew Jackson entered Peter Cartwright's church, the preacher was told to watch what he said since Old Hickory was in the congregation, whereupon Cartwright proclaimed, " 'Who cares for General Jackson. He'll go to hell as quick as anybody if he don't repent.' Supposedly Jackson was so pleased by the boldness that he said, 'Give me twenty thousand such men, and I'll whip the whole world, including the devil' " (Clark 154). The military solution was always a quick alternative for Old Hickory. Manliness and the ability to adapt to unexpected challenges were widely admired. Once when a young minister named Bascom saw all the men in his Kentucky congregation rise simultaneously to chase a bear that had just run by the meetinghouse, he himself joined in the chase and soon was ahead of all his people and not far behind the dogs. When the bear was killed, he returned to the house with the others and gave an "uncommonly good sermon" (Posey, *Development* 38–39). By midcentury, says Clark, "there were more enterprising and sporting clergymen on the frontier than those preachers who used homely terms to catch the attention of backwoods listeners." An announcement for services illustrates this point:

> "The reverend Mr. Blaney will preach next Sunday in Dempsey's Grove, at ten A.M. and at four o'clock P.M., Providence permitting. Between services the preacher will run his sorrel mare, Julia, against any nag that can be trotted out in this region for a purse of five hundred dollars!" The purse was made, and Julia, amid deafening shouts, won the day. Not only did the congregation stay for the afternoon services, but some two hundred joined the church: some from sincerity, some from the excitement of the day, and some because the preacher was "a damned good fellow!" [Clark 156]

Keeping score of converts began early. With ministers themselves now leading the assault on the Sabbath by engaging in horse racing, the Sabbath itself as a day of sanctity was endangered. "This was the frontier," says Clark, "and not puritanical New England; people had sporting to do, and there was no better day on which to do it than Sunday"(30).

I do not want to simplify the complex tension between what might be "the praying South" and "the sporting South." It is an old conflict and still much in evidence. Tennessee churches still mount effective campaigns against state lotteries and animal racing, for example, though surrounded by states where these are legal. Organized athletics are exceptional, in that prayer and competition have been joined together in holy matrimony, not only in the South but elsewhere too. In *Subduing Satan* Ted Ownby shows how recently that alliance occurred. In fact, in many areas of the South between 1865 and 1920 there was a spate of "legislation to ensure the quiet of the day [Sunday]. Not until the postbellum years did most states forbid the sale of alcohol on Sunday. Several states prohibited the Sunday enjoyment of specific activities such as baseball, football, golf, tennis, and bowling, and some banned any activity that involved shooting guns, including target shooting" (176).

In the recent South the tension between masculine sinfulness and evangelical control takes many forms. "Willie Nelson . . . can begin a concert with the line 'Whiskey River, take my mind,' and end it with 'Amazing Grace.' Elvis Presley, one of the more flamboyant sinners in American history, included gospel singers and evangelists in his train" (Ownby 211). How have modern sports, with their celebrated abuses, been able to escape the evangelical passion for, as Ownby says, "new laws dealing with everything from prayer and Bible reading in school, to abortion, to pornography, to the content of popular songs and television programs, to the old standby, the sale of alcohol"? (212). (I am not, however, suggesting that sports with all their problems be added to an evangelical hit list.) There are several reasons for the immunity extended to sports by religious reformers. By the emphasis upon victory, sports became a symbol (though a misplaced one) for spiritual success. As a consequence they offer a ready means of proselytizing in an age of simple imagery and uncritical acceptance. Sports suggest self-control, discipline, and obedience, while drinking and gambling have become almost synonymous with addiction and sin. Sports are manly, which squares nicely with the Pauline Christianity that evangelists prefer. Finally, organized sports, like evangelism, is big business and big entertainment. Any criticism of either the sporting industry or the evangelical empires would be bad business for both. The channels on our cable television must, it seems, coexist peacefully.

Just as sports and religion found common ground on the early frontier, so did evangelism and business. One of the most colorful and controversial figures was Lorenzo Dow, who announced at the first camp meeting held in the Mississippi Territory (1804) that he had the latest authentic news from hell! Dow entered the patent medicine game in 1820. Several preachers at the time were trying to learn medicine and to practice it (Posey, *Development* 41), but Dow seemed to have special skills in salesmanship, perhaps anticipating some of the commercial enterprises of the modern evangelical empires.

Worse by far than the business gimmickry of a few evangelists was the widespread animosity between denominations. The Protestants were fighting among themselves, and all of them were fighting the Catholics. Most celebrated were the attacks of parson William G. Brownlow, "the Fighting Parson of the Southern Highlands," who supported the Union and slavery as well. He castigated Catholics with the same wrath he directed at Confederates. He "characterized 'the Catholic Church' 'as a dangerous and immoral operation' which, 'if unchecked, will overturn the civil and religious liberties of the United States' " (Posey, *Religious Strife* 110). The parson claimed that Catholics had killed sixty-eight million Protestants simply because they were Protestants. Considering that each victim had four gallons of blood, he reckoned that the deluge would have been sufficient "to overflow the banks of the Mississippi, and destroy all the cotton and sugar plantations in Mississippi and Louisiana" (111). Apparently Brownlow still dreamed of putting all the imagined spilled blood to good use by washing away the wealth of the Confederacy.

The Catholics did not suffer all this abuse gladly. "They looked upon the camp meetings as 'heathenish assemblies' whose 'demoralizing effect' had been proved. 'What is the area around the camp,' a Catholic writer asked, 'but a scene for the exhibition of vice, where the profane swearer, the reeling drunkard, the rowdy, the pickpocket and such like to mix among the thousands who see only amusement?' " To the Catholics the camp meeting was a "Methodist Holiday" (ibid., 105). Though they often returned fire in a less provocative manner, sometimes the Catholics allowed Protestant ministers to be hoisted on their own verbal petards: The *Telegraph* of 6 March 1845 quoted from the *Millennial Harbinger* a description of the participants in a camp meeting as they sat "looking vacantly into space, with that strange, wild, and indescribable sort of grining [*sic*] smile that we have seen upon the unfortunate inmates of those asylums benevolently provided for the insane." Catholic readers of the *Telegraph* on 17 December 1846 must have enjoyed a reprint from the *Western Christian Advocate* that recommended a deputation of Methodist preachers be sent to Rome, for a "camp meeting in the Coliseum would recall vividly to the minds of the astonished Italians, the Pagan times when the amphitheatre re-echoed to the roar of the lions" (ibid., 106).

A Catholic country picnic in the latter part of the nineteenth century in upstate New York contrasts sharply, as described by Harold Frederic in *The Damnation of Theron Ware*, with the Methodist camp meeting. At the Catholic event, Ware, a Methodist minister, runs upon a baseball game, football, dancing to music, swinging, swimming, wading, and all manner of play, including primitive fisticuffs, which ended up, as was often the case down south, in "genial reconciliation." He also saw to his amazement "a rough narrow shed" where twenty men in shirtsleeves toiled "ceaselessly to keep abreast of the crowd's thirst for beer" (235). Says Ware to his Catholic friends he finds at the celebration, " 'I am in love with your sinners. . . . I've had five days with the saints over in another part of the woods, and they've bored the head off me' " (237). Had Ware been present at the southern camp meeting a few decades earlier he certainly would not have been bored, but he would not have found the official sanction by the churches of sports, games, and alcohol, the absence of which would not have kept the attendants from having a "holiday" anyway. To be sure, the Catholics found nothing wrong with a "holiday." What they objected to theologically was the over-lapping of worship and amusement, which, in the spirit of *eutrapelia*, should remain separate so that one can "turn well" from one to the other. Eventually many Catholics too will be seduced by the idea that sports, instead of providing fun and recreation at picnics, are, after all, serious enough to elevate one as a witness for Christ. The priest in Mary Gordon's *The Company of Women* calls sport a "Protestant Heresy." That is true enough, but it is increasingly becoming an ecumenical heresy as well.

The Civil War, in the view of some historians, ushered in a brief cessation of sectarianism (see Posey, *Religious Strife)*. Is this true, or was sectarianism merely removed to the battlefield? The Civil War was not after all a conflict between the nation's agnostics and atheists but primarily one between believing Christians who divided their churches and took to slaughter. The secretary of the New York YMCA told his counterpart in Richmond: "Your Christians will meet ours in battle." One of the speakers sponsored by the New York YMCA in 1862 was Parson Brownlow (Hopkins 87), the colorful pro-Union, all-American segregationist. In the days ahead Christianity would become increasingly muscular and militant under the twin influences of the YMCA and the national military establishment. The spiritual home of the YMCA was Yale, while the mecca of knighthood was West Point. The goals of knighthood and of the "Y" were completely compatible, and between the two of them the work begun by the muscular evangelists of the early frontier was officially complemented and completed, nationalized and sanctified. In other words, the turbulence of the campground gave way to the rules of the playing field and parade ground. Always knowing best, the English with their *organized* games, chivalry, and flow-chart types of religion had conquered after all. Still the old Celtic features of the revival remain, both in the sporting nature of our stadium crusades and in the evangelical but festive character of our big home games. The campground revival was our first tailgate party. We have institutionalized this activity in our culture along with opening prayers before our own organized "exercises" of falling, rolling, running, jumping, and leaping that we call sports.

What were, then, the essential features of American frontier evangelism? They are the same ones that characterize the muscular Christianity movement to this day, namely an unwavering emphasis upon the suffering of Christ on the Cross as opposed to the suffering of others induced by social conditions; the certainty of apocalypse; a sense of theater and entertainment; a preoccupation with numbers and growth; a selling-the-Gospel mentality; the endorsement of competition (*agon*)—including competition between denominations, or sectarianism—but the explicit denunciation of other forms of play, gambling (*alea*), and drinking (*ilinx*) (the classical terms are Caillois's); the general acceptance of emotional outbursts and bodily agitation ("exercises") as manifestations of gifts of the Spirit, which of course paves the way for the embracing of athletic ability as a form of Christian witnessing and cheering and applause as a display of religious conviction and enthusiasm; the virtual requirement of manliness in ministries; anti-intellectualism; and sectionalism and Americanism.

# 5

# The Soul of American Knighthood

In the first half of the nineteenth century two familiar figures led a battle against ignorance and the wilderness: the teacher-preacher from the eastern college or seminary and the army engineer, more than likely a graduate of West Point. Both believed in discipline and manliness. The Corps of Engineers, dominated by West Pointers, "legitimately traces its beginning back to the days of exploring, mapping, and conquering Indians in the West, and it takes full credit for the opening of the new empire"(Galloway and Johnson 221). In 1850 Wayland Brown, president of Brown University, summed up the engineering achievements of West Point: "Altho there are more than 120 colleges in the United States, the West Point Academy has done more to build up the system of internal improvements in the United States than all the colleges combined" (quoted in Dupuy 44).

While West Point is not now synonymous with the Corps of Engineers, it is hard to imagine one institution without the other even to this day. Nor can we imagine what our culture would have been without the Corps of Engineers, constructor of the Washington Monument, the Library of Congress, the Pentagon, the St. Lawrence Seaway, the Panama Canal, the Alcan Highway, the Burma Road, the Manhattan Project, NASA headquarters in Houston, and the JFK Space Center launching facilities at Cape Canaveral. More recently it has been responsible for mapping the moon. For this organization, the sky is no limit.

According to Stephen Ambrose, "The importance of the Academy to the development of American roads, canals, and railroads cannot be overstated. . . . The Academy's influence in the pedagogic aspects of civil engineering at least equalled its influence in the actual building process" of the country (122–23). West Point graduates helped to establish other schools, including the U.S. Naval Academy, whose graduates achieved glory of their own as inventors and educators. One member of the Naval Academy class of 1878 established the school of engineering at Harvard and became its first dean (Lovell 32), more than 250 years after the founding of our first university.

Controversial because of opposition to the idea of a standing professional army, West Point survived in the first half of the nineteenth century more because of its engineering excellence than because of its contributions to national defense. Davy Crockett of Tennessee introduced a bill in the House of Representatives in 1830 to abolish West Point because of the establishment of a "military nobility," and between 1833 and 1843 four state legislatures–Tennessee, Ohio, Connecticut, and New Hampshire–passed resolutions calling for the abolition of the institution for the same reason (Galloway and Johnson 143–44).

Almost certainly George Washington, our most famous citizen-soldier, could have anticipated the controversy, and for this reason his role in the creation of the Military Academy needs to be put in perspective. In response to a proposal by Alexander Hamilton for a complete system of military education with "a fundamental school" at West Point, another school for engineers and artillerists, one for cavalry and infantry, and one for the navy, Washington wrote just three days before his death, "The establishment of an institution of this kind upon a respectable and extensive basis has ever been considered by me as an object of primary importance to the Country." Though he declined to comment on details of Hamilton's plan, he did urge Congress to establish at least one academy (Ambrose 14). Hamilton's basic argument was simple, even archetypal. "Just as a farmer, if he 'would secure his flocks . . . must go to the expense of shepherds,' America had to have trained military men who could teach civilians the art of war" (ibid., 13). Hamilton's knightly emphasis on the threat of danger is, of course, consistent with his politics: he insisted upon a strong central government backed by an aristocracy.

There is no doubt that Washington, a professional surveyor, would have applauded the role of the Corps of Engineers in the development of the country. The imposing statue of Washington on horseback on the northeast corner of the Plain at West Point proudly proclaims the victorious rider as the "Founder," but what is not well known is that Washington expressed continued support for another type of school, "a national university" that would, in addition to "sciences," also teach "the different branches of literature and the arts." To be located in the Federal District, this university would have provided "young men from all parts of the United States" firsthand knowledge of the "science of government." In addition to receiving preparation for the professions, they should "get fixed in the principles of the Constitution, understand the laws and the true interests and policy of their country." Furthermore, the students from the various regions would, "by forming acquaintances with each other early in life," be cured of "those local prejudices and habitual jealousies which, when carried to excess, are never failing sources of disquietude." Fearing that in Europe young Americans might acquire "habits of dissipation and extravagance" and "principles unfriendly to the rights of man," Washington visualized bringing to America "the best European professors." Before 1795 he had drawn up a will in which he left shares from the Potomac Canal Company and the James River Canal Company toward the endowment of such a university (see Flexner 199–200). Washington, the Father of His Country as well as the founder of the U.S. Military Academy, while giving due homage to engineering knowledge, placed the science of government on an equal or even higher plane.

It would be wrong, even considering his contributions toward peace and stability, to portray Washington as a gentle shepherd. "Washington was roused and stimulated by the dangers of the battlefield, and utterly despised cowards, or even men who ran away in battle from a momentary terror which they did not habitually manifest." But he was also "a planter sportsman," "a country gentle-man" who "fished for profit," "lived very close to nature," and "was constantly on horseback"; he was an "out-of-door-man" (C.W. Eliot, *Four Leaders* 45). Although Washington is enshrined as a knight on horseback at the Military Academy, he was at the time of the Revolution more of a citizen-soldier or "guerrilla" fighter like Thomas Sumter, Andrew Pickens, Francis Marion, Ethan Allen, and John Sevier. To be sure, Washington, considering his British heritage, exhibited some features of the professional knight, especially before the Revolution; but from the outset Washington was also the farmer or shepherd (though as a slave owner, he was certainly not totally egalitarian). He fought in defense and for democracy, as flawed as his practice of that ideal was, rather than in aggression and for aristocracy.

While Washington is promoted as the founder of the academy, Jefferson, whose influence on the establishment of it was crucial, is demoted in part because he was not as easily brought into harmony with the image it sought to project. Jefferson was not much of a knight. He fought, one might say, with the pen rather than with the sword, and his interest in West Point came from his interest in education rather than from devotion to military affairs. As the president who signed the act creating the Military Academy, as the Father of the University of Virginia, and as the architect of public education in a fledgling democracy, Jefferson would have to rate as perhaps our greatest education president. He envisioned the Military Academy as a "model for training in the practical sciences" (Gallo-way and Johnson 146). Jefferson "wanted a national university, and as the foremost apostle of progress in America he wanted that university to teach science, not the musty classics that prevailed at other American schools. . . . Jefferson, therefore, decided that he would smuggle his national scientific school into the nation under the guise of a Military Academy" (ibid., quoting Fleming 16).

While Jefferson favored a strong emphasis upon the practical sciences and engineering at the Military Academy, he shared with his predecessors expectations for its military contribution. Washing-ton, Adams, and others who contributed to its founding envisioned it as a school for citizen-soldiers whose graduates would lead local militias and thus make up a democratic military. But this failure of the original idea of West Point became obvious even before the Civil War, since graduates of the academy held volunteer units in contempt (Ambrose 113). In 1837 a House Select Committee on Military Affairs concluded that "it must be apparent to all that the institution at West Point is not in principle, nor in practice, what it was under Washington, under the elder Adams, and under Jefferson, nor what it was only designed to be under Mr. Madison. What it now is it has attained to independent of the authority of their illustrious names, if not against their authority" (quoted in Galloway and Johnson 147).

At the time of the Revolution, military practice was dominated by aristocratic conceptions of order and formal tactics of engagement, which the war would subvert. Since the training of military officers was a primary goal in the establishment of West Point, the influence upon the academy of a knight in the old tradition, Baron Friedrich von Steuben, a colonel in the army of Frederick the Great and thus "one of the cogs in the most perfect military machine in the world" (Palmer 29) must be considered. Moreover, it was Steuben who presented to General Benjamin Lincoln, secretary of war, "detailed plans for a military academy which afterwards developed into the West Point establishment" (Doyle 299).

Upon invitation by Benjamin Franklin, Steuben trained Washington's suffering soldiers at Valley Forge in the European art of military discipline, a task for which Washington appointed him inspector general. Here on the frozen ground of Pennsylvania was the beginning of military drill in America, with its endless implications for our society. Praise for Steuben is often exuberant: "This new birth of the continental Army as a trained fighting machine is Steuben's contribution to the history of the War of Independence" (ibid., 161). His tactics for training were institutionalized, especially at West Point, and influenced every subsequent American army. "If you would catch the still surviving thrill of his personality, go to West Point some morning in mid-June when the new yearling corporals are drilling the plebe recruits. They do not know it but each of the young drillmasters is doing his best to follow the Baron's example" (142).

At first West Point operated like other colleges of its day, with little special attention given to the demands of military training. Then came Sylvanus Thayer, fourth superintendent (1817–33), a graduate of Dartmouth and the academy itself. The epithet "The Father of West Point," generally applied to Thayer, is quite appropriate, since he left an indelible mark upon the academy and its ideals of education and manliness. He established at West Point "an inflexible, Spartan rule" under which all phases of daily life were devoted to some disciplined activity, from drill to cleaning quarters. In 1817, the same year that Philip Lindsley asserted that students at Princeton would not riot if they had some relief from Bible study and prayer, Thayer began to apply the same principle in another direction. Since he believed that cadets would waste any spare time, he began the practice of requiring every cadet to attend Sunday chapel services, and of using cadet officers to enforce rules against other cadets and report them for violations. The overall intent of his system is best described in his own stern dictum: "Gentlemen must learn it is only their province to listen and obey" (Galloway and Johnson 148). Thayer took over at West Point after a visit to France to study the art of war, since the American army, in his view, had performed so shoddily in the War of 1812.

Near the end of the nineteenth century Theodore Roosevelt echoed Thayer in his defense of the idea of a professional army. While lavishly praising the mountaineers of Tennessee and Virginia for their victory at King's Mountain, South Carolina, in 1780, acknowledging that it was a "turning point" in the war that "gave cheer to patriots throughout the union," Roosevelt argues astonishingly in a footnote that "the mountaineers . . . would have done far better under another system. . . . If the states had possessed wisdom enough to back Washington with continentals. . . . the Revolutionary contest would have been over in three years. The trust in the militia was a perfect curse. Many of the backwoods leaders knew this" (8:504). Even when shepherds are victorious—Roosoevelt says their "sole sources of livelihood were the stock they kept beyond the mountains" (ibid.)—they still fall short in the view of knights. The reliance upon huge military machines with their inherent flaws and the underestimation of civilian militia faced with a do-or-die struggle was a costly lesson for the British and eventually proved to be just as costly for the United States during our own imperial phase, most notably in Vietnam. The term "standing army" is basically a misnomer. Professional armies rarely stand but sooner or later invade the territory next door usually under the slightest pretext. What the world would be like without them we can scarcely imagine.

A civilian army is no guarantee against atrocities and outrage, but it does not enshrine the well-drilled knight, as does the system of the professional or standing army. The battles of King's Mountain and of New Orleans showed something that Thayer did not want to admit, namely that the best fighters are often volunteers simply because they have a reason to fight. In 1817, the year Thayer began his reign at West Point, reporter Anne Newport Royall said Tennessee was known as "the land of heroes," owing no doubt to the victories of "Nolichucky Jack" at King's Mountain and "Old Hickory" at New Orleans. Thayer, though, could not have backwoods fighters as his heroes. His models had to be imperial; thus his hero was Napoleon, whose hero in turn was Caesar. Thayer went abroad to pay homage to a celebrated loser when upstart winners were all around him at home. What he brought back from France was far more than the French version of the art of war. He returned with ammunition for the official establishment in America of a professional military class, a knightly class, that has affected every aspect of our culture, especially sports, education, and religion. If West Point is "the key to America" (see Crane and Kiely), then the key to West Point is Sylvanus Thayer. Admittedly Thayer stressed academics more than bodily exercises, but his influence lies elsewhere—in the high seriousness with which he integrated the idea of physical conditioning with national defense and even manifest destiny, which depended on engineering genius and military might.

Thayer brought with him from France General Simon Bernard, one of Napoleon's engineers and at one time Napoleon's aide-decamp. He also brought over, as his first professor of engineering, Claude Crozet, an artillery officer under Napoleon. A close look at paintings reveals that Thayer even tried to emulate Napoleon in dress and appearance. This in itself would have been enough to disenchant John Adams, who in a letter to Jefferson on 10 March 1823 expressed an entirely different opinion of the Corsican, speaking of him as "tyrannical and immoral" and just like all other conquerors such as Alexander, Caesar, and "Zingis Kan" (Cappon 590). Thus did Thayer in a little over a decade Napoleonize the Military Academy and move it far to the right of what was intended by its founders, blending in typical knightly style the ideal of formal religious worship and a highly regulated system of physical training, as well as a tattletale system of honor. "Even Cadet Robert E. Lee remarked that cadets generally disliked Thayer because of his constant espionage" (Kershner 190).

All roads on the drillmaster technique of education lead back to West Point and specifically to Thayer. His philosophy permeated the first half of the nineteenth century. In 1826, the year of Jefferson's death, James Monroe, regent of the University of Virginia, turned to Thayer for advice on how to manage a "literary institution." Thayer saw little or no difference between a literary and a military education and advised Monroe first "to keep the students at their studies, and second, to prevent gambling, intemperance, and dissipation" (ibid.). To achieve these ends, Thayer recommended the following:

> First, leave no idle time on the students' hands. Assign each student an amount of study material equal to his capacity and have daily examinations to ascertain whether he has studied; occupy all time not devoted to sleep, meals or study with physical exercise, such as dancing, fencing, horseback riding, gymnastics or military exercise. Second, use roll calls and monitors to verify attendance. Third, make frequent inspections or visits to determine what students were doing with their study time. Fourth, remove all pecuniary means from the students' hands and forbid them to contract debts or receive funds except by permission of the school's executive government. Student expenses could be paid from funds deposited with the school treasurer. Fifth, apply to the state legislature for a law imposing restrictions on tavern keepers and others within a limited distance from the university. Thayer warned that these measures would be fruitless without a vigilant, active and energetic executive, a person of high character and attainment who possessed particular qualifications for governing youth. [ibid., 206]

Thayer had little faith in the idea of education as a quest for self-knowledge. Knowledge was information to be dispensed, not truth to be discovered. We are, in our educational system, still marching to the beat of his drums.

Though Thayer may have brought engineering excellence to the Military Academy, he also paved the way for the glorification of an American military aristocracy. Why did the country allow Thayer to get away with such regimentation? The answer is simple: "West Point survived because it was the first American educational institution capable of providing the critical engineering skills needed by a growing nation during the long peace following 1815" (Galloway and Johnson 151). Indeed, military regimen and engineering skills seemed to go together, and West Point was the grand institution where they merged with a vengeance. The engineering emphasis was in keeping with the dominant religious credo of the time, Calvinism, which, in contrast to Armenianism, was aristocratic, the doctrine of the elect. The doctrine of man's dominion over nature was more or less realized by engineers who seemed able to accomplish any imagined alteration of environmental conditions. This included, of course, both wild rivers and wild men. The Indians, "natural men," were not of the elect, and "internal improvements" of the engineers was a euphemism for flushing them out of their natural environments.

One of Thayer's star cadets, Dennis Hart Mahan (class of 1824), influenced both the academy's engineering emphasis and its Napoleonic cult. He became a professor at the academy and taught a course called "Engineering and the Science of War," a subject on which he was a world authority. During the superintendency of Robert E. Lee (1852–55), Mahan was president of the Napoleon Club, called by Ambrose the "crowning jewel of intellectual life at West Point" (138). Meetings were held with Lee's permission in the Academic Building, where members "discussed and argued over Napoleon's movements," which many, including George McClellan, tried without success to emulate in the war that soon began (ibid., 138–39). Mahan had many students, and his enormous influence upon American history can never be assessed. "Mahan never commanded troops in action, never saw a battle. . . . but through his teaching and writing he was responsible for the manner in which much of the Civil War was fought" (ibid., 101). According to R. Ernest

Dupuy, almost 1,100 graduates served in the war, 800 for the Union and 296 for the Confederacy. Of the sixty important battles, graduates commanded on both sides all but five (455). "Later tales of their feats reached heroic proportions, but, as a cynic might point out, West Pointers lost as many battles as they won" (Galloway and Johnson 139). Some have even gone so far as to suggest that without West Point the Civil War might never have occurred (Bowers 69).

During the war, with the signing of the Morrill Land Grant Act, Lincoln endorsed military education at land grant colleges. In theory this program was itself a check on the type of military education Lee had practiced as superintendent at West Point and one more in keeping with the thinking of the founding fathers, who had wanted to develop a well-trained militia for the defense of a democracy. On the day that President Lincoln signed the Morrill Bill, 2 July 1862, "the army of the Potomac began its retreat after the disastrous battle at Malvern Hill, and the fortune of war seemed to go against the preservation of the union" (True 106). Malvern Hill was actually a Union victory, but McClellan, despite the advice of his generals, made no attempt to follow up. Lee, on the other side, withdrew to Richmond, after his infantry and artillery had been blown to bits, leaving more than five thousand killed and wounded on the slopes (Blay 108). Graduates of the Napoleon Club were losing on both sides. The evidence is not overwhelming that those most committed to knightly forms and principles always make the most effective officers.

Lincoln did not directly criticize West Point officers, but he left little doubt of his disappointment in some of them, especially McClellan, who in Lincoln's view was undoing the whole Union cause by his classroom approach to campaigns that made the war seem like a game rather than the bloodbath it would have to become if the Union was to prevail. In signing the Morrill Act, Lincoln may or may not have given a lot of thought beforehand to the educational structure that it established in the colleges, but he could not have been unhappy with a feature that called for not only more officers for the Union but also a different type of military education than that supplied by the Military Academy. The fears of the founding fathers on this matter were haunting Lincoln as well. Not all was lost in 1862, however, and some of the sons of West Point were redeeming the political and military failures—in Union eyes—of others, specifically one Ulysses S. Grant. Of him Lincoln said succinctly in a letter to A.K. McClure, "I can't spare this man—he fights!" (Shaw 139). The same was true of William T. Sherman, who believed not so much in theory but in the wrath of God.

Lee also fought. Like Washington, he has the reputation of being one of our greatest generals. Lee's status of "aristocrat as hero" parallels his admiration for Napoleon, emperor and bestower of titles upon himself and his family. But Lee's aristocratic attitude was qualified by his admiration for Washington, who was inclined toward more democratic principles and refused in the end to be transformed from citizen-soldier to emperor. "In the home where Robert was trained," Douglas S. Freeman states, "God came first and then Washington" (quoted in Wecter 276). As the years passed, Lee's own ways blended with those of his hero. "He developed a passion for perfection which was not unlike the mainspring of Washington's life. He loved the precision of mathematics, map-making, engineering, logistics, the strategy of the field." Like Washington, he was athletic: "He swam and danced and even at the age of 40 was able to compete in high jumps with his sons. His large, muscular hands were expert in menage of horses. . . . Sometimes he slept on the ground when house and bed were near" (ibid.).

It will be said that in one crucial way Lee was not like Washington: he was a traitor to his country and to the West Point that Washington had "founded." It can be argued conversely, of course, that, like Washington, Lee stood up for his beliefs against an established government that he thought was in the wrong. Both were, perhaps, part knight and part shepherd. These points can be argued endlessly, never forgetting the self-judgment of the Marble Model (as Lee was called at West Point), made after the war: "The great mistake of my life was taking a military education" (Bradford 233). Lee's judgment here does not fit well with the simple image of him most wish to perpetuate: a Christian knight skilled in use of sword and horse and ever prayerful before battle, as other West Pointers often were. Bishop Leonidas Polk, for instance, after asking God's help at Chickamauga, sent human waves against the Union lines of

General George H. Thomas. The casualties of both sides of that one battle alone numbered 34,633 (Galloway and Johnson 140). Considering the total loss of life engineered under the leadership of numerous West Point graduates, including Lee and Grant, a military education did not include, apparently, a concern for human life deeper than that for winning at any cost. Among West Point graduates who became minsters of the Gospel was Michael Simpson Culbertson (class of 1839), who translated the Bible into Chinese. Had his Chinese converts seen the attacks of General Polk against the lines of General Thomas, they "might have been prompted to observe that 'Confederates don't seem to value life the way we Orientals do' " (ibid., 140). Lincoln himself became a victim of knightly thinking, which effectively guaranteed a bloodbath, in his concern to find commanders who would do what had to be done. Such thinking assumes a correlation between military might and righteousness, as illustrated in Julia Ward Howe's "Battle Hymn of the Republic" (1862).

Both military discipline and the emphasis on engineering at West Point had a direct connection to the rise of the cult of manliness and American sport. The inordinate influence of the academy upon American sporting culture reflects not a playful attitude toward nature but a spirit of conquest and crusade typical of the European knight. The overcoming of nature, a messianic endeavor careless of suffering—all in the name of religion and progress—and a glorification of organization—Christ, engineering, sports, and war—all easily overlap in the West Point tradition, and no one, as far as I know, has previously tried to sort out the rationale for their strange connections. The answer lies in the tradition of the Christian knight, who stands in sharp contrast to the archetype of Christ the Good Shepherd. Tellingly, the athletic teams at the military academy became the Black Knights of the Hudson.

Surprisingly, organized athletics, in contrast to drill, were relatively slow in catching on at West Point considering the fact that the academy was credited by the National Commission of Education in 1899 with being the first American educational institution "of importance" to establish bodily exercises as a part of its curriculum. This occurred in 1817, when Sylvanus Thayer became superintendent, which is not to deny the influence of Alden Partridge, the preceding superintendent, who was a well-known advocate of physical conditioning. In 1826 the Board of Visitors, undoubtedly influenced by Thayer, made an official recommendation for a gymnasium and a physical education program consisting of gymnastics, riding, fencing, and military drill. Still, the institution lacked a gymnasium for thirteen more years, and gymnastic instruction did not begin until 1846. The following year there appeared an official endorsement of sports, with the superintendent requesting cadets to form cricket clubs as a means of "healthful and manly exercise during the suspension of drills." Such clubs were "in vogue in the British service" and were "highly conducive to physical development." Cadets did not take too readily to cricket and turned instead to townball and early forms of baseball. Some reports indicate that cadets played soccer in the 1840s (Crane and Kiely 149).

If the Military Academy was short on organization and facilities in the decades before the war, it was long on philosophy, praising the vigorous life and steadily growing in its reputation for manliness. Indeed, West Point's influence in the shaping of manly ideals was as pervasive as its influence in engineering. Philip Lindsley began to champion physical education at the same time that Thayer was bringing change at West Point. In 1817 Lindsley became vice president at Princeton and began to recommend in part the West Point model in physical education, and in 1826, as if echoing among the Cumberland Hills of Tennessee the vigorous recommendations of the Board of Visitors at West Point, he exhorted the graduating class at the University of Nashville: "Let education be extended to the physical and moral, as well as to the mental faculties. Let agriculture, civil and military engineering, gymnastics, the liberal and mechanical arts—whatever may tend to impart vigour, dignity, grace, activity, health, to the body—whatever may tend to purify the heart, improve the morals and manners, discipline the intellect, and to furnish it with copious stores of useful elementary knowledge—obtain their appropriate place and rank, and receive merited attention in our seminary; so that parents may, with confidence, commit their sons to our care" ("Cause" 154). Sylvanus Thayer would have applauded vigorously.

In the development of sports West Point represented trends in the rest of the country. An observer of the American scene in 1869 claimed that "the taste of athletic sports in America is not over fifteen years old" (Paxson 144). Around midcentury, as in Victorian England, organized sports in the cities, in contrast to the unruly play of the backwoods, began to flourish at an astonishing rate, spurred in part by what John R. Betts called "technological change and the decline of agrarian isolation": "All in the population were affected. Immigrant and native, man and boy, woman and girl, capitalist and labor, Jew and Christian—all responded to the growing national consciousness of the great possibilities of organized games. More and more they realized that the great issue of the day in sport was not simply amateurism as opposed to professionalism (strong as the prejudice remained) but the moral and educational value to be derived. The American spirit was being modified, at least, by our athletic interests" (*Heritage* 188). In the aftermath of the industrial revolution the overall physical condition of the average citizen declined, thanks to the waning of the active life of the frontier and the new leisure that the cities and the industries afforded. Thus came the protest from the intellectual and academic circles that bodily conditioning should accompany mental development as it did for the Greeks (Lucas 56). This change can scarcely be overemphasized, for it represents a shift in emphasis from the scholastic life to the physical, signaling the beginning of a classic phase in the history of American culture, the official recognition of *mens sana in corpore sano*. The ancient ideal, however, becomes imbued with a military cast, and West Point, itself the creation of Ivy Leaguers, becomes the touchstone of all-around excellence.

Philip Lindsley, who died in 1855, would have been pleased with the new emphasis upon *mens sana in corpore sano* expressed by such luminaries as Harvard men Oliver Wendell Holmes and Thomas Wentworth Higginson. All deplored the same physically weak condition of young men that Philip Lindsley had lamented in his 1825 address in Nashville: "The colleges and universities have long been consecrated to literary ease, indulgence and refinement. In them, mind only is attempted to be cultivated, to the entire neglect of the bodily faculties. This is a radical defect; so obvious and striking too as to admit of no apology or defence. Youth, at most public seminaries, are liable to become so delicate, so effeminate, so purely bookish, as to be rendered, without some subsequent change of habit, utterly unfit for any manly enterprise or employment" (*Address* 24).

By 1858 the situation in the eyes of Holmes was, if anything, worse instead of better: "I am satisfied that such a set of black-coated, stiff-jointed, soft-muscled, paste-complexioned youth as we can boast of in our Atlantic cities never before sprang from loins of Anglo-Saxon lineage" (881). Emerson, while preaching balance, had been on the same tack for some time, trying to find some classical course of moderation, at least as revealed in "Montaigne; or, The Skeptic" (1844–45), where he noted that the "studious class . . . are abstractionists, and spend their days and nights in dreaming some dream; in expecting the homage of society to some precious scheme, built on a truth, but destitute of proportion in its presentment, of justness in its application, and of all energy of will in the schemer to embody and vitalize it" (*Selections* 287).

Like others of the time, Higginson in an 1858 *Atlantic* essay entitled "Saints and Their Bodies" expressed admiration for Dr. Thomas Arnold for defending the "athletic virtue" of the Greeks. Higginson liked the idea that the modern English Broad Church aimed at "breadth of shoulders as well as doctrines." He applauded Charles Kingsley for his new definition of a saint as "one who fears God and can walk a thousand miles or a thousand hours." He decried the prevailing belief of the time that "physical vigor and spiritual sanctity are incompatible." As examples of the imbalance of his times, he cited a young orthodox divine who lost his parish for swimming the Merrimack River and another who lost his for beating an influential parishioner at ten pins. Higginson's own times, he believed, were too heavily influenced by the medieval attitude of a strong soul in a weak body. He regretted that what he called "robust military saints" (George, Michael, Sebastian, Eustace, Martin, Hubert the Hunter, and Christian the Christian Hercules) were not adequately venerated and that the Greek honoring of "manliness" had been forgotten (T.W. Higginson 583–84).

To Higginson, famous now for his inability to appreciate the fragile and ambiguous poetry of Emily Dickinson, the service academies offered models to imitate for physical regimen. "Everybody admires that physical training of military and naval schools. But the same persons never seem to imagine that the body is worth cultivating for any purpose other than to annihilate the bodies of others. . . . Do not waste your gymnastics on the West Point or Annapolis student whose whole life will be one of active exercise, but bring them into the professional schools and the counting rooms" (ibid., 585; see also Hartwell 97-98). To Higginson's credit, he advocated a sound mind in a sound body for purposes of health rather than for national defense.

To Higginson, however, sports were a matter of class, gender, and race as well as health. "By placing sports and exercises under the imprimatur of the Greeks, Higginson stamps athleticism with the mark of high civilization. Sport elevates and celebrates the body by defining a physical ideal against the unenlightened embodiment of particular antitypes: the effeminate saint, the consumptive poet, the 'brainless' savage, the Irish 'muscle-worker', and almost all women. Sports and exercises constitute the 'labor' of the 'higher classes,' the means by which Anglo-Saxon men and—with caution—women cultivate the integration of mind and body" (Black 5). Here is the heart of the elitist ideology that kept the service academies all-white and all-male until recent times.

The Naval Academy, modeled upon West Point in its emphasis on physical discipline, was founded in 1845 by George Bancroft. In 1823, with Joseph Green Cogswell, Bancroft, at Round Hill School in Northampton, Massachusetts, had made the first attempt in America to introduce physical education as a regular part of the daily school curriculum, the goal being "to preserve the health and improve the morals and the mental powers" (Marburg-Cappel 236). Thayer, the Father of West Point, and Bancroft, the Father of the Naval Academy, institutionalized knighthood and the Guardian class of Plato's *Republic*, skillfully interweaving what they understood as classic ideals of excellence with Christianity, so as not to disturb the taxpayers who would be called upon to support their creations.

Things did not go smoothly at Annapolis, especially at first. Bancroft appointed Franklin Buchanan as the first superintendent, and within six months Buchanan dismissed "two midshipmen for insubordination, four for drunkenness, and one for delirium tremens" (Ambrose 127). Eventually the Naval Academy was able to get under way with its own adopted hero appropriately honored. Just as Washington is revered at West Point, so at Annapolis is John Paul Jones, the Father of the American Navy, whose remains lie in a crypt beneath the Naval Academy Chapel, his sword nearby in a lighted niche in the chapel wall. A knight of the sea, Jones, in a fashion characteristic of the age, stressed renaissance versatility for the future naval officer. In Jones's view he must be "a capable mariner" and "a gentleman of liberal education, refined manner, punctilious courtesy, and the nicest sense of personal honor" (quoted in Roberts and Brentano 16). Jones's famous victories at sea serve both the causes of the Revolution and knighthood with its cornerstone concept of "an officer and a gentleman."

Like Thayer, Jones did not dwell excessively on physical excellence, though it is implied in his words and actions. The Naval Academy authorities, however, knew early the importance of conditioning and training and in 1865 introduced organized athletics "in order to keep midshipmen out of Annapolis taverns during their free time." In 1878 Harvard built a gymnasium "for much the same purpose," and in 1885 Colonel Herman J. Koehler, a product of the Turner tradition from Germany and a graduate of the Milwaukee Normal School of Physical Training, came to West Point and established a program for the Fourth Class in calisthenics. In 1892, with the completion of a new gymnasium, Koehler, who was given the title Master of the Sword, extended his program to include riding, fencing, boxing, wrestling, and swimming. In 1905 Theodore Roosevelt thought so highly of Koehler's system that he ordered it for all classes (Ambrose 246).

It is difficult to determine just how movements in physical education and sports originate, but the military nationalistic connection is never far from view, whether in Greece, Rome, Elizabethan and Victorian England, or the United States. Important in the development of physical exercise, as in education generally, was Johan Heinrich Pestalozzi (1746–1827), a disciple of Rousseau. Pestalozzi was a strong advocate of "manliness" and the belief in the rational development of the child. After writing a text on physical education in 1807, he went to Berlin to integrate his program into German schools (Betts, "Mind and Body" 793). His school at Yverdon on Lake Neuchatel in Switzerland became world-famous and was mentioned favorably by Lindsley in his Nashville address of 1825. Jefferson learned of his work through John Griscom's *A Year in Europe* (1819). Jefferson, along with the organizing trustees, called for gymnastics at the University of Virginia in 1824 (ibid., 794).

The key figure behind the cult of physical culture was Friedrich Jahn, who established an open-air athletic field in Berlin in 1811, fought in the war of liberation, and emerged as the Father of the Turner Movement. Jahn's influence was enormous, especially in the United States, and the talk of gymnastics and the actual introduction of programs into the eastern schools and colleges can be traced back through Thayer and Bancroft to him. Harvard even considered hiring Jahn, but Jahn asked for the moon and immortality for his program: "Should the Gymnastic Art once be removed across the Atlantic it must flourish proper until another Atlantic sink" (Marburg-Cappel 245).

No doubt Jahn's program of physical fitness brought personal joy to many, but his theories were thoroughly elitist, racist, and nationalist, and parallels with the philosophy of the Third Reich are obvious: "This national-volkish ideology was disseminated in the new movement of which Jahn exerted such influence, and hence his early designs and visions are more than mere intellectual and historical curiosities. The education of the future was to be based on a popularized national history, on a language cleansed of all foreign words, on physical labor and military sports, on the glorification of national symbols and heroes" (Karl Bracher, quoted in R. Turner 32). Though America in the early 1800s was racist and elitist enough to conform to such an ideology, and while administrators in the colleges were applauding the physical programs promoted in Europe by Jahn and others, there is no direct evidence that his extreme moral and social views were adopted even at the Military Academy, where one would think they might have best taken root (see Hartwell 17-22).

In 1824 Karl Follen and Karl Beck migrated from war-ravaged Germany to the United States, and Beck, who had studied under Jahn, introduced gymnastics at Bancroft's Round Hill School. "Beck, upon his arrival at the school, constructed an outdoor gymnasium according to Jahn's plan just below the school buildings and began with a systematic training" (Marburg-Cappel 238). Of Beck's innovation at their school, Bancroft and Cogswell wrote: "We are deeply impressed with the necessity of uniting physical and moral education; and are particularly favored in executing our plans of connecting them by the assistance of a pupil and friend of Jahn, the greatest modern advocate of gymnastics. . . . The whole subject of moral and physical education is a great deal simpler than it may first appear. And here, too, we may say, that we were the first in the new continent to connect gymnastics with a purely literary establishment" (ibid., 239, quoted). Bancroft, however, notes a playful element in his belief that games and healthful sports should promote "hilarity" as well as good health (*Military Schools* 842). In spite of Jahn's influence, Bancroft seems far removed in his general approach to education and national defense from the obsessive methods of Jahn. Bancroft was relatively liberal in his educational views, which he may have brought with him from his Harvard student days, and this possibly accounts for the civilians who constitute half of the faculty at Annapolis, unlike the situation at West Point.

While evidence of a direct connection between West Point and Jahn in the early nineteenth century is lacking, his influence can easily be seen in its system of physical training. This system, though, may be more reflective of the thought of Alden Partridge than even of Thayer. Partridge had a healthy skepticism of military aristocracy, pointing frequently in his writings to the endless struggle of military despots in Europe. Still, Partridge probably did more to promote exercises in American military circles than anyone else.

Throughout his writings on military training Partridge championed fitness and health at every opportunity. Like many educators of his day, he lamented the sad physical conditioning of youth in seminaries and was convinced that military exercises would preserve good health and "a good figure and manliness of deportment." The cadet or student, he believed, should spend two hours a day in military and other exercises, including fencing. The goal of the cadet or student was "to possess a sound mind in a sound body" (*Military Schools* 843).

After leaving West Point, Partridge, a bitter enemy of Thayer, set about establishing other military schools with the zeal of a Jesuit priest. In September 1820 he founded the American Literary, Scientific, and Military Academy at Norwich, Vermont, which became Norwich University in 1835, the first U.S. civilian institution to offer military training, the forerunner of the ROTC program. Partridge, a Dartmouth alumnus like Thayer, made efforts to bridge the gap between the military establishment and the civilian population; Thayer, conversely, supported military exclusivity. Though he was probably influenced by the thinking of Jahn on physical training (see Betts, "Mind and Body" 792–93) and though he was a strong advocate of military preparedness on a national basis, Partridge seems to have retained a sincere appreciation of the value of civilian life (see Hartwell 98-100).

As different as Thayer and Partridge were in their views of West Point and the nature of the militia, West Point became the general model for the burgeoning military schools in the country before the Civil War, especially in the South. According to Rollin G. Osterweis, in 1839 the Virginia Military Institute was established "along the lines of West Point" (*Myth* 57), and VMI in turn influenced the founding of state-chartered military academies all over the South, including, in 1842, the Arsenal in Columbia and the Citadel in Charleston (*Romanticism* 125–26). Osterweis says that "the growth of state-supported military colleges . . . coincided significantly with an emerging spirit of Southern nationalism. The military cult fed the feeling of nationalism and nationalism gave impetus to the military cult" (*Romanticism* 93–94). With West Point at the top, the system of military schools in eastern America can best be symbolized by the ancient ziggurat, which was fortress and temple at once. The American ziggurat, to be sure, was beautifully decorated with flowers of chivalry, especially those nurtured by Sir Walter Scott, just as Mark Twain, who deserted the Confederacy, always argued (ibid., 41–53, 89–92).

According to Twain, "little sham castles" were everywhere in the South: the Female Institute in Columbia, Tennessee, for example, was pictured in the *Southern Literary Messenger* in 1838, "complete with towers, turrets, battlements, Gothic doorways and windows and placed in a melancholy setting of trees" (ibid., 89). White women may not have been enslaved like the black population, but they were certainly imprisoned within the ziggurat. Lest we blame Southerners entirely for the oppressive system of education that was leading the country toward its own "holocaust," as Faulkner called the war, we need to remember that West Point was in large measure the creation of the Ivy League. Knighthood was a national institution both before and after the Civil War.

Perhaps no one summed up the dangers of chivalry as well as James Longstreet before the battle of Gettysburg in Michael Shaara's *Killer Angels*: " 'God in Heaven,' Longstreet said, and repeated it, 'there's no strategy to this bloody war. What it is is old Napoleon and a hell of a lot of chivalry. That's all it is' " (251). Then for the saddest words of tongue or pen I would nominate the dying ones of Shaara's General Lewis A. Armistead after his capture on the last day at Gettysburg, after learning that his dear friend on the Union side had been hit: " 'Will you tell General Hancock, please, that General Armistead sends his regrets. Will you tell him . . . how very sorry I am' " (ibid., 329).

While faith in the religious "exercises" of the campground withered in the first half of the nineteenth century, trust in military exercises on the parade ground and athletic field blossomed. Though pagan either in origin or nature, gymnastic exercises, calisthenics, drills, physical education, and sports were gradually imbued with Christian morality, so that one soon got the impression that *mens sana in corpore sano* was in reality one of the Ten Commandments or a Beatitude, as the following excerpt indicates: "a systematic education of the body was a principle, and a practice, with all the civilized nations of antiquity. There was a constant attention to this in the training of youth; and the Olympian Games, their Gymnastic Exercises, and Gladiatorial Shows all had reference to the principle. If heathen nations could thus wisely attend to the healthy development of their bodies, can Christian people safely neglect it" (*Military Schools* 745). The anonymous author of this rationale incredibly associates gladiatorial combat with the idea of the healthy development of the body!

It is the tragic genius of John Milton and not the comic genius of Rabelais that is invoked in defense of military education in *Military Schools*:

Milton assigns to military drill, and use of swords and other weapons, at least an hour and a half each day, that his students may be equally good both for peace and war. "The exercise which I commend first is the exact use of these weapons to guard and strike safely with edge or point. This will keep them healthy, nimble, strong and well in breath; is also the likeliest means to make them grow large and tall, and to inspire them with a gallant and fearless courage, which being tempered with seasonable lectures and precepts to make them of true fortitude and patience, will turn into a native and heroic valor, and makes them hate the cowardice of doing wrong." [866; see Milton's pamphlet *On Education*, first issued in 1644]

With the use of the sword Milton would associate all athletic sports "wherein Englishmen are apt to excel." The reference to Milton also appeared in a plea at the start of the Civil War by Edward L. Molineux, major and inspector in the New York militia, for "Physical and Military Exercises in Public Schools," which he calls a "National Necessity." Such a program of calisthenics would bring young men properly into manhood, teach self-reliance and esprit de corps, and most of all make them "Christian soldiers in defense of truth, justice, and our country." A "righteous cause" and "Almighty God" would be the guide of those called upon to do the dying (*Military Schools* 884). For a model of the type of values such approaches were designed to teach, one need look no further than West Point.

Philip Lindsley did not live long enough to see the sprouting of the sporting revolution before and during the Civil War, and one cannot help but wonder whether he, Holmes, Higginson, or anyone else of the period saw any connection between the new craze in competition and the growing political (and religious) sectarianism that would lead to war. Lindsley wanted to educate "the farmer, the mechanic, the merchant, the sailor, the soldier" (Ambrose 88), and Higginson wanted the rest of society to imitate the gymnastic training of sailor and soldier at Annapolis and West Point. Neither man wanted a war. Did, however, a sudden proliferation of sports in the decade before the war and the celebration of manliness—the knightly exercises of West Pointers, for instance—have something to do with

intransigent attitudes North and South and the breakdown of comity
that inevitably precedes war?

The evidence is strong that both the frontier religious "exercises" and the physical exercises of the mushrooming military academies in the East and South before the war only led to sectarianism
and strife. Both were forms of social control. When one thinks of all
the marching done North and South in the years before the war, one
of the reverberating lines in Stephen Crane's "Do Not Weep,
Maiden, for War Is Kind" seems terrifying in its fateful implications:
"These men were born to drill and die." The men that Crane spoke
of in 1896 were "Little souls who thirst for fight" (Blair 2:665). In
short, the South that feared Romanism so much embraced the
Caesarism of West Point with open arms, and had in fact done so
from the days of John Smith, long before there was a West Point.

If you want to see the manly ideals among which America has
been forced to choose, put beside one another the portraits of Davy
Crockett, Andrew Jackson, and John Sevier, and then set these
opposite the Napoleon-lovers Sylvanus Thayer, Robert E. Lee, and
Dennis Hart Mahan. What Jackson, Crockett, and Sevier represented, as different as they were, is the idea of the citizen-soldier,
essentially an Old Testament idea (cf. the Gideons). Jackson, Crockett, and Sevier were lovers of rural sport, hunting, horse racing, and
wrestling, as opposed to the continental exercises, calisthenics, and
drill promoted by academy authorities that led eventually to organized tournaments such as the Army-Navy football game. Drills and
exercises, military or otherwise, are always preparatory to some type
of knightly contest. Just as two mentalities of sports are represented
by the groups, so too are two different types of warfare, one built on
the idea of the phalanx and the other on guerrilla action.

Andrew Jackson, I must admit, is not the best example of the
citizen-soldier to contrast with the profession for he too was a
professional. After his crushing defeat of the Creek Indians at
Horseshoe Bend in 1814, he was appointed major general in the
regular army, so hungry was the nation for winners, and at New
Orleans in 1815 he achieved lasting fame for his victory over the
British. Still he was enough of a homegrown hero to despise the
"alien system" of indoctrination practiced by Thayer. As president,

Jackson is reported to have said, "Sylvanus Thayer is a tyrant. The autocrat of all the Russias couldn't exercise more power" (Galloway and Johnson 150-51). Still Jackson had two nephews who graduated from West Point and one, Andrew Jackson Donelson, served his uncle as personal secretary for two terms (ibid., 153). While he was widely hailed as a champion of the ordinary person, Jackson was not a shepherd of the universal variety as seen in his tragic involvement in the Trail of Tears. Like Emerson, who "detested" him (Gay Wilson Allen 345), Jackson was a paradox. "Like the Old Southwest that spawned him, he carried within his nature the conflicting spiritual claims of the yeoman and Cavalier ideals, claims that exerted themselves on the entire region between 1815 and 1860" (Watson 19-20). As a southern Cavalier—that is, a knight—bent on achieving wealth and honor, Jackson continually added slaves to his expanding property. In 1794 he owned 10; in 1820, 44; at the time of his election to the White House in 1824, 95; and at the time of his death in 1845, 150 (16). As aspiring knights always do, Jackson put a great deal of stock in appearances, adding to the front of the Hermitage " 'columns big enough for the desired effect' " (Remini, quoted in ibid., 24). "The front of Jackson's Hermitage is fake, bearing no architectural relationship to the rest of the house. The grand portico is like a stage setting, a properly dramatic backdrop for Jackson-as-Cavalier" (Watson 24). While Jackson proved again that one could win in war without European training, he also proved that one did not have to go to Europe to be a military knight.

Sports took on religious significance in America not because they were fun for a growing number of civilians in the 1850s but because they became intimately connected with the ideal of the complete officer committed to duty, honor, and country. What happened in the British Empire in the late nineteenth and early twentieth centuries (see Mangan) was replicated in the United States during the same time. The whole Western world was marching to manliness. The rhetoric of war, sports, Christianity, and patriotism in America was not limited to West Point and did not even begin there; but it found its home on the banks of the Hudson, symbolized by the nine worthies in the Administration Building. The "worthies" are not the 1928 Yankees, as a friend observed, but famous warriors of the ancient world, as Johan Huizinga tells us: "three Jews (Joshua, David, and Judas Maccabeus); three pagans (Hector, Caesar, and Alexander); and three Christians (Arthur, Charlemagne, and Godfrey of Bouillon)" (*Waning* 61). In their military canonization they hold up the huge stone mantle in the Academic Board Room as if there had never been any conflict between them or what each represented. One wonders what they might say if they came to life. What would Judas Maccabeus ask of Alexander, whose descendants provoked the Maccabee revolt? Would good King Arthur whisper to Alexander that deep down he understood why Alexander had to crucify two thousand Tyrians as punishment for their resistance to his invasion of their city? What would David say to Godfrey of Bouillon concerning the Crusades that took so many Jewish lives as well as those of Muslims and Christians? In the perfect silence of stone, they glorify the solemn virtues of knighthood, as dubious as those virtues often are to those of a shepherd persuasion. They constitute a hall of fame of knighthood.

Theories other than the perpetuation of knighthood that try to account for the rise of sports in America, such as the catharsis theory, fall far short in explaining not the ubiquity of sports but the reverence paid to them. Frederick L. Paxson stated in 1917 that "between the first race for America's Cup in 1851 and the first American Aeroplane show of February last the safety valve of sport was designed, built, and applied" (145). Paxson's thesis has become a cliché, and the safety-valve theory of sport is widely accepted among the general population. Among sports psychologists, however, this thesis, also known as the catharsis, sublimation, or ventilation theory, is open to question to say the least (see e.g. Guttmann, *Sports Spectators* 154-58, Guttmann 17-18, and Russell 171 in Goldstein). I do not claim that the Catharsis theory has no validity; sanely interpreted and applied, it might yield positive benefits. In *Killings: Folk Justice in the Upper South* Lynwood Montell offers this observation. "There is no real way to gauge the extent, if any, to which the potential for and actual participation in varsity athletics reduced the homicide rate" in the "State Line Country" of Tennessee and Kentucky in the early and middle forties. "Nevertheless, the reality must be reckoned with: young men who might have been roaming the countryside at night and on weekends in search of hell-raising 'fun' could now [after the advent of high-school athletics] burn of nervous energy and frustration on the athletic floor or field. . . . Whether the changed behavior should be credited to athletic programs, to new courses offering in social studies, or to a multiplicity of interrelated social factors, something helped the young people of the 1940s to understand that moonshine whiskey consumption and gun possession were lethal concomitants that offered nothing to help them for the future" (133). Sports as a substitute for violence was also the argument advanced by John C. Campbell for the improvement of conduct of mountain youth in the twenties, and it is in the rationale for "midnight basketball" for our large cities. I do not wish to argue specifically against these ways of thinking. My argument at this point is that our institutionalized games have no possibility whatever for ventilating frustration as long as manliness and power are their goals and as long as these are seen as perfectly commensurate with Christian doctrine. The relation of sports to our wars, civil and foreign, can lead to no other conclusion. Catharsis as a principle *might* work if we keep in mind another theory that Jung called *enantiodromia*, the tendency of a virtue to become a vice. In organized sports this starts happening when coaches and administrators remove the fun and play from sports and start to yelp about their inherent value to God, country, and scholarship.

One can only wonder in amazement just what Paxson thought happened in American society between 1851 and 1917. If sports sublimate violence, why didn't they release enough steam to prevent, for example, the catastrophe of the Civil War? If that was not an "explosion," just what would be one? It can be said of course that before the war sports were not sufficiently organized to serve the healthy function of redirecting aggression. The other answer is that sports may not serve this purpose at any time, at least not at the scale attributed to them. Too often in our history, instead of siphoning off bellicose emotions and destructive energies, they have served cohesively the purposes of patriotism and state religion, especially during the formative years of a nation. Used in this way, sports are not so much a safety valve as the steam engine itself, if mechanical metaphors must be used. They inflate a society with a sense of power and glory and command the center of attention whenever they are in operation, like the steam engine on the old family farm. No doubt sports did allow for some elements of the population to "let off steam," but they became after the war a unifying symbol of national strength and purpose. They were consecrated not only at West Point but on the soil of our most exalted and most liberal institution, Harvard University. Once primarily esteemed for the training of clergy, Harvard, Yale, and Princeton all became famous for turning out athletes, soldiers, statesmen, and educators celebrating sports and Christian manliness.

# 6

# The Consecration of College Sports

While West Point became the soul and symbol of knighthood in the United States, the eastern colleges were also affected by the spirit of reform in physical education sweeping the Western world in the early nineteenth century. The response to the Napoleonic Wars in both Europe and the United States, as well as responses to the revolutions of 1848, rekindled reactionary thought that promoted militarism under the guise of educational progress. By the end of the Civil War the colleges, even traditionally liberal Harvard, had themselves become bastions of conservatism, championing the interlocking virtues of religion, sports, and military heroism.

Whereas it is difficult to explain the general movement in nineteenth-century America toward knighthood and the cult of the hero, it is somewhat easier to see that movement happening. This unhappy period was suffused with the idea of a cruel enemy that could only be defeated by superior physical strength and courage. Germany adopted athletic training for German interests, Great Britain for British interests, France for French interests, and so on. Sandhurst, the "British West Point," introduced athletic games in 1812, and the Grenelle gymnasium opened in Paris in 1818 (Betts, "Mind and Body" 793). In 1817 physical education was adopted as part of the curriculum at West Point. No one at the time would have

disputed Plato's dictum, a favorite of Douglas MacArthur, that only
the dead have seen the end of war.

   In 1824 Karl Follen and Karl Beck emigrated to the United
States, where Beck introduced gymnastics at Round Hill School in
Northampton, Massachusetts (Marburg-Cappel 238). Follen in turn
introduced the same system at Harvard in 1826 and set up an outdoor
gymnasium in the delta, producing curious responses among the
locals. One poet commented:

> . . . the Gymnasium mast, erected high,
> Which oft has made the country people pause,
> Or wonder, as they pass at slower speed,
> What can a college of a gallows need?
> [quoted in Morison, *Three Centuries* 207]

Follen, by one account, also "led the first cross-country run, 'all
college at his heels,' point-to-point across fields and over stone walls;
but before these pioneer Harvard harriers attained their destination
at Prospect Hill, Somerville, an irate farmer stopped them" (ibid.).
Country people, I have noticed, have usually preferred play (baseball, for example) to exercises, calisthenics, and running, perhaps
getting enough of repetitive movement in milking cows and other
farm chores. Gymnastics and calisthenics are largely an urban and
leisure-class phenomenon, promoted with good intentions by educators and with utilitarian purposes by militarists. Beck and Follen
may have had good intentions themselves, but their efforts smacked
of a commitment that was essentially alien to still rural and Puritan
New England.

   It was just as well that Friedrich Jahn did not accept Harvard's
offer to lead its new endeavors in physical fitness, since by 1830
enthusiasm for gymnastics at Harvard had waned, and most students
were "content to walk in the then lovely country around Cambridge"
(ibid., 207). After flirting with the idea of gymnastics of the Jahn
variety, Harvard, along with other Ivy League schools, embraced the
sporting competition that swept the nation before and during the
Civil War. One sport after another took hold in academe, and the
lingering piety of the Puritans could not prevail against these conspicuous displays of power, North or South.

First there was rowing. Yale had a boat club in 1843, Harvard in 1844, and in 1852 the first match occurred between them (Betts, *Heritage* 37). Without Lake Carnegie, Princeton was late in entering the water, but by 1858 it had a baseball team and in 1862 won the championship of New Jersey and later defeated the Athletics of Philadelphia "handsomely," as well as three teams from Brooklyn (Wertenbaker 279). In 1862 Harvard defeated a Brown class team in baseball and in 1865 beat Williams in the first intersectional match (Morison, *Three Centuries* 316). At Yale baseball replaced the football matches between classes; by 1857 the traditional contests had turned into free-for-all fights. The early morning chapel service had little effect on softening the intensity with which these games were played (E. Eliot 3). By 1859 baseball games occurred regularly. In the *Yale Literary Magazine* for 1863, "a posthumous paper by Blake '58, who was killed in the Battle of Cedar Mountain, extolled the value of football and pleaded for its return to favor in place of baseball, by which it had been superseded" (ibid.). Baseball survived at Yale, which played its first intercollegiate match in 1865 against Wesleyan (Kelley 299). The first intercollegiate football game, a turning point in the history of American culture, was played at New Brunswick on 6 November 1869 between Princeton and Rutgers.

In all the flurry of activity, the sporting spirit became virtually synonymous with the college spirit, in a mixture of competition, achievement, and leadership. When asked by a Harvard professor just what college spirit was, a young 1859 Yale graduate replied, "It is a combination of various elements—inspiration or faith with enthusiasm, sacrifice or self-denial, fidelity and loyalty, cooperation and patriotism." The Harvard professor responded: "We have not got that here" (ibid., 305). The professor was not quite accurate, for Harvard, like Yale, had its own heroes in the making. The impending war gave ample opportunity for the demonstration of the virtues of that ideal. The war helped transform and institutionalize the attitudes of a nation; before the war graduates of the eastern colleges were mostly trained in the "learned professions" in the care of ministers and teachers building up a flock of believers and training the mind (through drill, which was mostly an expression of ideas), while after the war the focus became training the body (and drills were physical).

(See Hartwell 92, 99-105.) The heroic spirit, reduced to "golden mottoes" that had led so many youth to their deaths, became the national spirit. Herman Melville clearly saw the irony of the almost universal acceptance of this ideal in "On the Slain Collegians." Troops "of generous boys," says Melville,

> Went from the North and came from the South,
> With golden mottoes in the mouth,
> To lie down midway on a bloody bed. . . .
> Apollo-like in pride,
> Each would slay his Python—caught
> The maxims in his temple taught. . . .
> Each went forth with blessings given
> By priests and mothers in the name of Heaven;
> And honor in all was chief.
> [110]

In a note on this poem, Melville, a keen observer of the war, wrote, "The records of northern colleges attest what numbers of our noblest youth went from them to the battlefield. Southern members of the same class arrayed themselves on the side of Secession, while southern seminaries contributed large quotas. Of all these, what numbers marched who never returned except on the shield?" (ibid., 155-56). The northern schools (that is, the best schools) also provided southern boys for the slaughter. By my count some 420 collegians from Harvard, Yale, and Princeton were slain in the conflict, almost equaling the number of battle deaths of West Point graduates, 445 (294 Union soldiers and 151 Confederates, according to Dupuy 455). The monument at West Point erected at Trophy Point in 1897 in honor of regular army officers who died in the war lists 2,240 names. Atop the monument is the statue "Fame," the most glorious of all "golden mottoes" for knights of any age. All of these figures here refer to the bright ones, the elite heroes. It was, after all, they and their teachers and preachers who led the hundreds of thousands of poor, ignorant farm boys from Maine to Georgia and sent them back on the shield as well.

The war was just one of the media, along with engineering, sports, commerce, and religion, through which the cult of the hero was articulated. And the ideal of heroic distinction for the few and

the proud defines that age. Part of the explanation for this phenomenon no doubt derives from the courtly tradition of knighthood, but
an adequate explanation for this flourishing, could one be given,
would involve an understanding of the development of individualism in democracy. In the United States individualism became partly
codified in a political system that at least claimed an importance for
each citizen, though at the same time there was a general and
continuing animosity (both a fear and a disrespect) toward "mob
rule," toward the collective action of those same individuals, and a
belief in and reliance on a so-called natural aristocracy of leadership.
The lessons of Shay's Rebellion in the 1780s as well as the excesses
of social upheavals in Europe moderated a trust in the great unwashed.

At the same time, in religion the movement toward individual
conscience and salvation was juxtaposed with a sustained reliance
on the authority of church law and orthodoxy, with Antinomianism
remaining the most dangerous heresy. That each pilgrim might find
his or her own way independent of established authority (and an elite
leadership), whether through personal experience (neither rational
nor universal) or an alternative community of interpretation, was
seen as a danger to both social and moral order.

A third force at work was the challenge of survival in a wilderness without a framework of established patterns of support and with
continuing risk from environmental unknowns, including the alien
cultures that both threatened and confused accepted standards of
civilization. Darwin's codification of the struggle and competition of
life came at midcentury, but he did not need to invent the concept.

These three forces—individualism, salvation, and struggle—combined with the ideology of knighthood to sponsor a growing sense
of the need for heroes. Together they also defined manliness. The
elitism of heroism is, of course, one of its most essential traits. A few
great souls became examples of achievement and daring and thereby
proved the value of individualism, demonstrated the value of democratic principles that made it possible for the best to succeed, and
fulfilled the promise of compatibility between piety and prosperity,
which had been the Puritan compromise (see Lang 172). These great

souls were prepared for their ascension at places like West Point, Harvard, and Yale.

The best example of the almost universal acceptance of the cult of the hero–though few could actually *become* heroes–was the popularity of Longfellow, who wrote the one great motto that almost everyone knew. Before the war Longfellow was a fixture at Harvard.

Though Longfellow was neither infatuated with soldiering nor much interested in sports (Wagenknecht 206, 198), his poem "A Psalm of Life" (1838), which seems to celebrate the heroic ideal, became one of the best-known poems of all time. Ordinary people knew the poem by heart and could recognize Longfellow's name at once. He became a celebrity, even beyond the borders of his beloved country. His poem, which he may have intended as a commentary on the dangers of the hero (see Hovey), was taken to represent a model of aspiration for the new democratic citizen. One stanza reads:

> In the world's broad field of battle,
> In the bivouac of Life,
> Be not like dumb, driven cattle!
> Be a hero in the strife!
> [Longfellow 5]

The elitism and the idea of struggle are both obvious. Another line advises us to "be up and doing," that one might become one of the "great men" who leave their mark for others to emulate. It does not seem to matter much what is achieved and pursued: "Act–act in the glorious Present!" Modern literary critics may find the poem too didactic, but the ordinary reader found it an inspiration.

To be a hero one had to have self-reliance, the celebrated credo of another Harvard literary hero, Ralph Waldo Emerson. Although it is notoriously impossible to pin Emerson down to a single position, his fascination with and continual devotion to the idea of the (romantic) poet and creative energy and power carry through all he wrote. He inspired "feelings of access to manly power" (Leverenz 135), and he sought always what he called in his essay "Nature" the "keys of power." It was the power that comes neither from authority nor from reason; its source was what he named, among other things, intuition. With this universally available force, which in "Self-Reliance" Emerson called "the essence of genius," it would be possible, Emerson thought, for anyone to succeed. For him, as one critic put it, "Life is a search after power" (Lopez 140). It is a search driven by conflict; as Emerson wrote, "Man was made for conflict; not for rest" (ibid., 145, quoted). We are "parlor soldiers," he said, while life ought to be, as knights insist, "a rugged battle of fate" (*Selections* 161). Our only true course is "to be strong and to prevail" (ibid., 167), since "man's life is of a ridiculous brevity and meanness" (quoted in Leverenz 139). And Emerson left no doubt about the goal in this motto for victory in the strife: "One thing is forever good, / That one thing is success" (quoted in Stessel 173).

A justly famous passage from "Self-Reliance" summarizes the position: "Trust thyself: every heart vibrates to that iron string. Accept the place the divine providence has found for you, the society of your contemporaries, the connection of events. Great men have always done so, and confided themselves childlike to the genius of their age, betraying their perception that the absolutely trustworthy was seated at their heart, working through their hands, predominating in all their being" (*Selections* 148).

Emerson had a deep antipathy to both conformity and imitation, and his great men are clearly an elite (Stessel 174; Leverenz 135, 142, 150), "a natural nobility of genius" (Leverenz 147). It should come as no surprise that one of Emerson's habitual metaphors for his poet-hero is the soldier (Stessel 167, 173, 174), the man of action who actually accomplishes something in the world. As with Longfellow, the emphasis is on practical achievement. And as with the Puritans, Emerson's project is one of self-testing and self-proving within the experience of life's trials (see Warren 17, 25). Emerson's hero is not, however, isolated; he is a patriot (Warren 32), a leader who brings "social cohesion" (Lang 179), not disorder. Like Longfellow's hero, he leaves a pattern to guide others, though he must not himself, it seems, follow any but his own genius. Unlike his neighbor Thoreau, Emerson was not athletic (nor an athlete), but he too had a playfulness of mind that on occasion strayed into humor (Leverenz 144). His influence on the rising fascination with sport, unlike his impact on (and allegiance to) commerce, may seem minimal (Warren 32). As "the patron saint of overachievers," as one critic called him, he continues to influence more recent knights, from Nietzsche to coach Woody Hayes (Leverenz 140, 135). Emerson did have a hand in the evolution of the gospel of wealth, though he was fond enough of excoriating materialism. He helped prepare the soil for Andrew Carnegie and other captains of industry who liked to sing the glories of self-reliance while robotizing their employees à la Napoleon and other masters of drill.

Emerson celebrated nature and the ordinary, but he was a hero-worshiper of the first rank, and his symbol of "worldly success" was none other than Napoleon, one of the reigning deities at West Point. Napoleon was in Emerson's view a splendid example of *mens sana in corpore sano*. "He had that '*plus* condition of mind and body' to the fullest extent–'What a force was coiled in the skull of Napoleon!'–and a fully developed understanding of the laws of the world, along with all the mental faculties of the worldly success: coolness, timeliness . . . careful calculation and the power of combining hard design with minute attention to fact" (quoted in Cawelti 90). Gay Wilson Allen, however, says that "Napoleon was never a real hero to Emerson though he admired his energy, his intellectual and executive ability and his determination" (460). Emerson also had a wide establishment streak running the length of him. A member of the Board of Visitors at West Point, where astonishingly he found self-reliance among cadets programmed like robots, he felt that the best way of developing power–that is, success–was concentration, "the stopping off decisively our miscellaneous activity, and concentrating our force on one or a few points," and "drill, the power of use and routine" (Cawelti 89–90). (One wonders what Emerson thought of Lee's cherished Napoleon Room, where so many battles had been replayed by knights on the Hudson.) Emerson, however, "grumbled" that the board visit to West Point in 1863 took sixteen days rather than a couple. From one perspective Emerson was a shepherd inspecting the school for knights in the darkest days of the republic, a condition brought on, Emerson realized, not because of inefficiency in the army, but because "the clerisy, the spiritual guides, the scholars, the seers have been false to their trust" (G.W. Allen 624). Emerson's life was a grand contradiction casting long shadows amid the beams of brilliance. He was eminently quotable for any purpose at hand.

By the end of the war Emerson had become one of those Representative Men of whom he wrote. On 16 October 1869, less than three weeks before the first football game between Princeton and Rutgers, Charles W. Eliot, taking over as president of Harvard, sought in his inaugural address with guidance from Emerson to define and establish at Harvard the heroic spirit that would direct education, commerce, sports, and religion in the years ahead. Eliot's speech expresses the heroic spirit in all its knightly glory.

Eliot did not say much that was new or different from what Philip Lindsley expressed in his inaugural speech at the University in Nashville in 1825, but following the Civil War, everybody was prepared to listen as Eliot unabashedly included sports as part of the Christian character and heroic ideals of America's oldest college. One did not have to look to ancient Greece and Rome for heroic models; they could be found among Harvard alumni. "There is," Eliot said, "an aristocracy to which the sons of Harvard have belonged, and let us hope will ever aspire to belong–the aristocracy which excels in manly sports, carries off the honors and prizes of the learned professions, and bears itself with distinction in all fields of intellectual labor and combat; the aristocracy which in peace stands for the public honor and renown, and in war rides first into the murderous thickets" (*Turning Point* 17). He could as well have been speaking to the Corps of Cadets at West Point.

It was, says Samuel Eliot Morison, "one of the greatest addresses in modern educational history, delivered with a precise diction and in a deep mellow voice that lent weight, and even beauty, to the speaker's simple, muscular English. The delivery lasted an hour and three-quarters, during which one 'might have heard a pin drop,' save when the Old Arches sang with thunders of applause' " (*Three Centuries* 329).

Eliot, an 1853 Harvard graduate, touched every topic that affected American education, but he did more than enunciate the academic course that Harvard, under his leadership, should follow. He defined the heroic behavior that had served the Union so well in the conflict just ended and that Harvard, as America's oldest university, should continue to engender in its graduates. "The founding of Harvard College," he said, "was an heroic act of public spirit" *(Turning Point* 29). Clearly he expected the heroic effort to continue during his administration.

What were the "old-fashioned virtues" that Eliot represented and desired to cultivate, not just in the colleges but throughout America? They are easily inferred from his inaugural address and other writings, for though he did not "preach," he did not wish to keep secret the ideals he most admired, all of which in his view served the cause of Christ. They were excellence, aristocracy, duty and service, and of course "manliness," which the Ivy League had promoted since the Revolution.

*Excellence.* When Eliot spoke of excellence in education, he did not mean merely academic excellence but a broader excellence, akin to the Greek concept of *arete* or virtue but not identical to it. What was important was the education of the whole person (the whole man, that is), for success, and almost a century before C.P. Snow, he attacked the idea of "two cultures." The division of knowledge was in fact the first object of concern in his inaugural address. "The three opening sentences smote like a sharp, clean sword through the controversy between the old, and 'new' education that had caused so many weary hours of discussion since 1825" (Morison, *Three Centuries* 329). Recognizing "no real antagonism between literature and science," Eliot embraced all branches of "mental training" and would have them "at their best" (*Turning Point* 1).

Eliot thus was interested not in what was old or new but what was "best" (for success), and one way of discovering the "best" was not by the rote study of history but by the study of great people. Taking his cue from Emerson, he sought to promote a study of those "who fill great historical scenes or epitomize epochs" with their accomplishments (ibid., 5). As different as he was from D.H. Lawrence, Eliot would have agreed with Lawrence's dictum "Give homage and allegiance to a hero and you become yourself heroic, it is the law of men" (quoted in Bentley 246). In literature Eliot gave homage and allegiance to the classics, believing that the best books, if diligently studied, would supply a liberal education. The fifty books that Eliot selected as the Harvard Classics in 1910 became commonly known as "Dr. Eliot's five-foot shelf of books." It might not follow from reading such classics that one would attain the excellence of accomplishment that merited the label *hero*, but Eliot (with Emerson) would have noted that the fact that many heroes had read them at least suggested that such an education was necessary if not sufficient for success.

*Aristocracy*. Thomas Jefferson, in a letter to John Adams dated 28 October 1813, stated that the word *aristocracy* comes from the Greek *aristoi*, which means "best," and the "best," he proceeded to point out, are those who possess virtue and talent, "natural aristocrats," as opposed to those who possess mere wealth and family name, "pseudo-aristocrats" (Jefferson 632–33). Eliot strongly endorsed this same idea: "Harvard College is sometimes reproached with being aristocratic. If by aristocracy be meant a stupid and pretentious caste, founded on wealth, and birth, and an affectation of European manners, no charge could be more preposterous: The College is intensely American in affection, and intensely democratic in temper." *Democracy* was a term Eliot defended throughout his career, but his democracy was one that provided opportunity for the best: "the community does not owe superior education to all children, but only to the *élite*–to those who, having the capacity, prove by hard work that they have also the necessary perseverance and endurance. . . . The poorest and the richest students are equally welcome here, provided that with their poverty or their wealth they bring capacity, ambition, and purity" *(Turning Point* 15).

*Duty and Service*. Actually, "Eliot's phrase for the elite in a democracy was less often 'natural aristocracy' than 'educated classes' " (Hawkins 147). The distinction between the two terms is revealing, since the latter puts proper emphasis upon the role of education in the civilizing process for poor and rich, both of whom, in Eliot's view, conferred benefits to the university: "The poverty of scholars is of inestimable worth in this money-getting nation. It maintains the true standards of virtue and honor. The poor friars, not the bishops, saved the Church. The poor scholars and preachers of duty defend the modern community against its own material prosperity. Luxury and learning are ill bed fellows. Nevertheless, the college owes much of its distinctive character to those who bringing hither from refined homes good breeding, gentle tastes, and a manly delicacy, add to the openness and activity of mind, intellectual interests, and a sense of public duty" (*Turning Point* 16).

Members of the "educated classes," whether rich or poor, would possess a keen sense of service to society, an attitude close to noblesse oblige. In producing its "educated classes," the university, said Eliot, "will make a rich return of learning, poetry, and piety. Secondly, it will foster a sense of public duty–the great virtue which makes republics possible" (ibid., 29). By *public duty* Eliot did not mean business and commerce, though service was possible in these fields too, but primarily the Senate, the cabinet, the diplomatic service, and the army and navy. The spirits of Sylvanus Thayer and Philip Lindsley were smiling.

Werner Jaeger in *Paideia* defines *aidos*, the moral quality often associated with the ancient athlete, as "the Homeric sense of duty, of obligation and willingness to conform to a transcendental ideal, which is the true sign of a nobleman" (1:7). By this definition Eliot clearly possessed a Hellenistic sense of duty, but he synthesized the classical view with the Christian, allowing Harvard to retain its liberal and progressive approach to education and the idea of service to society. "The worthy fruit of academic culture," he said, "is an open mind, trained to careful thinking, instructed in the methods of philosophical investigation, acquainted in a general way with the accumulated thought of past generations, and penetrated with humility. It is thus that the university in our day serves Christ and the church" *(Turning Point* 6). Eliot did not seem to be particular whether the sense of duty came from Plato or Christ, so long as the Harvard graduate felt a commitment to serve society unselfishly in some way, to "be useful," as Nathan Hale had said, for "every kind of public service, necessary to the public good, becomes honorable by being necessary" (quoted in Stokes 325).

In 1906 Eliot published *Four American Leaders*, writing about four men distinguished by their service or intellectual contributions to society. They were Franklin, Washington, William Ellery Channing, and Emerson. Washington, Eliot wrote, is especially to be admired because of his sense of duty: "For him, patriotism was a duty; good citizenship was a duty; and for the masses of mankind it was a duty to clear the forest, till the ground, and plant fruit trees. . . . We think more about our rights than our duties. He thought more about his duties than his rights. Posterity has given him first place because of the way in which he conceived and performed his duties; it will judge the leaders of the present generation by the same standard, whatever their theories about human rights" (43–44).

After the battle on civil rights and animal rights in the twentieth century, Eliot's views on duty seem narrow and antiquated. If he stressed duty and service for the "educated classes," what was his attitude toward the rest of society? According to Hugh Hawkins, Eliot did not want a "passive population" nor a society ruled by "the fierce passions of the multitudes." In many ways Eliot had a shepherd's view of society but one which gives us pause. Like Philip Lindsley, Eliot saw a fissure between the elite and the masses that the talented and deserving could jump over to the cheers of the upper class but still a gap that separated the many from the few. Eliot's gap between classes was not a chasm as in the case of knightly institutions. Further, it could be crossed by academic excellence without physical prowess in football. To Eliot, the shepherd and the flock could see one another and hear one another but they did not mix easily. "The university could serve the democratic society best by remaining somewhat separate and privileged. It was for the people but not of them" (Hawkins 167). While Eliot was not a knight, at least of the Roosevelt variety, he was a shepherd manqué.

*Manliness.* Basic to Eliot's concept of the heroic ideal was manliness. By this term he meant not only moral strength and courage but actual physical vigor and martial valor. He referred to "manly sports" (excluding football, at least eventually), and in the concluding remarks of his inaugural address he eloquently tied together manners, morals, and manliness:

> Honored men, here present, illustrate before the world the public quality of the service. Other fields of labor attract them more and would reward them better; but they are filled with the noble ambition to deserve well of the republic. There have been doubts, in times yet recent, whether culture were not selfish; whether men of refined tastes and manners could really love liberty, and be ready to endure hardness for her sake; whether,

in short, gentlemen would in this century prove as loyal to noble ideas, as in other times they had been to kings. [Eliot then points to the playground where Memorial Hall would later arise.] In yonder old playground, fit spot whereon to commemorate the manliness which there was nurtured, shall soon rise a noble monument which for generations will give convincing answer to much shallow doubts; for over its gates shall be written "In memory of the sons of Harvard who died for their country." The future of the University will not be unworthy of its past. [*Turning* Point 29–30]

This was Eliot's way of saying not only that the battles of the Civil War were won on the playing fields of Harvard, Yale, and Princeton but also that, if universities continued to do the job that he envisioned, young men, trained in honor and steeled by the virtues of manly sports, would continue to fight their country's battles for generations to come. Eliot himself had drilled a handful of "Harvard Cadets" in 1861 in the "old gymnasium," built in 1860. In the Civil War 1,311 Harvard men enlisted in the Union forces, and 138 were killed or died. There were 257 enlistments in the Confederate forces, of which 64 were killed or died (Morison, *Three Centuries* 303).

Twenty years after his inauguration address Eliot was still commemorating the valiant dead, as seen in his introduction of Henry Lee Higginson (son of Thomas Wentworth Higginson) at the dedication of Soldiers Field on 10 June 1890. Higginson, veteran and promoter of music in Boston, presented the land to the university as a memorial to his six schoolmates who died in the war. At this event Eliot stated that Higginson "wants to promote manly sports" among the students and "to commemorate the soldier of 1861" (H.L. Higginson, introduction 7). Obviously these goals met with Eliot's full approval.

The land or playground that Higginson presented adjoined land that Longfellow and others had given to the university for the purposes of play, "if wanted for that purpose" (ibid., 8). Higginson, though, had more in mind than Edenic play. The so-called playground would be both a memorial and a training ground for future knights. Indeed, he could not have been more explicit. Those honored by the memorial were men who "loved study and work, and loved play too. They delighted in athletic games, and would have used this field, which is now given to the college and to you [the students] for your health and recreation." Here comes the "but," a huge one: "But my chief hope in regard to it is, that it will help to make you full-grown, well-developed men, able and ready to do good work of all kinds; and that it will remind you of the reason for living, and of your own duties as men and citizens of the Republic" (ibid., 24).

The fallen heroes, Higginson pointed out, were exemplary in every respect, exhibiting individually and collectively the qualities Eliot had enumerated in his speech of 1869. They included James Lowell, first scholar in his class; Robert Shaw, who led the Fifty-fourth Massachusetts into the murderous thicket and into glory and was of "a simple and manly nature"; Stephen Perkins, a great oarsman, "wit and philosopher who delighted in intellectual pursuits"; Charles Lowell, a "first scholar," "brilliant and strong beyond compare," "always in the front" of his men; James Savage, who was "very fond of his books and of nature—much given to games and a great rusher at football from pure will-power and enthusiasm—courageous to the last degree," "a real knight—just and gentle to all friends, defiant to the enemies of his country and all wrong-doers"; and Edward Dalton, a physician, who "worked out his life-blood to save that of others . . . he played full-back and no one ever reached the last goal if human power could stop him" (ibid., 11–18).

The war in which these men died, Higginson reminded his listeners, was no "boy's play" (21, repeated on 23). He even issued a subtle caveat against the essence of true leisure and one type of play—idleness—when he warned the students: "Remember that the idle and indifferent are the dangerous classes of the community. . . . The useful citizen is a mighty, unpretending hero; but we are not going to have a country very long unless such heroism is developed" (26). Not surprisingly, Higginson closed with a lesson not from play but from sports. "And just here let me, a layman, say a word to you experts in athletic sports. You come to college to learn great things of great value beside your games, which, after all, are secondary to your studies. But in your games, there is just one thing which you cannot do, even to win success. You cannot do one tricky or shabby

thing. Translate tricky and shabby–dishonest, ungentlemanlike"
(28–29).

So competitive were the Big Three colleges in 1890 and so
intense was the rivalry, especially in football, that Higginson felt
compelled to remind his Harvard listeners that "Princeton is not
wicked; Yale is not base." He left them with this hope and challenge:
"Mates, the Princeton and the Yale fellows are our brothers. Let us
beat them fairly if we can, and believe that they will play the game
just as we do" (ibid., 30). With his affirmation of duty, the celebration
of manliness, and the warning against wealth and the dangers of
idleness, Higginson was encapsulating the ideal of the Puritan knight,
just as Eliot had with all his shepherd leanings. To a real degree the
commemoration of the field was the work of the Boston Brahmins.
Longfellow's injunction "Be a hero in the strife" ruled the time, and
others of the inner sanctum echoed the wisdom and valor that it, to
them, reflected. James Russell Lowell presented words of his own
for the stone, "Friends, comrades, kinsmen, who died for their
country," and quoted Emerson, who was in turn echoing Longfellow:

> Though love repine, and reason chafe,
> There came a voice without reply,–
> " 'Tis man's perdition to be safe,
> When for the truth he ought to die." [Quoted in H.L. Higginson 21]

Eliot, with political acumen as well as academic vision, touched
all the topics that a postwar Cambridge audience would have wished
for. Manliness, for example, was a proven value, and sports helped
to develop it. Hence Eliot approved, even if somewhat generally, of
athletics in the schools, later claiming that one of his intellectual
heroes, Emerson, had provided the rationale: "I find in Emerson the
true reason for the athletic cult, given a generation before it existed
among us. Your boy 'hates the grammar and grades, and loves guns,
fishingrods, horses, and boats. Well, the boy is right, and you are not
fit to direct his bringing up, if your theory leaves out his gymnastic
training. . . . Football, cricket, archery, swimming, skating, climbing,
fencing, riding are lessons in the art of power, which it is his main
business to learn. . . .' We shall never find a completer justification
of athletic sports than that" (*Four Leaders* 95).

Eliot, though, was thrown into a quandary by football. As he had stated publicly, sports in his view had played a role in the development of manliness in the warrior; and football, because it is the sport with the largest element of combat, should have been among those sports Eliot admired. Instead, he came to see the lesson taught by football as "driving a trade, as winning a fight, no matter how" (ibid., 2). It is doubtful that Eliot had football in mind as the highest example of "manly delicacy." It is easy to see why Eliot preferred crew over football.

While Eliot would remain an advocate of sports and games as well as physical education for purposes of both health and national defense, he would also remain a skeptic about the values of football for either war or peace, in contrast, for example, to Theodore Roosevelt, the most famous graduate of Harvard during Eliot's administration. In spite of his objections, however, Eliot would live to see the Harvard-Yale football game grow into an institution and football become a symbol of manly valor. Ironically this distinguished educator himself had helped to sanctify the relationship.

Graduates of the eastern colleges (and other colleges too) served in the Spanish-American War and in World War I, but by the end of the "war to end all wars" something had happened to the Ivy League ideal that Eliot had helped to define. There were no great educators such as Eliot to sing its praise, only politicians and professional patriots. Writers and intellectuals came to the same sad conclusion that Melville had in 1868, that young men in Europe and America had died in "their flush of bloom," "with golden mottoes in the mouth" and "maxims" in the "temple taught." Unlike the Civil War, though, which Melville thought tragic because of "man's foulest crime" (that is, slavery), World War I seemed pointless, with meaning being inversely proportional to the carnage wrought. Few poets after World War I had the heart to celebrate the ideal in elegy as Melville did in the late 1860s in "On the Photograph of a Corps Commander."

After the Civil War the apotheosis of heroes served to keep the ideal alive for others to imitate. Memory was connected to meaning. After World War I, however, that connection was largely severed. With Robert Graves, one writer after another seemed to say "goodbye to all that." The mottoes of sports and war, though "golden," were, as we have come to realize, gilded as they always had been, and not only gilded but also tragically seductive. Heroes were still admired but largely nostalgically, and they had little relevance for a "lost generation." The case of Princeton's Hobey Baker, the epitome of the Ivy League ideal, is illustrative: "a combination of Tom Brown and Sir Galahad, a clear case of life imitating art: the superb athlete, mannered, modest, handsome, who was actually a gentleman and an amateur and a sportsman. . . . When he was killed in France in 1918, the 'old-fashioned' virtues he personified took on a legendary, eternal quality" (Davies 135).

Just as the virtues of Baker were "old-fashioned" by 1918, so were those of Eliot, as *Time* remarked, by 1926. The all-around man began to yield the field to specialists and celebrities—Red Grange in sports, for example, and Billy Sunday in religion. By the end of his life Eliot had become a legend, a type of Harvard classic himself. Like all true classics, he belonged more to the past than to the present.

This is not to lament the passing of the old order. While there was much to admire about Eliot's idealism, it was, in spite of his relatively enlightened position, still tainted by sexism, racism, and chauvinism, though not so much as the more manly idealism of his most famous student and quondam antagonist, Theodore Roosevelt, who would also at the end of his life look like and feel like an anachronism himself. The influence of both men and the groups and positions they represented—basically the old intellectual Harvard and the new muscular Yale—lived after them. With his talk of "manly delicacy" Eliot sought in academe the old ideal of two hearts, "one as hard as stone, the other soft as wax." Glorifying the war dead by recalling their sporting past, he, like Roosevelt, romanticized the noble tradition of the courtly warrior.

Again, sports between the wars had not been a safety valve for relieving tension, not a psychological mechanism, as Frederick Paxson argued, but an Anglo-Saxon icon. If sports have ever been real fun in America, the fun was slowly drained out of them as they were increasingly eulogized and prayed over. Like war and religion, sports became serious business as business itself was increasingly lauded from rostrum and pulpit.

Thomas G. Bergin, Sterling Professor of Romance Languages

and Literature emeritus at Yale, writing on the occasion of the one hundredth birthday of the Harvard-Yale football game, said that "the past four decades have witnessed an impressive enrichment in the ethnic origins of combatants. Slavs, Scandinavians, Hungarians, Lithuanians, Greeks and Hispanics have joined the ever-more prominent Ausonian segment (Yale's Pagliaro and Diana, Harvard's Gatto and Champi) and the already comfortably installed Irish to reinforce the original Yankee stock" ("To the Game" 33). At the same time, there has been no relaxation, according to Bergin, of academic standards: "The roll call of players over the years includes poets, men of letters, governors, senators, diplomats, college presidents, and more distinguished doctors, lawyers, and captains of industry than you can shake a goal post at. And doubt not gentle reader, that the delegations of '83, though the elite is not so restricted as of yore, will achieve their share of renown in the years to come" (29–30).

Here in Bergin's view is heroic virtue. Here too is optimism that would have warmed the heart of Charles W. Eliot, his skepticism of the values of football notwithstanding. Eliot would have been puzzled, though, as to why soldiers and sailors had not also been included in the list of distinguished Harvard and Yale men. In the post-Vietnam era and in a time of strife in Central America, Bergin apparently thought it chauvinistic to dwell on military heroics, which Roosevelt and probably Eliot as well would have placed first on the list. In contrast especially to the Civil War, the Spanish-American War, and World War I, the Vietnam War was not generally a college war, being instead a poor man's war and generally denounced on American campuses, especially in the East and in California. What was popular on campus was the dissent of Thoreau and not the imperial policy of Theodore Roosevelt to extend American influence around the globe. The idea of the elite had reached a turning point in American culture.

What had happened in the wake of the civil rights movement, the Vietnam War, and the feminist revolution was a compromise with a generally positive outcome, one foreshadowed by the idealism of Frank Merriwell and Dink Stover. The old aristocratic order was democratized, demilitarized, and "demasculinized," for lack of a better term, while emphasis upon competitive sport and academic achievement remained. Both women and members of ethnic minorities may now strive for classic versatility with a reasonable assurance of being evaluated on their own merits. The drive for financial success and power, though, which troubled popular writer Owen Johnson so much, is still held in high esteem and still calls forth critics. Kurt Vonnegut in *Jailbird,* for example, writes of Harvard graduates who show up in all sorts of questionable positions: one, a Chinese Communist, is in charge of a military prison in North Korea. For those who take comfort that the humanist and classical ideal of *mens sana in corpore sano* is still evident at Harvard and Yale, the skepticism of George Santayana of a century ago does not go away. Updating his question, we may ask, are we still going partly in the wrong direction? Yes. While the ideal of excellence or virtue has clearly been democratized, it is still far removed from the world of nature and the ideal of the shepherd. The transcendental vision of Thoreau and Whitman and their own forms of personal heroism seem to have made no more impact upon American educators than they did in the latter half of the nineteenth century. Are not knowledge of nature and knowledge of self the only alternatives to the pursuit of war and the pursuit of a bland business ideal?

# 7

# Manliness Moves West

In 1606 King James I of England granted a charter for two companies of "Knights, Gentlemen, Merchants, and Other adventurers" to plant colonies in parts of North America claimed by England, and the following year Jamestown was founded in Virginia. King James's classification of types is intriguing and prophetic, for after three hundred years the types were still flourishing, moving west as the country expanded.

Perhaps chief among all American knights was Theodore Roosevelt. Athletic, learned, brave, and adventurous, he was one of America's most vocal advocates of manliness, devoting one of his essays to the topic: "The Manly Virtues and Practical Ideals." Here he claimed that any man "desirous of doing good political work" stands in need of "the rougher, manly virtues, and above all the virtue of personal courage, physical as well as moral" (13:32). The same note is sounded in "The Strenuous Life," an address he delivered before the Hamilton Club of Chicago on 10 April 1899. "I wish to preach," he told his audience, "not the doctrine of ignoble ease, but the doctrine of the strenuous life, the life of toil and effort, of labor and strife; to preach that highest form of success which comes . . . to the man who does not shrink from danger, from hardship, or from bitter toil, and who out of these wins the splendid ultimate triumph" (13:319). Roosevelt did not "shrink from danger," and his life displayed what the phrase "splendid ultimate triumph" had come to mean on both the playing fields and killing fields of modern knights.

In following "the strenuous life," America would be imitating the example of England, which "trained up generations of men accustomed to look at the larger and loftier side of public life" (ibid., 13:330), a tradition that in Roosevelt's view was of great benefit to England and even greater benefit to India and Egypt. The great goal was the "uplifting of mankind," which Roosevelt said would require establishing "the supremacy" of the American flag. In order to achieve "true national greatness," Americans must boldly "face the life of strife, resolute to do [their] duty well and manfully" (13:331).

"A man must be glad to do a man's work, to dare and to endure and to labor; to keep himself, and to keep those dependent upon him. The woman must be the housewife, the helpmate of the homemaker, the wise and fearless mother of many healthy children. . . . When men fear work or fear righteous war, when women fear motherhood, they tremble on the brink of doom; and well it is they should vanish from the earth, where they are fit subjects for the scorn of all men and women who are themselves strong and brave"(13:320–21).

Roosevelt in circumscribing women's roles in society reflected the thinking of some leading social Darwinists such as Stanley Hall, who ironically has been called America's premier psychologist. In an address in 1903 to the National Education Association, Hall interpreted the liberated woman as free *from* masculine ideals rather than free to attain them, emphasizing as well a procreative duty. The mantle of greatness would, Hall asserted, "ultimately go to that country that is most fecund [for] the nation that breeds best, be it Mongol, Slav, Teuton or Saxon, will rule the world in the future" (quoted in Vertinsky 69–70). To be sure, Hall advocated strong programs of health and fitness for women, but such programs were means to a higher end. He went so far as to imagine a program of selective breeding to improve the overall fitness of the race (ibid., 82).

All of Hall's philosophy was based upon a scientific and muscular interpretation of Christianity. "In as concise a statement of muscular Christianity as can be found, Hall spoke for progressive physical educators as a group: 'We are soldiers of Christ, strengthening our muscles not against a foreign foe but against sin within and without us' " (ibid., 92). The work of Hall sounds like a modern enchiridion for a state of supermen. It was made to order for a president who believed that America was destined to triumph through manliness.

Charles W. Eliot, a "gentleman," would have objected to Roosevelt's narrow and simplistic classification of the role of women, and he did disagree in fact with Roosevelt and Henry Cabot Lodge (another Harvard knight) on the nature of manliness in competitive sports, especially football. Lodge defended the game in response to Eliot's efforts to suspend football in 1895–he would try again in 1905–with the sweeping testimony that "the time given to athletic contests and the injuries incurred on the playing field are part of the price which the English-speaking race has paid for being world-conquerors" (Hawkins 114). Another Harvard knight, Charles Francis Adams, echoed those sentiments when he declared that "football was more important than genius in national development because the game built character." Even death on the gridiron was cheap, the *New York Times* said, paraphrasing Adams, "if it educated boys in those characteristics that had made the Anglo-Saxon race pre-eminent in history" (Weeks 113). Much more was at stake, then, than a threat to the future of football; at issue, at least among the leading voices of the debate, was the prestige and power of WASP, especially Ivy League WASPs like Adams, Lodge, and Roosevelt.

In 1895 Roosevelt, reacting to the charges of violence in football, wrote Walter Camp that he "would a hundred fold rather keep the game as it is, with the brutality, than give it up" (quoted in Smith 95). In 1905 the football season "left 18 dead and 159 with 'more or less serious injuries' " ( Lawrence 8). In that year Roosevelt called two White House meetings to deal with the violence in football, and with his backing, the game survived with important changes. As would be expected, the Military Academy led the defense among the colleges to preserve football (see Lawrence 9), and as if in payment to knights for their services, Roosevelt, also in 1905, ordered that all classes at West Point, not only the plebe or Fourth Class, participate in the gymnastics program of Colonel Koehler, who in 1892 had added to his calisthenics requirement riding, fencing, boxing, wrestling, and swimming (Ambrose 246). In 1906 Roosevelt received the Nobel Peace Prize for negotiating peace in the Russo-Japanese War.

In spite of the changes he made at Harvard in education, Eliot was relatively traditional, Roosevelt clearly progressive. TR saw the dangers in football but, like Lodge, wanted to preserve it for reasons that went far beyond the playing field. Eliot in his inaugural address stressed the sacrifice of the sons of Harvard in the Civil War to save the Union; in the Spanish-American War TR stressed service that was needed if the United States was to be a world power. In "Raising the Regiment" in *Rough Riders* he left no doubt about the connection in his mind between service and sports, or more specifically service and Ivy League sports:

> What particularly pleased me not only in the Harvard but the Yale and Princeton men, and, indeed, in these recruits from the older States generally, was that they did not ask for commissions. With hardly an exception they entered upon their duties as troopers in the spirit which they held to the end. . . . So it was with Dudley Dean, perhaps the best quarterback who ever played on a Harvard Eleven; and so with Bob Wrenn, a quarterback whose feats rivalled those of Dean's, and who, in addition, was the champion tennis player of America. . . . So it was with Yale men like Waller, the high jumper, and Garrison and Girard; and with Princeton men like Devereux and Channing, the football players . . . and with scores of others whose names are quite as worthy of mention as any of those I have given. [11:8–9]

Time after time TR extols the gallantry of the Ivy Leaguers. In an address at the Yale Alumni Dinner in Brooklyn on 3 March 1899, he rhapsodized about the glory of Yale men in battle. They were among "the best soldiers," "the gamest men" who "could be depended upon for bravery"; where one gave his "life for the flag that he held dear," a "hundred" other Yale men were anxious themselves "to have the chance to win honor." Honor, honor, honor—TR never gets tired of the word, and apparently neither did his listeners. "All honor to Yale men, who went out to win glory and to come home to feel all their lives that they had added to the honor, not only of their university, but of the Nation. An even higher meed of 'honor' to those who went out and did not come back. An even higher meed of 'honor' to those who 'ventured life and love and youth for the great prize of death in battle' " (11:170–71). Then he cites the example of Theodore Miller, who was on his way to help a comrade when the end came. In TR's view, in this war as in Melville's poem "On the Slain Collegians," "honor in all was chief."

One is stunned by TR's ringing rhetoric, which is not to deny the brave, gallant, and courageous their bravery, gallantry, and courage. We are not talking about those qualities here but about understanding that might prevent the tragedy of such conflicts from occurring. The truth, if we care to admit it, is that TR sounds demented in these speeches. His words have that rambling, disjointed rhetoric that characterizes drunkenness of power, and this, I am afraid, is the only way to explain such ethnocentric hyperbole at this point in our nation's history. We were going through an expansionist phase that called for glorification of a heritage of hardy strength and resolve and the giddy justification of foreign adventure or knight errantry. With the emergence of a nation from obscurity to empire, sports themselves underwent significant change.

Decidedly to the right of Eliot, Roosevelt is the key figure in the development of the knightly tradition in the United States. Roosevelt, though, was both exemplar and chronicler. For instance, he reminds Americans of the valor of those who wrested independence from the British, including Princeton man Samuel Doak, who inspired the heroes of King's Mountain. Doak, says TR, "was possessed of vigorous energy" and was "admired" for "his adventurous and indomitable temper; . . . the stern, hard, God-fearing man became a most powerful influence for good" (8:452; also in vol. 10). Of Sevier and the Overmountain Men, whom Doak sent off to battle, Roosevelt had unbounded admiration, heaping encomiums upon them and never letting his reader forget that Sevier was a lover of sports: "Sevier had given a great barbecue, where oxen and deer were roasted whole, while horse-races were run, and the backwoodsmen tried their skills as marksmen and wrestlers. In the midst of their feasting Shelby, hot with hard riding, arrived to tell of the approach of Ferguson and the British" (8:477). The Overmountain Men, the first Tennessee Volunteers, were the prototypes of TR's own Rough Riders. Though Roosevelt's account calls attention to the importance of sports on the frontier, one gets the distinct impression that he never had much fun playing such sports. To him sports were an instrument of foreign policy, not something one simply enjoyed. In any event, TR's message is clear: America cannot survive without manly heroes, and American heroes must now be willing to fight in foreign lands.

In Roosevelt is illustrated clearly what had happened since 1869 to the "manly delicacy" of Eliot. By the turn of the century "manliness" had gone one way and "delicacy" another, forming the advocates of the "strenuous life" on the one hand and the "genteel tradition" on the other. While one group stressed decisiveness and action, the other turned toward inquiry and introspection. Harvard men Roosevelt and William James demonstrate the difference clearly. In many ways the split between Eliot and Roosevelt was between the word and the deed, which for the ancient warrior–according to H.D.F. Kitto–had joined together as *arete*. In the Ivy League the split was mirrored in the years 1892–1909 between athletics and debate. The winner, not surprisingly, was athletics: "Athletes literally *embodied* ideologies of discipline, control, courage, 'sand,' power, and efficient organization *in action*" (Park 285). Through a man's actions on the field of combat, it was assumed, his real character would be revealed, and his "manliness" would be displayed and reinforced. By the end of the nineteenth century "the deed" had taken precedence over "the word"–especially when these were "mere words" and not the agonistic words of "real men" (ibid.). According to the prevailing view at the end of the century, Eliot would not have been a representative of manliness, having seen no battlefield action. Roosevelt, therefore, was the one who embodied *arete* or excellence, since he was both "a maker of speeches and a doer of deeds." His speeches, however, were a long series of patriotic clichés, the very thing that Socrates warned against in orators.

Still another split in Eliot's old ideals that came into view in the 1890s was the conflict between two models: that of the businessman and that of the soldier. Business was not a glorious undertaking, but it was constantly a necessity in a democracy and a capitalist society. Eliot had always kept a place in his hierarchy of values for the businessman and even for the wealthy, provided they maintained a sense of duty to Harvard and society and saw that the mere making of money was not the highest good to which an individual could aspire. He was a brilliant exponent of the Protestant ethic. In an address in Chicago in 1893 he made it a point to show that George Washington had put duty ahead of financial gain. Similarly, Roosevelt in his speech in Chicago in 1899 on "the strenuous life" gave due homage to the captains of industry and the architects of "our material prosperity," but he reminded his audience that "the highest type of man is to be found in a statesman like Lincoln, a soldier like Grant." In his praise of the statesman and especially of the soldier, Roosevelt celebrated the man of action, who was not the same as the man of business. Certainly the man of action stood in contrast to the man of letters, such as William Dean Howells and Henry and William James, though Roosevelt in his own way was a man of letters too. In addition to timidity and introspection, Roosevelt also feared "the violence of . . . business individualism," which others like novelist Harold Frederic "hoped to harness for social good" (Ziff 220). Frederic tended to play down the vigorous gentleman's merits and in so doing took a stand opposed to Roosevelt's military-athletic doctrines. Frederic's faith in the merchant class as reasonable and diplomatic would not take prominence, however, over the muscularity that brought about the Spanish-American War (ibid., 219).

In "The Strenuous Life" Roosevelt catalogued all the types that in his view impeded national destiny: "The timid man, the lazy man, the man who distrusts his country, the over-civilized man, who has lost the great fighting, masterful virtues, the ignorant man, and the man of dull mind, whose soul is incapable of feeling the mighty life that thrills 'stern men with empire in the brains'—all these, of course, shrink from seeing the nation undertake its new duties" (13:323). Of all these types Roosevelt probably feared and detested the over-civilized man the most, for in such a man was conscious and articulate dissent. By *overcivilized* Roosevelt meant a reluctance "to harm others in order to fulfill one's destiny" (Ziff 222). Roosevelt shared this judgment with other graduates of Harvard; though Yale had achieved dominance in athletics and even had cornered the market on "honor," the leaders of "the strenuous life" were graduates of Harvard. "After 1895 Brooks Adams, Henry Cabot Lodge, and Theodore Roosevelt all addressed themselves vigorously to maintaining an air of militancy in America which would lead the nation to its new role as competitor for colonies" (ibid., citing Arthur F. Beringause in *Brooks Adams*). According to Ziff, "Brooks Adams would be publicist, furnishing the platform of manifest destiny abroad and centralized government at home with a theory of history which demonstrated that civilization was dependent upon the warrior. Lodge would push for the necessary legislation in congress, and Roosevelt would organize capital and labor" (ibid.). While Brooks Adams, Henry Cabot Lodge, and Theodore Roosevelt were the triumvirate, "many other men of more or less consequence cooperated . . . in an effort to make America a world power before the turn of the century" (Morris 568). Other Ivy Leaguers among the expansionists were, to name a few, John Hay (Brown), William N. Taft (Yale), and from Harvard Brooks Adams's more famous brother Henry, whom Eliot had hired to teach history at Harvard in 1871, an episode that is called "failure" in *The Education of Henry Adams.*

Most of his adult life Henry Adams was disenchanted with Harvard and America, his despair perhaps the perfect expression of *fin de siècle* psychology and certainly the funniest. Like Roosevelt, he saw money mentality as one of the menaces of the time, but unlike Roosevelt, he could not see in President Grant a representative hero, especially a statesman. "Grant's administration wrecked men by thousands," Adams wrote, "but profited few." In it "one could not catch a trait of the past, still less of the future. It was not even sensibly American." Grant himself was "inarticulate, uncertain, distrustful of himself. Still more distrustful of others, and awed by money" (*Education* 297). In Grant, Adams found further testimony of the fracturing of mind and energy. Grant, who was all energy, was as far from the ideal of the Adams family and of Eliot as one could imagine. Grant, Adams concluded, "should have been extinct for ages" (266). Grant, Adams claims, said in seriousness that "Venice would be a fine city if it were drained" (ibid.).

In his despair over cultural and economic conditions in the 1890s, Henry Adams came to accept the theory of history set forth in his brother's *Law of Civilization and Decay* (1895) in which the poet and the soldier were seen as kindred spirits, their ascendancy in contrast to the petty and small-minded spirit of the merchant (Ziff 219). At the same time Henry Adams expressed that view, many Southerners were becoming convinced that business and commerce were the only escape from the old plantation system and Reconstruction. In a letter to Charles Milnes Gaskell in 1894 (quoted in part by Ziff 222) Henry vented his rage:

> My generation has been cleaned out. My brothers and their contemporaries are old men. I am myself more at odds with the time. I detest it, and everything that belongs to it, and live only in the wish to see the end of it, with all its infernal Jewry. I want to put every money-lender to death, and to sink Lombard Street and Wall Street under the ocean. Then, perhaps, men of our kind might have some chance of being honorably killed in battle and eaten by our enemies. I want to go to India, and be a Brahmin, and worship a monkey. [*Letters* 2:34–351]

Thus while the expression "men of our kind" had traditionally meant to Henry Adams "men of disinterested devotion to public policy, men who were statesmen not politicians," by 1895 it meant "warriors" (Ziff 222-23), though Henry Adams himself was anything but a warrior. Ziff is right in claiming that Henry Adams may have shared "the muscular simplifications which his brother was promulgating and Roosevelt was putting in action" (ibid., 223), but certainly any hope for improvement that Adams held was temporary. He was an eternal pessimist and had as little faith in simple approaches to problems as in complex ones. Still, he was attracted to the man of action, especially Eliot's hero, George Washington. Though Washington was "a mere cave-dweller" in education and experience, he had known enough to organize a government and to select "Jeffersons and Hamiltons to organize his departments" (*Education* 265). With all his limitations, George Washington for Adams "was . . . an ultimate relation, like the Pole Star, and amid the endless restless motion of every other visible point in space, he alone remained steady . . . to the end" (ibid., 47). Roosevelt, by contrast, was "lost."

Though Roosevelt and Adams shared a belief in the warrior ideal and a skepticism of a business culture, they did not hold each other in the highest esteem. To Adams, Roosevelt was an amateur historian, his "lectures childlike and superficial" (Morris 23). Adams saw him as "pure act" (ibid., 580) and "repulsively fascinating" (ibid., 416). In later years Roosevelt would write of Adams "and that other 'little emasculated mass of inanity,' Henry James, that they were charming men, but exceedingly undesirable companions for any man not of strong nature" (ibid., 416).

It can hardly be said that Henry Adams saw any candidates on the American scene befitting the old warrior ideal, certainly not Grant with his view of Venice. For the rebirth of "the instinctive man, artist and warrior," there would have to be a revival of the worship of the Virgin, who inspired and controlled such men (Saveth xxix). This, he knew, would not happen except in historical imagination and idealization. In his view, it was not the artist or warrior who shaped society but the opposite, the moneymaker, which, sadly, he equated with the Jew. Like men of less intellect, he "ascribed enormous power to the Jew" but "never proved what he alleged." He even, in the view of one scholar, "wanted to hang Rothschild from a lamp post. Evidently Adams felt guilty about these thoughts. He expressed them only in his letters, and deals more kindly with Jews in his books. Adams seems involved in a love-hate relationship with the Jew that went to the core of his personality. However, as we peel off the layers of his consciousness, the trail of the subconscious source of his anti-Semitism becomes increasingly obscure" (ibid., xxviii). Still it is sad to see a distinguished historian of a great American family uttering, even in private, ethnic prejudice that would cause so much tragedy in the twentieth century. Ethnic prejudice, however, was as much a part of the theme of *Götterdämmerung* of the age as was the belief in the degeneration of men and morals. In contrast, Roosevelt seemed free of what Ernest Samuels, editor of *Education*, calls "Adams's highly ambivalent attitude toward Jews" (see *Education*, n. 10, 620). Of Roosevelt in this regard, Morris writes, "Jews all over the world revere him for his efforts to halt the persecution of their coreligionists in Russia and Romania, and for appointing

Secretary of Commerce and Labor Oscar Straus, the first Jewish Cabinet officer in American history" (14).

The reaction to overcivilization by the Roosevelt–Lodge–Brooks Adams group brings to mind the same complaint by Walt Whitman, who in "Democratic Vistas" said that he would not be made a "civilizee," one, that is, who had been refined and cultured to such an extent that all naturalness had been drained away or repressed (481). To counter that excessive civilizing tendency in modern society, Whitman would, he says in "Song of Myself," "go to the bank by the wood and become undisguised and naked" (25). This is not the type of naturalness that Roosevelt was calling for. Whitman calls for a return to nature, as did Thoreau; but Roosevelt was always conquering nature, killing the beasts of nature for trophy, even while, like Thoreau, singing the praises of wildness. Thoreau gave up the gun (and eventually the fishing rod) and became a hunter for truth, the self-appointed "inspector of snow storms," but Roosevelt strove to carry the ideal of the hunter forward into a commercial age—not just the ideal of the hunter but of the warrior too. His model was closer to Beowulf than to Francis of Assisi (who constantly invites comparison with the persona in Whitman). It is true that Roosevelt did much for the conservation of wilderness, but one cannot escape the conclusion that he did so in order to maintain a supply of game and provide territory where manliness could thrive, an altogether different attitude from Thoreau's conservationism, though Thoreau, like others of his era, did equate heroism and manliness (*Journal* 1:329, 529). At the end of his life Thoreau had made his one exploration of the still wild West, where the image of the warrior had already taken hold.

The Far West as a theater for adventure was crucial to the idea of the strenuous life, and each advocate of the code had to spend time there, almost as if to prove his mettle. Roosevelt set the pattern as early as 1884, sometimes spending sixteen hours a day tending cattle on his two ranches in the Dakota Territory. It was no accident that his Rough Riders comprised not only former college athletes but Western cowboys as well.

If in the concerted effort to make America more manly, Brooks Adams was to be publicist for the warrior, the publicist for the Westerner was to be Owen Wister, another Harvard alumnus (1882). Roosevelt, in fact, wanted him to become the "Kipling of the West," and while not a Kipling, Wister was a talented writer who in his masterpiece *The Virginian* (1902) achieved a synthesis of myth and reality that was immensely popular and quite acceptable to Roosevelt, who praised him in 1907: "Grim, stalwart men stride through Wister's pages. It is this note of manliness which is dominant through the writings of Mr. Wister. Beauty, refinement, grace are excellent qualities in a man, as in a nation, but they come second . . . to the great virile virtues—the virtues of courage, energy, and daring: the virtues which beseem a masterful race—a race fit to fill the forests, to build roads, to found commonwealths, to conquer continents, to overthrow armed enemies. It is about the man who can do such deeds that Mr. Wister writes" (quoted in White 197). Though one understands the sense in which Roosevelt meant it, such a term as *masterful race,* in light of twentieth-century horrors, evokes the same revulsion as does Henry Adams's talk of putting moneylenders to death.

Two fictional modes of Wister's literary career, early and late, have been identified by G. Edward White, using the terms *picaresque* and *heroic.* Wister's early writings show "the violent and rustic aspects of the West and a sneering at the false trappings of eastern civilization, while his later work, the heroic, tended to view the West not as anticivilized but precivilized, and to portray his protagonists as precursors to more cultured times, even possessing some smattering of culture themselves" (131). The distinction is not absolute, but evolution is discernible, leading to the creation of his "most heroic" western protagonist in *The Virginian.*

The heroic qualities of the Virginian are precisely the same, excluding excellence in academics, as those identified by Eliot in 1869. Wister must have heard these extolled any number of times. The first of these, as might be expected, is "manliness," a quality valued in the Civil War and even more in the industrial age. "The triumph of industrial enterprise paradoxically produced a heightened consciousness of women as delicate flowers and men as their defenders against the evils of a strange new world, resulting in a nationwide assertion of masculinity" (ibid., 141). The women re-

garded as "delicate flowers" would obviously be those of the middle
and upper classes, since women toiling on the farms and in the
factories of the nineteenth century would scarcely qualify for such
chivalric beautification any more than men of the lower strata would
qualify as knights. The development of knighthood in America has
been a project of the ruling class. As a symbol of the manliness of
that class, Wister's Virginian excels; he is gentle but powerful and
authoritative in his dealings with women. Thus he wins the affection
of Molly Wood, who rejects civilized Vermont society in favor of "a
man who was a man" (ibid.).

Though the Virginian was not of the educated classes, he
nevertheless represented Eliot's faith in a natural aristocracy. Indeed,
the ideal of Jefferson's natural aristocrat is part of the myth that Wister
helped to enshrine in *The Virginian* (Vorpahl xviii). The hero's rise
from humble beginnings to the status of "an important man" is
analogous to the poor boys at Harvard, who, because of talent and
dedication, also become important. The Virginian is a competitor
and a believer in self-reliance, but he is also a gentleman, a quality
highly prized at Eliot's Harvard and even at the more competitive
Yale. Athletes may be gentlemen, and so may cowpokes, a point
insisted upon by Wister:

> "You're from Virginia, I understand?" said Molly Wood, regard-
> ing him politely, but not rising. One gains authority immensely
> by keeping one's seat. All good teachers know this.
>
> "Yes, ma'am, from Virginia."
>
> "I've heard that Southerners have such good manners."
>
> "That's correct." The cow-puncher flushed, but he spoke in his
> unvaryingly gentle voice. [77]

In spite of all his natural and civilized virtues, the Virginian retains
some ingrained racist attitudes, singing derisive songs about Negroes, calling Germans "Dutchmen" and Jews "hebes," and considering Indians subhuman (White 143). His Americanness is
emphasized not by the integration of minorities but by unification
of what has been called "Saxon blood."

Henry Adams himself went to Colorado in 1871 to observe the

work of the Fortieth Parallel Survey and "to spy upon the land of the future." There he met Clarence King who, in Adam's view, was the most remarkable man of his age. Founder of the U.S. Geologic Survey, he was not only a scientist but a prolific writer of science, mainly of geology: he wrote the "epochal" *Systematic Geology* (1878). He published work on other topics as well, and his *Mountaineering in the Sierra Nevada* (1872) is regarded as a minor literary classic. He was also a lover of art, a patron and collector, at home in the great galleries of Europe as well as in the Sierra. Judging from accounts, however, he was more than the sum of his achievements. Says Adams, "The charm of King was that he saw what others did and a great deal more. His wit and humor; his bubbling energy which swept everyone into the current of his interest; his personal charm of youth and manners; his faculty of giving and taking, profusely, lavishly whether in thought or money as though he were nature herself, marked him almost alone among Americans. He had in him something of the Greek—a touch of Alcibiades or Alexander. One Clarence King only existed in the world" (*Education* 311).

Adams here gives clear proof of the type of man of action he admired, the man who, according to Carlyle's definition of a hero, could be "all sorts of men." This, in Adams's view, was King to the letter. "Whatever prize he wanted lay ready for him—scientific, social, literary, political—and he knew how to take them in turn" (ibid., 313).

Indeed King, an 1862 graduate of Yale and member of the expansionist lobby, epitomized the excellence that Eliot defined, since he was "almost equally" at home, in words of Anson Phelps Stokes, "in the world of art, letters, and science." At Yale, says Stokes, he "was a good student, had a taste for field work in his vacations, derived an enthusiasm for science from his instructors, and was prominent in the social and athletic life of the college community, being stroke oar of one of the crews, and captain of the baseball team" (76).

King lived up to his promise sufficiently to be invited to give the commencement address at Sheffield School (Yale Scientific School) in 1877 and to gain seven laudatory pages in Stokes's *Memorials*, but he himself became increasingly disappointed in his own efforts to succeed in the fashion of a true renaissance man.

Utilizing his vast knowledge of geology and mining, King wanted to turn a fortune, but not for the mere purpose of making money. Says his biographer Clarence Wilkins, "He dreamed of gaining millions from his Mexican mines; he dreamed, too, of turning millions to the uses of contemporary artists, and of making himself a new Lorenzo" (297). Almost at every turn in mining enterprises, though, King failed.

Henry Adams deplored the preoccupation with wealth in others, but he quickly excused it in King. From King's example he drew the familiar conclusion, "that the theory of scientific education failed where most theory failed—for want of money" (*Education* 346). In King, Adams had further proof that while the ideal, as defined by Eliot, posited an integration of the drive for wealth and the love of learning, the two instincts are virtually irreconcilable. If King couldn't reconcile them, Adams and his friends seemed to say, then there was no need for anyone else to try. Inquisitiveness and acquisitiveness simply did not go together.

Clarence King was sincere in his desire to patronize art and artists, and he was equally sincere in his defense and even praise of Indians and Negroes, a rare attitude for one of his class and time. He kept a Negro valet "who spoke like a cultured Englishman," he "praised Cable's stories about the people of color in New Orleans," and in 1888 he secretly married "Ada Todd," a young Negro woman more than twenty years his junior, in whom he found all "the energy that spelled the essential woman" (Wilkins 320). Though interracial marriage was legal in New York, King chose to keep his secret for fear of the scandal such an announcement would create, especially for his mother who was in ill health (ibid., 321).

Though King seemed kind and even solicitous toward Ada and their children, the secrecy with which he guarded their relationship sheds light on the times and the patronizing attitudes toward women on the part of the manly upper class. The patronage of women was much like the patronage of art. Both were to be revered and protected and, if need be, kept from public view—like Ada Todd, a treasure too rare to show.

In the words of Henry Adams, King "had no faith in the American woman." She had been overcivilized, just as, in the view of Roosevelt, Lodge, and Brooks Adams, the educated male had been. Christianity and doting mothers had made her too refined. King saw the young female of his own class as "a prim little Puritan maid, sharp as a stockbroker and with an unabridged dictionary of a mind," while the girl of the West had "something of the same flatness and sugary insipidity that marked the California grape" (Wilkins 318). In spite of his idealization of dark-skinned women, King sounds at times almost misogynistic, reflecting the male confusion of the age about the other half of humanity. King also reflected the traditional Ivy League view of women: Thomas Wentworth Higginson, for example, remarked that "no person who has never left America can appreciate the sensation of living among healthy women." In Boston, by contrast, there reigns a "lovely invalidism": "Morbid anatomy has long enough served as a type of feminine loveliness; our polite society has long enough been a series of soirees of incurables" (Black 5). Higginson advocated "high physical training" for women as well as men, but there was a purpose behind his program: "In a republic, a woman's physical condition will determine the 'temperament' bequeathed to 'our next president' " (ibid., 6). Few if any of the muscular graduates of Harvard or Yale ever moved beyond a utilitarian or idealistic view of women.

If the surveys of Clarence King provided a comprehensive view of the geologic history of mountain regions of the West, then Frederic Remington, another Yale man (1900), provided through his painting, sculpture, and fiction a comprehensive view of the man of the West. While King's pioneering work has been overshadowed and dated by the advances of science, Remington's art becomes more valuable with the passage of time. Few people would disagree with Owen Wister, who called him "a national treasure," or with Roosevelt, who said,

> I regard Frederic Remington as one of the Americans who has done real work for his country, and we all owe him a debt of gratitude. It is no small thing that such an artist and man of letters should arise to make permanent record of certain of the most interesting features of our national life. . . . The soldier, the cowboy, and rancher, the Indian, the horses and the cattle of

the plains, will live in his bronzes for all time. [quoted in White 197–98]

Roosevelt had a special admiration for the manliness of Remington's art, as he did for that of Wister's fiction. When the Rough Riders gathered for the last time, in September 1898 at Montauk Beach on Long Island, they gave Roosevelt a copy of Remington's "Bronco Buster," which, Roosevelt told his men, "represented 'the foundation' of their regiment" (Vorpahl 237).

The manliness that Remington portrayed in his art was in part part of a "cowboy philosophy" that seemed almost reserved for Anglo-Saxons. Like Clarence King, he denounced the "torrential vulgarity flooding America," and, like Henry Adams, he was ready to do violence to the culprits:

> Jews, Injuns, Chinamen, Italians, Huns–the rubbish of the Earth I hate–I've got some Winchesters and when the massacring begins, I can get my share of 'em, and what's more, I will. . . . Our race is full of sentiment. We invite the rinsins, the scourins, and the Devil's lavings to come to us and be *men*–something they haven't been, most of them, these hundreds of years. I don't care a damn how a man gets to Heaven–how he takes care of his soul–whether he has one or not. It's all nothing to me. But I do care how he votes and lives and fights. [quoted in White 109; Remington's italics]

For Remington, manliness meant actual physical strength and ability and almost a love of fighting, certainly a love of sports. He especially loved football and was glad to see Roosevelt defending it during the trial of the game in 1905. He even loved the destructive side of football and hoped it would never be changed to suit critics like Eliot. In a recent study of his art, Remington was described as "a natural athlete, displaying strength and skill which enabled him to excel in all sports, including boxing and horsemanship. As a rusher he knocked heads on the line, and although his brawn should have been sufficient, he employed psychological tactics as a means of bringing his team to victory. On the occasion of the 1879 Princeton-Yale game, Remington reputedly dipped his jersey in blood at a local slaughterhouse 'to make it look more businesslike' " (Hassrick 19,

101). Stokes mentions Remington's "fine physique" and membership on the football team. He also cites one authority who called Remington "the authoritative chronicler of the whole western land . . . and of all men and beasts dwelling therein" (127).

In his fiction Remington also chronicled the women of the West, as seen in his *Crooked Trails* and *Sundown* stories and especially in *John Ermine of the Yellowstone*, published only a few months after Wister's *The Virginian* and by the same company. Remington, in fact, was a friend of Wister and an illustrator of his work, including an edition of *The Virginian*. Indeed, the friendship of the two men and the similarity of their novels raised several questions, but there were differences between the novels, if not "a thousand," as one reviewer said, at least some significant ones. Both John Ermine and the Virginian were "historical" characters, but they "operated under different laws." Though both were manly, natural men, the Virginian was a Southerner while John Ermine "was born white . . . but had a Crow heart" (quoted in Vorpahl 312).

Katherine Searles of *John Ermine* is the beautiful and desirable daughter of the commandant of a unit who employs John Ermine as a scout. Wister, had he written the novel, would have united the two in marriage, since Ermine possessed "a white skin" and all the visible attributes of quality. In Remington's philosophy, however, no peaceful union could exist between the civilized and the uncivilized, and thus Katherine Searles rejects Ermine. In the wake of this refusal Ermine grasps that "I am all alone," as Remington believed was only proper (ibid., 314).

But the lament of Ermine applies to Frederic Remington as well in his last years. Predictably, he had been drawn to the Cuban War at the beginning because of an unending desire for physical action, but he ceased to see a kinship between the winning of the West and the Cuban campaign. That former spirit he felt to be tied to youth—his own and that of his country—which were both lost by the time of the war (ibid., 237). "Cowboys! There are no cowboys anymore!" was Remington's cry. For Remington the West was no longer a reality but a symbol, and his work was to help preserve and upraise the romance (White 121).

The famous graduates of Harvard and Yale in the last decades of the nineteenth century extended to the American West heroic ideals and to a large degree twisted them out of shape so that unanimity about the meaning of certain aspects of the ideal never emerged. Though all proclaimed themselves champions of democracy, they manifested a thoroughgoing elitism that frequently took the form of racial and ethnic prejudice. All were from "good," "old," and powerful families, and their faith in the potentialities of "equality" was not always the highest, to say the least. The "manliness" that attracted them all may have served well Roosevelt's goals of establishing the "supremacy" of the American flag and "uplifting mankind" around the world, but it did not exactly uplift womankind at home. Woman was seen either as a source of energy or a refiner of energy. For Henry Adams she was divine energy in the form of the Virgin Mary, for Clarence King primitive energy in the form of the African Sibyl, and for Roosevelt domestic energy in the form of "housewife" and "helpmate" and "mother of many healthy children." For Owen Wister in *The Virginian* she was the gentle modulator of energy who instructed the rugged Southerner and Westerner in the finer things of "quality." In every case, though, man is the protector and woman the object of the protection and idealization. Natural relationships seem impossible.

The living legend of western manliness was Buffalo Bill, William F. Cody. He was the hero of all heroes and "in the eyes of the world the greatest idol out of the West. . . . For almost fifty years, in more than a thousand dime novels, in melodramas, in his own Wild West Show, Cody remained the finest figure of a man that ever sat a steed." He made a career of his image, accepting most of the "yarns told about him, including the 137 wounds he had received from the Indians. (His wife in her old age, somewhat disenchanted with her hero, revealed that he had suffered only one casualty, a scalp wound in his skirmish with the Sioux)" (Wecter 353–54).

As a young surveyor for the Kansas-Pacific Railroad, Cody, who was later known as the Knight of the Plains, won buffalo-killing contests while a gallery of excursionists toasted him with champagne. In his exploits on the plains and in his shows Cody, like Wild Bill Hickock and General Custer, wore his hair long, not as any sign of effeminacy–an interpretation that enraged them all–but as a taunt to the scalping knife of the Indians: Come and get it! (ibid 355-56). In revenge for Custer's death, Cody supposedly killed the young chief Yellow Hand; he was enraged, Cody said, at the sight of the Indian wearing an American flag wrapped around his groin and the scalp of a blond woman attached to his hair as a trophy (Sell and Weybright 118). "Scientifically" taking his enemy's scalp, Cody displayed it for years as a promotional device in his shows.

Apparently there was never anything like Cody's Wild West Show before or since. According to one billing, it contained "more Ladies, Gentlemen, and beasts than ever seen in one exhibition." One act of the troop known as the World's Rough Riders was "Football on Horseback, between Indians and Cowboys." Cody wanted to perform in the "Colosseum of the Caesars" but found it too shabby and small. In 1893 he was one of the great attractions at the Chicago World's Fair, and in 1895 he was compared on posters to Napoleon (Wecter 361), both men shown on horseback separated only by a century. After the Spanish-American War, Buffalo Bill reenacted the battle of San Juan Hill, playing the role of Roosevelt himself and hiring some of Roosevelt's Rough Riders for the performance. The show helped to elevate Roosevelt's popularity and to help audiences forget the tragedy of General Custer, whom Buffalo Bill also portrayed in another show: "Teddy Roosevelt was triumphant at every performance" (Sell and Weybright 208).

Just as the Spanish-American War elevated Roosevelt to fame, so it sealed the fate of Buffalo Bill. The great hero of the plains kept saying he was ready to fight in that war at any time, but he never got around to it despite the urging of his image makers. When General A. Miles cabled Cody, telling him he would like for him to take the first steamer from Newport News for Cuba, Cody grumbled at the cost of one hundred thousand dollars that closing his show would entail, suggested that peace was near anyway, and asked the general if it wouldn't be better to wait. Miles concurred. Thereafter Cody's luck began to fail. Of his increasing financial and domestic troubles, Cody said, "I do not want to die a showman. I grow very tired of this sort of sham hero worship sometimes" (Wecter 361–62).

The lament for the heroism of a passing age was one of the chief characteristics of the period. Unless the glory of a nobler past could be revived, Roosevelt and his group seemed to say, there was no hope. Wister salvaged something of the ideal in *The Virginian* but kept it safe within the Saxon family. Henry Adams saw no hope in any event, and Clarence King, though he maintained a sense of humor to the last, slipped more frequently into "enervating 'spells of depression' " in a "hostile milieu" in which William James's "bright Bitch Goddess" of success reigned supreme, a goddess that both attracted and repelled King (Wilkins 308–9). The "gentleman's world of Anglo-Saxonism degenerated into squalling nationalism and xenophobia; the technocratic paternalists gave way to an administration which believed that 'the business of government is business'; and small town America became Main Street" (White 201). Instead of that ideal of the warrior or artist, the millionaire became the national model, his merit measured purely by material acquisition (Wilkins 309). Frugality and diligence, the restraining virtues of the Protestant ethic, also fell victims. The triumph of the conspicuous millionaire meant the proliferation of sports, for economic competition, as Caillois shows, is an institutional form of *agon* or competitive sports (54). In corrupt form they represent a will to power, which was widely evident in America among the barons of business, politicians, and intellectuals wanting to extend the dominance of the Anglo-Saxon race to the Far West and beyond. Indeed, as Thorstein Veblen argued at the turn of the century in *Theory of the Leisure Class*, sports, government, warfare, and religion, all barbaric traits of conservative groups, reinforced each other. The expansion of the American frontier did not present evidence to refute his theory.

The role of religion, specifically Protestantism, upon the frontier was subtle and profound, as Sacvan Berkovitch reveals in *The American Jeremiad*. Berkovitch cites John Juricek's important definitions of the word *frontier*. At first, *frontier* meant "a 'military line,' and then 'a cultural confrontation between whites and Indians'; finally *frontier* referred to only one of these populations, the (white) Americans,' and it was this meaning that Frederick Jackson Turner drew upon" in *The Significance of the Frontier in American History*. "After all, 'conquest of the continent' was for him [Turner] also an enterprise of the spirit. It was to 'dream as our fathers dreamt and . . . to make their dreams come true' " (Berkovitch 164). Since Turner was a professor at Harvard from 1910 to 1924, it should not surprise us that his view of the frontier was essentially the same as that of Roosevelt and Wister.

Berkovitch cites other examples of the peculiar use of "our"—as in "our fathers" in the passage from Turner. In *Landscapes of Frederic Edwin Church*, for instance, David Huntington speaks of the opportunities of the frontier in this way: "The genius of our people is required to declare itself after a fashion of its own. . . . 'This heritage of ours is without a parallel.' . . . It is a wondrous impulse to the individual, to his hope, his exertions and his final success, . . . to be taught that there is nothing in his way;—that he is not to be denied because of his birth or poverty; that he stands fair with his comrades, on the same great arena,—with no social impediments,—and that the prize is always certain for the fleetest in the race. This is the *natural* influence to the democratic principles of our Revolution" (quoted in Berkovitch 165).

The western experience of Roosevelt, Remington, Wister, Adams, and King confirms the observations of Berkovitch in his response to the passage from Huntington: "*Our people* in this passage is as ambiguous as the *frontier* is barrierless. It stands for a remnant of visible saints become a remnant of visible WASPs—an American consensus that has broadened, in accordance with the broadening American landscape, from non-separating congregationalists to include all denominations of *our* (Anglo-Saxon Protestant) *race*" (165).

The experience of the moving frontier, Berkovitch argues, "was shaped not by Rousseau but by New England Puritanism." Crucial to the idea of a New England was the idea of a New Israel. Says Berkovitch,

> The biblical Hebrews were nationalists. Although they claimed their land by promise, Canaan itself was a country (like any other) with fixed boundaries; and though they defined themselves as chosen people, the definition was itself based (like that of any other people of their time) upon genealogy and a certain form of religion. The Christian concept of New Israel did away with genealogy; the Puritans' concept of wilderness and frontier allowed their "walled garden" to expand (after Washington—Joshua's "conquest of Canaan") into the "Western garden of the world." . . . In their view they represented not a particular sect

but the vanguard of Protestantism; and Protestantism was not just a religious movement for them, but the last stage of the work of redemption. [165-66]

While theoretically the "garden of the world" was open to all, genealogy did matter very much to the sons of New England. Huntington argued that "birth and poverty" had no bearing on admission, but history tells a different story. The terms we use to describe our myths are themselves revealing, for there is a huge difference between the West as "garden of the world" and as a "great arena," as Huntington called it. Anyone can walk into a garden, but going into an arena requires training, background, practice, even privilege and invitation. A garden is a place of play and recreation; an arena is a stage for sport and theatrics. Instead of a garden, the West became a playing field and a killing field featuring stalwart knights from the East in leading roles.

Though its view of America is profoundly ambivalent, *A Connecticut Yankee* by Twain is classified by Berkovitch as an anti-jeremiad: one of the books that reflects more than it solves. In that novel, for example, Twain shows how in essential ways Arthur's England and the Confederacy are mirror-images of each other, with all the abuses and outrages to the human spirit that such hierarchal systems permit and promote. The captions for Dan Beard's illustrations in the first edition of the text show some of the similarities between the cultures. "This is a picture of an ancient tournament; when, for want of something better to do, the nobility used to kill each other, while the ladies looked on and enjoyed it" (Twain, *Yankee* 527). Under a drawing reflecting the system of rewards in a monarchy, which Twain thought we would eventually embrace, there is this: "The Yankee establishes both military and naval schools, but the king, in the appointment of officers, persists in favoring only those of noble birth, no matter how meritorious the others may be. The artist here has represented a crown of laurels as a reward of birth, and a crown of thorns as a reward of merit" (531).

Knighthood in all its American forms remained a favorite target for Twain. In 1904 Twain wrote a short story called "The Horse's Tale," which, like the majority of his works, reminds us how far adrift we are from common sense in our entertainment and in our notions of aristocracy.

> I am Buffalo Bill's Horse. I have spent my life under his saddle—with him in it, too, and he is good for two hundred pounds, without his clothes; and there is no telling how much he does weigh when he is out on the war-path and has all of his batteries belted on. He is over six feet, is young, hasn't an ounce of waste flesh, is straight, graceful, springy in his motions, quick as a cat, and has a handsome face, and black hair dangling down on his shoulders, and is beautiful to look at; and nobody is braver than he is, and nobody is stronger, except myself. . . . He is chief of scouts of the army of the Frontier, and it makes us very important. In such a position as I hold in the military service one needs to be of a good family and possess an education much above the common to be worthy of the place. I am the best-educated horse outside of the Hippodrome, everybody says, and the best-mannered. . . . Buffalo Bill taught me the most of what I know, my mother taught me much, and I taught myself the rest. . . . My mother was all American. . . . she was the best blood of Kentucky, the bluest Blue-grass aristocracy, very proud and acrimonious—or maybe it is cere-monious. [Twain, *Complete Short Stories* 525–26]

Roosevelt, who admired Buffalo Bill, placed Cody in the tradition of Boone and Crockett, but this linkage is misleading. Boone and Crockett belong to a yeoman tradition, while Cody's prototype is Jeb Stuart—gallant, military scout, and expert horseman. Boone and Crockett are frontiersmen afoot, but Cody, like Stuart, is a mounted darling of derring-do. Just as the cavalier tradition suffocated the yeoman tradition in the South, so it did in the West, with its endless implications for Hollywood, the great American dream machine. The "West" as we have come to know it is not a "stage of redemption" but another kind of stage, a theater of rivalry and revenge wherein the Marlboro Man can ride and rope, John Wayne can shoot and strut, and Clint Eastwood can cover the ground with corpses, making his day. After barbed wire the cowboy became a myth, but it was the myth of the knight rather than of the shepherd. Every western movie would end either with a war between natives and newcomers, with predictable results for the white knights, or with a showdown tournament between gunslingers with scarcely a clue as to how men and women might live in harmony with nature and one another.

The heroic past that Roosevelt, Henry Adams, and others lamented and wanted to revive was to Twain a sham in itself, a nightmare from which society was trying to awaken. Instead of a new start, America west of the Great River became a repeat of failures in the East. The first civil war had been fought over slavery; the second in the West was over land. The "winning of the West" was a contest, as the phrase reveals, against natives, native animals, and the land itself, and the language was often the same as that which appears in sporting rhetoric: "The prize is always certain for the fleetest in the race." When victory was announced, even the star of the great Wild West Show said that he was tired of the parade. With Adams, King, and Remington, the idol of the West himself was uttering *Götterdäm-merung*. There are many forms of heroism, and at the same time that the West was passing into legend a more democratic brand was emerging within the gates of the oligarchy that offered a form of "manliness" morally superior to that of the gentlemen, knights, merchants, and other adventurers of the prevailing cultural order, East and West.

# 8

# Playful Alternatives

In both popular culture with its fascination for reform and practicality and in more elite intellectual establishments, the idea of the hero captured the imagination of an age. The hero became the ideal of the individual in triumph by the turn of the century. As Emerson said in "Education," "Victory over things is the office of man" (*Complete Works* 10:127). But in a democracy elitism is always a problem. Parallel to the cult of the heroic elite were the growing legends of the more ordinary hero, the common person, whether outlaw or simple citizen, who demonstrated a more democratic embodiment of the struggle to succeed. These heroes offer something new, an open affirmation of the rights of minorities and sometimes a sense of appreciation of the natural gift of play. Their impact may be minimal compared with the pervasive legacy of competitive knighthood distinguished for military glory, the setting of records in business and sports, and the conquest of nature; but these heroes, increasingly presented in the stories for boys that have now mostly become mere artifacts of popular culture, seem in crucial respects considerably more virtuous than their real-life contemporaries, like Theodore Roosevelt, whom we still honor.

Mark Twain wrote the most important stories for boys filled with satire of chivalry and knighthood and heroes. "Twain's imagination dwelt, at times obsessively, on play and childhood throughout a lifetime in both conventional and unconventional ways" (Oriard,

*Sporting* 400). The play Twain most admired might be called Edenic play, in contrast to the agonic, highly competitive knightly contests of the elite. Edenic play yields a natural gift, agonic a cultural prize. Edenic nurtures communion and seeks delight in nature; agonic finds meaning in victory. The first seems almost to favor seclusion such as that found on a river raft. Knightly games require arenas and display of prowess so that winners can be distinguished and records established. Edenic play is private and recreational, pointing toward meadows and enjoyment; agonic play, public and self-promotional, moves toward the urban, toward coliseum and trophy rooms.

Between them, Michael Oriard and Ralph Cohen in Part 2 of the Bantam Pathfinder edition of *Huckleberry Finn* identify at least five types of play in Twain: that of Huck and Jim, characterized by total freedom but mutual respect without written rules; the romantic play of Tom Sawyer, which requires adventures and made-up rules but is not democratic; the murderous feuds of the Grangerfords and Sheperdsons and of Arthur's knights; the play of the King and the Duke on the raft; and the play of Young Satan (in "The Chronicle of Young Satan" and "The Mysterious Stranger"), which is constant re-creation but without any rules whatever (Oriard, *Sporting* 400–410; R. Cohen 282–91). Edenic play, in contrast to these other forms, is always presented lyrically with a sense of transcendent joy. When play in Twain is not working, when it is cruel and destructive, he is at his satiric best, revealing how those often grown-up Tom Sawyers (Cox 220), who aspire to set moral examples for others by means of the shows and hunts they stage, equate manliness with morality. An incurable knight, Tom Sawyer plays by the romantic books. Even among young knights, Twain shows, there is destructiveness. "When the doctor asks Huck how Tom was shot, Huck replies, 'He had a dream ... and it shot him' " (R. Cohen 290). The play of the grown-up Tom Sawyer was perhaps the most troubling for Twain, since national heroes not only engaged in it but raised such play to new levels of foolishness and tragedy. Such a one was Theodore Roosevelt, whom Twain called "the Tom Sawyer of the political world of the twentieth century" (*Twain in Eruption* 49). Ironically, Twain received an honorary degree from Yale in 1902, along with Roosevelt. Here at the same ceremony were representatives of the two poles of play in American culture, the Edenic play of Twain and the knightly adventure of Roosevelt.

When Roosevelt was presented his honorary degree, the public orator proclaimed that while Roosevelt was "a Harvard man by nature . . . in his democratic spirit, his breadth of natural feeling, and his earnest pursuit of what is true and right [he] possesses those qualities which represent the distinctive ideals of Yale." These remarks were received, says Yale historian Brooks Mather Kelley, "not with gales of laughter, but with prolonged applause" (314). Mark Twain may have been the only one present who was amused. Of the event he said, "There was a freshet of honorary degrees at Yale and the President was there to be part of the ducking, and I was there on the same errand, . . . gowned and hooded for baptism" (*Twain in Eruption* 30). In order to grasp the implications of these two poles of adventurous play, it is helpful to look at the heroic attitudes at Harvard and Yale at the turn of the century. Military and athletic glory was still pretty much determined by class, but a new spirit of equality was in the air, opening up possibilities for those formerly excluded for reasons of birth or wealth. The democratic consensus was beginning to widen for the young and the young at heart just as the old order was chanting *Götterdämmerung*.

Even in elite establishments like Harvard and Yale, there was a gradual movement toward acceptance of the ordinary hero, at least partly because of the influence of sports. Excellence, aristocracy, sense of duty and service, and manliness were the essential features of the Harvard ideal, as defined by Eliot. It was basically the same as the Yale ideal, which was as old as Nathan Hale, "the hero" of Yale. Perhaps the biggest difference between the ideals of Harvard and Yale was that Yale stressed "manliness" even more than Harvard. In his description of Hale in *Memorials*, Stokes links the words *spirit* and *football*, and the linkage in 1915 is probably deliberate. By this time "spirit" had become the distinguishing feature of Yale, especially in contrast to Harvard and especially in sports. "From 1872 through 1909 in all games of soccer, rugby and American football, the fantastic Yale teams ran up a record of 324 victories, 17 losses, and 18 ties. Yale's success against Harvard was so great that Cambridge men began to think of Yalies as nothing but muckers while Yale men had serious doubts about the manliness of the Harvards" (Kelley 322). It was in fact the Yale dominance in sports that led to such clichés as Yale "spirit" and Harvard "reserve" and Yale "brawn" and Harvard "brains." Both universities, of course, valued both brain and brawn in accordance with the heroic myth of the age, but Yale men, for whatever reasons, were more confident and optimistic than their Harvard counterparts, certainly more ebullient, at least in the eyes of a Yale historian: "Sociable and enthusiastic, Yale men believed in friendship and each other" (Pierson 15).

The emphasis on athletics was a way of improving actual quality and not, at least in the mind of Walter Camp, one of Yale's most famous graduates (1880) and coaches, merely an effort at showmanship and glamour. The effects of organized sports were much deeper, since they promoted, in his view, "the establishment of an all-round standard of clean morals and health, and an *esprit de corps* that carries the typical Yale man far towards the best goal in all his efforts" (ibid., 33). At Yale little difference seemed to exist between spirit in sports and the spiritual values associated with religion. *Spirit*, or *sand*, was an all-encompassing word that applied to every part of college life.

Religion and football always coexisted comfortably at Yale and even grew up together. While Yale was compiling its amazing records in all sports, Dwight L. Moody led in the formation of the Christian Social Union in 1879. Two years later it became the YMCA, and the same year Thomas Hughes published *The Manliness of Christ*. By 1901 the YMCA at Yale had a thousand members, "the largest college Christian association in the country" (Kelley 304). Perhaps it is accidental, but at approximately the same time, in 1900, the university had its greatest football team, which had seven All-Americans, won thirteen games, and was unscored on (Bergin, *Game* 73). The mission work of the university extended not only to the poorer sections of New Haven but all the way to the Far East. In religious and sporting enthusiasm, Yale at the turn of the century was undisputed champion and had been, considering the two activities collectively, for a number of years. From Harvard, Eliot had to be wondering what had caused him ever to make the association between Christ and manliness.

To be sure, Yale was in many ways still like Harvard, but it was quite different also. In 1892 distinguished Harvard philosopher George Santayana visited Yale to see just how different it was and whether or not the Yale spirit was fact or fiction. He found it to be a fact that impressed him immensely. Not only was Yale in 1892 what Harvard used to be, in Santayana's view, but it was a great deal more:

> If there is a difference, as of course there is, between the Yale undertone of crudity and toughness and the sweet melodiousness of studious and athletic life in England, that is not the fault of Yale, but is due to the fact that English and American society are at different intellectual stages. . . . As American society approaches maturity, and all human interests gain representation in it, a college like Yale will gradually ripen too. Its curriculum will be extended, its outlook will be widened and its barbarism will disappear; but the initial intention and function will remain. The continuity of the past will not be broken and the sympathy with the national life will never be lost. [quoted in Ballowe 54]

Santayana did not downgrade Harvard in contrast, but in a companion piece to "A Glimpse of Yale," titled "The Spirit and Ideals of Harvard University," he penned words that were no doubt music to President Eliot's ears. The Harvard "reserve" had virtues, said Santayana, like "steady self-restraint." He continued, "It is not only moral independence and worth that we find here: we find very generally a certain maturity and balance. This is another virtue which underlies 'Harvard indifference.' What seems coldness is often justice, and tardiness of perspective and a steady sense of what is best" (ibid., 66–67).

Santayana was optimistic about Yale and Harvard and the ideals of both schools in the 1890s. There is, however, at the end of the Harvard essay a cautionary note rendered almost as a further compliment to "Harvard reserve" that is telling and prophetic: "All is tentative, and the goal, the final truth, is not clearly seen. This sense that we are experimenting, exploring, that our efforts are partial, imperfect, and partly, perhaps, in the wrong direction, and that the totality of our mind is chaos–this sense is what imposes upon us an attitude of expectancy, or reserve" (ibid.).

Certainty on any issue is as elusive for any thinking person today as it was in the 1890s, but from a perspective of democratic idealism and the advantage of a century of hindsight we can see, I think, that the codes and goals of Harvard and Yale between the Civil War and the end of World War I were imperfect and were "partly . . . in the wrong direction." The heroic ideal was warped, as were the well-meaning and talented people who took it seriously and tried to abide by the severity of its demands. In each of the aspects of the heroic code there was finally an unbridgeable gap between opposite tendencies that the heroic ideal tried to reconcile, so that any serious advocate of the ideal, such as Eliot, had constantly to engage in a sort of funambulism to keep the ideal alive.

On the matter of excellence it was necessary to champion the synthesis of arts and sciences to produce the whole man, a task that became an increasing challenge with the growth and specialization of scientific knowledge. In regard to natural aristocracy, the charges of preferential treatment of the privileged classes would not go away no matter how much Harvard, and especially Yale, proclaimed a commitment to democratic principles. Money was also the problem as far as duty was concerned, private financial gain, as Eliot well knew, being more of a lure than a career in government service. Finally, the concept of manliness was riddled with problems. In essence, manliness meant maleness, which meant the virtual exclusion of women in any heroic endeavor, military or civilian. Eliot was, relatively speaking, a progressive liberal on "the intellectual emancipation of women," as he was on most issues. Because of conservative attitudes of the Harvard Corporation and society in general, however, progress in educational opportunities for women in Cambridge and elsewhere moved slowly.

In contrast to the real Ivy League heroes, the young fictional heroes of some of the boys' books of the period may somewhat redeem the democratic idealism of Yale in particular. A good example is Gilbert Patten's Frank Merriwell, who made his appearance in 1896. What Patten wished to revive was not the stock theatrics of the plains, which had served as the testing ground for manliness of the graduates of Harvard and Yale, but the simpler and older form of entertainment centered on "athletic sports." With Frank, Patten started where the old order finished. He went east, back to roots, to tradition, to Yale, the school of Nathan Hale. There in the person of Merriwell he produced an innocent hero who was truer to Charles W. Eliot's dream in many ways than the distinguished graduates who left their marks upon the nation's arts, letters, and political destiny. Indeed, Frank had all the sterling attributes that Yale held dear.

> Frank Merriwell . . . stood for truth, faith, justice, the triumph of right, mother, home, friendship, loyalty, patriotism, the love of *alma mater*, duty, sacrifice, retribution and strength of soul as well as body. Frank was manly; he had "sand." He was tolerant. Although he neither smoked nor drank—"Frank had proven that it was not necessary for a man to drink at Yale in order to be esteemed a good fellow"—he gladly blew off his chums to fizz at Morey's while he quaffed ginger ale. He was honest. When some prankish classmates stole a turkey from a farmer's coop, Frank risked capture to stay behind to nail a five-dollar bill to the roost. "Have all the sport you like over it," he told his laughing friends, "but I feel easy in my mind." [Boyle 242]

Merriwell too found the heroic ideal in sports, as his creator explained:

> Believing the old-fashioned dime novel was on its way out, I decided to set a new style with my stories and make them different and more in step with the times. As the first issues were to be stories of American school life, I saw in them the opportunity to feature all kinds of athletic sports, with baseball, about which I was best informed, predominating.
>
> Such stories would give me the opportunity to preach—by example—the doctrine of a clean mind in a clean and healthy body. [Patten, *Merriwell's "Father"* 178]

Just as Frank was a great athlete, so too was his brother Dick:

> Frank won every big game in Fardale's history and Yale's, and so did Dick after him. Each was at Yale nine years, and each graduated with honors. Both were fullbacks, both were pitchers, both stroked the crew—Frank threw a "doubleshoot" ball that curved twice before it reached the plate, while Dick possessed a "jump ball" that rose a full foot as it approached the batter. In

track meets the Merriwells ran the dashes, the half mile, the mile, did the pole vault, the broad jump, the high jump, and threw the hammer. In vacation periods they hunted big game, punched cows, explored the jungle, mined gold, and so on. [Nye 75]

In *Frank Merriwell at Yale* (1903) Patten has a chapter entitled "The Yale Spirit," in which he comes to the defense of Yale in response to the "cry . . . that the spirit of democracy was dying out at Yale" (257–S8). Frank acknowledges that while Phillips men "as a rule" were given preference at Yale, he had also "discovered that in most cases a man was judged fairly at Yale, and he could become whatever he chose to make himself, in case he had the ability." Frank also discovered that "the democratic spirit at Yale came mainly from athletics. . . . Every class had half a dozen teams—tennis, baseball, football, the crew and so on. Everybody, even the 'greasy' grinds, seems interested in something." Another promoter of democracy was, appropriately, religion. "Compulsory chapel every morning brought together the entire college, and had its effect in making everybody acquainted with everybody else." Then too there was the Old Yale fence where "men read the newspapers, crammed for recitation, gossiped, told stories, talked athletics, sung songs, flirted with passing girls, and got acquainted" (ibid., 259–61).

Last but by no means least in the promotion of democracy were "the drinking places." At Harvard the men drank in their clubs, most of which were very expensive places, and in Boston cafés. The Yale men drank at Morey's, Traeger's, and Billy's: "Traeger's, where from a score to fifty students may be seen any afternoon or evening, is furnished in exact mutation of German students' drinking places. In the back room is heavy furniture, quaint paintings, and woodwork and carvings. It had a sort of subdued cathedral light, which fell softly on the mugs which decorated the shelves and mantels" (ibid., 261).

Frank's character profited from all these democratic influences, excepting Traeger's, perhaps. Whereas the dream of dollars wrecked the lives of others such as Clarence King, Frank rose easily above such temptation. Patten, in fact, provided another set of values that parallel nicely those of Eliot and are entirely different from those of the Horatio Alger novels, which praised distinction and wealth. As one critic explains, "Implicit in the Merriwell books is a concept of success markedly different from that stated in Alger. The Alger hero's rise is measurable in accountable material terms; we know where our hero starts, where he will end, and we can measure his progress in the size of his wallet. The Merriwell books recognize success as something quite different, in terms of the personal satisfaction of excellence, of the assumption of authority through virtue, of establishing leadership by example, of excelling under the rules, of 'doing the right thing' and 'playing the game' " (Nye 76).

Frank also seems an improvement over his real-life contemporaries in other ways. Though Patten allows Merriwell "an occasional pointed comment," the books never, like those of many of his contemporaries, use Negro or Jewish types for purposes of low comedy. "No Italians, Jews, or Poles appear in his books"; Frank's companions were "Irish, English, Dutch, and Scots, and so on." Sports were a form of democracy at work, and success called for compliment. "Frank once outraged a crowd by shaking hands with a Negro jockey who had ridden a good race," and in 1939 in a radio script for the Council against Intolerance "Frank defended a Jewish baseball player at Fardale" (ibid., 77, 104). The editors of *Frank Merriwell's "Father"* note that "by being friendly with characters who happened to be Negro or Jewish or members of other minority groups, Frank helped to erase prejudice and intolerance from growing minds, without preaching. The same was true of the handicapped, as in the case of Harry Rattleton, famous for his comic spoonerisms. He was used for comedy relief, as were various others, but never as the butt of cruel ridicule in Frank's way of life" (see Patten, *Merriwell's "Father"* 303). Patten, by his own words, set out to preach *mens sana in corpore sano*, but he also knew how to show or illustrate values of fair play and good sportsmanship. The "Frank Merriwell model of geewhiz modesty" declined over the course of this century. It was replaced on the football field, especially since the 1970s, by "the finger-pointing, fist-pumping, elaborately choreographed antics" we now see, revealing, as Oriard says, "the transformation of football for an age obsessed with self-presentation and self-fulfillment" *(Reading Football* 280).

Frank had many admirable qualities, but the pursuit of academic excellence was not one of them. One cannot, for example, imagine him matching the achievement of either King or Remington. Though intelligent, Frank was not really that interested in sciences or arts. His strengths lay not in the intellectual virtues but in the heroic ones, which accounted for his wide appeal.

Theodore Roosevelt, by selecting college athletes from the East and cowboys from the West to make up his Rough Rider Regiment, hoped to draw the attention of youth everywhere to the manly ideal that could be followed in sports, ranching, or war. Frank Merriwell may have had an even wider influence than Roosevelt. Patten said there were logical reasons to believe the Merriwell books had sold nearly 500 million copies. A more accurate measurement, Patten suggested, might be the following: "You know Dr. Eliot's famous five-foot shelf of immortal books? You ought to see the Frank Merriwell twenty-seven-foot shelf!" (*Merriwell's "Father"* 181). One of those reading at least some of the novels on the twenty-seven-foot shelf was Eddie Eagan, "outstanding Yale athletic star and college boxing champion" who was later U.S. attorney in New York. Said Eagan, "I lived 'way out in Colorado where Yale was something you did when you shouted good and loud—that's all it meant to us—and college was a place where sissies went. It wasn't until I began sneaking in . . . novels on Frank Merriwell that I got the big yearn to be like him, and that's how I came to go to Yale—something I'll never regret" (ibid., 307). Here is an example of the eternal cycle, the expectant youth, as opposed to the aging and despairing intellectual, going east to learn and to play and, later, to enter public service. In Frank, then, there is a revitalization of the heroic ideal, a naive innocence and optimism, and an affirmation of the democratic principles of Yale and America.

While the Merriwell novels emphasize fair play as opposed to material success, another set of stories for boys presents the established model, arguing that fair play is not inconsistent with the basic Horatio Alger theme. Among these is the Baseball Joe series, featuring Joe Matson, who succeeds at Yale and in Major League Baseball, illustrating in the view of author Lester Chadwick the dual meaning of *good* as "moral and material triumph." The "historical analogue" is Bucknell man Christy Mathewson, with his "matching virtues of temperance, fair-play, intelligence, and pressure perform-ance" (Sojka 116, 121). Mathewson has also been compared, not surprisingly, with Merriwell, as in Jonathan Yardley's "Pitcher: The Real Frank Merriwell." Another real-life analogue of Frank Merri-well, Patten points out, is Albie Booth, noted for last-minute heroics. Patten, though he might not have stressed the acquisition of wealth as much as Chadwick or Alger, would not have disagreed with the American truism, growing out of the Protestant ethic, that virtue, skill, and hard work should have their rewards. Patten would insist, though, that cultural awards are empty if the participant does not first truly appreciate the intrinsic gift of play, which Baseball Joe does not do in the manner of Frank. In an examination of the theme of heroism in three Chadwick novels, Greg Sojka points out that Baseball Joe embodies the best of Ralph Waldo Emerson's "self-reliance," Theodore Roosevelt's "strenuous life," and Horatio Al-ger's "grit and pluck." With no outs and the bases loaded by three errors, Joe snags a liner to start the game-ending triple play. Yet the climax of the novel is not the series victory, but what this success enables Joe to achieve: a wife of high social stature. When he tells her that " 'these victories are nothing to me unless I win you, too,' Mabel collapses in his arms." Sojka concludes: " 'Decidedly, it was Joe's winning day.' His hard work, initiative, and humility all con-tributed to his pilgrimage up the long hard road to material, domestic and moral success" (119).

The "moral success" symbolized by Joe is pagan or primitive rather than Judaic or Christian. It is not fully illustrative of the Protes-tant ethic, which traditionally views material success more as a by-product of virtue rather than a primary award and even does this with a skeptical eye. The wife of high social stature also compounds the issue, raising the suspicion that Joe may be as much a victim of conspicuous display as of romantic love. Joe's ethic is one of "having" rather than "being," which is the ethic of Frank (which also differs from the Protestant ethic but in another way). Frank's ethic empha-sizes the joy of play; Joe's, the rewards of effort and achievement. Joe is the young man from the provinces who becomes a knight, gains a throne, wins a princess, and lives happily ever after. It is, as Lord Raglan points out in *The Hero*, one of the most primitive of all stories;

but it does not reflect the basic wisdom of the prophets or the Greek philosophers. What Joe seeks is what "the nations of the world seek after" (Luke 12:30). As admirable as Joe is, he is warped at a fundamental level: "One familiar thought 'kept pounding away at his consciousness' and at the reader's attention. He thinks, 'I've *got* to make good! I've *got* to make good!' " (Sojka 118). Making good is not exactly doing good, and both might seem to differ drastically from the scriptural idea of seeking the good.

Another fictional Yale man highlighted the democratic ideals, not by heroic action in the manner of Merriwell or by dogged perseverance in the manner of Baseball Joe, but by skepticism, by noting the discrepancy between the ideal and the actual, by a form of revolt against the system much in the manner of Thoreau. This was Dink Stover, titular hero of Owen Johnson's novel *Stover at Yale*, which first appeared in *McClure's Magazine* in 1911, three years before Frank disappeared from the pages of *Tip Top Weekly* after a run of seventeen years. *Stover at Yale* is, like *A Connecticut Yankee*, an example of an anti-jeremiad, one of those books of unflinching frankness that, according to Berkovitch, reminds us of the distance between what is and what ought to be. Like Frank, Stover is a star athlete and a leader on campus, but unlike Frank, he is credible, and the issues that the novel addresses were real, especially at the time. Here are only a few of the shortcomings of the university "glaringly revealed in the novel":

On choosing friends:

> You may think the world begins outside of college. It doesn't; it begins right here. You want to make the friends that will help you along here and outside. Don't lose sight of your opportunities and be careful how you choose.

On conformity:

> Directly, clearly visualized, he perceived for the first time, what he was to perceive in every side of his college career, that a standard had been fashioned to which irresistibly, subtly, he would have to conform.

On college life:

> And yet, what completely surprised him was the lack of careless, indolent camaraderie which he had known at school and had expected in larger scope at college. Every one was busy, working with a dogged persistence along some line of ambition.

On the effect of a year at Yale:

> By the perfect averaging system of college, he had lost in one short year all the originality and imagination he had brought with him. [Kelley 310]

In a review of a modern edition Michael J. Halberstam calls *Stover* a "bitter, almost subversive" book that "starts us thinking about our own condition." It is a book "where American higher education is split open like a Delicious apple and then allowed to turn brown and rot under the reader's eye" (470). That such will happen with every reader is unlikely, but that the values and assumptions of Yale and America are called into question cannot be denied, as, for example, when one of the characters, Brockhurst, gives the following opinion of football, as timely today as in 1911:

> I say our colleges today are business colleges—Yale more so, perhaps, because it is more sensitively American. Let's take up any side of our life here. Begin with athletics. What has become of the natural, spontaneous joy of contest? Instead you have one of the most perfectly organized business systems for achieving a required result—success. Football is driving, slavish work; there isn't one man in twenty who gets any real pleasure out of it. Professional baseball is not more rigorously disciplined and driven than our "amateur" teams. Add the crew and the track. Play, the fun of the thing itself, doesn't exist; and why? Because we have made a business out of it all, and the college is scoured for material, just as drummers are sent out to bring in business. [O. Johnson 195]

Brockhurst is speaking for Johnson in the novel but only partly. Brockhurst, "the champion of individualism," is also an unashamed elitist, sounding at times like an apologist for the Roosevelt–Lodge–

Brooks Adams group in their fight against "over-civilization."
Though he is no doubt sounding off in the discussion among peers,
he believes in "a smashing war every ten years," for war, he says,
has "two positive advantages: It teaches discipline and obedience,
which we profoundly need, and it holds up a great ideal, the ideal
of heroism, a sacrifice for an ideal. In times of war, young men
such as we are inspired by the figures of military leaders, and their
imaginations are turned to noble desires by the word 'country.'
Nowadays what is held up to us? Go out–succeed–make money"
(ibid., 193). There is an irony here, in that Brockhurst, the intellectual
and thinker in the novel, would probably not be one to ride "first
into the murderous thickets," as old heroes of Harvard and Yale had
done. Still he sounds like an aggrieved old patriot who sees the
corruption of the heroic ideal in every phase of American society,
replaced by the business ideal: "Twenty years ago we had the ideal
of the lawyer, of the doctor, of the statesman, of the gentleman, of
the man of letters, of the soldier. Now the lawyer is simply a
supernumerary enlisting under any banner for pay; the doctor is
overshadowed by the specialist with his business development of the
possibilities of the rich; we have politicians, and politics are deemed
impossible for a gentleman; the gentleman cultured, simple, hospi-
table, and kind, is of the dying generation; the soldier is simply on
parade" (ibid., 192).

Certainly Johnson did not want a war every ten years nor even
a return to the warrior ideal. What he did want he makes clear at the
end of the novel, giving the lines to Brockhurst, appropriately, since
he had been the most critical of Yale: "I'm not satisfied with Yale as
a magnificent factory on democratic business lines; I dream of
something else, something visionary, a great institution not of boys,
clean, loyal, and honest, but of men of brains, of courage, of
leadership, a great center of thought, to stir the country and bring it
back to the understanding of what man creates with his imagination,
and dares with his will. It's visionary–it will come" (O. Johnson 308).

Brockhurst, though he ends the novel on an optimistic note, is
for the most part an extremist who by virtue of his independence
and intelligence directs a withering attack at Yale and America.
Stover, by contrast, is a moderate who, impressed by Brockhurst,

must work out for himself the conflicts he finds at Yale between quality and equality. Like Frank Merriwell, he is thoroughly decent. Likable and open-minded, he is drawn to the outsiders, "to Regan, a gruff older freshman, working his way through Yale in order to go into reform politics back West. He comes to respect Gimbel, a classmate who is politicking to overthrow the sophomore societies. (Johnson hints that Gimbel may be Jewish—despite being an Andover athlete he has no chance of making a society—but never uses the word.)" (Halberstam 472–73).

Just as Stover discovers the discrepancy between the ideal and the reality in scholarship, so he finds an inherent conflict in the values of athletic training or competition in sports, as when he beats out a bigger, stronger upperclassman for a place on the first team.

> It was not play with the zest he loved, it was a struggle of ambitions with all the heartache that lay underneath. He had gone out to play and suddenly found himself in a school for character, enchained to the discipline of the Caesars, where the test lay in stoicism and the victory was built on the broken hopes of a comrade.

> For the first time, a little appalled, he felt the weight of the seriousness, the deadly seriousness of the American spirit which seizes on everything that is competition and transforms it, with the fanaticism of its race, for success. [ibid., 476, quoted]

Stover comes to terms with Yale but with misgivings that linger in the reader's mind, misgivings based upon Johnson's persistent theme of the mad race for material success.

According to Kelley, when *Stover* appeared, faculty, students, and alumni were aware of what was happening, and the situation was "already changing" for the better. How rapidly it was changing toward equality of opportunity may remain a matter of opinion, but that positive change occurred over the long run seems undeniable, at least in the eyes of Kingman Brewster Jr., former president of Yale, who wrote the introduction for the modern edition of *Stover at Yale*. Johnson, he thinks, perhaps "would like the new Yale better than his own" (in O. Johnson vii).

The boys' books of the Roosevelt era were just that—books for *boys* who would grow up to be manly and heroic white boys. If there were few women as models of behavior, there were no blacks. In spite of these omissions and the almost pathological emphasis upon winning and succeeding, the books were not without merit. Some of them stressed service to others and heroic action in times of danger, such as the courageous deeds of firemen and policemen. The Frank Merriwell stories went squarely against the Horatio Alger genre by stressing playing fair instead of getting rich. They also taught acceptance of others' differences. The didactic books were a mixed bag, reminding us one more time that the challenge to education and society is to find the best models, as Mr. Sammler says (Bellow 148–49).

The dominant model in the United States at the turn of the century was Theodore Roosevelt, who epitomized the traditional heroic virtues. In 1904 he was elected president "in his own right" by two and a half million votes. His life, it was said, was the dream of every typical American boy: he fought in a war, became president, killed lions, and quarreled with the pope (Wecter 374). Perhaps we could say that his became the dream of every typical American boy except Huckleberry Finn. To Twain the president was a classic case of arrested development, but he was not the only one who saw a problem of maturation in the chief executive. Said one Englishman, "You must remember that the president is about six." Eliot said he had known Teddy as a boy, and after Teddy's election, he still knew him as a boy. And like Tom Sawyer and Francis McComber, the great American boy-man, Roosevelt loved romantic adventures. Roosevelt saw little difference between sports and war, but he did not see this connection as ironic. Of the Spanish war he said, "It will be awful if we miss the fun," a theme that carried over for many to World War I.

Twain's complaints about Roosevelt are much too long for invoicing, but among many insights Twain notes that Roosevelt "admires the dime novel hero and has always made him his model . . . ; he has always been ready to do the fine and spectacular hero act and he has always been equally ready to wish he had let it alone when he found that it pleased only half of the people and not the other half" (*Twain in Eruption* 29–30). As early as 1865 Twain had ridiculed the Horatio Alger concept of success in "The Story of a Bad Little Boy" and "The Story of a Good Little Boy," but he lived to see a continuing avalanche of such books in the first decade of the next century. Twain's judgment of Roosevelt is at times more severe: "I think the president is clearly insane in several ways, and insanest upon war and its supreme glories. I think he longs for a big war wherein he can spectacularly perform as chief general and chief admiral and go down in history as the only monarch in modern times that has served both offices at the same time" (ibid., 8–9).

In his denunciation of Roosevelt, Twain was perhaps the first to relegate sports to what Howard Cosell called the Toy Department. "Hasn't the President," Twain asked, "kept up such a continual thundering from our Olympus about football and baseball and mollycoddles and all sorts of little nursery matters that we have come to stand in fear that the first time an exigency of real importance shall arise, our thunders will not be able to attract the world's notice or expect any valuable influence upon ourselves?" (ibid., 20). The president's celebrated hunting exploits came under a withering satire when Twain claimed that Roosevelt, instead of killing a bear in Louisiana, actually tracked a helpless cow and shot her as she pleaded for her life with tears streaming down her face. The fact that the president swore the animal he killed was a bear did not diminish any doubt but only enlarged it (11). No mercy for a cornered cow, no mercy for humans, Twain seems to argue in criticism of the capture of Aguilando in the Philippines–where "six hundred helpless savages" had been "butchered" to the president's approval. The man behind this "brilliant feat of arms," as Twain called it, was Major General Leonard Wood, whom Roosevelt praised for upholding the honor of the American flag (33–34). Edmund Morris, in his biography, says that Roosevelt "hero-worshiped Wood . . . as a fighter of Apaches and vanquisher of Geronimo." A doctor by profession and a soldier by choice, Wood was "tall, fair, lithe, and powerfully muscled," walking "with the slightly pigeon-toed stride of a born athlete," forever "compulsively kicking a football around an empty lot, the leather thudding nearly flat as he drove it against the wall." Wood's other obsession was driving the Spaniards from Cuba and extending American influence to the Far East (Morris 577). It is no accident that Twain's "War Prayer" was written in 1904, the year of Roosevelt's election in his own right.

Playfulness was becoming deadly serious. And the democratization of heroism has turned out to mean little more than permitting more competition for success, now defined as gaining ground and making good, in stark contrast to the idea of being good in the present, which Thoreau had offered as an alternative image. As a social model of success Thoreau was an ultimate American failure. As a person of virtue, one who loved creation and rejoiced in it, he may be one of our greatest "successes." Thoreau did not champion the value of athletics; rather, he saw beneath "the games and amusements of mankind" an "unconscious despair." Like Whitman, Thoreau emphasized the union of body and soul throughout his works, but it was a synthesis that placed great emphasis upon the instructive power of nature. Like Twain, Thoreau valued unstructured play in the great outdoors as opposed to organized sports in designated spaces.

If Emerson is the founder of the "cult of athletics," as Eliot suggests, then Thoreau, as much as anyone, would be the creator of American play. Emerson quietly kindled several power impulses in the American psyche, including, in addition to a sporting spirit, ethnocentrism and imperialism, even as he became a celebrated spokesman for the one doctrine he said he preached, "the infinitude of the private man." While a strong supporter of the Union in the Civil War, "he continued to believe," says Berkovitch, "in the inherent inferiority of blacks." In fact, Emerson shows many of the same prejudices toward non-WASPs as did other Ivy Leaguers who were taming and recording the American West. " 'No candid person, could maintain that the African race have occupied any very high place in the human family. . . . The Irish cannot; the American Indian cannot. The Chinese cannot. Before the energy of the Caucasian race all other races have quailed and done obeisance.' Such statements attest not only to Emerson's provinciality, but to the *mythic* limitations of his claims for representative individualism" (Berkovitch 200, quoting Emerson, *Journals* 2:48, 12:152).

Thoreau, in contrast, did not participate in the rating game. Instead, he was willing to extend equal rights to trees, for without them there would be no race of any kind. Like Twain, however, Thoreau was not any more reluctant to criticize Native American culture than he was that of transplanted Europeans. For Thoreau, the wild game of nature were the best playmates, as seen in his famous hide-and-seek with the loon in *Walden* and his chase of the fox in *A Week:*

> Suddenly looking down the river, I saw a fox some sixty rods off making across the hills to my left. As the snow lay five inches deep, he made but slow progress, but it was no impediment to me. So yielding to the instinct of the chase, I tossed my head aloft, and bounded away, snuffing the air like a foxhound and spurning the world and human society at each bound. It seemed the woods rang with the hunter's horn, and Diana and all the satyrs joined in the chase and cheered me on. Olympian and Elean youths were waving palms on the hills. In the meantime, I gained rapidly on the fox, but he showed a remarkable presence of mind, for instead of keeping up the face of the hill, which was steep and unwooded in that part, he kept along the slope in the direction of the forest, though he lost ground by it. Notwithstanding his fright, he took no step which was not beautiful. The course on his part was a series of graceful curves. It was a sort of leopard canter, I should say, as if he were nowise impeded by the snow, but were husbanding his strength all the while. When he doubled, I wheeled and cut him off, bounding with fresh vigor, Antaeus-like recovering my strength each time I touched the snow. Having got near enough for a fair view, just as he was slipping into the wood, I gracefully yielded him the palm. He ran as if there were not a bone in his back, occasionally dropping his muzzle to the snow for a rod or two, and then tossing his head aloft, when satisfied of his course. When he came to a declivity, he put his fore feet together, and slid down it like a cat. He trod so softly that you could not have heard from any nearness, and yet with such expression that it would not have been quite inaudible from any distance. So hoping this experience would prove a useful lesson to him, I returned to the village by the highway of the river. [*Thoreau* 424]

Lest it be assumed that such spontaneity is the sole possession of romantics, Heywood Hale Broun in *Tumultuous Merriment* points to the example of Dr. Samuel Johnson, who on the spur of the moment once set himself rolling down a grassy hill like a "great laughing brown ball" and at the bottom "arose haystreaked and refreshed" (11).

A more recent example of the gift of play as opposed to the prize of sport is seen in the experience of Loren Eiseley, the poet-anthropologist. On one of his many excursions into the natural world, Eiseley came upon a young fox under the timbers of a foundered boat who "innocently" took a chicken bone in his mouth and shook it invitingly at Eiseley while placing his forefeet together. "Gravely" Eiseley did likewise with a whiter bone, getting down on all fours and facing the fox with his own "forefeet" arranged appropriately. "Round and round," he says, "we tumbled for one ecstatic moment." For Eiseley, it was the gravest, most meaningful act he would ever accomplish, leading him to a view of the universe "as it begins for all things. It was, in reality, a child's universe, a tiny and laughing universe" (210).

Thoreau, Twain, and Whitman endeavored to awaken this universe within us. With their own examples of Edenic play, they remind us that gifts of play are hidden in contrast to cultural prizes, which are always tantalizingly before us. Neither Eiseley nor Thoreau would endorse modern play theology any more than muscular Christianity. Neither was a pantheist, Thoreau dismissing that possibility with one unforgettable line: "The red-bird which is the last of nature is but the first of God" (quoted in Wolf 158). Play is not simply worship nor worship a form of play, but play in nature, pursued in proper spirit, might offer keys to the kingdom within. Charles S. Prebish and others argue that competitive sports can bring on the same effect. In my view the thrill of victory in athletics is a universe apart from the conscious immersion in nature, the "oceanic feeling"–the one stemming from the explosion of ego, the other from obliteration of it. To be sure, there are dangers in the extremes of both emotions and in societies that celebrate one over the other. In contemporary America the routes to the "oceanic feeling" seem largely limited to drugs, alcohol, and sex, none of which Thoreau depended on for the natural highs that on occasion gave him glimpses of the divine. Even the "oceanic feeling" is a natural mysticism different from but a step toward the highest orders, characterized by vision as well as an "*ineffable* moment" before which "words recede and understanding cannot penetrate" (Otto 5).

Thoreau loved to spend afternoons doing nothing but sitting in his doorway. Yet he also celebrated the active life as well as the contemplative. Whereas Emerson had honored "drill" and "concentration," Thoreau, his most famous disciple, believed most firmly in "walking" and "meditation." Along with Whitman, he was a precursor of the gospel of nature, which contrasts sharply with the gospel of wealth. Like Owen Johnson and the official Emerson, both Thoreau and Whitman celebrated the individual, Whitman making a special point to include women and to place them on a level equal to men. In contrast to Thoreau, Whitman also celebrated competitive games, calling himself "the teacher of athletes." As much as he admired Whitman and as prone as he was to humorous boasting himself, Thoreau would never consider such a claim. When he crowed as lustily as Chanticleer, he was cheering us on to some vision of the world that had little to do with competitive games. In this regard especially, he differs from Emerson, and Whitman differs even more with his inherited culture of Western Europe. Thoreau's transcendentalism, for instance, clashed dramatically with the renaissance heritage emphasizing honor and renown, especially when honor and renown include "captains of industry." The highest rank that Thoreau ever attained was "captain of a huckleberry party," a position that apparently did not impress Eliot, Roosevelt, or many other Harvard men, including Emerson, whose original use of the phrase was meant to criticize Thoreau's lack of achievement.

Roosevelt seemed almost oblivious to the works of Thoreau. Henry A. Beers said that he does not even mention Thoreau in his writings, but a member of the Roosevelt Memorial Committee brought one reference to his attention in *The Wilderness Hunter*. "As a woodland writer Thoreau comes second only to Burroughs." Beers says that Francis Parkman had contempt for philosophers like Emerson and Thoreau and that Roosevelt had a similar inclination (13–14). There is in fact no mention of Thoreau's name in the national edition of Roosevelt's works of 1919, nor of Emerson's or Eliot's. Roosevelt was too far to the right of all of them to take much notice of what they were saying or to observe the differences in what they were saying. In contrast to Roosevelt, who was a party for all, Thoreau for the most part was a party of one. At Harvard he wore green while all his classmates wore black. His advice is "Simplify, simplify"; Roosevelt's would be "Achieve, achieve"–in academics, sports, business, or war. As the founder of the Boone and Crockett Club in 1888, named for two of his heroes, Roosevelt endeavored to encourage among his aristocratic friends " 'inquiry into and recording of observations of the natural history of wild animals' and 'the preservation of forest regions . . . as nursery and reservations for woodland creatures.' " Though an ardent conservationist, Roosevelt never gave up "the manly sport with rifle." The relish for blood sport "remained strong in him through old age, although an apologist claims 'he then no longer spoke of hunting as a pleasure, rather an undertaking in the interest of science.' Roosevelt was a complex man, and . . . his complexity grew apace during the middle years of his life" (Morris 384). Thoreau and Roosevelt both were Harvard graduates and conservationists, yet the latter would never fully appreciate the dying, playful words of the former: "Moose . . . Indians" (quoted in Krutch 19).

# 9

# Sportianity versus Mountainity

In the attitude toward the world that Thoreau and other "shepherds" personify, both play and worship, if not always carefully distinguished from each other, are certainly different from sport or business and labor. Starting with the industrial revolution, however, business and industry encroached boldly upon the domain of both recreation and worship, as Arnold Toynbee observed in *A Study of History*. The Sabbath, once a time for rest and religious reflection, became the day ordained for "organized games" of all sorts as people sought respite from the numbing repetition of factory labor. The quasi-religion sportianity found its followers. Professional athletics have of course tended to integrate industrialism with sports, the athletes becoming technical specialists of the first (and best-paid) order (see Toynbee, *Breakdown* 242).

Toynbee writes that "the spirit and rhythm of Industrialism have become so insistent and so pervasive that they have invaded and infected sport itself" (ibid). This, according to Owen Johnson, author of *Stover at Yale* (1912), would include athletics, "one of the more perfectly organized business systems for achieving a desired result—success" (195). With characteristic genius, Johnson hit upon the key word—*success*. A business must succeed; it must turn a profit, that is, and grow in prestige. This is rather far from Thoreau's simplicity.

Schools and religious groups would, one would think, also have entirely different missions, but not in the mind of the knight who sees sports, learning, religion, government, and commerce as inevitable allies and in some cases virtually indistinguishable. By 1906 William James could conclude that "the *exclusive* worship of the bitch-goddess of success . . . is our national disease" (Lynn, epigraph). (The implication that success might instead be a whore-goddess further suggests the revelation of "manliness" as essentially involving a gender bias.) One can trace the roots of the idea of success from the thought of Franklin and Jefferson through the philosophy of John Dewey (as John G. Cawelti has done), showing all along the way how competition and cooperation have fared in relation to each other, with the cult of success winning over the older ideas of the sense of duty of the founding fathers as seen in Mark Twain's "Revised Catechism," which appeared in the *New York Tribune* in 1871:

> Q. What is the chief end of man?
> A. To get rich.
> Q. In what way?
> A. Dishonestly if we can, honestly if we must.
> Q. Who is God, the only one and True?
> A. Money is God. Gold and greenbacks and stocks—father, son and the ghost of the same—three persons in one; these are the true and only God, mighty and supreme.
> Q. Who were the models the young were taught to emulate in former days?
> A. Washington and Franklin.
> Q. Whom do they and should they emulate now in this era of enlightenment?
> A. Tweed, Hall, Connely, Camochan, Fisk, Gould, Barnard, and Winans.
> Q. What works were chiefly prized for the training of the young in former days?
> A. Poor Richard's Almanac, The Pilgrim's Progress, and The Declaration of Independence.
> Q. Do we progress?
> A. You bet your life.
> [Cawelti; 140, quoted]

To the gods of mammon listed in the "Revised Catechism"

Twain could have added others, which in his autobiographical writing of 1906 he did, including himself. "It is my belief that there isn't a single male human being in America who is honest. I held the belt all along, until last January. Then I went down, with Rockefeller and Carnegie and a group of Goulds and Vanderbilts and other professional grafters. . . . I believe the entire population of the United States—exclusive of the women—to be rotten as far as the dollar is concerned" (*In Eruption* 258). What lay behind the drive for wealth was the cult of success or in Twain's term "progress," that which could be quantified. Though the word "success" is scarcely noticeable in the King James Version used in Twain's time, in contrast to its widespread appearance in contemporary editions, as I will show in chapter 14, knights of Twain's day worked sedulously to give the idea Christian dignity by smuggling it into Sunday school guide books, which Twain abhorred. One example f such instruction, which Twain may or may not have seen, is *New Cyclopedia of Prose Illustrations Adapted to Christian Teaching Embracing Allegories, Anecdotes, Aphorisms, Emblems, Fables, Legends, Metaphors, Parables, Quotations, Similes, Biblical Types and Figures, Etc.* by Reverend Elon Foster and dedicated to "The Christian Instructors of the Age, Both Clerical and Lay" (1877). Under the subject of "success" there are examples, among others, of Martin Luther, John Jacob Astor, and Admiral David Farragut, who, after becoming a Christian, gave up swearing, drinking, smoking, and gambling. Foster asks why these men were "winners" and then supplies the answer: "They made their minds up as to what they wanted. . . . You may call them a bull-dog race of men but it is the bull-dog, after all, that brings down the prey, not the graceful spaniel. 'Here stand I,' says Luther, 'and if all the tiles in Worms were devils, I could do no otherwise" (716). Notice in this passage the reference to "prey," which is absolutely crucial to the knight, Christian or otherwise. We can be sure that Mark Twain, who, like Kafka, wrote a lot about dogs, would be wondering what was going on in the mind of the poor "graceful spaniel" among all the bull-dog sound and fury going on around him or her.

As indicated in these examples, success was directly associated with heroism, which many of the books attempt to inspire—American heroism. Among these were *American Heroes and Heroism* (1903),

*American Hero Stories* (1906, 1920, and 1926), *Little Visits with Great Americans* (1903)—this published by "The Success Company"—and *Winning Their Ways: Boys Who Learned Self-Help* (1909).

The basic principles of knighthood are everywhere evident in the widespread acculturation represented in these books, which is why Twain despised them. The idea of "success" as another name for the "works," which in our own age has come to include people who "play" in their "work"—that is, athletes—whose "success" provides the foundation for their spiritual testimony. There is an irony here in regard to Protestantism itself. The verse that changed Luther's life and the course of history was Romans 1:17, "the just shall live by faith," yet in practice, Protestantism, especially the American variety, has embraced a theology of works of which the cult of success and Muscular Christianity are examples. To be sure, Protestantism is not alone in this as Catholics quite often seem just as prone to point to victory in sports as evidence of works approved by the Almighty. Sport is a latecomer to the literature of success, which was dominated previously by stories from the battlefield and the marketplace. For this to have happened the element of play in leisure, which Twain cherished, had to be minimized or eliminated.

The doctrine of success stands in contrast to the social gospel; it also contrasts with a gospel of nature. Whereas the gospel of wealth glorifies competition and approves the subjugation of nature in the name of profit, the gospel of nature values cooperation and living without abuse of nature's resources. Sports and play respectively serve as symbols of the two contrasting gospels, both derivable from Matthew; one heads for the stadium, the other for the hills.

Twain's "Revised Catechism" reveals his unfailing insight into the transformation of values occurring in his time as millionaires became models of emulation. In 1906 in his autobiographical writing Twain repeated the message of the "Revised Catechism." Though he indicted the Gospel of Gould *(In Eruption* 77) as the new religion of the time, Twain excoriated Carnegie as well (ibid., 35-60). Carnegie, unlike "other grafters" of the plutocracy, as Twain called the super rich, did something special—he wrote a bible for the transformation called *The Gospel of Wealth* (1900). His philosophy, though, had a long history on the sawdust trail. The position of Dwight L. Moody, an evangelist of Carnegie's era, is typical of the tradition that had absorbed success into reverence: "It is a wonderful fact that men and women saved by the blood of Jesus rarely remain subjects of charity, but rise at once to comfort and respectability. . . . I never saw the man who put Christ first in his life that wasn't successful" (quoted in McLoughlin 252–53). Billy Sunday believed exactly the same thing: "It pays to serve God. I never saw a Christian hitting the ties and panhandling; I never saw a Christian that was a hobo. . . . They that trust in the Lord do not want for anything" (ibid., 415).

Not only did our most noted evangelists have a hand in the evolution of the doctrine of success and the gospel of wealth, but so did Mr. Transcendentalist, Emerson himself, Thoreau's neighbor, who was fond enough of excoriating materialism and conformity but who was also a hero-worshiper, as seen in *Representative Men.* Emerson had a hand in preparing the culture for Andrew Carnegie and other captains of industry, though Emerson lamented the " 'careless swagger' with which America marched to power, seeming only to care for its selfish ease and little for human rights" (G.W. Allen 625). Emerson would not have applauded Andrew Carnegie, but Carnegie could easily justify the heroic vitalism of transcendentalism as easily as he could transfigure the meaning of the Gospels. In *The Gospel of Wealth* Carnegie saw civilization dependent upon a triple law of the sacredness of private property, open competition, and unrestrained accumulation of wealth. The man of wealth, he says, "becomes the mere trustee and agent for his poor brethren, bringing to their service his superior wisdom, experience, and ability to administer, doing for them better than what they could do for themselves." In opposition to the idea of being good in the present, which Thoreau offered as an image of success and which may be the shepherd's chief virtue, Carnegie substituted another Gospel: "Five words spoken by Christ so interpreted, if strictly obeyed, would at one blow strike down all that distinguished man from the beast, 'take no thought for tomorrow' " (25).

The high priests of sportianity stress winning, drive, discipline, hard work, and the benefits of victory for one's self and society, and so did Andrew Carnegie. He utterly transformed the image of Christ: "The highest life is probably to be reached, not by such imitation of the life of Christ as Count Tolstoy gives us, but, while animated by Christ's spirit, by recognizing the changed conditions of this age, and *adopting modes of expressing this spirit suitable to the changed conditions under which we live*, still laboring for the good of our fellows, which was the essence of his life and teaching, but laboring in a different manner" (ibid.; italics added). Lenin at approximately the same time criticized Tolstoy as a misguided prophet. Though acknowledging his power as an artist, Lenin inveighs against Tolstoy, calling him "a country squire acting the fool in Christ," a "washed-out hysterical cry-baby known as the Russian Intellectual." Lenin feared the "historical sin of Tolstoyism"—the striving for personal moral perfection rather than public, social victory—as a force that would keep "the democratic masses of peasantry" from developing "steeled" warriors necessary for the triumph of the revolution (1392–95). For Carnegie and Lenin, as well as for Hitler a generation later, steel was a favorite metaphor for the knight's strength.

The philosophies of Tolstoy and Carnegie, diametrically opposite, derive from the Gospel of Matthew. Tolstoy's can be found in Matthew 5:39: "But I say unto you, that ye resist not evil: but whosoever shall smite thee on thy right cheek, turn to him the other also." The basis of Carnegie's theology is Matthew 25:14–30, the parable of the talents. Carnegie seems to forget that the parable is based on a simile; he has taken the story literally (not to be confused with taking the message literally). Carnegie, to support his interpretation, appeals to a sermon from John Wesley:

> Gain all you can by honest industry. Use all possible diligence in your calling. Lose no time. Gain all you can by common sense, by using in your business all the understanding which God has given you. . . .
>
> Having gained all you can by honest wisdom and unwearied diligence, the second rule of Christian prudence is, "Save all you can." Do not throw it away in idle expenses—to gratify pride, etc. . . . first provide things needful for yourself, food, raiment, etc.
>
> Second, provide these for your wife, your children, your servants, and others who pertain to your household. If then you have an overplus, do good to all men. [quoted in Carnegie 73]

Upon this sermon, says Carnegie, "the gospel of wealth seems founded" (ibid.).

Max Weber has pointed to Wesley's view as one model for the idea of the Protestant ethic.

> I fear, wherever riches have increased, the essence of religion has decreased in the same proportion. Therefore I do not see how it is possible, in the nature of things, for any revival of true religion to continue long. For religion must necessarily produce both industry and frugality, and these cannot but produce riches. But as riches increase, so will pride, anger, and love of the world in all its branches. How then is it possible that Methodism, that is, a religion of the heart, though it flourishes now as a green bay tree, should continue in this state? For the Methodists in every place grow diligent and frugal; consequently they increase in goods. Hence they proportionately increase in pride, in anger, in the desire of the flesh, the desire of the eyes, and the pride of life. So, although the form of religion remains, the spirit is swiftly vanishing away. Is there no way to prevent this–this continual decay of pure religion? We ought not to prevent people from being diligent and frugal; *we must exhort all Christians to gain all they can, and to save all they can; that is, in effect, to grow rich.* [Southey's biography, quoted in Weber 175; Weber's italics]

Note that Carnegie does not recognize the tension between religion and wealth, as do Weber and Wesley. Nor does Carnegie see the conflict between sports and religion that Weber finds inherent in the Protestant ethic (166–71). Wealth is not the temptation for Carnegie that Wesley knew it inevitably was. Carnegie sees neither the danger in wealth nor the irony of having to give it away to save one's soul. Thus the gospel of wealth is by no means identical to the Protestant ethic, and in some ways is its opposite. The easy connections that Carnegie establishes between the Gospels and the making of money, his sense of noblesse oblige, his almost casual dismissal of Jesus' metaphors of nonviolence and love of nature, as interpreted by Tolstoy and John Muir, bring Carnegie's gospel to the doorstep of Veblen's theory of the leisure class, with its emphasis upon "conspicuous waste" and "invidious distinction." While Carnegie's vast donations to the American public cannot be called "waste," they have certainly been "conspicuous," which makes them hard to square with the spirit of the Gospel that requires that giving be done in secret.

The annual spectacle of the United Way is a classic example of conspicuous donations quite in keeping with the manner of Carnegie's gospel, philanthropy on parade and even deductible on income tax returns. Recently professional football players are used at half-time to endorse on television the United Way, attempting to elevate the moral status of their sport as well as the practice of public charity but unwittingly flying into the face of basic Christian doctrine. Hannah Arendt explains why: "When goodness appears openly, it is no longer goodness, though it may still be useful as organized charity or an act of solidarity. Therefore: 'Take heed that ye do not your alms before men, to be seen of them'. . . . Whoever sees himself performing a good work is no longer good, but at least a useful member of society or a dutiful member of a church. 'Therefore let not thy left hand know what thy right hand doeth' " (74). Arendt goes on to say, as if in refutation of the Gospel of Wealth, "It may be the . . . lack of outward phenomenal manifestation . . . that makes Jesus of Nazareth's appearance in history such a profoundly paradoxical event; it certainly seems to be the reason why he thought and taught that no man can be good: 'Why callest thou me good? none is good, save one, God' " (Luke 18:19, Matt. 19:17). Arendt says that "the same conviction finds its expression in the talmudic story of the thirty-six righteous men, for the sake of whom God saves the world and who also are known to nobody, least of all to themselves. We are reminded of Socrates' great insight that no man can be wise, out of which love of wisdom, or philosophy, was born; the whole life story of Jesus seems to testify how love of goodness arises out of the insight that no man can be good" (74–75).

Following in the path of Carnegie, the National Football League contributed $40 million in advertising to the United Way in 1986 and $255,000 in direct grants since 1975 (Fraser). When informed that evidence points toward an increase in battering of women on Super Sunday, a league spokesperson said that the NFL gives to the United Way and that they do what they want with the money. Of the 2.3 billion the charity raised in 1986, $13 million went to women's crisis agencies (ibid.). The recent crime bill provides $50 million for women's shelters and $3 million for domestic violence programs. The hidden human costs of institutionalized violence may never be known. The same can be said of the same type of costs, to say nothing of the visible carnage, stemming from the collision of the great international political, economic, and social systems of our era, each certain of its supreme virtue. What are these? Among others, communism, fascism, capitalism, monarchy, and chivalry, to name a few, all examples of fortified thought, all self-righteous systems of closure, all requiring combative frames of mind and enormous sacrifice at public expense—all requiring knights.

Wesley, Carnegie points out, accumulated about $250,000 by his writings. It was not, though, the example of its enterprising founder that led Methodism to the comfortable bed of the gospel of wealth, since few Methodists knew of Wesley's wealth any more than Dwight L. Moody's admirers knew the truth about his income, which at one time was an embarrassment to him. Neither man sought wealth, and Moody was penniless at the time of his death. Certainly the poverty-stricken frontier circuit riders were not prototypes of material gain, since they had little or no money to save. However, there was for the ministry a more subtle but related problem, another type of trap, not so much the love of money but the love of numbers, the numbers of converts. Bishop Asbury demonstrates this measure of success in his journal from 1805: "At Duck Creek camp-meeting five hundred souls; at Accomack camp-meeting, four hundred; at Annamesssex chapel, in the woods, two hundred; at Somerset, line Chapel, one hundred and twenty; at Todd's Chapel, Dorset, two hundred; at Carolina Quarterly meeting seventy five; all, all these confess to have received converting grace" (quoted in Sweet, *Revivalism* 129–30).

Herein lies the origins of the litany of successes in numbers that televangelists are so fond of quoting. It is religion's way of keeping score, of making points. It is a type of vanity, as much a temptation as wealth itself. In *Crusades: 20 Years with Billy Graham*, scarcely a page appears without numbers expressing in some form Graham's great success as a minister. For example, "At the final service of the Sydney Crusade, on May 10, 1959, no less than 150,000 people were present: 80,000 in the Showground and 70,000 in the adjoining Cricket Ground, linked by amplifiers. It was estimated that a further one million Australians listened either by landline or by the live radio broadcast. There was an exciting added touch to the service when the two choirs, one of 1,500, the other of 2,000 with Bev Shea, sang 'How Great Thou Art' in alternate verses, one from the Showground, the next from the Cricket Ground. . . . 5,683 people made decisions" (Pollock, *Crusades* 199). Thus the campground revival reached other continents with the implied message "God's in the stadium, all's right with the world." Like sports, modern religion has gone "from ritual to record," to use Allen Guttmann's phrase. That such a condition has evolved in sports is bad enough; in religion it constitutes a heresy.

Carnegie does not discuss sports and play in connection with the gospel of wealth, but the parallels are clear. Sports, stripped of fun and commercialized, are a veritable symbol of open competition. As noted in a recent introduction of Carnegie's classic book, "Few men wanted more intensely to win than Andrew Carnegie; none was more certain his destiny was success. In 1868, at the age of thirty-three, he wrote in an introspective note a sentence of self-analysis: 'Whatever I engage in I push inordinately.' Thirty years later he was trumpeting his triumphs in golf: 'So all goes well. I played eighteen holes today with Taylor. Beat him! Beat Murray Butler Saturday. Beat Franks the day before' " (in Carnegie vii). How strange, almost bizarre, that a man of Carnegie's wealth could relish so strongly victories over other old men in a mere game.

For Carnegie sports also offered a useful metaphor and a means of inspiration to get his employees to work longer hours at reduced wages. In the late 1870s at the Edgar Thompson steel works in Braddock, Pennsylvania, the captain—what is revealed in this title?—one William Jones, who was already driving his men hard on twelve-hour shifts, seven days a week (even in the heat of July and August), resisted Carnegie's efforts to lower costs and increase production even more. But Carnegie knew how to motivate for success. The story reveals much about the way manliness, sports, and success support one another:

Captain Jones was a particularly easy victim for Carnegie's constant goading on costs and production, for he carried much of the fierce competitive sportsmanship that he demonstrated in playing baseball, which he dearly loved, into the mill. Carnegie knew this and played upon it effectively, making wagers of a new suit of clothes or a $50.00 gold piece that Jones could not beat Cambria in tonnage for the coming month, or if that was too easy, could not reduce his own costs from what they were the previous quarter. With a snort of defiance Jones would take up the challenge, usually win it and then write back in triumph that Carnegie owed him two new suits. "Now in conclusion you let me handle this nag in the race. I think I will keep her on the track, and may keep her nose in front. I think at the end of this year I will have her ahead, and when we stop to rub down, you will find her in excellent condition." [Wall 344]

After some ministers complained about the breaking of the Sabbath, Jones proudly reported to Carnegie: "I have notified our bigoted and sanctimonious cusses that in the event of their attempting to interfere with these works, I will retaliate by promptly discharging any workman who belongs to their churches and thereby get rid of the poorest and most worthless portion of our employees. If they don't want to work when I want them, I shall take good care that they don't work when they want to. We bet a dollar that they will be glad to drop the agitation" (ibid., 345, quoted).

Jones would have won his bet, for he, being a betting, sporting man, knew the odds. Such insensitivity as his and Carnegie's led to the celebrated Homestead strike in 1892, and long after that tragedy Sunday work remained a policy of Carnegie Steel. In 1899 the general sales agent said that local ministers applied no pressure, since "Carnegie Steel has always been generous to churches throughout the area." Though the board of the corporation voted to discontinue Sunday work after improvements in the mills were made, the practice continued for several years. It had not occurred to the managers "to consult with the workingmen as to what a seven-day week, month in and month out, meant to them not only in physical well being but also in mental health, family relaxations, and community life" (ibid., 629).

One can only wonder what the nature of American culture might have been had the churches focused as much attention on labor abuse as on blue laws. Blue laws in Pennsylvania were repealed on 7 November 1933, allowing major league Sunday baseball in Philadelphia and Pittsburgh. It is obvious that these absurd laws were not overthrown until it was determined that Sunday sports were not only enjoyable for many but also a profitable business. If it is all right to work for pay on Sunday, as Carnegie taught us, it is certainly all right to play for pay on the same day. We can never know just how much Andrew Carnegie influenced our attitudes toward Sunday work and play. He "had been the one boy in his neighborhood allowed to skate on the river on Sundays" and "as an adult had imbued his entire business with secularism" (ibid., 345). Carnegie blurred all distinctions between traditional "times," that is, between time for labor and time for rest and meditation. The fires of sport, like those in the steel mills, never go out.

Carnegie believed that his gospel of wealth was justified in Scripture, but it seems a far cry even from the Christian advice for businessmen that Charles M. Sheldon offered in *In His Steps: What Would Jesus Do?* (1896). According to Sheldon, Jesus would, as a businessman, follow these principles:

1. He would engage in business for the purpose of glorifying God, and not for the primary purpose of making money.

2. All money that might be made he would never regard as his own, but as trust funds to be used for the good of humanity.

3. His relations with all the persons in his employ would be the most loving and helpful. He could not help thinking of them all in light of souls to be saved. This thought would always be greater than the thought of making money in his business.

4. He would never do a single dishonest or questionable thing or try in any remotest way to get the advantage of anyone else in the same business.

5 The principle of unselfishness and helpfulness in all the details of the business would direct its details.

6. Upon this principle he would shape the entire plan of his relations to his employees, to the people who were his customers, and to the general business world with which he was connected. [90–91]

Sheldon's book shows just how difficult it would be to conduct a business on this scriptural ethic, yet Carnegie made it all look easy. He did so, though, by not looking honestly at the conditions in his plants or at Scripture either.

In his later years Carnegie seemed to make an effort to redeem the tragedy of the Homestead strike of 1892, which "has become a part of the American Union man's legend, a symbol of the injustice and perfidy of 'the bosses' " (Wall 557–58). Though union men distrusted him and accused him of speaking with "a false tongue," Carnegie had even before Homestead "celebrated the dignity of labor, the sanctity of a man's job, profit sharing, the gospel of wealth, and democracy triumphant" (560), all the while sedulously trying to get his managers to push ever harder for success. Eventually he became the high priest of philanthropy, giving more money to institutions than any other American, and the grand promoter of peace, trying desperately to ward off World War I by means of arbitration of national grievances.

Carnegie, though, had in mind power as well as peace. When Theodore Roosevelt left office in 1908, Carnegie funded for him an African safari, with the understanding that Roosevelt in return would later meet with the Kaiser and work for the alliance of which Carnegie dreamed. Notice the behind-the-scenes shenanigans in the whole operation, keeping in mind that Roosevelt secretly had almost a monkish disdain for the corporate giants:

> Roosevelt's mass slaughter of African wild life would be done in the name of science under the auspices of the Smithsonian Institution, but financed by Carnegie, Morgan, and a few other selected "money-making" friends. In return Roosevelt would visit the Kaiser and press the cause for a "League of Peace." From there he would go on to Britain and meet with the league of both parties and again talk up a multilateral pact that would tie the Teutonic nations together in "a great power" alliance. [Wall 929]

Though he used Carnegie's money, Roosevelt was not keen on Carnegie's peace plan and was less keen on Carnegie himself. To him Carnegie was one of the "whiners" like Wilfred Owen would be after the war, and Roosevelt was a "Newbolt man" through and through. The great champion of sports and outdoor life wrote to his close friends Henry Cabot Lodge and Arthur Hamilton Lee: " 'All the male shrieking sisterhood of Carnegies and the like are quite powerless; and the professional apostles of peace, like Carnegie, are both noxious and ridiculous.' The sentimentalist is by no means always a decent creature to deal with; if Andrew Carnegie had employed his fortune and time in doing justice to the steel workers who gave him his fortune, he would have accomplished a thousand times what he accomplished or ever can accomplish in connection with international peace" (ibid., 982).

Carnegie in turn had reservations about his hero, though he treated Roosevelt more generously than Roosevelt did him. On the back of one of Roosevelt's letters inviting him to Oyster Bay, Carnegie wrote: " 'President Roosevelt. If he would only act as he tells one that he feels. Plenty good advice given & apparently taken & then some wild erratic outburst on the stump. . . . But one can't help loving him. He has pure and high ideals' " (ibid., 927).

How just was Roosevelt in his harsh and rather hypocritical denunciation of his benefactor? Carnegie seems almost the better man in some ways. It must be said, though, as Roosevelt claimed, that though Carnegie gave much to society, he, like all philanthropists, took a lot to return a little. The books in the libraries he gave to American towns are not read by athletes, many of whom, even those in college, can barely read, so low is reading and writing regarded in our society. The Commission on American College Athletics named in Carnegie's honor concluded as early as 1929 that "the workings of commercialism have almost obliterated the non-material aspects of athletics" (Savage et al. 310). Since 1929 the commercialism the commission identified as the villain of college sports has gotten worse, and it is fair to ask how much Carnegie contributed to these conditions by his own example. Unlike the Lord, Andrew Carnegie taketh away and then giveth. Carnegie was a knight with two hearts, one hard as stone toward the workers in his plants, the other soft as wax toward the great general public from whom he expected eternal thanks and praise for his boons.

In contrast to Carnegie's knightly gifts to social welfare, the gifts of shepherds—or those at least closer in attitude to this abstract ideal—carry a different kind of expectation. John Muir, for example, is more or less forgotten by those who still profit from his far different bequest (parks that preserve the wildness whose preservation Thoreau called "the preservation of the World" [*Essays* 112]), a bequest that transcends both receiver and giver. And even if Muir did "compromise," as is sometimes charged, he did so from a definite position, passionately wanting to preserve nature and make its wonders available to all. In his embrace of wildness he went even beyond Thoreau in practice and in theory, but politically he was more conventional than Thoreau (Hoagland 45–46), perhaps making him susceptible to compromise. On the spectrum between nature and culture he was a transitional figure between Thoreau and Roosevelt, just as Roosevelt might be said to stand between the extremes of Muir and Carnegie. Whereas Muir was the naturalist and Carnegie the knight as tycoon-philanthropist, Roosevelt was always the knight as hunter-warrior, loving the wilderness for the possibilities of excitement it afforded and hating business until he needed the fruits of it for his campaigns or hunting expeditions. While Roosevelt admired Muir, he did not seem to like Carnegie, even when Carnegie was trying to do better, and he more or less ignored Thoreau. Roosevelt did not dwell on philosophical distinction but on manly action. He was the chief exponent of the cult of activity that found a secure place not only in our national parks, where, Muir hoped, people would not only be renewed but changed upon seeing God's handiwork, but in our schools and churches as well. Now there is scarcely sanctuary anywhere from the incessant busyness Thoreau called the Saint Vitus's dance.

Leo Tolstoy, as if he had read Carnegie's *Gospel of Wealth* (1900) and the reference to himself, made a rebuttal in 1901 concerning his nonviolent struggle in Russia: "I should like to thank [the American people] for the great help I have received from their writers . . . Garrison, Parker, Emerson, Ballou and Thoreau, not as the greatest, but as those who I think specifically influenced me. . . . And I would like to ask the American people why they do not pay more attention to these voices (hardly to be replaced by those of financial and industrial millionaires, or successful generals and admirals), and continue the good work in which they made such hopeful progress" (quoted in Harding 198).

The followers of Henry David Thoreau have been comparatively few in number, but they are an impressive company. In addition to Tolstoy and Muir, others who have acknowledged a debt to him include Mohandas K. Gandhi and Martin Luther King Jr. The emphasis of all these men was not upon the acquisition of wealth but equality of rights or the stewardship of the natural world. Theirs was not a gospel of wealth but either a social gospel, in the case of King and Gandhi, or a gospel of nature, in the case of John Muir and John Burroughs.

In an essay called "The Gospel of Nature," published in *Century* in 1912, Burroughs wrote,

> We load ourselves up with so many false burdens, our complex civilization breeds in us so many false or artificial wants, that we become separated from the real sources of our strength and health as by a gulf. . . . For my part, as I grow older I am more and more inclined to reduce my baggage, to lop off superfluities. . . . The show and splendor of great houses, elaborate furnishing, stately halls, oppress me, impose upon me. They fix the attention upon false values, they set up a false standard of beauty; they stand between me and the real feeders of character and thought. . . . How the contemplation of nature as a whole does take the conceit out of us! How we dwindle to mere specks and our little lives to the span of a moment in the presence of cosmic bodies and the interstellar space! . . . Behold the infinite leisure of nature. [quoted in Shi 192]

At odds with dogmatic assertions of organized religion, Muir also engaged in a private quest in nature, which led to a belief that he almost playfully called mountainity. In an essay entitled "Mountainity, Reciprocal Action of Men and Mountains," Muir wrote, "the expressions of God in Nature cannot mean love to one hate to another. The sermon of Jesus on the Mount is on every mount & valley besides, unmistakable joy & confidence beams from mtn flrs redeeming the storms that fall upon them & the mtns on wh[ich] they grow from dominion of fear to love. They are great strong tremendously fateful John Baptists proclaiming the Gospel of harmonious love in the cold realms of ice" (quoted in Limbaugh 26).

Muir differed with John Ruskin, who doubted "the consistency and sufficiency and everlastingness of God's love as written in nature." To Muir, "Christianity and mountainity are streams from the same fountain." Mountainity might be most vulnerable to criticism that it is a form of pantheism and hence unchristian and that it does not give proper consideration to God and humans. In regard to the first, Muir had "an unshakable faith . . . in a creator–God both transcendent and immanent, personally and majestically transcending the universe, yet spiritually immanent and indwelling, both in nature and man. This was essentially New Testament monotheism geared to a belief in divine love as the ruling principle of creation" (ibid., 24).

In relationship to others, Muir embraced what might be called a Christian humanism based on the Sermon on the Mount:

> The central message of the sermon is anthropocentric man: man, as the highest order of creation, uses nature responsibly for human ends. Far from rejecting that doctrine Muir personified sermon scripture in his concern for both the natural environment and the people that inhabit it. His personal lifestyle seemed patterned after sermon teachings on such things as Christian Witness, Virtue, Pacificism, Charity, Private Worship, Modesty, Humility, Non-utilitarianism, and Pastoralism. In criticizing the moral bankruptcy of modern, industrial Christianity, Muir joined the call for Christian reform and echoed the words of fellow creationist Alfred Wallace: 'Let us hope that the twentieth century will see the rise of a truer religion, a purer Christianity . . . ' in which morality prevails over money-making, exploitation gives way to equity, and life's values are measured by quality instead of quantity. [ibid., 27]

In his acceptance of transcendence and immanence, God above and within, Muir again reflected the influence of Thoreau (see Fleck; Schofield). It is a religious philosophy theologians now call *panentheism*, a term coined in Europe when Thoreau was a young man. It is, as William J. Wolf points out, as old as St. Paul (1 Corinthians 15:25) and as modern as Teilhard de Chardin. Thoreau gave striking testimony of the idea before he knew it had a name. According to this analysis, "Emerson chose the consistent alternative, the complete immanence of God, or pantheism. Thoreau, on the other hand, kept the transcendence of God but brought God so intimately into the world that most thought him a pantheist. Note the retention, however, or transcendence in the following quotation: "By usurer's craft . . . we strive to retain and increase the divinity in us, when infinitely the greater part of divinity is out of us" (Wolf 172).

With his emphasis upon self-reliance, individual power, competitive games, and the god within, Emerson ironically had some influence upon the thinking of the captains of industry such as Carnegie, who brought industrial Christianity into full production. Thoreau's perspective was quite different and helped to shape Muir's mountainity. Some modern land planners and scientists such as Lynn White Jr. (see "Historical Roots") have blamed environmental damage on the anthropocentricity of Christianity, but this is not the anthropocentricity of John Muir. What White indicts is a type of industrial Christianity that differs from the nature gospel of Thoreau and Muir as day from night. Further, the Bible is not the authority for abuse of land but the source of a Christian stewardship, as is abundantly illustrated in Loren Wilkinson's *Earth Keeping: Christian Stewardship of Natural Resources*. I do not say that Thoreau and Muir are saints—though this is precisely what Wolf says of Thoreau—but only that their language and vision in regard to conservation are entirely scriptural. It is not surprising that Thoreau's collected works contain over 500 references to the Bible (KJV) with 116 as reference to Matthew, Wolf observes (163). Perhaps it is safe to say that Muir and Thoreau are saints to the extent that both heeded fully the advice of St. Bonaventure as given in *The Mind's Road to God*: "He, therefore, who is not illumined by such great splendor of created things is blind; he who is not awakened by such great clamour is deaf; he who does not praise God because of all these effects is dumb; he who does not note the first principle from such great signs is foolish. Open your eyes, therefore, prick up your spiritual ears, open your lips and apply your heart, that you may see our God in all creatures" (quoted in Wilkinson 203).

I have taken some pains to trace the scriptural foundation of

Muir's mountainity, which was fertilized abundantly by New England transcendentalism, to show that it is a doctrinal alternative to sportianity, which essentially repeats the sanctified business philosophy of Andrew Carnegie. Mountainity emphasizes enjoyment of nature rather than the exploitation of it, but it does not confuse play with religion any more than it confuses nature with God.

What a striking contrast Carnegie (1835–1919) and Muir (1838–1914) make. Born in Scotland within three years and forty miles of each other, Muir at Dunbar and Carnegie at Dunfermline, both came to America as young men, Carnegie at thirteen and Muir at eleven. Muir walked thousands of miles over the length and breadth of the land, and Carnegie walked far less on exclusive golf courses. Their impact upon American culture has been inestimable. In one year, 1912, Carnegie gave over $130 million to institutions and foundations (see "Carnegie, Andrew"). Altogether Muir persuaded Theodore Roosevelt to set aside 148 million acres for forest reserves (see C.B. Baker). They derived totally different religious philosophies, the one based on the administration of wealth and the other on the preservation of nature, the one on inordinate striving and the other on casual observation. While Carnegie thought that planning and control were the special preserve of "man," Muir believed that there were already too many man-made distinctions between man and beast to start with, and his famous thousand-mile walk was in effect an illustration of the take-no-thought-for-tomorrow attitude, drawing as it does, almost uncannily, upon the same passage cited by Carnegie (Matthew 6:19–34).

In the book that recounts his walk Muir denounces hunting, much as Thoreau did in his journal in 1861 (see C.R. Anderson). Muir comes to the defense of alligators, bears, and deer, referring to deer hunting as the "–est work to slaughter God's cattle for sport. 'They were made for us,' say their self-approving preacher; for our food, our recreation, or other uses not yet discovered. As truthfully we might say on behalf of a bear, when he deals successfully with an unfortunate hunter, 'Men and other bipeds were made for us, and thanks be to God for claws and teeth so long.' " Muir's powerful sense of irony must have emerged out of years of struggle for the preservation of wild lands from hunters, trappers, and miners" (Fleck 62–63). For Muir, walking was avocation and vocation, and the same was true of Thoreau, who at least on one occasion was also a runner, as seen in his chase of the fox.

Thoreau and Muir espoused the "playful, joyful life" of nature (Fleck 62). In "Natural History of Massachusetts" Thoreau put it best: "Surely joy is the condition of life" *(Essays* 4). Success for Thoreau is defined not as winning and accumulation. "If the day and night are such that you greet them with joy, and life emits a fragrance like flowers and sweet-scented herbs, is more elastic, more starry, more immortal,—that is your success" *(Walden* 265). Like Thoreau, Muir would have seen beneath the games and amusements of mankind "an unconscious despair," but the park system that he helped to bring into being would in the end have plenty of games and amusements that showed how deeply Americans were caught up in sports and play and how they confused activity with leisure. "Even as he extended the contemplative tradition, Muir revealed its potential for linkage with the cult of activity—namely their common fondness for the concrete." To a degree he might have been caught up in " 'monumentalism' (the perception of natural monuments as if they were the psychological and emotional equivalents in America for man-built structures . . . such as the Parthenon or the Cathedral at Chartres)," which "was a prime motivation for the establishment of the parks in the first place" (Mrozek, *Sport* 185). Donald Mrozek feels that Muir by his grand descriptions was even partly responsible for the heavy intrusion of recreation into the park system: "Encouraging city-dwellers to journey to the Bitterroot Wilderness, he promised obligatory 'lofty mountains steeped in lovely memophilia-blue skies and clad with forests and glaciers, mossy, ferny waterfalls in the hollows . . . '; but he moved swiftly to assure the visitor: 'when you are calm enough for discriminating observation, you can see the larches' " (183–85).

Mrozek speaks of "Muir's compromise," which means that while Muir was decidedly in the contemplative tradition of Thoreau, he shared some habits of mind with Roosevelt, who had some rather un-Thoreavian attitudes on the purpose of the parks. Mrozek argues that

> the proponents of the play-park . . . gave greatest importance to obviously man-made facilities for . . . recreation through games,

play, and sport. Carried into the national parks from the city parks, this impulse justified the maximum possible facilities, which would provide the widest range of activities from which the visitor could choose. Again activity and experience were set against contemplative passivity.

These perceptions of the national parks became particularly important to understanding the connection between notions about recreation and the sense of nationalism because parks were considered not only treasures to be saved but key devices through which the purported national values could be regenerated. From the more contemplative vantage, Muir certainly believed this; but Theodore Roosevelt also subscribed to this view, proving it in an ironic way when he incinerated an ancient tree near his campsite while on a hike with Muir. The exhilaration he felt seemed to him to be part of the sense of renewal and regeneration that he wanted for all Americans. The constant round of activities–hikes, drives, sails and the like–that typified Roosevelt's outings represented something of the marriage between landscape and human kinetics. . . . Life was equated with doing rather than being; and the rising interest in sport was paralleled by the shifting interest in national parks as playgrounds rather than sanctuaries. [*Sport* 187]

If we look at the biggest names at the turn of the century, we can infer how pathetically mountainity fared in contrast to the highly trumpeted ideals of sportianity. Sportianity embraced Andrew Carnegie (the knight as banker), who preached a gospel of wealth and internationalism; Billy Sunday (the knight as priest), who taught muscular Christianity and evangelism; and Theodore Roosevelt (the knight as professional patriot), who touted chivalry and nationalism. Mountainity, on the other hand, had John Muir (the naturalist as tracker), who taught stewardship. Clearly those practicing sportianity espouse triumphalism. They are not only doers but conquerors as well, extractors of ore, slayers of demons, exemplars of faith, and sportsmen all. Though it might be argued that the "monumentalism" Muir directly or indirectly supported is a type of triumphalism, the conquest of nature and others is not his credo. Mountainity emphasizes being and learning, observing rather than having. The gospel of stewardship is clear in Scripture, yet every strain of sportianity is haunted by some explicit verse that flies in the face of the heroism it embraces. On making money: "For the love of money is the root of all evil" (1 Timothy 6:10). On blending sports and religion: "For bodily exercise profiteth little: but godliness is profitable unto all things" (1 Timothy 4:8). On knighthood and the rhetoric of war: "A soft answer turneth away wrath: but grievous words stir up anger" (Proverbs 15:1). Yet Thoreau, Burroughs, and Muir are forever "excommunicated" in mainline Christianity, perceived at best as pantheists. It could be argued that Christianity in its original form is "lost" but sportianity lives on, and in fact thrives.

# 10

# Builders of Character and the YMCA

Because of the YMCA connection, Springfield, Massachusetts, is our American Jerusalem, the site common and sacred to three of our major "religions," football, basketball, and baseball. At one time or another their three founding fathers, Amos Alonzo Stagg, James Naismith, and A.G. Spalding, either taught there or held workshops there or used the town as a base from which to civilize and/or convert, or at least to impress, the wild Celts in the hinterland and the hordes of poor Catholics and Jews with strange-sounding names streaming into the cities through Ellis Island.

The YMCA made its most significant inroads on American campuses during the period following the Civil War, when both military training and sports became dominant. The colleges began to stress "citizenship" and the development of "character" as goals in addition to the more traditional goals of education (Nash 50). These two words, *citizenship* and *character*, reverberate throughout YMCA doctrine; indeed, they lie at the heart of its fourfold program. Under the influence of William Earl Dodge, a philanthropist and merchant, the program expanded in 1866 to include the word *physical.* Thus the object of the association became "the improvement of the spiritual, mental, social and physical condition of young men" (Hopkins 107). "Onward Christian Soldiers" was published the year before.

*Condition* is another name for *character*. C. Howard Hopkins's monumental study of the YMCA, published at the middle of this century, repeatedly illustrates this. For example, in 1897 the Athletic League of the YMCA, under the direction of Luther Gulick Jr., worked out "the idea that Christ's kingdom should include the athletic world, that the influence of athletics upon character must be on the side of Christian courtesy" (ibid., 265). In the 1880s and 1890s "the YMCA was completely immersed in the task of explicating the fourfold program, which seemed to be the answer to all problems. Its all-round activities were expected to develop good citizenship as well as Christian character." This was not, as the study points out, such an admirable goal. During this period, the YMCA "leadership was so completely identified with the cult of material success that any suggestion that its goals might be questioned would have been regarded as communism, then, as later, a bad word. . . . this blindness to the tragic circumstances in which millions of young men in the American working classes were caught was also the result of institutional myopia" (393).

What was true for the leadership of the YMCA was also true for the leadership of military education. In 1908 Charles W. Larned, a general and graduate of West Point, wrote in *Education from a Military Viewpoint:* "Throughout the whole system there looms the dominant and controlling purpose of character development for citizenship." Larned had no difficulty whatever in relating the education of the Greeks to the teachings of Christ. "There is but one system of character-education in which the methods and results are perfect; that is the one founded by the Master of Nazareth. That is wholly a school of character and supreme wisdom"; it is "a school of discipline," "obedience," "simplicity," "devotion," and "sacrifice" (4–5). The best exemplar of the type of education Larned had in mind was Theodore Roosevelt. As a "Christian," Roosevelt was "reverent and faithful." "He has embodied in the person of the First Citizen of the United States the highest type of American manhood and made it renowned among all nations of the earth" (1).

Yale opened Dwight Hall, its YMCA building on campus, in 1886, when Amos Alonzo Stagg was a sophomore. Two years later he was the secretary of the Y as he began postgraduate study and a new devotion to football, having dedicated himself to baseball as an undergraduate. So seriously did Stagg take baseball that he uttered a prayer with each pitch: "*Help me do my best*" (Lucia 72). Originally planning on the ministry but passionately involved in sports, Stagg found a solution to his predicament in the YMCA, which in his view would allow him to play ball and serve God at the same time. Stagg was the most famous of the evangelists of the gridiron, but he was not alone. In the last decade of the nineteenth century and the first decade of the twentieth, a virtual army of Christian football coaches from the eastern colleges brought muscular Christianity to the West and South on a scale second only to that of the U.S. Army in assignment of troops to the western forts. "Yale and Princeton led the football missionary effort of the late nineteenth century just as they had led the earlier religious one; Harvard lagged, as it had at the beginning of the century" (Lester, "Rise" 11). Other notable gridiron missionaries were Fielding H. "Hurry-Up" Yost and John W. Heisman. Of all these "evangelists," however, the most famous was Stagg, Mr. Football.

As head coach of the YMCA Christians of Springfield, Stagg introduced the game's first hidden ball play against rowdy Harvard, and to Stagg's delight, it worked like a charm. Stagg called it his dead man play, while opponents and sportswriters called it "most unchristian" (Lucia 93; some claim that it was Glen S. "Pop" Warner who came up with the hidden ball trick at the Carlisle Indian School [see Steckbeck 129]). Trickery on the field became Stagg's forte. He became known as "the man with a thousand plays." His sleight of hand, however, was not confined entirely to the playing field.

In 1890 Stagg accepted an appointment as coach and director of physical culture at the newly created University of Chicago offered to him by president William Rainey Harper, who had been Stagg's professor of biblical literature at Yale Divinity School. Stagg registered his acceptance with typical piety: "After much thought and prayer I feel decided that my life can best be used for my worker's service in the position which you have offered." Harper, like the man he hired, had an eye for worldly glory as well as for divine, and in the negotiations with Stagg, a champion of "moral athletics," he reportedly wrote, "I want you to develop teams which we can send around the country and knock out all the colleges. We will give them a palace car and a vacation, too" (Lawson and Ingham 42). Thus the University of Chicago's athletic program would serve the dual purpose of promoting Stagg's brand of morality as well as Harper's idea of a university, a university of "system" and "order," two of Harper's favorite catchwords.

Stagg's fierce love of sports and his bag of tricks seem innocent enough in retrospect, and his contributions to the game of football are extensive. They include—in addition to the hidden ball trick—tackling dummy, Statue of Liberty play, T-formation, place kick, jersey numerals, slip-proof jersey, and padded uniforms (see Lucia 36-37). Yet Stagg, admirable as he was in sticking to his amateur status and refusing to sell the story of his life, helped to put football on the hazardous course it has maintained ever since.

Note, for example, the familiar and questionable features of modern college athletics that Stagg either perpetuated or initiated:

1. The autonomy of the athletic director and the secrecy of his budget. In the letter to Harper in 1896 Stagg wrote, "I understand that I am not to be hampered in my work in any way. . . . I am not compelled to explain for what purpose certain money is to be used."

2. Tailoring the curriculum and specialized recruitment. Together with Harper, Stagg "established a requirement in Physical Culture which, in Stagg's words, would aid him to recruit 'many special players who otherwise would not appear' and would enable him 'to develop players for teams.' "

3. The importance of winning. In a coauthored book on football as a science, Stagg proclaimed that "the objective of football was to win rather than to play merely for pleasure. And winning required planning, specialization and coordination—in short, 'system' and 'order.' . . . In characteristic progressive tenor, both Harper and Stagg were in the business of saving souls by administering lives—Christianity, democracy, and scientific management presumably could co-exist."

4. Special treatment for athletes. In a letter to Harper on 5 July 1901 Stagg complained about Harper's decision to terminate the

athletic dorms, citing the inconveniences of athletes with injuries and bruises having to walk long distances to classes. Also, "as a way of conferring distinction upon his athletes, Stagg also helped to organize in the 1905–06 academic year the first athletic letter club, the Order of C." In 1905 Harper had to remind him "not to hold football practice on the afternoon of convocation."

5. Using ineligible players. "Stagg was charged, as early as 1895, with employing professional athletes and over-emphasizing winning." Harper himself reprimanded Stagg "for using an ineligible player in the 1896 football campaign and in 1898 scolded Stagg for exceeding his authority on the issue of player eligibility." [Lawson and Ingham 42–44]

In 1933 Stagg was forced out by a retirement rule and a complicated set of circumstances, but he took his bag of football tricks and went west to the tiny College of the Pacific at Stockton, California, his fame and legacy secure (see Lester, "Rise" 232–33). His former players were everywhere, so that early in the century the University of Chicago was regarded as the home of both razzle-dazzle football and muscular Christianity. The famous Notre Dame shift came from Jesse Harper, who was Knute Rockne's predecessor at Notre Dame and a Stagg player. Harper, said Rockne, got the shift "from Stagg who got it from God" (Lucia 37).

While at Chicago Stagg was in a position to influence another hiring that constituted a turning point in the history of U.S. college sports. Asked by President Francis Snow of Kansas if he could recommend someone to be athletic director, Harper in turn asked Stagg if he knew someone like himself, who could "direct athletics and pray." Stagg promptly wired: " 'Recommend James Naismith, inventor of basketball, medical doctor, Presbyterian minister, teetotaler, all-around athlete, nonsmoker, and owner of vocabulary without cuss words. Address 80 YMCA Denver, Colorado.' " Hurry-Up Yost had been added to the Kansas coaching staff: "He made it clear that he was willing to lead the K.U. football teams to victory, but he felt he was not properly qualified to lead the student body in prayer" (Webb 104). Naismith was qualified, as his friend Stagg well knew.

Yost gave us "Winning is the only thing," and Naismith and Stagg gave us pregame prayer.

Naismith had been the center for "Stagg's Stubby Christians" that had held mighty Yale to 16–10 in the first indoor football game at Madison Square Garden in 1890. Stagg was the fullback. Think of it—these two men, Mr. Football and the Father of Basketball, lined up one behind the other on every play. Once Naismith asked Stagg why he put him in the lineup. Stagg's answer was memorable: "Jim, I play you at center because you can do the meanest things in the most gentlemanly manner" (ibid., 49). Though he was not aware of it, Stagg was describing the heroic features of chivalry, not in the abstract, but in practice. Naismith also coached fencing and track as well as basketball at Kansas (ibid., 126). He was a perfect Christian knight.

Just as Mr. Football and the Father of Basketball were involved in the YMCA movement, so too was the Father of Baseball, A.G. Spalding, though not so directly. The YMCA was actually only one of several organizations concentrating on building "manly Christian youth." Another was the Playground Association of America (PAA) and the Public School Athletic League (PSAL). These organizations were either headed by or strongly influenced by the thought and action of Luther Gulick Jr., Henry Curtis, G. Stanley Hall, and Joseph Lee. (on PAA see Cavallo 34–35). All of these men knew that Americans worried about their physical and moral condition, believing that both were eroded by "overcivilization" and that the great influx of European immigrants, many of whom had fought for the cause of labor, presented a threat. Sports represented a method of meeting that threat through acculturation in the wake of the disappearance of the frontier (Levin 110).

For the playground theorists, most of American society from 1850 to 1917 was in need not so much of ventilation as of rectification. This could only come about by structured systems of games such as those proposed by the playground movement, which enjoyed the backing of leading capitalists Andrew Carnegie, J. Pierpont Morgan, and John D. Rockefeller Jr., themselves champions of competition.

With James Sullivan, who served as chairman of PSAL's game committee, Gulick asked A.G. Spalding to donate trophies for the baseball competition. Since the gesture promoted both his business and his own image, Spalding accepted the offer. Talking to a group of schoolchildren in 1906 in Manhattan, he said that baseball developed confidence, concentration, aggressiveness, alertness, and self-praise. A game so sapped "a boy's youthful vitality" that "after a hard fought game" he had "no inclination for anything except a good meal . . . and bed." He referred to Theodore Roosevelt as "our first athletic president," emphasizing that his "sportsmanlike qualities, energy, and 'square deal' brand of integrity inspired the Nation's Youth and were available to them through the PSAL" (ibid., 111), which, after all, stood for "duty, thoroughness, patriotism, honor and obedience" (ibid., 110).

Between October 1888 and April 1889 Spalding sponsored an around-the-world trip of professional baseball players, his own Chicago White Stockings and their opponents, the "All Americas," selected mainly from National League clubs, to promote American culture abroad. At a dinner at Delmonico's in Manhattan celebrating their return, "a host of toastmasters" praised the players for their manliness and citizenship, one speaker calling them " 'gladiators . . . covered with their American manhood' " (Levin 107). Both Roosevelt and Mark Twain were present as they would be at Yale in 1902 to receive honorary degrees, but the spirit of Spalding was much closer to that of Roosevelt the knight than to that of Twain the humorist, who in his speech at the dinner commented "amusingly" upon the "incongruity of bringing baseball, 'the very symbol, the outward and visible expression of the drive and push and rush and struggle of the raging, tearing, booming nineteenth century . . . to places of profound repose and soft indolence' " (ibid., quoted). Twain never favored big stick diplomacy, and a bunch of big sticks was precisely what Spalding had shipped around the globe in his efforts to promote manliness, American style. As a humorist Twain was in the service of Thalia, muse of comedy, who is always pictured with a shepherd's crook, which symbolically stands in sharp contrast to baseball bat, sword, and gun.

In 1904 Spalding made similar speeches before the Springfield, Massachusetts, YMCA, referring to baseball as a sentiment whose spirit had "permeated into every part of our strenuous life" (ibid.,

167). The reference to the "strenuous life" comes no doubt directly from TR. Spalding's spiel contains an element of safety-valve rhetoric, but it is minor compared with the heavy rhetoric of duty, honor, and country, the building blocks of manly acculturation. It is interesting to note that when the safety-valve language did emerge, the speaker always assumed that if a youth was not competing in organized sports, perhaps for one of Spalding's trophies, he would be doing something else physical that was much worse. Walking the streets or country lanes or swinging on a front porch swing were rarely mentioned as other recreational possibilities. These types of leisure activities offered no prizes.

Northern as well as southern schools near the turn of the century reflected the new attitudes toward the muscular Jesus, scholarship, and athletics. At the University of Michigan, for example, a group of students split from the Students Christian Association, citing doctrinal differences as well as a desire to affiliate with the YMCA at state and national levels. At roughly the same time, in 1890–91 "the management of all athletic sports was entrusted to a central organization called the University of Michigan Athletic Association" (Hinsdale 127–28). The record there of Hurry-Up Yost proved, from the point of view of success, that all the changes had been in the right direction. In four years in the early part of the century Yost's teams scored 2,271 points against 42 for their opponents.

Yost personified the stated ideals of the YMCA, at least in the eyes of his admirers. In a book of pure hagiography J. Fred Lawton says that "as an example of clean living he had no equal. He was a symbol of upright manhood. He believed in athletics, properly supervised, as a builder of men" (50). Similar testimony came from players like Bob Brown: "The Old Man was a great builder of men. His influence will live on through future generations as an inspiration toward clean living and sportsmanship which he frequently defined as 'The Golden Rule in Action.' " How the Golden Rule applied to Yost's lopsided scores is never made clear, but never mind. Said Supreme Court justice Frank Murphy, "Fielding H. Yost has done more to inculcate high ideals of clean, Christian living in the minds of Michigan students than any other one man" (ibid., 52).

The same type of adulation followed in the wake of Amos

Alonzo Stagg's career at the University of Chicago. While students criticized Stagg in an "unprecedented fashion" (Lester, "Rise" 229), his former players and businessmen were profuse in praise.

"George Matthew Adams, a leading writer of twentieth century success manuals and favorite of Henry Ford, had recalled: 'Many years ago, when Eckersall, the brilliant quarter-back for the University of Chicago, finished his college course, he paid this tribute to Mr. Stagg: "Stagg teaches character as well as football!" ' " (ibid., 233).

Character meant obedience, and obedience generally meant machinelike behavior. Yost, a student of war as well as a builder of character, even a lover of the strategy of war, made of the machine not merely a metaphor but a model to emulate, and the same was true of Stagg. "It is striking how often Yost's team was termed a 'machine' by himself or others.... Yost referred to it as 'My ... beautiful machine'.... aggregations of student-athletes became 'machines' of athlete-students." In reporting the outcome of the famous 1905 Chicago-Michigan game, won by Chicago 2-0, the *Chicago Tribune* reported that "Stagg had 'out-machined' Yost's eleven" (Lester, "Rise" 105-6). In the well-drilled machine, military or athletic, there is no place for play, or, in other words, for freedom.

If the YMCA, a WASP phenomenon, had triumphed in the colleges, there was reason for some to believe that it might also work in the countryside as well. It might, in fact, work right in the buckle of the Bible Belt, the southern Appalachian Mountains. In 1921 no less a figure than John C. Campbell astonishingly expressed almost to the letter the exercise and athletic theories of Gulick, Hall, and others, as if admitting defeat of all the preaching based on the relatively simple conversion experience that had gone on in the hills since the last years of the eighteenth century.

The young people of the mountains as a whole do not know how to play, Campbell argued. "Even when they do play, he says, they wish passionately to win and are inclined to take whatever means necessary to reach a goal." What is missing, says Campbell, in addition to sportsmanship, is "organization": "The Young Men's and Young Women's Christian Association might also find a special field for service for supplying and stimulating recreation. The young people of the mountains ... need to be directed into lines of wholesome vigorous activity. There must be definite fostering and supervision, and in places a traditional and religious opposition must be overcome, sympathetically and tactfully. The greater use of music—of community in particular—would be helpful, as well as the encouragement of games in which all may take part, folk dancing and sports of various kinds" (319–20). It may have been true that "as a whole" the mountain children in 1921 did not know how to play, but there is good evidence that many did, including much activity that did not include competition, a clear divergence from the dominant American culture (see Henson).

Campbell would argue that overall the highland boy of the 1920s had "little knowledge of play as play," resorted too quickly to the knife or, when he was older, to the pistol, and was overall "a poor sport" without any knowledge of the art of "playing the game to a finish." "No man in any country" makes a more valiant soldier, Campbell says, but "he needs to learn the code of honest sportsmanship which can best be taught through games which bring him into touch with his fellows in team-play and healthful competition" (126).

Campbell called for the Anglicization of Appalachia, using the same British process that was at work everywhere else in America at the time through sports and other activities of the Y. So thoroughly British was Campbell's advice that he included the British idea of "the good loser," which, according to some, the British invented and came to admire almost as much as the idea of the good winner (see Gardiner). There is a trick here, though. What is really at issue is not the value of being a good loser, which we all claim to admire, but the difference between two ways of life—one unregulated that emphasizes play, freedom, and creativity, the other highly regulated with emphasis upon competition, obedience, and discipline. One is essentially rural in nature, the other urban. One is shepherd's play, the other contests of knights. The basic assumption on the part of Campbell and other champions of the YMCA is that the great unwashed do not know how to play. In 1921, however, the same year of the publication of Campbell's book, Ring Lardner voiced exactly the same complaint about mainstream America. We do not know how to play in America, said Lardner, because we lack imagination and we are a nation of hero-worshipers: "But hero worship is the national disease that does more to keep the grandstands full and the playgrounds empty. To hell with those four extra years of life if they are going to cut in on our afternoon at the Polo Grounds, where, in blissful asininity, we may feast our eyes on the swarthy champion of Swat, in an excess of anile idolatry, 'Come on, you Babe, come on you Baby Doll!' " (461).

Lardner, characteristically, was accurate to the letter in naming hero-worship as the culprit undermining the spirit of play. Heroes and hero-worship, after all, are the essence of knighthood, and it was the knight in history—Caesar, Alexander, Napoleon—that served as the model for our own athletic knights—John Smith, Robert E. Lee, Theodore Roosevelt, and Douglas MacArthur. In contrast, Henry David Thoreau was not a knight, athlete, or hero. He was merely a walker and a player. His was the spirit of play closest to that of the mountain children and of the vanquished Indian. This is not an effort to romanticize either the mountaineer or the Native American, both of whom, like all human beings, have plenty of faults, but the two had much to tell us about living in unison with nature, playing on the earth rather than conquering it. Campbell's call for the YMCA, by the way, came only five or six years before Robert Neyland came to Knoxville to build a winning football tradition at the University of Tennessee, at the foot of the Smoky Mountains. The call for the YMCA and the desire for a highly organized system of intercollegiate sports grew out of the same mind-set. It is no accident that George Williams, founder of the YMCA, was knighted or that Neyland was a star player for the Black Knights of the Hudson.

Just what was wrong with the YMCA in the 1920s? The problem was the same that we encounter today: the belief that exercise and games build character. They can, of course, but the type of "character" that emerges is the question. The qualities generated by preoccupation with physical exercise and intense athletic competition tend everywhere to bury rather than cultivate the fruits of the spirit. How did the YMCA make this error? The harmonious integration of body, mind, and soul, the goal of the YMCA, is a tricky, if not impossible, undertaking, as Robert M. Hutchins, who successfully led the fight to end football at the University of Chicago, tried to explain in an address to officers of the YMCA.

"If the YMCA is not a business, neither is it a club nor the Boy Scouts nor a gymnastic organization. . . . Although I subscribe heartily to the doctrine of *mens sana in corpore sano,* we must agree, I suppose, that the physical aspects of the Association's program have the same relation to it that we have already allocated to the physical plant. That is, these items go to make up a rounded development; they are not, and ought not be, central. . . . I do not urge the withdrawal of the YMCA from a field in which it has provided leadership and preeminent service. I do urge these things be relegated to their proper place and subordinated to the primary aim of the movement. . . ." Advocating adult education and especially religious education that would command intellectual respect, Hutchins advised, "nor do we need to worry if this kind of education does not conform to what we ordinarily call 'character education.' Education that sets as its stated and obvious aim the development of character is likely to degenerate into sloppy sentimental talk about character. The result is neither character nor education. Rigorous intellectual activity remains the best character education; and the less said about character in the process the better." [Lawson and Ingham 53–54]

Much about the YMCA philosophy, however, was more troubling than "sloppy sentimental talk about character." To begin to comprehend it, it is necessary to consider the thinking of perhaps its most important missionary of sports, Luther Gulick Jr. It was Gulick who hired Stagg to his staff at the YMCA College in Springfield and Gulick who assigned James Naismith, an alumnus of the class of 1891, the task of inventing a game that would serve as "an indoor substitute for football. The result, of course, was basketball. Under Naismith's influence, W.G. Morgan came to Springfield and, finding basketball too strenuous for business men in his evening gymnastic class, developed a game called 'mintonette,' later called volleyball" (Hopkins 263). The invention of both games "resulted from Gulick's inspiration and suggestions" (Rader 126).

In one way or another Gulick was directly involved in all aspects of the recreation movement within the YMCA. In addition to his work in the Playground Association of America and the Public School Athletic League, Gulick also assisted in the founding and administration of the Child Hygiene Department of the Russell Sage

Foundation and the American Campfire Girls, and he was even a leader of the American Boy Scouts movement (ibid., 125). Finally, Gulick invented the famous emblem of the YMCA, the inverted triangle signifying the spirit supported by mind and body. This symbol, by the way, should not be confused with the fourfold mission that unites the social goal with the ideals of body, mind, and spirit.

Gulick's threefold philosophy was not so much an effort at a synthesis of Hellenic and Christian thought as a procrustean squeezing of the latter into the familiar pagan triangle of Plato. Like so many muscular Christians after him, he transformed the body of Christ into a Hercules or Apollo, for which there is no scriptural foundation. Christ, he said, foreshadowing the theology of Billy Graham, was a perfect man, "body, mind, and spirit; he worked for the whole man, body, mind, and spirit, and he saves the whole man, body, mind, and spirit." But the universal need to be kept in sight is that of symmetry—a proportionate development of man's whole nature. "Use what you have, and God will give more—spiritually, mentally, and physically." Three principles govern all the work of the physical department and recreation movement: unity, symmetry, and development. Therefore, when gymnastics and athletics are taught, they must "tend toward symmetry of form, and symmetry of function, so that a man may become strong, quick, enduring, skilled all in proportion." Anyone who directs such activity must "be an all-round man, physically, mentally, spiritually" (Hopkins 255).

Even if one grants Gulick his thesis that the resurrected Christ was perfect in body as well as mind, a more serious problem arises with his theory of play, called the recapitulation theory. In this, Gulick followed the thinking of G. Stanley Hall, drawing connections between the moral and physical development of the athlete and the skills of the citizen of modern society. Thus his whole effort as a physical educator was away from "Germanic" gymnastics and exercises for the individual and toward physical programs stressing "social" aspects of recreation (Cavallo 34). Note that it was "team play" that Campbell thought was needed by mountain children, and it was "team play" and "technical skill" that Neyland brought to Knoxville. If a master theoretician lurked behind the spread of games, it was Gulick, whose motto was, essentially, "Good bodies and good morals go together." Hollywood, as well as the daily sports pages, should be proof enough that the idea is heretical, yet it persists with amazing popularity.

According to the evolutionary view of Gulick, the development of the individual reflected the evolution of the species (Rader 123–24). For instance, adolescent games—baseball and basketball, among others—were supposed to reflect the hunting instinct and an increasing awareness and need for cooperation. Gulick concluded that complex motor behavior became a reflex through repetition. "For example, the awkward, more or less conscious throwing of young children with time and practice became smooth and unconscious, thus freeing the body for the efficient playing of adolescent ball-games" (ibid., 124–25). The training of the body was not the only thing or even the most important thing. Building moral character was the goal. The key, however, to the development of moral character was not reflection or rote learning of creeds but physical activities that served in an allegorical manner to enforce moral precepts. "Life for others is rendered far more probable, natural, and tangible," Gulick wrote, "when it comes as the gradual unfolding and development of that instinct that has its first great impulse of growth in the games of adolescence" (ibid., quoted).

The recapitulation theory had several practical implications. It justified the creation of special institutions for boys supervised by adults; it brought a de-emphasis on prayer meetings, sermons, and soul-searching while bringing about an increase in games and play in the churches, settlement houses, and playgrounds; it permitted boys to subordinate ethnic, religious, and class differences to a "presumably universal expression of maturation," thus, ideally, transforming a gang tendency into a higher civil consciousness; and it provided a rationale for segregation of organized play. "So it is clear," Gulick wrote, "that athletics have never been either a test or a large factor in the survival of women; athletics do not test womanliness as they test manliness" (ibid., 129, quoted). The recapitulation theory remained a potent argument against involving girls in sport until after the mid–twentieth century (ibid.; also Vertinsky). In his attitudes toward women in sport, Gulick was echoing Hall, who believed that "womanliness" was tested by motherhood. "Ritual rites of passage assisted girls to learn that only pain of motherhood could make women of them. Said Hall, 'just as a man must be ready to lay down his life for his country, so a woman needs a heroism of her own to face the pain, danger and work of bearing and rearing children' " (Vertinsky 93). It is frightening to think how similar Gulick's thinking was to that of Hall, who believed that "for most of us the best education is that which makes us the best and most obedient servants. This is the way of peace and the way of nature, for even if we seriously try to keep up a private conscience at all . . . the difficulties are so great that most hasten . . . to put themselves under authority again" (ibid., 84, quoted). In this way he sounded like another noted advocate of sport and religion in our time, Adolf Hitler, who said, "I am freeing man from the demands of a freedom and personal independence that only a few can sustain." Hall's philosophy, particularly as it concerns the role of women, thus predicts and underlies the aggressively antifeminist doctrines of national socialism (ibid.).

Though its legacy lingered on in elitist thinking, by the 1920s the recapitulation theory was in decline, with Gulick himself down-playing in a published paper the instinctual base of this play theory (Rader 132-33), ironically at the same time that Campbell was recommending the Y method for the mountains. "Disillusioned with the extreme forms that organized athletics had taken, the YMCA abandoned sponsorship of sport at the championship levels," leaving a vacuum to be filled in the 1930s and afterwards "by national voluntary boys' work organizations such as Little League Baseball, Pop Warner Football, and Biddy Basketball" (ibid.). Thus, just as Stagg lived to see the stadium named for him at Chicago torn down in the 1950s, so Gulick would see his theory of play largely rejected by educators and psychologists, though the belief that "Good bodies and good morals go together," which he helped to articulate, remains a supposed truism. Further, in fairness, it is certain that neither Stagg nor Gulick would have welcomed all the extreme forms that sports or muscular Christianity have taken in the last quarter of a century. In any event, both men, along with many others, helped to popular-ize and democratize muscular Christianity, though neither was probably as famous in his own day as another contemporary laborer in the same cause. This was Dwight L. Moody, one of America's great evangelists, who did not buy into the argument that physical exercise leads to godliness and eventually broke with the YMCA, putting his belief not in theories of acculturation or recapitulation but in the Word (see chapter 13).

The role of the YMCA in World War I staggers the imagination. It was not simply an association but an army with global outreach, as if it were living up to the faith that Woodrow Wilson placed in it in 1914: "You can test a modern community by the degree of its interest in the Y.M.C.A." (quoted in Hopkins 484). In the Spanish-American War and in the Mexican campaign of 1911–14, the YMCA had dutifully followed the flag and bidding of the ranking generals. The association responded to the orders of General John J. Pershing during the Mexican incursion as if it were part of the military itself (ibid., 486). In fact, while at West Point, Pershing became friends with John Raleigh Mott, a graduate of Cornell, who upon Moody's death, was called "the outstanding YMCA evangelist." Almost at the same time that Pershing was punishing the Mexicans, Mott became general secretary of the International Committee of the YMCA, in addition to holding key offices in several other evangelical and missionary groups. Thoreau said if someone would bring him a list of the world's organizations he would resign from them all at once; Mott's motto seemed to be "Bring me a list and I will *join* them all at once." Mott became a confidant of wealthy men through his organizing and promoting efforts and funded his many projects via these contacts. He was called "the pre-eminent leader of our world brotherhood in this century" (ibid., 433).

The involvement of the YMCA in World War I, determined to a large degree by the efforts of Mott, began officially with Executive Order 57, signed on 28 April 1917 by President Wilson, an avid Princeton football fan and an admirer of Frank Merriwell. The order enjoined officers of the armed forces to "render the fullest practical assistance and co-operation in the maintenance and extension of the Association, both at permanent posts and stations, and in camps and fields" (ibid., 487). Service centers, the presentation of entertainers, popularized athletics designed to maintain morale, educational materials, and recreation centers resulted (492).

Wherever war or even the threat of war occurred, the YMCA was there, not only in the main theater of operations but all around the world, echoing the prevailing belief that it was sweet and glorious to die for one's country. YMCA groups were in Brazil, China, the Dardanelles, Egypt, Mesopotamia, India, East Africa, Poland, and the Balkans. Like knights of the Middle Ages, YMCA workers entered Jerusalem with British conquerors, and they were on the Russian front in 1918–19 to support Allied efforts to stop the Bolshevik revolution, a war, like those conducted by the modern CIA, never officially acknowledged that went on after the armistice of 11 November 1918, a war "without a flag," a war that helped to force, in the view of some, the revolution itself. Of the Allied effort, Ralph Albertson wrote, "Suspicion, recrimination, tale-bearing, jealousy, hatred of Russian for Russian is the harvest our intervention has left behind it" (120). It was an intervention that few Americans outside the government, the army, and the YMCA ever knew about.

Almost as far-reaching as Wilson's executive order was General Order 33, issued from General Headquarters of the American Expeditionary Force on 6 September 1917, which granted the YMCA authority "to establish exchanges for American troops in France to be operated along the general lines of post exchanges" (Hopkins 489). Just as most Americans did not know of our war in Russia before and after 11 November 1918, so most soldiers in France were not aware of business concessions awarded to the Y. Few realized that the YMCA was not conducting charitable work but was in fact performing contracted army business. As a result, the YMCA received considerable criticism for selling articles in exchanges that were given away "free" by other welfare organizations. In an official investigation in 1919 the army concluded that *"The work of the YMCA was so much larger than that of any other organization that there was no basis of comparison.* It gave away more than all the other welfare organizations combined, but the fact that it was engaged in the canteen business and sold the same supplies that others gave away was a fact that … many soldiers … could not understand, and because of their misunderstanding, the YMCA received considerable unmerited criticism" (ibid., 500). The Knights of Columbus jumped to exploit the situation by advertising a policy of "Everybody

Welcome and Everything Free"–later shortened to "Everybody Welcome"–at their own huts and centers, far fewer in number than those
of the Y. "Everything" for the Knights included "tobacco, cigarettes,
candy, chocolate, and hot drinks as well as free entertainment,
athletic and welfare services" (ibid., 499). The Knights provided 18
percent of the total athletic events offered, the Y the rest.

In addition to its other myriad activities in World War I, the
YMCA, in cooperation with chaplains and church leaders, held over
100,000 bible classes in home camps and distributed over 3 million
testaments and 15 million special religious books and pamphlets
prepared by church leaders (Hopkins 492). One of the "most important" of the "devotional books" during the years 1910-20 was *The
Manhood of the Master* by Harry Emerson Fosdick (505). At the
beginning of this book Fosdick sets out to demolish the idea of Jesus
as uttered by a "noble pagan" in Swinburne's "Hymn to Proserpine":
"Thou has conquered, O pale Galilean,/The world has grown grey
from thy breath." In chapter 3, entitled "The Master's Indignation,"
Fosdick illustrates the value of wrath, showing how God used it for
his purpose, citing the words of the Psalmist, "Hot indignation has
taken hold of me, / Because of the wicked that forsake my law." By
the next chapter Jesus has taken up the sword. "Think not that I came
to send peace on earth but a sword" (Matt. 10:34). Then we learn
that the fact that Jesus stirred up the people (Luke 23:5) was really
an act that would impress people like Napoleon! (55). Other people
may rejoice in Jesus' friendship and home-loving affection for Mary,
Martha, and Lazarus, but "Napoleon thinks of him as a great leader."
Fosdick doesn't bother to point out to the troops that when in his
youth he heard a sermon proclaiming that Caesar and Cato were
burning eternally in hell for not having practiced a religion they
knew nothing about, Napoleon decided he could no longer call
himself a believing Christian (Cronin 36). The young men Fosdick
writes for stand in need of "leadership calling for knightly adventure," a quality "we find in Christ" (ibid., 175). Christ thus becomes
the ideal battalion commander.

In 1844 George Williams and other young men established the
YMCA in London to help improve the "spiritual condition of young
men engaged in drapery and other trades by introduction of religious

services among them" (Hopkins 4). In the centuries that followed, the Y changed dramatically, becoming athleticized, nationalized, and finally militarized. Not surprisingly, the founder, an urban shepherd, was knighted in 1896 by Queen Victoria and honored again after the war. A window dedicated in Westminster Abbey in memory of Williams and others in 1921 "showed our Lord preaching the sermon on the Mount, balanced on the right by a representation of the Transfiguration. Above were medieval knights–St. Michael and St. George, and in quatrefoil was our lord in Glory. . . . At the bottom . . . were portraits of George Williams as a young man and at the time of his own knighthood, 'in recognition of his service to the young men of the world' " (Binfield 315).

The muscularization and militarization of Jesus continued in the western world for both victors and losers of World War I so that on the surface at least it was difficult at first glance, judging from propaganda, to tell the difference between the ideologies that in the next great war would tear the world asunder. Dorothy Parker explains in her review/preface that the 1939 English Edition of *Mein Kampf* intended to awaken the nation to the dangers in Germany at the time. In regard to Hitler's repeated references to *mens sana incorpore sano*, Parker asks, "Is not conception of a sound mind in a sound body perfectly sound? In the midst of this guilt-drenched search for redemption, we stumble upon YMCA clichés. And then lose sight of the fact that the author of *Mein Kampf* has abolished the whole concept of the *citizen* as we have known it from the days of Pericles! In its place is the man of the Tribe, ruled by Totem and Tabu" (xi). As we all now know, the fundamental Christian doctrine of pity, love, and forgiveness was under the Nazis completely repudiated by contempt, hate, and revenge. In their theology Jesus was transformed from a Jew into an Aryan (see Shirer 152-64), a transformation that all the imperial nations had been pointing to for over a century, often under the auspices of the YMCA.

# 11

# Cloning West Point on the American Campus

$A$s the YMCA spread in the last decades of the nineteenth century from its urban hearth into every part of the country, it brought with it a new consciousness of sports and of a new muscularized Jesus as well. Wherever the YMCA appeared, there was almost at the same time the rapid development of organized sports, a shift from "turbulence to rules" or from unorganized play into structured competition.

The Y made its first appearance at the University of Tennessee, for example, on 2 February 1877, according to one history of that college, to assist the university–then called East Tennessee University–in "counteracting somewhat the general impression among the public that East Tennessee University was not only non-sectarian but also a 'Godless' institution. Consequently, the catalogue for 1876–1877 proudly announced that the organization of the Y was 'exerting a happy influence on the students.' A year later the catalog announced in more detail that the institution was 'not sectarian, but is intended to exert a decided Christian influence upon the students, and to cultivate among them a healthy moral tone.' " In a sense the YMCA competed with the churches, but apparently with their blessings. "Not only did the churches in Knoxville welcome them [students] but the YMCA, in active operation, had opened 'a reading room, which is free to all students' " (Folmsbee 126).

College athletics also made their appearance in the 1870s. "Spasmodic efforts were made to maintain a boat club in the river, but more important was the organization as early as 1875 of the University baseball team. It was called the Riverside Club, and since there were no other college teams near enough to play, it contested with city teams of Knoxville and other East Tennessee towns. . . . As was the case with the cadet band, however, the baseball team also fell under the faculty restrictions regarding travel" (ibid., 127).

The reference to the word *cadet* is an important reminder that after the Civil War the state colleges, under the provisions of the Morrill Land Grant Act of 1862, became essentially military institutions. As happened at other land grant colleges, the militarization of the campus in Knoxville coincided with the advent of the YMCA and organized athletics in the 1870s. In 1871 the War Department assigned Lieutenant Thomas T. Thornburgh as commandant of cadets, and for the next twenty years "the whole school was under military discipline similar to that in effect at West Point" (ibid., 116). In April 1872 the Knoxville *Press and Herald* gave the following picture of life at the university:

> Most of the students wear a military uniform of cadet gray at the present time, and after the first of September they will all be required to wear it. The cadets are divided into four companies and parade and drill under arms, every day. In fact, the discipline of the whole institution is military. . . . Delinquents are punished by extra drill, or extra duty of some sort. Lights are extinguished at half past ten and immediately afterwards every room is inspected "to see that all occupants are in their proper places. . . ." The deportment of the cadets is highly commendable. The military duties which they have to perform serve them for exercise. Besides, they have some time each day for voluntary exercises. [ibid., quoted]

In 1830 Davy Crockett tried to abolish West Point; had he lived to a ripe old age he would have witnessed the cloning of that august institution in his native east Tennessee. Though the spirit of West Point triumphed across the country, ironically it was the ghost of Alden Partridge, not that of his enemy Sylvanus Thayer, who shadowed the militarization of the American campus. Thayer symbolized the professional army, while Partridge, strongly opposed to a standing army, believed in a trained citizenry, liberally educated. Partridge was also the driving force for the establishment of the archipelago of military schools in the South in the 1820s and 1830s, as well as the founder of Norwich in 1820. He was a friend of Representative Justin S. Morrill of Vermont, who coauthored the bill that would transform American education through money received and invested from the sale of public lands (Nash 20). According to Morrill, the bill "proposed to establish at least one college in every state upon a sure and perpetual foundation, accessible to all, but especially to the sons of toil, where all the needful science for the practical avocations of life shall be taught, where neither the higher graces of classical studies, nor the military drill our country now so greatly appreciates, will be entirely ignored, and where agriculture, the foundation of all present and future prosperity, may look for troops of earnest friends" (quoted in Eddy 34).

The provision for military training by the colleges in the Morrill Act reflected to some extent the victory for the proponents of the idea of the citizen-soldier as envisioned by the early presidents. Morrill explained why it had been added: "Something of military instruction has been incorporated in the bill as a consequence of the ... history of the past year [1862]. A total unpreparedness presents too many temptations even to a foe otherwise weak. The national school at West Point may suffice for the regular army in ordinary years of peace, but it is wholly inadequate when a large army is to be suddenly put into service. ... The state must have the means within itself to marshall its own forces" (quoted in Nash 18).

Samuel Eliot Morison and Henry Steele Commager called the Morrill Act "the most important piece of agricultural legislation in American history." Said Andrew D. White, "In all the annals of republics, there is no more significant utterance of confidence in national destiny" (quoted in Eddy 44–45). During the darkest hours of the nation, when knights North and South were engaged in wholesale slaughter, the promoters of the Morrill Act tried to awaken in the consciousness of the country a shepherding responsibility, by focusing attention upon agriculture and mechanical arts.

While the Morrill Act did bring new opportunities for "the sons of toil" and the "industrial classes," knights seized upon the reference to "military tactics" to spread their doctrine of discipline. After the war West Point and Annapolis enjoyed great popularity in Congress and elsewhere, and three of the new colleges were modeled after the federal institutions: Texas A&M (1866), Clemson (1868), and Virginia Polytechnic Institute (1870). Elsewhere the military manner was also much in evidence, as seen in the description of life at the University of Tennessee (see also Hartwell 100-105).

Virginia Polytechnic Institute and State University (VPI), for instance, the school first known in 1872 as Virginia Agricultural and Mechanical College (VAMC), was represented in baseball in 1876 by the Allegheny Baseball Club (Tillar 10). The first football team was formed in 1892 (17), and the cornerstone for the YMCA building was laid in 1899, the first edifice on campus to be erected by alumni contributions, with the campaign headed by the same individual—Lawrence Priddy—who raised money for the War Memorial Gymnasium (31). Beginning in 1872 all the able-bodied undergraduates were required to take military training, a practice that continued until joining the corps of cadets was made optional in 1964 (5). The cadet gray of West Point was the fashion.

Universal approval did not greet the militarization process in the new A&M schools. At VAMC in the mid-1870s the issue led to a fistfight between first president Charles Landon Carter Minor, a Confederate veteran and graduate of the University of Virginia, and Brigadier General James Henry Lane, the first commandant of cadets and also a Confederate veteran but a graduate of Virginia Military Institute (VMI), who wanted to organize the new school along military lines like his alma mater. It is not known who won the fistfight, but Lane and his supporters won the argument, bringing VAMC into the consensus of knighthood. The first VAMC-VMI football game was played at Staunton on Thanksgiving Day, 1894, only four years after the beginning of the Army-Navy game. The entire corps of cadets attended the first "military classic of the South," which VMI won 10-6 (ibid., 20). Though it lost the war, the South retained two traditions dear to its heart: military training and sports. The conflict between Minor and Lane recalled in some ways the old feud between Thayer and Partridge at West Point, but these feuds and fisticuffs did little to impede the militarization of the American campus. Partridge, after all, was the great advocate of the idea of a civilian militia, and Minor, a former professor of Latin at the University of the South, was a "robust and athletic man" (5). Ironically the Morrill Act succeeded more in helping to create a militarized citizenry than a civilian militia. The balancing act of knight and shepherd was not easy in the Reconstruction South.

Not only did the Morrill Act allow for the survival of sixty-nine colleges, but it also created a new emphasis on physical activity. As different as military drill, physical education, and sports are from each other, they all grew up together in the state colleges between the Civil War and World War I, relating symbiotically more than antagonistically. Thus, by the time of the Carnegie Commission report in 1929, departments of physical education were dominated by intercollegiate athletics (Nash 44). In the Big Ten, for example, such departments were set up in every school except the University of Chicago between 1910, when Wisconsin led the way, and 1929, when Purdue followed suit. Most were founded in the early 1920s; they permitted football players to retain academic eligibility while concentrating almost entirely on sports (W.H. McNeill 95, 117).

And just as athletics and physical education programs in colleges merged, military concepts also influenced athletics (Nash 103). Indeed, much of our sports vocabulary comes from the military: *drills, recruit, draft, offensive, defensive,* and so on. The list is long and goes far deeper than mere words. General von Steuben is honored at every football game in the game itself, with the well-drilled combatants contending against each other, and in the pregame ceremonies often performed by the ROTC (which grew out of the Morrill Act), and certainly in the halftime shows of marching bands. The distribution of *Drill and Ceremonies,* published by the Department of the Army, is even now "unlimited."

In large measure the goals of the land grant colleges paralleled those of the YMCA. The stated aims for both military and physical education departments included the physical training benefits of military drill, the preparation of reserve officers and soldiers for leadership in national emergencies, citizenship training, discipline, character training, health and corrective work, "carry-over" values of athletics, educational values of military science, and military science useful in industrial and professional careers (ibid., 50–51).

As vague as the terms are, a pattern is discernible, and it is quite compatible with the objectives of the YMCA. Both the YMCA, a private organization, and the Morrill land grant program, a public plan, were designed to lift up the fallen, a traditional shepherd challenge in the teeming cities and in the vast rural heartland of the country. To be sure, the Morrill Act may well have been designed in part to develop officers for the Union army, but according to one study, "it took Congress about forty years to make full provision for carrying out the military clauses of the Act of 1862" (ibid., 25).

That the YMCA and the Morrill Act met the shepherd challenge to some degree is acknowledged. The YMCA has aided legions by providing inexpensive shelter, athletic facilities for exercise and the fun of competition, and spiritual consolation by its programs in counseling and reading. The Morrill Act directly influenced the development of American agriculture, which the hungry of the world have long depended upon for survival. These are notable shepherding accomplishments, yet the knight exploited both programs for his own autocratic purposes. The knight made sure that neither the YMCA nor the land grant acts went too far in promoting the general welfare and that under no conditions should shepherds be established as national models. The A&M schools promoted leaders for industry, especially the textile industry in the South, as W.J. Cash observed:

> The young men who attended them were often poor; but they were not poor within the meaning of the term as the original sponsors of such schools had used it. And many times they were not poor at all. For during the first decade of the century, the cotton-mill chiefs and powerful stockholders in the mills began more and more to send their sons to them for training as textile experts–perhaps adding two or three years at such Yankee schools as the Massachusetts Institute of Technology and the Wharton School of Finance to round off the process. [246]

To this day we have no memorials to the American farmer or the agricultural researcher, the two types, as Jefferson and Lincoln realized, we depend upon the most. Halls of fame proliferate, but not for those who labor or study. All honor and renown still goes to the knight, the military hero, the corporate executive, the politician, the film star, and the athlete.

In fact, the land grant colleges even suffered the disdain of the private schools, becoming increasingly associated in the minds of the elite with what are now two archetypal dummies in our society, the hayseed and the dumb jock, who in the land grant colleges were often considered one and the same. "Cow colleges" and "football factories" became interchangeable. Clemson and Texas A&M, it seems, have had to bear most of the burden of much of this humor—for example, the bumper sticker "Honk if I'm an Aggie"—but it abounds everywhere rivalries arise between the land grant schools and either an older military order—VPI versus VMI—or a private school—the University of Tennessee versus Vanderbilt. This humor does not reflect contempt for either sports or the military tradition but for an agricultural tradition that Jefferson wanted to honor instead of a military aristocracy or one smacking of sterile scholasticism. The path we have taken has been far more Hamiltonian than Jeffersonian.

The provision for the teaching of military tactics in the Morrill Act of 1862 and the amendment of 1866, which specified numbers of officers and students, became the little tail that wagged the big dog. The same can be said of the addition of the word *physical* in 1866 to the YMCA triangle of goals. Instead of promoting peace, war always promotes the thought of more war, even in the minds of the victors. In spite of shepherd intentions and achievements by the YMCA in the cities and of the Morrill Act in the farm country, the knight exploited both programs to extend his domain to playground and campus. The military-academic alliance, previously limited to the Ivy League and the service academies, was extended throughout the country under the banner of knightly virtues: character, citizenship, obedience, discipline, teamwork, military readiness, and success. There was less emphasis upon play, relaxation, enjoyment of nature, or the possibility of sectional and international cooperation instead of combat.

Nor was there much evidence of Paxson's safety valve at work, except perhaps in returning veterans who looked for exciting forms of athletics to satisfy their restlessness. The dominant theory at work was acculturation, the molding of the masses into a conservative mentality. It is perhaps more accurate to say that the ventilation theory worked in concert with acculturation. If in the ventilation theory anger is ignited at intervals so that it can escape like steam from an engine, acculturation emphasizes fueling the machine in the first place. Thus the whole operation becomes a mechanical function, a taking in and a letting go. By the late 1920s the inevitable metaphor of the soldier in military manuals was that of the well-drilled and well-oiled machine, like the football teams of Yost and Stagg. "The military writers stress explicit obedience to orders of superiors, promptness in carrying out such orders, respect for authority of superior officers so that no question of the wisdom of the orders will delay action; in other words, to these writers, the well-trained man is an automaton, whose habits have become so fixed that upon hearing the word of command the muscles respond with a minimum of consciousness and thought" (Nash 77). Thus did the knight triumph on our campuses, contemporaneous with the arrival of the muscular Christ of the YMCA.

Jesus and Mars, though, had got on famously for over a millennium in the form of Christian knights. The most renowned of such groups in Western history were the Templars or Knights of God, who for "nearly 200 years prior to their suppression in the year 1312 on charges of heresy and magic practices were the most formidable and feared fighting machine in Christendom" (Burman, cover). Yet it is clear that these militant knights personified the heroic qualities that the expansionist oligarchy wanted to revive and that both the YMCA and the military establishment endeavored to bring to American campuses: obedience, discipline, courage, manliness if not misogyny, legitimation of killing for Christ, elitism, and, of course, the two-heart theory: "They were lions in war, and gentle as lambs at home . . . they were harsh and savage to the enemies of Christ, but knightly and gracious to Christians" (ibid., 59; see also 47, 58–59, 32, 37, 46). The embrace of such attitudes by advocates of the strenuous life, coupled with immense wealth and political power, which the Templars themselves achieved (2), could only spell trouble for Jews, Africans, New World Indians, and women. "The principal scapegoat" of the hatred of the long adaptation of a profit economy in the middle ages was "the Jewish community" (83), an attitude still evident in the thinking of influential figures in the cult of the warrior at the beginning of the twentieth century. As military knights always do, the Templars regarded themselves as the natural superiors of all who worked the land: "The huge army of non-knightly workers served a single purpose: 'The Templars employed farmers and agricultural laborers, shepherds and millers, gardeners and artisans, but over all they exercised the same central control, directed by the same motive, the increase of the common revenue and the financing of the Holy War' " (97). The pattern is all too familiar.

Even the democratic features of the Morrill Act and the YMCA, which had the expressed intent of opening doors of opportunity and hope to the lower classes, were sabotaged by the reactionary mentality of the national leadership between the Civil War and World War I. This conservatism also harked back to the proto-Fascist assumptions and practice of the Templars.

Initially, Native Americans and former slaves did not benefit from the land grant legislation, failing to qualify in 1862 as members either of the "industrial classes" or "the sons of toil." In the Morrill Act of 1890, seventeen land grant colleges for blacks were established. (Alcorn University in Mississippi had been created in 1871.) Though the assertion is open to question, one view is that the "Morrill Act of 1890 accomplished for Negroes what the first act of 1862 had accomplished for men and women of other races" (Eddy 258). Before 1890, humanitarian efforts to assimilate Indians and blacks into the general population were for the most part private, as seen in the notable work of two knights turned shepherd (or part shepherd): General Samuel Chapman Armstrong, founder of Hampton Institute in Virginia (1868), and Richard Henry Pratt, founder of the Carlisle School for Indians in the military barracks in Carlisle, Pennsylvania (1879). Some government money was available for the establishment and maintenance of Hampton, but figures differ on the amount (see Pratt 314-15 and Tillar 3). In any event, according to Pratt, "money for Hampton was largely sustained by charity." In order to raise money for this school, General Armstrong, who had commanded a black regiment in the war, would make expeditions to New England

and New York to appeal for help, "with an Indian or two and a colored student or two, as samples and to speak" (Pratt 214).

As one of the most famous experiments in acculturation, Carlisle offers ample illustration of the uses and abuses of football, especially the latter. In her study of the school Carmelita S. Ryan observes that "during Pratt's superintendency [1879–1904] football had been a means to win support for the school; after his departure it became an end in itself" (259). The same problems threatening the integrity of football in universities today were present at Carlisle; these were not so much the fault of the players as the administration, as is the case today as well. "More harmful to the school's discipline and morale than payment to the school's football players were the special treatment and privileges granted to these athletes" (263). As further evidence that sports lie close to the soul of culture, Ryan offers this observation: "In promoting football at the expense of everything else," the administration after Pratt "had seriously weakened the moral fiber of the student body. The main purpose of Carlisle—that of providing an education to the Indians—was forgotten and the special tone and ascendancy of the school was lost forever" (206). In the debate over the closing of the school in the second decade of the twentieth century, one is not surprised to find that "the most common suggestion put forth was to make the school an Indian college or an Indian military training school, 'a miniature West Point' " (268). Nor is it surprising that Theodore Roosevelt admired the team's success in football. After defeating Georgetown in 1902, 21–0, the team met with the president, who, according to the players, "was all football and asked many questions about the teams they defeated, including his alma mater, Harvard" (Steckbeck 74; also cited in Ryan 255).

While more studies need to be done on the role of sports and military training in the black land grant colleges, it is revealing to contrast two different attitudes toward sports as articulated by Pratt and Booker T. Washington, perhaps Hampton's most famous graduate, who idolized Armstrong and who himself founded Tuskegee Institute in Alabama. In 1890, after banning all games away from Carlisle because of injuries on the field, Pratt, upon appeal by athletes, reconsidered and agreed to let sports continue on two conditions: that the Indians never slug and play so fair as "to set an example ... for the white race" and that they "whip the biggest football team in the country" (Pratt 317–18; cited in Oriard, *Reading Football* 234). In gridiron success, the rest is history, the Fabulous Redmen accumulating a record of 269–169 (with 13 ties) from 1894 to 1918, when the school closed (Steckbeck 144). Furthermore, they succeeded by a legendary spirit of fair play that Frank Merriwell himself would have applauded. There is, however, a caution here, and a double irony, as Michael Oriard has observed: "In a narrative of civilization and savagery, the savage emerges as the exemplary sportsman. But their sportsmanship serves to confirm more than the spirit of fair play in American football." Though an example of good sportsmanship, especially in defeat, the Carlisle player represented, Oriard explains, "an honorable, uncomplaining and wholly reconciled loser in a fair fight, the overt stake football but the implicit one a continent. . . . For Theodore Roosevelt, and others of his class and race, that narrative of fair play and racial destiny was a necessary fiction" (Oriard, *Reading Football* 247).

Like Pratt, Booker T. Washington emphasized the value of vocational training and manliness, but sports had little or no place in his vision. Asked by Lyman Abbott, editor of *Outlook*, to talk about sports in his life, Washington dismissed the whole subject: "Games I care little for. I have never seen a game of football. In cards I do not know one card from another. A game of old-fashioned marbles with my two boys, once in a while, is all I care for in this direction. I suppose I would care for games now if I had any time in my youth to give to them, but that was not possible" (Washington 266). Washington was basically a shepherd, though he became a controversial one over the years in the black community as well as the white. Echoing the wisdom of Thoreau, Washington wrote, "I pity the man or woman who has never learned to enjoy nature and to get strength and inspiration from it" (265).

To Washington sports belonged to the Toy Department, while for Pratt they were close to the soul of culture. Both, though, reflected the dominant myth of the white majority: the necessity of success. As Louis Harlan says in his introduction to *Up from Slavery*, Washington's book is in "reality the Black version of the American success-hero," with Washington being "the exemplar of the Puritan work-ethic he believed in" (vii). "It was the Horatio Alger myth in black" (xlii). Whether in work or play, the experiences of minorities seemed to confirm the knightly values of competition and success of the transplanted European culture.

By 1930 the result of "manly" thinking in the "leadership," a common goal of colleges and the YMCA, was solidified in official government documents, such as the booklet of the Reserve officers Training Corps Association: "Patriotic inspiration has given birth to every forward step in our national life, therefore we may well stop to examine and consider those other 'isms', so commonly heard on every hand these days, such as bolshevism, communism, radicalism, pacifism, and many other brands of 'internationalism', to find, if we may, to what extent and in what way the followers of these various 'isms' are devoted to the welfare of one's country. The answer is obvious, internationalism is directly opposed to nationalism and patriotism" (Nash 64). The War Department's *Manual on Citizenship* for 1931, designed for use in classes of the Training Corps, had this to say about citizenship:

> There is no place for the doctrine of "non-cooperation." Religious beliefs will not excuse any citizen from rendering service in defense of the country although Congress has power at its discretion to exempt him. . . . Socialism kills; the doctrine of "socialism" is "collectivism." It tears down the social structure, weakens the individual's responsibility by subjection to or reliance upon the state in all material, social, and political matters. It compels the thought that at best man is not better than the worst; he loses his self-respect and his keener sense of seeing moral and ethical values. Socialism aims to save individuals from the difficulties or hardships of the struggle for existence and the competition of life through calling upon the state to carry the burden. [ibid.]

Such documents were read by significant numbers. In 1928 more than fifty-four thousand students were enrolled in military science at fifty-two land grant institutions, almost half of the total male population of the colleges (ibid., 29).

In addition to the systems of forts mentioned in this study I would like to draw attention to one more system, the NCAA

(National Collegiate Athletic Association), coordinator of televised sports, which since the early fifties has been a boon companion of televised evangelism, each reinforcing the other in a doctrine of success and salvation. With its forts of athletic departments across the nation the NCAA maintains headquarters, the pentagon of college sports, in Kansas City, Missouri. The YMCA and the FCA brought a muscular Jesus to the American campus, the Morrill land grant act and the ROTC brought the army, and the NCAA and the CFA (College Football Association) brought television. The CFA is a sort of superstructure of sixty-two highly visible NCAA colleges seeking since the early eighties to maximize television revenue in football for its members.

That the NCAA, with its endless rules, "divisions" of competition, and investigators of rumored abuses acting like inspector generals of the armed forces, should have a military configuration should come as no surprise. In the debate over the abolishment of football in the Murray Hill Hotel in 1905 Captain Palmer E. Pierce of West Point "characterized football as an excellent test of character and vowed that the U.S. Military Academy (Army) would continue to play the game whether other colleges did or not" (Lawrence 9). Along with Lieutenant Colonel Howze, also of West Point, Pierce "*dominated* the proceedings and after a *hard battle* secured a two-third vote to continue the game and make such changes as were recommended by the athletic association of West Point for its improvement" ("Army-Navy Game Here" 10, italics added, paraphrased in Lawrence 9). Astoundingly, Pierce did not play football at West Point but was the manager of the first Army team in 1890 and returned as graduate manager from 1902-7 when he was active as a leading advocate of the game's virtues. Pierce was the first president of the NCAA, but Roosevelt was the major force behind the effort to keep football without which we would have had another type of culture. In the battle over football Harvard-Yale man Roosevelt triumphed over genteel Charles W. Eliot, who "failed to convince his own trustees to ban the game, something that a small group of colleges accomplished, including Columbia, New York University, Union, Northwestern, California, and Stanford" (Smith 206).

Throughout the twenties Pierce, a retired general, was active in the NCAA, twice serving as president. He was also president of the AAU. At Pierce's retirement from the NCAA Dr. Steadman V. Sanford of the University of Georgia praised him for his heroic service in China, Cuba, the Philippines, and in World War I and for his "successful, eventful" life and his many contributions to the NCAA, noting that he was graduate of the Military Academy and a former professor there (Dougherty 79-80). Sanford himself was a force in the NCAA, serving as president, and as Dean of the Henry W. Grady School of Journalism; he pushed for an adequate football stadium at Georgia and pushed for funds to build it. On 12 October 1929 the stadium was named for him when Georgia defeated Yale (Coleman 868 ). The Bulldogs had arrived. The year 1929 of course was the year in which the Carnegie Commission catalogued the many abuses in college athletics, including "subsidization," which the commission found in 81 of the 112 NCAA institutions (Lawrence 27).

This is not to blame Pierce and the NCAA for those abuses. Indeed the NCAA tried to promote high knightly standards of sporting competition without intruding upon the authority of member institutions. Says Ronald Smith, "As mandatory eligibility rules were 'judged impracticable' by Palmer Pierce and the NCAA, they were left to each institution to enact and enforce.... Home rule dominated the NCAA for the first half century of its existence. The individual colleges agreed collectively to act individually" (207). Smith goes on to add that "moral force, not political force, was the keystone of NCAA power in the early years" (ibid.). Nathan Dougherty, himself a former knight, compared the situation in which the NCAA found itself in the twenties to "King Arthur and his Round Table: King Arthur bound his knights to oaths that many of them never kept" (ibid. 79). The NCAA, Dougherty suggests, was naive on the subject of amateurism and especially on matters of recruiting and subsidization, which was going on practically everywhere. At least Pierce and the NCAA were advocating compliance to a code of "clean athletics" during our imperial or High Roman phase.

What changed the character of the NCAA was television, the ubiquitous symbol of the Low Roman or commercial age. "At the same time that television was enhancing the expansion and financial status of openly professional sports, it was also furthering the professionalization of a self-proclaimed amateur sport enterprise—intercollegiate sport. When collegiate football became one of the most popular viewer events on early TV, the NCAA . . . quickly stepped in. . . . The NCAA began regulating television coverage of collegiate football games in 1951. . . . With a view toward receiving television money and public exposure, universities throughout the country threw enormous human and financial resources into their football and basketball programs while frequently severely restricting or even omitting other sports from their offering" (Eitzen and Sage 234). Today the NCAA is regarded by some as a "monopolistic cartel" (Smith 206, Eitzen and Sage 219 and 281, citing James V. Koch; also Lawrence, ch. 5).

While Paul R. Lawrence in his book about the NCAA called *Unsportsmanlike Conduct* gives the NCAA credit for making football considerably safer since 1905, he says that in other areas the organization has caused more problems than it has solved. If, he asks, amateurism continues to be "such a good policy, why is it good only for the athlete?" As for the NCAA's monitoring of intercollegiate athletics, "the highly publicized efforts . . . indicate that the enforcement mechanism has never worked and that most cheaters escape." Most damning of all charges by Lawrence is the following: "When rationalizing its control of intercollegiate sports, the NCAA has always cloaked itself in altruism, and, not infrequently, patriotism. Yet it stood convicted of using the same tactics generally associated with the robber barons of the twentieth century. Moreover, President Roosevelt, who encouraged the formation of the NCAA, rode into office on a reputation for busting the trusts that dominated and manipulated markets in much the same way the NCAA controlled televised football." Lawrence adds that the NCAA has its own legal office and an active "committee to lobby the government, just like any other for-profit industry" (151-52). Allen Guttmann in *A Whole New Ball Game* shows that the NCAA has not exactly been a pioneer in the development of equal opportunities for women in sport (155-56).

Television is the Pandora's box of college sports. Whatever problems we had before television have multiplied in the electronic wasteland. Let us take just one school, our most famous in the world of football, which is exceptional but also representive of aspirations of other "powers." Because of television Notre Dame is now in the national goldfish bowl with no way out. Its involvement in the world of entertainment only deepens. First, there were the bowls, then membership in the College Football Association, with its complicated television packaging. Then in 1990 Notre Dame arranged its own private package for televising its games, including the annual lopsided one with Navy, as if both schools were still living in the High Roman period. (Even Father Hesburgh has started pulling for Navy, at least for Navy to score, in memory of the good old days no doubt). For the right to televise Notre Dame's home games through 1995, the National Broadcasting Company agreed to pay the University around $37.5 million. In making this deal, Notre Dame reneged on its promises to be part of the College Football Association made three weeks earlier (Jaeger and Looney 276). One does not feel sorry for the CFA, however. On the Prudential College Scoreboard for September 18, 1982 Jim Lampley reported that at a meeting of presidents to discuss the new CFA alignment not a word was said about academics or the education of the athlete. The only subject, he said, was money. Now another lucrative possibility looms on the horizon, the NCAA football playoff, which will come as sure as the sunrise. The plan involves "a six-team, three game scenario to include one game on New Year's eve, one on New Year's night, and one on January 2" in order to determine the national champion. Since Notre Dame is usually in contention, it would more than likely be involved in every playoff. A report on this project indicated that as much as $62.5 million could be realized from the playoff (Tucker 17).

In an age of "public relations" television provides a means of spreading football propaganda, paying lip service to the old clichés while contracts are negotiated and coffers stuffed. At every opportunity the old knights are trotted out to exemplify the old pagan virtue of a sound body in a sound mind and by indirection the Christian virtue of good will, as practiced, say, by Chevrolet. One Saturday in the fall of 1988 at half-time of a Notre Dame game, a member of the Notre Dame Board of Trustees, also the chairman of the board of Coca Cola, came on television to remind us that Knute Rockne had been a chemist and that synthetic rubber had been discovered in the laboratories of Notre Dame. These seemingly innocent remarks contain much that is wrong with college football. First there is the implication that when we watch college football we should break out the periodic table instead of Budweiser. Second, there is the more than faint suggestion that Rockne is also the father of science at Notre Dame, maybe even responsible for synthetic rubber. Third, there is the indication that the current arrangement between power football and academics is sane and healthy, not only at Notre Dame but everywhere, since it meets with the approval of the lords of Coca Cola. Here is the familiar patronization by the athletic business complex of the arts and sciences.

During our High Roman, pre-television period sports were linked more with patriotism than with business, but the three have been entangled in some ways during most of our history—and with religion and education as well. At the service academies the linkage of sports and patriotism was not merely pabulum for public consumption but a sacred formula. Knights, though, always have their eye on the buck and on drama as well. Few schools profited more from television than the military and naval academies during the early days of television owing to what was for decades "football's biggest show," the Army-Navy game. The game for 1964, for example, was the highest rated broadcast of the season, reaching 16.2 million people. (Lawrence 97), a figure that makes the mere 111,000 at Soldier Field, Chicago, for the 1926 game seem paltry. Little did knights know it in the early days of televised football but for citadels of military tradition television was the Trojan horse within the gates. Today the Army-Navy game may remain colorful and well played but inconsequential in terms of power ranking, which has become a prime consideration of value in the public mind. Still the military motif remains an essential ingredient in the Disneyfication of patriotism evident in pregame and half-time ceremonies such as those at the Super Bowl. The obligatory pregame flyover by Air Force or Navy jets as much as says, "Thanks, Palmer and Teddy and West Point and Harvard trustees, too, for not listening to a wimp like Charles Eliot who would have had us all rowing and reading classics." If the spirit of Roosevelt is alive in the sensational displays of patriotism in the Super Bowl, so is that of Mark Twain as seen in the hilarious satire of a half-time Super Bowl game by Coach Shoat Cooper in Dan Jenkins's *Semi-Tough* (137-38).

One major casualty—possibly—of our move into the commercial age of college sport is the belief that football makes good warriors. In its early days football was viewed as a substitute for war and as a training ground for war. Strangely, the three staunchest promoters of the football-war metaphor, Palmer Pierce, Douglas MacArthur, and Teddy Roosevelt, never played the game in college for one reason or another (though Roosevelt boxed at 135 pounds), yet all were highly decorated soldiers. More recently, an attack on the association of sports and football came from Admiral Hyman G. Rickover, a nuclear knight in a new kind of warfare, who "kicked at football" as a military aid in an interview before the 1965 Army-Navy football game, claiming that there was no evidence the Duke of Wellington ever said that "the battle of Waterloo was won on the playing field of Eton" and adding that "the Duke probably learned the spirit of adventure by jumping over a ditch on horseback or perhaps tobagganing around corridors, drawn by a bevy of young women" ("Admiral Kicks"); While no exact figures are available on the correlation of football and military success, the belief of service academy officials in the mid-fifties was that as officers "the football men do just as well (as others), if not better. The number who have been decorated for heroism is high" (Paxton). There is ample evidence to support that claim. Some of the figures are stunning. For example, thirteen of approximately fifty members of the Navy football squad of 1935 were killed in action in World War II (Schoor 94). To what extent the United States helped to provoke the great wars by its foreign policy, particularly by its expansion in the Pacific early in this century and by its modernization of Japan in the nineteenth, will remain a topic of argument among historians, but there is no argument about the sacrifice of both the professional soldier and the citizen soldier to help bring those conflicts to an end. In our High Roman period sports were used to foster a sense of duty and sacrifice; in the Low Roman phase, they serve the ends of money and success. In the age of television it has been extremely difficult for the NCAA with its long military connections to walk a line between the old, amateur, patriotic use of sports and the new, professional, commercial use. That there might be other, saner options, particularly the idea of sport as fun, education, art and self discovery, does not seem to be a possibility that the NCAA, whose initials according to one joke mean Never Compromise Anywhere Anytime, is seriously considering.

Even those who have been in the NCAA trenches and show some appreciation of the complex issues facing that organization have reservations about the system. While Edwin Cady, humanities professor at Duke and NCAA representative from the Atlantic Coast Conference and before that the Big Ten, said that without "counsel of perfection" it is better to "muddle along with good, messy old human problems" (170), he was displeased with the matter of rules. In a list of "some suggestions" about what to do in "our present confusions and paralysis," he "would start by sending all the books of rules for the conduct of intercollegiate athletics, including the NCAA's, to archives" and begin again with a well-written, unmistakable text for Rule 1, providing that nobody shall compete who is not a bona fide student. It might take two and one-half pages to spell that out"(223-24). Or two and a half decades. The word "student-athlete" lies at the heart of many of our problems. Why not eliminate the term entirely and speak of those who play to go to college as well as those who work to do the same as "students," if they prove worthy of the designation?

According to Thomas K. Hearn Jr., president of Wake Forest University and proponent of academic reform in the NCAA, "the character of the regulations and rules of the NCAA inhibits or even forbids the development of thoughtful ethical judgment on the part of those who participate in intercollegiate athletics. The NCAA environment dictates a circumstance in which the only question is, 'is it permitted by the rules?' Conformity to the rules has replaced ethical and moral judgment" (8; see also Chaudoin). This preoccupation with rules as opposed to critical inquiry is further evidence of the long shadow of Sylvanus Thayer just as the separation of the athletic forts from academic departments on our campuses is reminiscent of the disdain for civilians exhibited at West Point for nearly two centuries. Civilians, especially civilian faculty, tend to ask questions.

With characteristic insight of the philosopher, Hearn has identified two paradigms that help to explain the perpetual dilemma between sports and education, that of the family and that of a military model. "The basic difference is that family systems regard cooperation as the basic social necessity while the military scheme takes competition as the requirement for human organization. The metaphors of war and conflict are everywhere in sport, which glorifies competition and seeks victory over the foe in surrogate combat. . . . The aim of conflict is victory, not virtue or happiness. . . . The virtues of compassion and kindness, rooted in the family paradigm, have little place on any field of conflict. Our student athletes are soldiers on real and symbolic fields of conquest"(4). Though Hearn cites Judeo-Christian ethics as source for the moral imperative to love the "family of mankind," there is a parallel between his distinction between a family and a team in Aristotelian ethics, as I'm sure he knows. "The correct test of a man's character is what he does when he is not acting for an ulterior object, viz. when he is acting for the sake of the activity" (Hutchinson 103). An example of acting for an ulterior object would be victory in sports; of acting for the sake of activity, cooperating or loving other members of a family, immediate or extended. If athletes are soldiers of sorts, and I agree that beyond a certain point of specialization they certainly are, then the effort of the FCA and other proselytizing groups has been to make them Christian soldiers, the ideal of the service academies from the days of Sylvanus Thayer. Therefore, let us march and run and forget about walking and the lessons of the lilies of the field.

The major question facing universities is this: are sports primarily a form of art and education or of business and entertainment? Sooner or later decisions turn on differences between honor and honesty, the same dilemma that faced the Military Academy in 1951. It is no accident that the West Point cribbing scandal and the beginning of NCAA regulation of televised football occurred the same year when the long-building tension between amateurism and professionalism, between honor and honesty, peaked. It may well be that honesty will win out over the old imperial code of honor with its inherent corollary of a sound body in a sound mind, but this is not necessarily a victory for virtue, only for specialization. "In time, we may see an end to hypocrisy, i.e., the admission that it is difficult, if not impossible, to compete in "big-time" college sports and still obtain a decent education. If the sham ends, the universities will be free to amuse the public by sponsoring openly professional sports" (Guttman, *Whole New Game* 188). It is possible that many universities could go the other way, deprofessionalizing, cutting costs, establishing sane, well-balanced, in-budget programs serving the health, happiness, and education of individuals, or, perhaps, even giving up football. We could, after all, live without major college sports just as we've done quite well without major league baseball, a situation that argues for the theory of sports as a form of adiaphora, "things indifferent." Almost no help can be expected in these hard decisions from advocates of Sportianity who "have not spoken out against racism, sexism, cheating . . . or any of the other well-known abuses in the world of sport" (Eitzen and Sage 153-54). A question by *Wittenburg Door* as to whether the role of the FCA was to seek to "change athletics" brought this reply from the communications department of the FCA, which was founded in 1954 at approximately the same time as the beginning of televised sport: " 'The FCA board and officers would not see that. . . . Stick with the positive, don't deal with the evils in athletics. . . . The board would rather have us not stir the waters. Just print the good story about the good ole boy who does good things' " (ibid., 54). This sounds exactly like the credo of Billy Graham—just preach the gospel, the gospel of salvation. Triumphalists, whether in sports, war, or religion have never been noted for subtleties of thought. When, though, did television ever expect more? Meanwhile, our college athletes struggle on not as students but as soldiers and, increasingly, as soldiers of the cross, just as leading knights had always wished.

# 12

# Symbols of the Union of Caesar and Christ

The relationship between sports, war, and Christianity in our society is a troubling one since the central figure in Christianity was, as far as we know, neither athlete nor warrior in the literal sense but was instead a figurative shepherd, again as far as we know. How this figure gets transformed into a knight militant is one of the mysteries of history and is apt to remain so. Why, for instance, are there "things of Caesar" to start with? Why are not the "things of God" everywhere and for all time so evident that other kinds of things would be literally unimaginable? What seems sure is that the founder of Christianity wished for things of God, that is, things of the spirit, and for things of Caesar, not shepherd things of the world by any means but things of imperial power, to remain separate and clearly distinguishable. At West Point the distinction between things of the spirit and things of power are blurred and nowhere else in our land is the transformation of Christ from shepherd to knight more evident as a look at the academy gymnasium and the Cadet Chapel will confirm. The following lines are inscribed upon the gymnasium.

> Upon the fields of friendly strife,
> Are sown the seeds
> That, upon other fields, on other days,
> Will bear the fruits of victory. [Crane and Kiely 155]

The author is General Douglas MacArthur, the American Caesar. This quatrain serves as America's version of the alleged remark of the Duke of Wellington that the battle of Waterloo was won on the playing fields of Eton. The words have also taken on a holographic authority reminiscent of the first stone edition of the Decalogue.

Though MacArthur never played football in college, serving as manager for the Army team while a cadet, he was a recipient of a gold medal from The National Football Foundation and Hall of Fame. Never has there been a more avid advocate of the game nor a more devoted Army fan than MacArthur as seen in his comments to Pete Dawkins, Army All-American and Rhodes Scholar, about what Army football has meant to him.

> *Since our earliest gridiron victories, the story has been the talk and the boast of every campfire gathering–every barracks mess hall–every garrison assemblage of the American Army.*
>
> *In my twenty campaigns, covering more than twenty-five years of foreign service, from the Rhine to the Yalu, from Vera Cruz to Tokyo, through the muddy sludges of Europe to the blistering jungle trails of Asia, in all that welter of breathless struggle between life and death, always a central topic of discussion and of paramount interest was–will the Army team win this year?* [quoted in Schoor x-xi]

In all these years we thought the enemy was the Germans and Japanese. How surprising to discover that all along it was the Navy. I jest here in part but the rivalry between the services, symbolized by annual football competition for the Commander in Chief's Trophy between the three major academies, is sometimes no laughing matter in terms of redundancy and inefficiency of joint operations and competition for taxpayers' dollars. Knighthood for the defense of land, sea, and air does not come cheap and much of the expense is subtle almost beyond imagination.

MacArthur may be considered the heir of Theodore Roosevelt as the renowned American knight. In typical fashion of the nineteenth-century romantic revivalist, MacArthur stressed wholeness or the all-round man, not only for himself but also for those he trained. At West Point, Commandant MacArthur, instead of specialized knowledge, favored a program in which "military bearing, leadership, and personality, military efficiency, athletic performance, and cadet participation in such activities as choir or the YMCA all counted" and indeed went hand in hand (Mrozek, "Habit" 230–31). He left no doubt about the connection he saw between military efficiency and athletic performance, two essential knightly qualities.

The Cadet Chapel at the Military Academy, dedicated on 12 June 1910, during America's High Roman phase, is an ingenious marriage of war and Christianity. At the opening ceremonies, "The Corps," the cadet hymn, was sung for the first time, and the processional hymn, as the congregation moved from the old chapel to the new one, was "Onward Christian Soldiers." Not surprisingly, the service included the reading of the Twenty-fourth Psalm with its apparent affirmation of war by the Almighty, "Mighty in battle" (Pappas, *Chapel* booklet, 16). In a footnote in the Ryrie Bible, editor Charles Ryrie says that "these verses speak prophetically of the ascension of Christ after his victory over sin and death and of his coming reign as king over all the earth."

How Ryrie arrives at such a conclusion is open to question, but West Point's official commitment to Christ the King or Christ the Knight is not. The stained glass of the sanctuary symbolizes " 'the Genius of West Point' and its motto, 'Duty, Honor, and Country,' by portraying the Old Testament antetypes of Christ, who is the personification of the highest type of patriotism" (Pappas, *Chapel* booklet, 35). These antetypes are invariably warriors: Eleazor, Abishai, and Shammah (David's three companions), who illustrate duty; Gideon and Hur, who convey a sense of honor; and Jephthah, who exemplifies love of country. Christ, ergo, is not merely a warrior but a fulfillment of type. The result is a classic case of warping, the deliberate association of Christ with American patriotism or the patriotism of any country, the equation of the theological virtues of faith, hope, and charity with the knightly ones of duty, honor, and country. If Caesar is the chief of the worthies in the Academic Board Room of the Administration Building, his spirit has also been smuggled into the magnificent chapel, where his presence reigns in the stained glass celebration of every military triumph.

More correctly, it can be said that Christ and Caesar have been fused. Directly above the center door is "a Crusader's sword embedded in a cross. Just as Galahad's sword was embedded in stone which bore the inscription, 'Never shall men take me hence, but only he by whose side I ought to hang, and he shall be the best knight in the world,' so is this sword embedded in the Cross to be drawn forth by the Christian knight only in defense of those things the Cross represents, and the defeat of evil" (ibid., 27).

King Arthur is abundantly represented in carved figures above the clerestory windows on the east and west faces of the chapel. Arthur is seen finding Excalibur, donning his armor for his last battle, and receiving his fatal wound. "The last two panels on the east face show first, the Holy Grail, and, then, the knight's armor stacked for the last time. This is emblematic in that, after life's struggle is complete and the soldier's armor put aside for the last time, the Holy Grail symbolizes the reward for the Christian knight" (ibid., 29; for fuller discussion, see Pappas, *Cadet Chapel* book). In contrast to Christ the Knight, our society's symbology offers almost no encouragement for one to follow Christ the Shepherd. The only symbol is a staff cut from the woods (Walt Whitman's sign) which, in a society preoccupied with power and prestige, carries almost no glory at all.

The victories of Old Testament warriors are abundantly dramatized in the Cadet Chapel's window scenes, but two of the ancient worthies are commemorated in individual windows sponsored by classes, David by the class of 1837 and Joshua by the class of 1858. Still the chapel is not "Jewish" by any means or even ecumenical. There are a Catholic chapel and a Jewish place of worship at West Point, but there is only one "real" chapel–the Protestant one (Galloway and Johnson 61).

For most of the history of West Point, worship attendance has been required: "Because the Military Academy accepts responsibility for the total development of the cadet–mental, physical, moral, and spiritual–and because biblical faith is one of the foundation stones of honor and integrity, every cadet is required to attend the chapel of his faith each Sunday" (ibid., 62). When one cadet (unsuccessfully) challenged the mandatory worship services in 1969, he encountered strong behind-the-scenes opposition from President Richard Nixon (ibid.), also noted as a sports fan. Obligatory worship for American soldiers began in 1775 and was abolished in 1916

(Atkinson 99–100). For West Point knights, the ties proved stronger and longer-lasting. Begun by Sylvanus Thayer in 1817, obligatory attendance did not end at West Point until 1973. At West Point on 14 January, following the decision of federal courts that compulsory chapel at the service academies violated religious freedom under the First Amendment, it was estimated that about 50 percent of the Catholics and 30 percent of the Protestants were in attendance (Ellis and Moore 218).

As expected, most of the chief chaplains, by tradition civilian, have been Protestant, particularly Episcopalian. "With its emphasis upon authority, ceremony, and mission," Episcopalianism "had long been considered the denomination most appropriate for Army officers. Until World War II, nine out of every ten generals were Protestant and about half were Episcopal. In the nineteenth century Catholics had been barred from worshipping on post. In recent years, the increased size and egalitarianism of the Army had eroded that elitism considerably, and Protestant sects were gradually melding into the ecumenical worship of what was sometimes called 'the Army God'" (Atkinson 99). Behind the so-called good-natured rivalry of the Army–Notre Dame game lay the history of the religious wars of Europe. We should not, however, jump to the conclusion that football is a good, clean subliminal substitute for war.

At the Naval Academy the same connections between religion and war are immediately evident. Worship attendance somewhere at the Naval Academy has been obligatory throughout most of the academy's history, most midshipmen choosing to worship in the Chapel, generally recognized as the most beautiful building in the Naval Academy Yard. Built originally according to the plans for Grant's Tomb and later enlarged, it is, like the chapel at West Point, a "symbol of the ideals of honor, loyalty, courage, and duty in the service of God and country." The two stained glass windows facing the altar portray "Sir Galahad, the symbol of the highest motives of the Service; the other is the Commission Invisible" (see *Reef Points* 55). Three stained glass windows are dedicated to three great admirals, Admiral David Dixon Porter, Admiral David Glasgow Farragut, and Rear Admiral William Thomas Sampson. Below is the crypt of John Paul Jones, surrounded by eight columns of Pyrenean marble.

The chapels at the service academies are not the only places of worship where knighthood is enshrined. The Episcopal Cathedral of St. John the Divine in New York City contains a sports bay, formally called Hubert's Chapel, where Hobey Baker is memorialized in granite, along with Walter Camp, Christy Mathewson, and Bob Wrens, as representatives of sporting ideals (Willis and Wettan 201–3). Baker was a football and hockey hero at Princeton who, in the words of F. Scott Fitzgerald, was "an ideal worthy of everything in my enthusiastic admiration yet consummated and expressed in a human being who stood within ten feet of me" (Davies 135). So impressed with Baker was Fitzgerald that, as John Davies observes, he patterned Allenby and to some extent Amory after Baker in *This Side of Paradise.*

The words of MacArthur on the gym at West Point and the granite statue of Baker and other athlete-heroes in the cathedral are evidence of the old school ties with duty, honor, country, and God. Bob Wrenn, Harvard quarterback and tennis champion, was praised repeatedly by Theodore Roosevelt for his athletic ability and service in Cuba. Also a veteran of a foreign war, World War I, and a noted Christian was Christy Mathewson, one of the great pitchers. "In 1913 he pitched 68 consecutive innings without walking a man . . . In our national mythology he occupies a place alongside Frank Merriwell and Dink Stover" (Yardley 70).

Walter Camp, who picked Baker on his 1911 team, was not a knight of combat but definitely one in character and behavior. Time after time in testimonies given in honor of the Father of American Football, the metaphors of chivalry are invoked as well as the words of King David, St. Paul, and the supposedly amateur philosophy of the Greeks. Baker, in Fitzgerald's view, was "an amateur and a gentleman and a sportsman," and so was Walter Camp, at least in the opinion of his admirers (Powel 199–201). He was said to be fond of rising at banquets and quoting Thackeray's stanza from "The End of Play":

> Who misses or who gains the prize
> Go, lose or conquer as you can;
> But if you fail or if you rise
> Be each, pray God, a gentleman.
> [ibid., 199, quoted]

We know now that Greek sport was far more commercialized (see D.C. Young) than Camp imagined and that knighthood in practice, as opposed to literary representation, was a system of rape and pillage, but Camp apparently was sincere in his belief in amateurism. Just as Stagg refused to exploit the story of his life, so Camp refused to exploit his "Daily Dozen" exercises used by naval recruits in World War I because he did not want to be one of those "woolly-headed physical culturists." He was instead an idealist of the sentimental variety.

> Camp was intensely romantic in spirit, and . . . he had only to close his eyes to see the lists and the barriers where champions rode to unhorse their rivals, with only fame and glory for reward. From those gallant competitions he saved as much romance and courage and glamor as he could, and wove these qualities into the game of football. His insistence that the code of honor must be transferred from the knighthood of old on to the modern football field was as enduring a contribution to the development of the sport, if a less visible one, as any of the rules he caused to be enacted for the regulation of the game.
>
> Football became in his hands a game of honor as well as of pluck, a knightly game as well as a manly one. [ibid., 201-2]

In all his talk about rules and honor, a favorite term of knights, Camp may have had a problem with honesty or at least with openness. "Until 1905 Yale was paying for athletic tutors out of a secret fund kept under Walter Camp's control. Yale, though, was only one of a number of institutions which tried to keep its athletes academically eligible using professional means" (Smith 170). Charles Eliot said Camp was "deficient in moral sensibility—a trouble not likely to be cured at his age." To Eliot, Camp was "directly responsible for the degradation and ruin of the game" (quoted in ibid., 200).

Camp's emphasis upon the idea of the gentleman carried with it exclusiveness of all kinds common to his day—social, cultural, and racial. As admirable as Camp sounds regarding fair play and sportsmanship, he epitomizes the type of refined chauvinism that has been more entrenched and more difficult to deal with than that of the redneck variety. His code of the amateur separated gentlemen from players, the Ivy League tournament form the earthy play of common folk. The barriers that Camp implicitly erected in his knightly order were the same ones that came under attack at Yale in Owen Johnson's *Stover*, a book more about honesty than honor.

The sports bay of St. John's suggests a vital connection between sports and religion stretching back to biblical authority, as seen in the final design of the chapel window with scenes of Jacob wrestling with the Angel, David conquering Goliath, and the commandment of St. Paul to "run a good race" (Willis and Wittan 201). Notice how the literalness of Paul's words distorts, almost reverses, his meaning. "Interspersed between the biblical scenes are twenty-eight representations from modern sport" (ibid., 201-2). In the formal assignment of the sports bay in 1928, Episcopal Bishop William Thomas Manning justified the union of sports and religion by arguing that (1) the bay "is a witness against the mistaken view . . . expressed in the Puritan Sabbath and the old Blue Laws," (2) "it proclaims God is interested in . . . our games and pleasures as well as our work and our progress . . . , and (3) it "is a symbol of the place of youth in the life of the church" (ibid., 199-201). From its inception the chapel has been more than a shrine for competitors before contests; it also hosts the weddings and funerals of former athletes (ibid., 203).

In its use in rites of passage, matrimony and apotheosis, the cathedral perpetuates the solemn ceremony so essential to knighthood. "Following the Persian Gulf War, St. John's paid homage to those who had lost their lives, including the thousands of Iraqi civilians and soldiers. The interfaith service incorporated prayers, music, and readings by Generals Norman Schwarzkopf and Colin Powell as well as Secretary of Defense Dick Cheney" (d'Aulaire 42). At St. John's where "anything goes" in an atmosphere of "radical hospitality" what might be called shepherd events are also held regularly, including since 1985 the Annual Blessing of Animals. In 1991, "after a sermon . . . by Senator Albert Gore, the great bronze doors were opened and in came the official entourage of beasts that had been trucked in from far and wide. The church fell silent as the creatures made their way to the altar, among them an elephant, a hedgehog, a pig, a particularly grumpy-looking camel, and a 3.5-billion-year-old rock from Australia covered with bacteria and reverently borne on a pillow. They were followed by a man in a choir robe, pushing a wheelbarrow and shouldering a shovel 'in case one of the animals decides to make an offering to God.' Bishop Grein blessed them one and all" (ibid.). Receiving animals at the altar probably makes as much sense as enshrining athletes in marble in the chapel, but in any event one must ask whatever happened to *eutrapelia* (well-turningness), in this case between cathedral and athletic fields and ball courts on the one hand and cathedral and jungle, desert and pig farm on the other? Certainly animals are God's creatures too, but this does not give humans the right to make them captive in places where they show no inclination to enter such as zoos and churches.

The individual assisting the architect in planning the original window of the sport bay was R. Tait McKenzie, the famous sculptor who was himself a renaissance man. Also charged with designing the altar of the sports bay, he died before completing either task (Willis and Wittan 201). McKenzie did live to complete another memorial vividly connecting sports, war, and religion in honor of another Philadelphian who, like Hobey Baker, was killed in World War I. It is described in detail in a McKenzie biography:

> *The Altar of Dedication* commemorates Captain Howard C. McCall, one of the first American officers killed in France. . . . He was a football man at college, and a friend and student of the sculptor. This memorial, unlike any other of McKenzie's work, is executed in white marble, and forms the front of the elaborate altar of Siena marble for the Church of the Saviour in Philadelphia. The side panels represent St. Michael, clad as a French soldier, with his foot upon Apolyon, and St. George, dressed as an English officer, bayoneting a wivern or dragon. Behind St. Michael is the figure of Joan of Arc, presenting in dedication her sheathed sword . . . and behind St. George a woman's figure with upraised hand symbolizing dedication. The central panel shows the Christ with outstretched arms. [Hussey 631]

Though the religious theme is not as evident in the statues and statuettes McKenzie made of other Canadian and American heroes, such as Captain Guy Drummond, Lieutenant Colonel G.H. Baker, and Lieutenant Norton Dawnes, there is no doubt that they boldly represent Christian knighthood. Each man was an athlete and a war hero. Thomas Wentworth Higginson would have been mighty happy to know that at last the military saints, St. George and St. Michael were reemerging.

As in the service academies and in the Ivy League, football in other parts of the country was invested with manliness and godliness. At the University of the South at Sewanee, Tennessee, 150 miles from Rugby, where Episcopalian Thomas Hughes, the author *of Tom Brown's School Days* (1857) and the *Manliness of Christ* (1879), attempted to establish a Utopian community for young Englishmen deprived of inheritance by laws of primogeniture, a shrine depicts the same values stressed by the sports bay in St. John's. The dean of the college, W. Brown Patterson, described for me the stained glass windows in the University Chapel:

> The window is one of those depicting significant figures in the arts and sciences. More often than not these figures are known for Christian interests as well. One of the windows depicts a figure in the traditional vestments of an Episcopal or Anglican bishop. He is holding a football (marked '02) in one hand and a book—presumably the Book of Common Prayer—in the other. A baseball bat is leaning against the frame of the window; a baseball is at the bishop's feet. Over his shoulder is the title Athletics. At the bottom of the window is the identification of the bishop: Bishop Henry Disbrow Phillips. . . . "He ministered to men with all his might."

In the aesthetic depiction in stone or glass celebrating the relation between sports and religion and in the correlation between modern athlete-military heroes and ancient warriors and muscular saints, Episcopalians, considering their long dominant influence at West Point, were undisputed leaders in the imperial phase of our culture. There are at least three reasons for this: (1) the long alliance between the Anglican church and chivalry dating back in America to Jamestown (2) a long tradition of a richly symbolic ritual and (3) a cathedral consciousness that traditionally has differed sharply with more Puritan attitudes of other Protestant denominations in the United States and especially with the campground tradition of the Methodists which to Episcopalians would seem both unhealthy and desperate. Even today a statue of an athlete, no matter how famous or popular, even a statue of Elvis, would be as out of place in both mainline and backwoods Protestant churches as an Uzi under a Christmas tree, which may not be a good example since apparently the majority of congress would not see any contradiction in such a scene. In any event the Puritan injunction against "graven images," as narrow as that attitude may seem at times to Anglicans, may be the last defense against the final absorption of Protestantism by the Church of Sport. Weight rooms and softball tournaments and testimony by living athletes—yes. Even a vespertine video of the Super Bowl followed by a buffet—but graven images of stone or metal? Not yet. To their credit and good sense, Episcopalians, with the rise of commercialism of sports, have ceased to sanctify the athlete in stone, glass, or otherwise. In the interest of history, however, it must be remembered that Congregationalists (Harvard and Yale), Presbyterians (Princeton) and Episcopalians (Sewanee) helped to get us into our sports dilemma to start with.

Once a power in southern football, Sewanee gained legendary distinction by winning twelve games in one year, in Yostian fashion holding all opponents except Auburn scoreless; five of the games were won in six days during a road trip through Texas, Louisiana, and Mississippi. A charter member of the Southeastern Conference, founded in 1933, Sewanee withdrew in 1940 after losing forty-four consecutive conference games (Givens 115). This transformation to amateur status alone speaks volumes about the shift in the South from an emphasis on academics to power football and the exploitation of the athlete for the benefit of coaches, with winning rather than education of players becoming the most important thing.

How different the situation at Sewanee is from that at Notre Dame, where power football enjoyed increasing significance. Rockne, as he said, learned everything about football from Amos Alonzo Stagg and Yale and then beat the WASPs at their own game: the great defeat of Army in 1913 induced many Catholics to begin praying for their team on a weekly basis (McCullum and Castner 14). Where Episcopalians feared to tread, Irish Catholics rushed in like the Baptists (Baylor) and Methodists (SMU), and glorified for the masses (the subway alumni) what eastern and southern aristocrats esteemed so highly—the knightly ideal. High church "English" aristocrats have paid a certain price by withdrawing from the fray. While Episcopalians enjoy the reputation of intellectuality, they suffer the image of wimpiness. At the Naval Academy, the Episcopal Church is known as "Catholic Junior Varsity," the terms of reference being not intellect but power, form, and influence.

The Notre Dame memorial to knighthood and the ideal of the all-around man is far more obvious than the isolated picture on the mountain at Sewanee and far more elaborate and far-reaching. It stands at the heart of America in honor of America's archetypal football coach, Knute Rockne. Thomas J. Schlereth describes the memorial:

> The Athletic facility contains a swimming pool, handball and squash courts, a solarium, apparatus rooms, basketball gyms, the golf shop, various athletic offices, and . . . the Institute for Urban studies. Over the building's front entrance are two stone bas-relief plaques honoring Robert de La Salle and Leopold Pokagon; over other entrances are the seals of the United States and the University, the coats of arms of Norway (Rockne's home), France (origin of the C.S.C. or Congregation of Holy Cross) and West Point and Annapolis (traditional Notre Dame athletic opponents). Inside is a Gothic foyer, dedicated to "the Rock." Here in glass-enclosed cases displaying the numerous athletic trophies won by Rockne are the other artifacts of Notre Dame's football prowess in the 1920s. Over the shrine broods a bronze bust of Rockne done by Nison Tregor in 1940. [144]

Army, Navy, Notre Dame—as the Rockne Memorial suggests, there was almost a mystique about this trinity. The names suggest a cohesiveness of church and state, Protestantism and Catholicism, knighthood and priesthood, a certain all-around excellence reflective of the old invidious dictum "Either a soldier or a priest be, all else is mediocrity." That they were bastions of white male exclusiveness was generally ignored, considering the national sense of excellence (*arete*) they symbolized. Even though the knightly ideal they collectively represented in sports has been democratized to some extent, something else has happened that is not so commendable, and again, the change has to do not with improvement of social rules but with the increase in public prizes. In many ways the democratization of American sports since World War II, still not complete by any means, is unrelated to the proliferating commercialism that accompanied it. Certainly the latter is not the result of the former. The "something" that happened to Army, Navy, and Notre Dame was not, then, loss of "racial purity" on the football field and male exclusiveness in the classroom but loss of the relative purity of the ideal of sacrifice and service, an ideal both pagan and Christian that lies at the heart of all three institutions, and that may well vary inversely with emphasis upon winning ball games.

There is no coat of arms of the Military Academy in the shrine of knighthood that I now wish to discuss, but the academy's influence is far more pervasive at this shrine than at Notre Dame. Directly or indirectly, West Point has had an extensive influence upon our entire educational system, in sports, physical education, military drill (ROTC programs), technology, and engineering. The military mindset is still the prized attitude of college presidents and executives, generals in pinstripes. In the classroom, the Socratic method (civilian method) wherein the student is taught to track knowledge by means of the question technique is almost extinct, while the lecture and regurgitative method is itself enshrined. One, the Socratic, is creative and playful; the other, Caesarian, is sterile and doctrinaire. The symbol of the authoritarian method is the guard dog, the German shepherd, an ironic choice. The symbol of the other is the coonhound, who sings as he tracks, full to the brim with the joy of scenting and seeking.

In May 1970 Neyland Stadium, the shrine of knighthood in east Tennessee, took on special religious and military significance as the site of the Knoxville Crusade of Billy Graham. Joining him on the platform was President Richard Nixon, and though Graham denied any political intent, insisting only on spiritual motivation, the occasion was a perfect opportunity for Nixon to appear in public following the recent killings at Kent State and repeated protests against the war in Vietnam. Graham's advisers also thought that the event provided "just the right touch" in a traditionally Republican section of Tennessee and the conservative South to boost the Senate chances of Bill Brock against Democrat Albert Gore Sr. and to help derail

George Wallace's troublesome presidential ambitions. During Nixon's appearance, the Fellowship of Christian Athletes joined with the Secret Service to protect the honored visitors against a band of protesters (inside) who responded to Graham's scriptural plea for obedience and Nixon's speech with chants of "Bullshit! Bullshit!" The hecklers too resorted to the Bible, displaying placards that recalled scriptural injunctions against killing. They called for an end to the war and knelt on the sidelines in memory of those who had died in it. In spite of the disturbances, the crusade from Nixon's perspective was a success; later in the evening, after Air Force One had landed in California, Henry Kissinger called Graham from San Clemente to thank the evangelist for including the president in the service (Martin 369–70).

Nothing like the Graham crusade had ever been seen before in east Tennessee, and nothing like it has happened since. Championship football, it should be remembered, made it all possible. Dianne Barker, in *Billy Graham in Big Orange Country*, provides a picture of the numbers involved in the operation. The petition asking Graham to come to Knoxville was signed by 129,000 people and was over a mile long. Some 40 people constituted the delegation to get Graham to come, "an effort that culminated 17 years of praying and hoping for the event" (6). Graham preached to 552,000 in the ten-day crusade. *The East Tennessee Crusade News*, a monthly publication with a circulation of 90,000, pictured Neyland Stadium as "a vast arena where the cross of Christ will be lifted up nightly and Jesus Christ presented as the savior of the world" (Barker 36). Says Barker, "God was at work in East Tennessee. His holy spirit came and dwelt among us, and we beheld his glory" (8). The field had been covered with artificial turf. The stadium was described as an "open air cathedral." Johnny Cash brought along the entire cast of his television show, including the Statler Brothers, the Carter family, and the Tennessee Three. Cash warned youth about the danger of drugs (30–31). A poll at the time reported that "President Nixon is considered the Number 1 person in the world and Billy Graham the Number 2. For the first time the top two men in the world appeared together on the same platform" (60). Said Nixon in his introductory remarks, "We can have what can be described as complete cleanliness and yet have a sterile life unless we have the spirit, a spirit that cannot come from a man in government, a spirit that will be represented by the man who follows me" (61).

Several Christian athletes gave testimonies: Charlie Rosenfelder, a member of "God's Team"; Coach Raleigh Wymon, athletic director at Knoxville's Austin East High School; John Westbrook, the first black football player to play in the Southwest Conference (for Baylor University); and John Keller, "a giant of a player," who said, "I wrapped my arms around Jesus and I told him I loved him and I was willing to do anything I could for him" (ibid., 66–67). Also on hand was Bill Pierson, "a husky football player from San Diego State College with a contract to play for the New York Jets. Bill was invited to Knoxville as a guest of Dr. Graham, who learned about Bill through the newspaper. When a group of about 150 dissident students attempted to lower the American flag at half-mast at his California School in protest of the war in Vietnam, Bill stood them off singlehandedly" (68).

Graham took time out during the crusade to play golf with Dr. Andrew Holt, president of the university, and with Charles Trentham, pastor of Knoxville's First Baptist Church (ibid., 87). "In every way the Crusade was a complete success. Total contributions during the meetings surpassed the $300,000 mark. Thousands streamed down the aisles to make their personal commitment to Christ . . . 12,306 all told" (8). "Who can tell the true effect of this great crusade in Big Orange Country? By means of Television the nation heard the message of hope and salvation in Jesus Christ as some 300 TV stations carried four of the services on prime evening time in June" (87). Some 200 demonstrators heckled President Nixon during his fourteen-minute speech. "It was the first time in history," Barker said, "that a chief executive spoke at a public religious gathering" (7). Tennessee head coach Bill Battle stood "up for Christ and Country and . . . led the Pledge to Allegiance to the American Flag at the Saturday Memorial Day Services" (65).

The next year Battle was fired by the university in spite of a 7–4 record and in spite of being one of the winningest coaches in the school's history so that Neyland's former player, Johnny Majors, could return to his alma mater. Bill Battle was not, it was deemed, "successful" enough. Neither, eventually, was Majors, who in the early 1990s returned to the University of Pittsburgh, where he had previously won a National Championship. Love of God and country will carry one only so far in Knoxville, where for coaches, winning ball games is the only thing.

In Knoxville, as in South Bend, knighthood had been brought to the common folk and, appropriately blessed by the leading evangelist and authorized by the commander in chief, himself a fan who constantly drew messages and morals from the world of sports. As Billy Sunday would have wished, dissenters were not welcomed. Beside Nixon on the platform, the impeccably dressed Graham was a magnificent knight himself, not a "rube" like Billy Sunday but a resplendent promoter of sports, a celebrated lover of God, and an eternal consort of the rich and powerful of his time.

To be sure, the charm of Notre Dame, West Point, Annapolis, and other such shrines to knighthood is still contagious. After a televised game at South Bend on a late fall afternoon, something of the magic of Notre Dame can still be seen and felt in the light glow permeating the campus at dusk, a golden time around the Golden Dome and the "Touchdown Jesus," the same feeling the chapels at West Point and Annapolis can fetch in spring or fall when colors are right and the mind off guard. In the same vein, consider this masterpiece of nostalgia describing West Point in 1862 by Major E.D. Mansfield, class of 1819:

> No imagination is necessary to clothe it with hues of poetry; no books to recall the lost pages of history; no labored eulogies to bring up the memories of the dead. You can no more forget them than you can the pilgrims when standing by the Rock at Plymouth. Yon gray and moss-covered ruin was once the fortress of the Revolution. Yon scarcely perceptible pile of stones marks the spot where its soldiers were hutted in the winter. . . . Yon little valley under the shadows of the mountain recalls the illustrious name of Washington. Yon blue mountain-top tells of the beacon fires he lit. All around are memories; all around are sacred spots. If the Greek remembers Marathon; if the Jew lingers at Jerusalem, or the Christian pilgrim grows warm at Bethlehem, so should the American remember West Point.
> [*Military Schools* 750]

Almost we are persuaded that Camelot lives and that knighthood is forever in flower. The romance, though, has faded, and the villain, as always, is power and money. We should look carefully at our shrines and see what they might tell us about our future as well as our past. We may still be able to change without tearing down a statue or breaking a pane of stained glass.

# 13

# Power in the Sweat

The YMCA, like Protestant denominations, West Point, and the colleges, was split wide open by the Civil War. The more militant associations turned a deaf ear to those few associations that pleaded for Christian love and brotherhood. "Many of the country's Associations," said one observer, "were entirely broken up, almost every member responding to the call of Abraham Lincoln to go forth and stand by the government" (Hopkins 85). Some associations produced entire companies from their membership and fanned the political flames with theological self-righteousness. During the fighting the Richmond Association featured a speaker who gave an address titled "The Southern Church Justified in Its Support of the South in the Present War." In 1862 the New York Association featured a speech at Cooper Union by parson William G. Brownlow of east Tennessee, who spoke on "The Irreligious Character of the Rebellion" (ibid., 7). Like the leaders of the Union and Confederate armies trained at West Point, the YMCA believed in Christ and exercises, but it would also fight both for and against slavery.

The YMCA also provided an institutional framework for a new type of evangelism after the war, one much more sophisticated and organized than the camp meeting affairs of an earlier time. The Second Great Awakening of 1787–1805 was a rural phenomenon; revivalism after the mid–nineteenth century was directed toward the cities, where the YMCAs usually pitched camp. Some of the techniques of frontier evangelism still applied in the city mission, and the man who made them work best in a new wilderness of American cities was Dwight L. Moody. In Moody the pincer forces of the muscular Christian movement came together, the frontier tradition reaching back to John Wesley, and the urban YMCA tradition also reaching back to England to George Williams. What Great Britain could not do through arms—suppress the American Revolution and maintain British dominance in the New World—it did indirectly through evangelism, the YMCA, and the export of athletics. These elements blended together into the model North American WASP, who carried upon his broad shoulders more than a smattering of Prussian and Napoleonic militarism. The problem with American evangelism in the post–Civil War era was that it made of religion a commodity, as it remains for many sport-loving evangelists to this day. For all his heralded virtues, Moody kept religious showmanship alive and worked unfailingly on the principle that whatever would get people into church was acceptable. "He would try anything, he spared himself nothing, and he never let up," one biographer noted (Weisberger 184).

Born in 1837 in Northfield, Massachusetts, Moody was inured to poverty and hardship and as a child drove cattle to and from a pasture for a penny a week. Leaving the farm, he became a shoe salesman on Court Street in Boston; after a conversion experience in the shoe store, he became the most noted winner of souls in American history. He was the Horatio Alger of religion, but money was not his aim, though he made so much it became an embarrassment to him. The royalties of $1.25 million from his hymnal with Ira D. Sankey, his musician, he poured into his schools at Mount Herman and Northfield, the Bible Institute, and the church at Chicago, where Moody had settled after leaving Boston. When he died, he had only five hundred dollars, the repayment of an old loan he had apparently forgotten (Loud 234).

After his conversion, Moody's career became intertwined with the YMCA. He said he owed more to the YMCA than to any other agency for his training in Christian work (Hopkins 187–88), and the indebtedness of the YMCA to him was equally deep. With another Massachusetts farm boy, John V. Farwell, Moody extended the facilities of the Chicago Association in the direction of mission and Sunday school work. From his experience at Northfield came the college summer conference, the student volunteer movement, and the American YMCA's World Service (187–89). Perhaps the greatest contribution Moody made to the movement was "economical and spiritual." Wherever he preached he brought together Protestant leaders and YMCA leaders, creating unity of purpose and promoting the goals of the YMCA and spreading its message. Before the Y secretaries in 1879, he publicly endorsed the fourfold idea of the movement: "There are many ways of reaching young men," he said. "I would recommend a gymnasium, classes, medical lectures, social receptions, music, and all unobjectionable agencies" (188, quoted).

Moody employed other measures to reach the unsaved:

> He kept his pockets full of maple sugar on his excursions into the alleys [of Chicago], and when word got out, children gravitated to him, after which it was an easy matter to get them into the school. It was not always so simple to get the consent of the parents. Many of the fathers were burly loafers with a wholesome distrust of slumming Christians bringing gifts and respectability. A good many, too, were Irish Catholics, who were all too willing to strike a blow for the faith by pummelling a Protestant heretic looking for converts among them. Now, Moody himself was a figure to command respect, with a physique of a logger or stevedore, but fighting was against his Christian principles. A mere look at Moody discouraged a potential attacker, but more than once he went sprinting through back streets, dodging barrels, carts and boxes, with a bellowing Irishman in pursuit. "If they persecute you one place, flee into another," was a favorite text with him. [Weisberger 1851]
>
> Weisberger adds that Moody got a pony to cover more ground, and thus he rode, the new model circuit rider, through the urban wilderness (ibid., 187).

Though his frame was far from athletic, Moody himself used games or contests to reach potential converts. At the Northfield conference of the college delegates of the YMCA, an event that Moody hoped would begin to turn the great state and national universities into "Christian Institutions," he demonstrated clearly that in spite of his solemn calling he had a sense of humor. While the mornings focused on prayers and lectures,

> the afternoons were devoted chiefly to recreational activities. Despite his huge bulk, the evangelist threw himself into the games and sports of the students. Foot races were his specialty, with the proviso, laughingly added, that all his young challengers had to carry ballast equal to his own considerable poundage. In a later conference he took a special interest in Amos Alonzo Stagg, then a delegate from Yale and later a famous football coach, whose athletic prowess was already much in evidence. Spiritual enthusiasm lasted even into the closing moments of his first student conference, and Moody as usual was at the center of things. [Findlay 347]

The interplay between Moody and the YMCA helped to ensure the success of both, at least for a time. Yet Moody, like Stagg and Gulick, would experience a rebuttal of many of his efforts on behalf of the YMCA, especially ironic in Moody's case, since he made enormous contributions to the organization. In the heyday of the YMCA, Moody's enthusiasm for preaching the Gospel to all the world had generally coincided with the organization's aims, but by the 1890s the YMCA's emphasis upon personal evangelism was weakening, replaced by the new enthusiasm for secular services and facilities, which of course grew out of the recapitulation and acculturation theories of Gulick and others.

The debate came to a head in Chicago, and recreation and sports were at the heart of it. His bulk notwithstanding, Moody believed in a sound body and a sound mind, but never for a moment did he entertain the idea of Gulick and others that sports were a means of inculcating moral training. For Moody they were a way to reach young people, to get young people into the church. The means of conversion were and always would be not the body but the Word—prayer, lecture, Sunday school, and Bible study. In the midst of innovation Moody kept looking to the past, calling for the need for the old-time religion. He was as little impressed by play theory as by the new liberal theology. He was not interested in building character but in saving souls, and he dismissed any theology or physiology that countered that fundamental belief.

By the nineties Moody was out of step with the YMCA leadership in Chicago as well as the national organization. He could not accept the new ideas of science or religion and the new organization and approaches they called for. He made his position clear at a conference to discuss his doctrinal differences with the YMCA. "I am an old man," he said, "too old to change and positive in my convictions." Moody's irrational refusal to entertain new opinions, his intransigence in matters of orthodox doctrine, spelled the end of his career with the Chicago YMCA, which now virtually disowned him (Findlay 405). Moody's work in the Y was undone in part by Gulick, despite the fact that both men professed to believe essentially in the same goals. Only the routes differed.

If we look at the logo of the YMCA and seek figures to represent spirit, mind, and body, we could find none more appropriate than the three in Chicago—Moody, Robert M. Hutchins, and Stagg—all of whom exercised a profound influence not only upon Chicago but indeed upon American culture at large. All believed in a principle of wholeness, but their emphases differed. While Moody was not averse to using athletes for purposes of proselytism, he showed a very un-Stagglike attitude in his letters to his son Will, who was trying out for the scrub football team at Yale: "It seems to me like running a great risk of being crippled for life for the sake of an half hour's fun and exercise" (ibid., 378).

Moody, Hutchins, and Stagg illustrate the dilemma of American ideals. Hutchins put much stock in great books (humanism), and Moody put all stock in the Bible (fundamentalism). Stagg believed both in the pagan ideal, a sound mind and a sound body, and the Christian ideal of love, but as a coach he showed behavior at times not entirely conducive to either. We may speak of the three as Mr. Evangelist, Mr. Great Books, and Mr. Football; more than a brook continues to separate what each stood for individually when compared with the others. Today "Mr. Evangelist" and "Mr. Football" have joined hands and left "Mr. Great Books" (also read "Mr. Secular Humanist") out in the cold, where his legacy hangs by a thread.

Hutchins shared friendship and many philosophies with Mortimer J. Adler. Adler, a true believer in great books, failed to graduate from Columbia, not because of his ideas but because he refused to attend physical education classes that were required for graduation. Later as a graduate student in psychology, he became the third Jew on the Columbia faculty (W.H. McNeill 35). Hutchins had something of the same aversion to athletics and exercises. In 1939, during the height of the controversy over football at the University of Chicago, Hutchins wisecracked that whenever he felt the need for exercise, his policy was to lie down until he felt better; this remark did not endear him to angry sportswriters (ibid., 97). The son of a Presbyterian minister, Hutchins remained "a preacher at heart" and in 1936 even called for "an evangelistic movement." "Its object was 'the conversion of individuals . . . to a true conception of general education. . . . I despair of converting our graduates and trustees,' Hutchins wrote early in November, 1939, from believing 'the excellence of a university is determined by its football scores,' but he vowed to continue the good fight" (Lester, "Rise" 254–55). Like Adler's, Hutchins's texts were the classics, especially Greek classics, and he left it to others to carry on the athletic tradition of the Greeks. This tradition, in Adler and Hutchins's view, had become warped, as evidenced by the growing commercialism of college football. Through their works on the great books curriculum, says William McNeill, Adler and Hutchins "had a powerful afterburn at Chicago and, after 1937, at St. John's in Annapolis, Maryland as well." Across the street from St. John's is the U.S. Naval Academy, which exhibits another kind of history entirely. Appropriately the two Annapolis schools are called Athens and Sparta.

Chicago was also the setting for a spate of "What Would Jesus Do?" books, published in the last decade of the nineteenth century. These books were designed to provide a model of conduct and success for young and old. Emphasizing a social gospel, they endeavored to measure the material progress of civilization using Scripture as a touchstone. The most prominent were *If Christ Came to Chicago: A Plea for the Union of All Who Love in the Service of All Who Suffer!* (1894) by the London journalist William T. Stead, *If Jesus Came to Boston* (1895) by Edward E. Hale, and *In His Steps: What Would Jesus Do?* (1896) by Charles M. Sheldon. These certainly were not great books such as Hutchins could recommend, but they were certainly popular. Sheldon's was among the most widely read books of all time. All of them were reminders of the contrast between the simple message of the Gospel, love, and the material success that the modern world had come to worship; but they also championed a new commitment to the improvement of the lives of all, not just a few.

Stead's book is even compelling in places, filled with facts and recommendations. The problem in Chicago (and elsewhere) in Stead's view was "lack of faith in God" plus an "every man for himself ethic." The solution was equally simple but difficult to implement: a revival of "civic faith" or "a civic church" was needed, "a banding together of citizens for the public good" (343). "For God is love and this service is sacrifice of self in helping others" (444). Reform was called for because the Catholic Church in Stead's view had forgotten its social and human responsibility. "The evils which afflict the city as the result of our forgetting God fall with heaviest weight upon the poorest citizens. The majority of these belong to Archbishop Feehan's flock. Yet so far as they are concerned, he might as well be the Archbishop of Timbuctoo as Archbishop of Chicago" (267).

Stead's book created much controversy, and book distributors refused to sell it in Chicago. Since it listed the houses of ill repute in the city, some felt the book would become a guide to fornication instead of a warning against it. While the book was not banned in Boston, it did create "much alarm" and spurred another type of response from Edward E. Hale, who wanted "to present another picture," an obvious effort to show Jesus that there was much in America to appreciate. In Chicago, says the narrator of *If Jesus Came to Boston*, one Dr. Primrose, "they took the saviour into very bad places. I could do it here. Hells and slums and dives,–opium, gambling, adultery, and murder,–I could show it all to him here, as I could have showed it to him in Jerusalem or Tiberias, or as they can in Chicago now. But I could show him other things, too, which I could not have shown him in Jerusalem or Nazareth or Bethlehem– and they could have done so there" (6).

To make up for what Jesus did not see in Chicago, Hale brings him over on an ocean liner and places before him "such marvels" as books and telephones, which he took "as though they were a matter of course" (12). This savior, though, is just the type to appreciate progress, for he himself is a man of the world, ready to hold his own. "He had that firm, strong look that you have seen among the Druses. Tall–six feet high,–as dark as some Italians in complexion, this charming smile I tell you of, and a perfect sympathy as he listened. Strong? Yes, as Julius Caesar; but affectionate, almost caressing" (8). We see in this passage from Hale a major problem with the "Jesus books," the familiar two-heart trope of the European knight. Hale in fact is echoing the Nietzschean ideal of the Roman Caesar with the heart of Christ; this combination–as old as the watchdog metaphor in Plato–is a warped dream at best and an unimaginable nightmare at worst, for the knight's soft, second heart is a myth that merely helps conceal and excuse the pitiless triumphalism of competitive manliness.

Stead's work focuses upon the need for a social gospel, but Hale concentrates on the person and his tour of Boston and its wonders, such as the well-stocked bookcases with glass doors at the YWCA! Hale's Jesus is on a particular mission to America to find a "lost" friend and his family but–guess what? "It was clear that he was used to success, and he meant to succeed. 'Legions of people to help, you know.' he said" (ibid., 9). Here is the first connection between a physical representation of Christ in America and the idea of success that I have found, but many more followed. The next milestone in the evolution of that doctrine is Bruce Barton's *The Man Nobody Knows* (1925), which, says Sinclair Lewis in *Gideon Planish*, "inspired a generation and enriched an age." According to Lewis, Barton proved that "Christ Jesus was not a rebel or a peasant, but a society gent, a real sport, a press agent and the founder of modern business" (179). Lewis called the book that celebrated Jesus' manliness an "epistle to the Babbitts," but it was an epistle fully anticipated in Hale's *If Jesus Came to Boston*. The Man Nobody Knows is the same stalwart gentleman in Hale's book who hails from "the east of the Mediterranean."

Instead of great books, Moody believed in the Great Book, the Bible or the Word. Nor did he have the faith in the value of games that Stagg continued to declare until his death. How Moody came to feel about the YMCA, the social gospel, and the new theology was best summed up by Billy Sunday, the most celebrated evangelist to succeed him, in a 1916 sermon called "The Second Coming": "The trouble with the church, the YMCA, and the Young People's societies is that they have taken up sociology and settlement work but are not winning souls to Christ." "Soul winning" and not social reform and "godless social service" was the one answer to all questions. "All human schemes of reconstruction must be subsidiary to the Second Coming" (quoted in McLoughlin, *Modern Revivalism* 439). With Moody and Sunday the emphasis in muscular Christianity shifted away from recapitulation and acculturation theories to triumphalism, from building character to saving souls. Actually, in frontier evangelism salvation had always been the main order of business. Today both heritages, that of the YMCA (building character) and of the evangelists (saving souls) are clearly evident in our sportianity, reflecting both our rural roots and urban experience but also the evolution of a democratic knighthood.

In the view of Sunday, a crusade against sin was at the same time a campaign for social reform, but only the Gospel could guarantee success in any endeavor. He himself was a success story, "a graduate of the University of Poverty" who called himself "the rube of rubes." His autobiography, he said, could be summed up in one line from Thomas Gray's "Elegy in a Country Churchyard": "The short and simple annals of the poor" (ibid., 407).

A gifted athlete, Sunday played right field for different major league teams and broke several records for stealing bases. After a conversion experience in 1886 he left professional baseball and a salary of five hundred dollars per month for a job with the Chicago YMCA at eighty-three dollars. "They didn't call me a grafter then," he was fond of saying. During his work with the central branch of the Chicago Y, he often heard Dwight L. Moody speak but never became intimate with him. After three years he himself became an evangelist, attaining fame approaching that once enjoyed by Moody himself, applauded by many liberals as well as conservatives, by the rich and powerful as well as by "the people." At the height of his career, Sunday received the public praise of such figures as Theodore Roosevelt, William Jennings Bryan, and Woodrow Wilson. Said John D. Rockefeller, who had funded the founding of the University of Chicago where Stagg achieved his fame, "Mr. Sunday is a rallying center around whom all good people interested in good things may gather" (ibid., 402, quoted). In 1918, John Leland, president of Cadillac Motor Company, called Sunday "this great plumed knight clothed in the armor of God" (ibid., quoted).

Whereas Moody devoted time in his sermons to the meaning of such terms as *compassion, grace, repentance, the Blood,* and *assurance,* (see, for example, *The Way Home*), Sunday reduced theology to a simple choice: "You are going to live forever in heaven or you are going to live forever in hell. There's no other place—just the two. . . . It's up to you and you must decide now" (ibid., 409). Like Moody, he believed the Bible was inerrant and detested the theory of evolution as much as any modern creationist. When a Reverend Dr. Wallace, a modernist, remonstrated in private with Sunday for being so intolerant on the subject, Sunday retaliated the next day by confronting Wallace from the stage: "Stand up there you bastard evolutionist! Stand up with the atheists and the infidels and the whoremongers and the adulterers and go to hell!" In the 1920s he repudiated intellectuals and intellectualism entirely, declaring with the authority of a papal bull, "Science and religion can never be reconciled" (ibid., 412).

Nor in Sunday's view could professional sport and religion be reconciled, especially if baseball persisted in breaking the Sabbath commandment. In the 1870s as an outfielder in Pittsburgh, he participated in "Athletic Sundays" arranged by Henry H. Webster of New York City, but these were evangelistic endeavors aimed at men in New York who did not go to church. Sunday along with Stagg and members of the Princeton football team spoke to capacity audiences, confirming by their presence that manliness and Christianity were not in the least incompatible. Sunday rejected Sabbath sports along with dancing, drinking, card playing, and theatergoing, but manliness was desired every day in the week, and his was "a masculine, aggressive muscular Christianity." He was said to match "even Mr. Roosevelt himself" in his insistence "on his personal, militant masculinity." Sunday expressed admiration for " 'the man who has real, rich, red blood in his veins instead of pink tea and ice water.' After pointing out that 'I'm still pretty handy with my dukes,' he would declare that Jesus 'was no dough-faced, lick-spittle proposition. Jesus was the greatest scrapper that ever lived.' The conclusion was patent: 'Let me tell you, the manliest man is the man who will acknowledge Jesus Christ' " (ibid., 427).

Just as the theme of manliness ran through Sunday's sermons, so did the theme of patriotism, especially after 1917. "I think that Christianity and patriotism are synonymous terms and hell and traitors are synonymous." He called himself "God's recruiting officer," and in 1919 when Attorney General A. Mitchell Palmer began imprisonment and deportation of alien "radicals," Sunday approved, sounding like the Okie from Muskogee, "If they don't like the way we do things, let them get out of here and leave." By the middle of the twenties he was telling crowds, "America is not a country for a dissenter to live in" (ibid., 444).

It is important to note that Sunday was truly a sporting apostle rather than, like more recent preachers Jerry Falwell, Billy Graham, and Oral Roberts, an apologist for sports. He drew few lessons from sports in the pulpit but was himself a sport, a player, and an actor. While the content of his sermons and early on the manner of delivery recalled those of Moody, after 1900 his presentations were characterized by stagy humor, florid rhetoric, and often "horseplay." "Evangelist Does Great Vaudeville Stunts in Tabernacle Pulpit" read one headline in 1904. One Iowa newspaper in the same year said his sermon was as good as Keystone Comedy or "The Perils of Pauline" (ibid., 407–8). In a superb chapter titled "Corybantic Christianity" in *Evangelized America*, Grover C. Loud presents a brilliant picture of player Billy Sunday in action on the Sawdust Circuit:

> Billy crouches on the platform, knocks on the floor and shouts an invitation for the Devil to come up and take his medicine. Billy admits his own fearlessness and when the bid to Beelzebub is not accepted the audience shares with the champion the delight and conquering pose. Cheers ring for the tower of physical strength and spiritual righteousness whom the Boss of Hell dares not meet in combat.
>
> This is no gentle Galahad going a-grailing; it is a Jack the Giant Killer gunning for Fiery Griffins. He isn't standing there and merely talking about sin and sinners. His occasional pensive moods are statuesque. The rest of the time he is in action,

now stalking his game, now impersonating the characters of this tremendous one-man drama.

He "snuffs the coke" or "jabs the needle" and lops over the pulpit. His snoring can be heard all over the tabernacle. He gulps poison, writhes in agony and stiffens out dead on the floor. Up he springs, both feet on the chair or one foot on the chair and the other on the pulpit, shouting—"Break away from that old bunch of the damned."

. . . "Come on Naaman, it's up to you to jump seven times into Jordan! Hold your nose, shut your eyes! Eeyow! You've stubbed your toe on the brink. Oo-ee, a big sand-fly biting between the shoulder-blades!" In and out the seventh time, stamping, spluttering, shaking the water out of his ears. But— Naaman William Sunday D.D. does a handspring and lands with legs wide apart and shoulder arched back—"My flesh is made whole, my leprosy is healed!"

No posture is impossible for this versatile go-getting Gospel gymnast. Squatting on his toes, his knees brushing the floor, his fingers flicking the green carpet for balance, for a split second he is the man who is "no better than a four-footed brute."

. . . In the prize ring with the Devil—the knockout blow—the slow count, eight, nine, ten and "OUT!" On the Marathon race to heaven the runner, Billy in the role, without an understudy in the world, lunges prostrate at the goal. The greatest base-stealer in old-time baseball knows how to slide. [305–7]

If Moody was a transitional figure in evangelism, representing a shift in focus from the frontier to the city, Sunday was a reversion to type. He was not only the muscular frontier minister come to life again but the frontier clown, the devil-fighting, fun-loving, rip-roaring somersaulter all at once, Davy Crockett and Sut Lovingood in the same skin.

There seems little doubt that Sunday is the general type under attack in Sinclair Lewis's *Elmer Gantry* (1927), though Stagg and the University of Chicago come in for some withering fire too, since one of the characters, Judson Roberts, "the praying fullback," had been a star player at the university. Roberts had also played baseball, captained the debating team, commanded the YMCA, and report-edly boxed with Jim Jeffries. Because Elmer too is a football hero,

Old Jud seeks him out at Terwillinger College and in manly fashion challenges him to a fight in the Christian cause. Whether Lewis had Sunday specifically in mind or not, Billy reacted as if he did, calling Lewis "Satan's cohort," "Mencken's Minion," and "Judas" and shouting that he "could have socked Mr. Lewis so hard there would have been nothing left for the devil to leap on" (Schorer 474–75).

Like Elmer Gantry and Sharon Falconer, Billy Sunday was an entertainer, and competing forms of entertainment spelled his doom. Radio and the motion picture did to Sunday's ministry what they did to vaudeville: they killed it (D. Cohen 162). Though he had continued success in small towns, Sunday no longer drew large crowds in cities—a development that darkened his mood and dispelled much of his American optimism. He preached increasingly of the end of the world, which he predicted for 1935, ironically the year he died (ibid.).

Things have a way of coming full circle. By winding up preaching in the small towns of the South, Sunday was returning, though not voluntarily, to the roots of frontier revivalism, but without the blessings of the high clergy that the manly, highly educated ministers coming out of Princeton to the South before 1830 had had. In the 1870s Sunday had participated with Stagg and the Princeton football team in the "Athletic Sundays" as examples of Christian manliness, but by 1915 President John Grier Hibben of Princeton refused to let Sunday speak on campus because of "the breaches in taste" Sunday committed in his use of sporting slang to describe the battle between David and Goliath: David, he said, "put one of them [a stone] in his sling, threw it, socked Goliath in the coco between the lamps, and he went down for the count" (McLoughlin, *Modern Revivalism* 428). Such a prissy attitude as that of President Hibben almost throws us on the side of Sunday in this regard, but Princeton was virtually the only college that refused him permission to speak at the time.

That refusal, however, illustrated a wider breach that had grown between the great universities and popular evangelism, so that today there is almost no dialogue between them, just as there is little or no dialogue between academic and athletic departments. Evangelism merged not with the mind but with the sporting body and the bromidic world of business. Just as Walter Camp would, I suspect, reject the hype and hoopla of modern college football, so would the old teacher-preacher "Thundering" Samuel Doak disdain the same features of modern evangelism, the PTL Heritage Park–containing the boyhood home of Billy Graham–the television "healing" extravaganzas of Oral Roberts and others, the saccharine piety of the Pat Robertson show. Regardless of how the founders of our cultural institutions might feel about our situation today, there is no denying that American evangelism and American football found common ground in show business. Billy Sunday was an important link in the long show business of revivalism that features such recent performers as Jimmy Swaggart and Jim Bakker. This is not to imply that Sunday was guilty of the same transgressions as they, but as a showman he outstripped them.

What Owen Johnson saw occurring on campus, which he described in *Stover at Yale*, merely reflected what was going on throughout the culture, including evangelical religion. While the ties between business and religion are ancient, not until this century did evangelical groups begin to take advantage of the sophisticated selling techniques of organized business. " 'To hell with the twentieth century!' cried Billy Sunday, but his show was undeniably a product of the promotion methods of the 1900's–a truly modern blend of enterprise and salvation, 'religion C.O.D' " (Loud 309). "At the flood tide of high-power revivalism, 1914–1917, the churches with the aid of a charitable public were spending twenty million dollars a year for the purported saving of souls by one thousand evangelists, great and small. The campaigns cost the communities an average of five thousand dollars but Dr. Sunday and other star performers came higher, all the way up to one hundred and fifty thousand dollars" (358).

Almost simultaneously business began to lubricate the machinery of sports and evangelism, making fans and saving souls and, in the case of Billy Sunday, doing both at the same time. "Frank Luther Mott designated the years 1892–1914 as a period in newspaper history when sporting news underwent remarkable development, being 'segregated on special pages, with special make-up pictures, and news-writing style' " (Betts, *Heritage* 68). Thus the specialists appeared in religion, sports, and sportswriting all at once. Billy

Sunday described things best: "You can't conduct business as you did twenty-five years ago, neither can you religion. This is a day of specialists." In 1900 he hired his first singing assistant and added a "new staff of specialists, each of whom dealt with one particular phase of the revivals" (McLoughlin, *Billy Sunday* 73). Henceforth the Gospel would also be a commodity. As George Wilson of the Billy Graham Evangelistic Association stated, the association was "selling . . . the greatest product in the world" (Bestic 137).

The "Jesus books" of the late nineteenth century had anticipated the controversy in the YMCA concerning the social gospel. The doctrine of success was inherent in the social gospel, since social or shepherd programs depended in large measure upon the success of knights and government in producing wealth. While the shepherd seeks equality, the knight seeks excellence, which unfortunately in history has too often been confined to the pursuit of arms, wasting wealth that could go to the support of the general welfare. The alliance in balance of the two archetypes is crucial in any good and just society. What happened in the YMCA and in the whole country in the years between the world wars is that the doctrine of success succeeded fabulously as an expression of capitalism while the social gospel, accused of ties with communism and socialism, faltered sadly. Due to its "institutional inertia, close ties to wealth and business, and the belief that the traditional attitude was adequate," the YMCA did not officially commit to the basic principles of the social gospel until after World War I (Hopkins 532). Even the earlier efforts of the YMCA toward improvement of living conditions of the poor were decried by Billy Sunday, who stressed instead salvation–the so-called personal encounter with Christ–manliness, and, like Dwight L. Moody, success. Sunday's attitude toward social reform appealed to the middle-class churchgoers (*Billy Sunday* 138) and the wealthy. "Revivalism was backed by the wealthy and hence bore the odium of possible ulterior motives on the part of that particular class of society toward the lower classes" (ibid., 109). When Sunday decried "sociology," "settlement work," "godless social service," and "all human schemes of reconstruction," he was giving voice to the clichés of the manly religious right still familiar to us today. As an athlete and an evangelist, Sunday embodied the doctrine of success that all classes applauded, even the poor themselves.

By the early thirties the muscular Christian from the college YMCA began to yield in popularity to the intellectual (F. Allen 120), who often found influence in the progressive programs of the Roosevelt Administration. Beset with more urgent problems of surviving the depression and World War II, Americans in these years were not exactly panting for the roaring evangelist. All things pass away but return again in different forms or on another channel. This is as true of revivalism as it is of everything else. If radio and the motion picture put an end to the ministry of Billy Sunday, driving him to the backwoods where his ministry began, then television revived revivalism under the leadership of the household names of our times, Jerry Falwell, Billy Graham, and Oral Roberts.

# 14

# Field Generals of
# the Crusade

The alliance of religion and sports in America presented new problems with which we still struggle. They are well illustrated in the careers of some of America's greatest coaches, field generals of the crusade, who transformed the mission inaugurated by the founding fathers such as Stagg and Naismith from building character to building winning dynasties. The problems inherent in this transformation appear in almost every dimension of our public and private lives, from gender issues to politics, from education to morality, from ecology to economics.

Fielding H. "Hurry-Up" Yost (1871–1946) was born in Fairview, West Virginia, where he attended the Normal School; after additional training at Ohio Normal in Ada, attracted by lucrative possibilities in petroleum law, he attended West Virginia University Law School, from which he graduated in 1897. Having played the newly developing game of football in Ohio, Yost took a coaching position at Ohio Wesleyan and then Nebraska (1898), Kansas (1899), and Stanford (1900), winning the conference championship at each school. In 1901 he went to the University of Michigan as head coach and remained there for the rest of his career. He was head coach until 1923 and again from 1925 to 1927, and he served as director of intercollegiate athletics from 1921 to 1941. His overall record at Michigan was

165–29–ll. His teams went undefeated eight times, and eight times they won the Western Conference, commonly called the Big Ten. Most remarkable were his "point-a-minute" teams from 1901 to 1905, which averaged 49.8 points per game (compared with 0.7 for their opponents) in fifty-five games played (Lester, "Yost" 917). According to one historian of the game, it was Yost (rather than Vince Lombardi or Paul "Bear" Bryant) who gave us "Winning is not the most important thing; it is the only thing" (Merchant 109). Yost built at Ann Arbor "the largest collegiate athletic enterprise in America," including the Yost Field House and Michigan Stadium, the largest in the nation. In the view of Robin Lester, Yost was one of the "Eastern College Evangelists of the Gridiron Gospel."

Noted for running up the score on opponents, Yost won his most lopsided victory at the expense of his alma mater, West Virginia University (130–0 in 1904). Thereafter Yost carried a clipping of the game that described West Virginia players speaking as if they had been invaded by Martians instead of Wolverines. With "gurgling satisfaction" Yost liked to read from the clipping, which was itself a sort of Appalachian tall tale: "It is declared that every player on Yost's team weighed eight tons and had an average speed of 96 miles per hour. They breathed forth smoke and flames" (Lawton, 33).

Yost not only made the big score respectable; he sanctified it. In 1929 the coach at Dobyns-Bennett High School in Kingsport, Tennessee, with Bobby Dodd as quarterback, followed Yost's example by beating Norton, Virginia, 128–0. Likewise, in 1916 John Heisman's Georgia Tech team beat little Cumberland University in Lebanon, Tennessee, 220–0, possibly in revenge for a loss to Cumberland in baseball 22–0 the previous spring. Heisman, also a gridiron evangelist fond of drawing metaphors from war, threatened Cumberland with a lawsuit if the team did not show up for the football game. All Cumberland had to do when it gave up football in 1949, said one Tennessee wag, was to let the air out of the ball. Running up the score in the attempt for national ranking has become part of the American sports scene, with church schools such as Brigham Young as guilty in this regard as state colleges (R. Fitzgerald 11). Wake Forest University has been trounced so often by "national powers" that some disgruntled alumni reportedly changed a road sign near Winston-Salem to read "U.S. Interstate 85–Wake Forest 0."

Yost often drew parallels between war and football and cited moral and religious reasons for his approach to coaching. He liked to refight the battle of Waterloo, and his acquaintances considered him an authority on the maneuvers on the Western Front during World War I. He preceded skull practices with a twenty-minute lecture on military strategy, reading dispatches from the front and making predictions about the outcome with, it was said, uncanny success. He was also fond of lecturing on "football's four corner-stones of success: 'brains, heart, courage, and character' " (Lester, "Yost" 917). Yost claimed that his job gave him a "pulpit" from which to preach his message of football as a "sanctified instrument for the good." Opposed to smoking, drinking, and swearing, he was widely hailed as a moral force. When Yost died, "his funeral service was an appropriate conclusion to his life." Boy Scouts formed a color guard, politicians and All-Americans served as pallbearers, and his frater-nity brothers sang his favorite song, "The Sweetheart of Sigma Chi" (ibid., 918).

In spite of his success, Yost sparked controversy. Until 1921 he worked only ten weeks each year, for which he was paid more than the annual salary of a full professor. During the rest of the year Yost pursued a profitable career in business, seeking out natural resource deposits for development companies, selling oil and gas leases, and, from 1901 to 1914, supervising the construction of a hydroelectric plant in Tennessee. "So lucrative were these ventures that he was loath to give them up when in 1906 the Intercollegiate Conference resolved that coaches in member schools should have full-time academic appointments. Michigan stood by its coach, and after two years of debate left the conference, remaining out until 1917. The controversy continued, however, and in 1921 Yost's position at Michigan was finally legitimized with his appointment as director of intercollegiate athletics" (ibid.).

His coaching also caused controversy. In his zeal to acquire quality athletes, he sometimes recruited players before they had graduated from high school. As early as 1903 Stanford's president had denounced such practices, identifying Yost as a practitioner of the "kind of corruptions in athletics that colleges should eschew" (ibid., quoted).

Yost was not America's most famous coach, however. The man who wins this distinction was a Protestant who became a Catholic, a Norwegian who was called "the Swede." According to John Kieran, he was "a serious student of chemistry" and "an excellent Latin student." He "was well-rounded. He was a builder of spirit, the finest spirit the gridiron has ever known" (Katz 13). Whether he was all this—as well as a businessman too—with the degree of excellence that his admirers proclaim is open to question. Says one critic, "He was a rah-rah team man who felt at home with screwballs and loners. . . . He was a brainy, nit-picking perfectionist with the broad appeal of a circus clown. He was quite a man but not quite the man legend would have us believe" (Phinizy 100).

Here I am not interested so much in Knute Rockne the man as in Knute Rockne the legend. In *The Hero*, Lord Raglan shows that the mass of us are far more interested in dramatic truth than in historical truth, and this is certainly true for Rockne. What then is the nature of the Rockne legend? He was both renaissance man and the chivalric ideal with a grand American common touch, according to Father Charles L. O'Donnell in his eulogy carried on nationwide radio following Rockne's death on 31 March 1931:

> When we say simply, he was a great American, we shall go far towards satisfying many, for all of us recognize and love the attributes of the true American character. When we say that he was an inspirer of young men in the direction of high ideals that were conspicuously exemplified in his own life, we have covered much that unquestionably was true of him. When we link his name with *this intrinsic chivalry and romance of a great college game*, which he, perhaps, more than any other man, made finer and cleaner in itself and larger in its popular appeal, here, too, we touch upon a vital point. But no one of these things, nor all of them together, quite sum up this man whose tragic death at the age of 43 has left the country aghast. [quoted in Katz 57–58; italics added]

Rockne's legend, like his memorial at Notre Dame with its coats of arms of West Point and Annapolis, is chivalric to the core.

Normally chivalry and business do not seem to go together, but in Rockne's case they do. At the time of his death he was director of sales promotion at Studebaker, and at the height of his career, says Sperber, he made more than the president of Studebaker (*Shake Down* 238). Rockne exploited his success in ways that Stagg and others did not, as a coach and salesman, but he too valued loyalty. Though he had received offers to coach at other colleges, which would have more than doubled the ten-thousand-dollar annual salary Notre Dame paid him, Rockne preferred to stay at the school he loved (Katz 112). Rockne became the symbol of the great American winner, and it was he that the American Caesar once had in mind for the Military Academy itself. MacArthur, while military governor of the Philippines, wrote to coach Earl H. Blaik in 1924: "I agree personally with what you say that the system of play at West Point is antiquated, too involved and totally lacking in flexibility and adaptiveness. Had I stayed at West Point, I intended introducing new blood into our coaching staff. Rockne of Notre Dame was the man I had in mind" (quoted in Blaik and Cohane, *Price* 70).

To become a rival of both Army and Navy was no little achievement in itself, and Rockne always had a sense of the national pulse as well as an inordinate drive for recognition. In 1926 the Army-Navy Game at Soldier Field in Chicago was advertised by Christy Walsh as "The Game of the Century" with "The Big Three of Football" (Rockne, Pop Warner and Tad Jones) serving as commentators (see photographs in Sperber, *Shake Down*, after 298). Rockne was also doing a series of syndicated articles while he dispatched his assistant coach Heartley Hunk Anderson to direct Notre Dame against low-rated Carnegie Tech in Pittsburgh. "You can imagine Rock's feeling when the score (Carnegie 19, Notre Dame 0) was relayed to him in the press box at Soldier Field" (Blaik and Cohane, *Price* 76). Rockne was criticized from several quarters for commentating in Chicago instead of coaching in Pittsburgh, an episode that, says Sperber, fell into "the black hole of sports history," so intent have Rockne's hagiographers been to portray their hero as perfect (*Shake Down* 220). Thus Rockne the knight is flawless, almost machine-like in the efficiency with which he simultaneously leads youth to victory and to "high ideals."

As is customary with knights in real life, Rockne jumped on the bandwagon of success, a favorite vehicle for all American celebrities. "In his standard Studebaker speech . . . he offered a few remarks on the psychology that is necessary for success in a football organization (because that) same psychology will make for success in any organization, and particularly in a selling organization" (Sperber 238). Rockne met the prime requirements for a knight of the highest class, an epic hero, for he was a maker of speeches and a doer of deeds. Says Sperber, he "loved sports-as-life metaphors, and at the same time when most Americans believed that religious leaders explained life's complexities far better than athletic figures, the N. D. coach pioneered with his sports analogies" (ibid). He along with Camp and Stagg, perhaps the reigning trinity in our gridiron pantheon, must shoulder some blame for delivering us into our present predicament wherein worth in sports is measured primarily in terms of money.

There is an interesting sidelight on the 1926 Army-Navy game which ended in a 21-21 tie. The Navy "field general" for that game, Eddie Hannegan, became a rear admiral in charge of "all American atomic strike forces" (Schoor 75). Little did Hannegan or anyone else realize that "the bomb" would be developed in part under a stadium named for "Mr. Foootball" across town from "The Game of the Century" at Soldier Field where Colonel Koehler, the old Master of the Sword at West Point, "paced up and down the Army sidelines in a quiet rage" (Blaik and Cohane 76) and where, from high in the sky, our most famous coach reported the excitement and color. Such have been some of the lines of force in our knightly culture.

In our Low Roman age, where "the game of the century" occurs almost every year, the service academies, owing to high academic standards and military obligations, have been unable to compete with modern football industries, but their influence, especially that of West Point, has been enormous. One who played a major role in the development of championship football was Earl H. "Red" Blaik, longtime coach of the Military Academy. In addition to building outstanding records himself, Blaik trained or at least influenced numerous coaches. In a ten-year period beginning in 1948 Blaik lost fourteen assistants to "head-man opportunities," including such well-known coaches as Herman Hickman, Andy Gustafson, Sid Gillman,

Murray Warmath, Stuart Holcomb, Paul Dietzel, Bob Woodruff, Bobby Dobbs, and, most celebrated of all, Vince Lombardi (ibid., 250–51). This is not to say that all (or any) of them exhibited specific Blaik-like techniques in coaching. But the West Point drumbeat reverberates throughout the American football camp, with one recurring message, "There is no substitute for victory," which sprang from the mind of Douglas MacArthur and which helped to give to American sports, especially football, a compulsive, neurotic character. The cliché, echoed by Lombardi, fails to take into account the difference between sports and war as distinguished by Paul Weiss (177). Instead it assumes a total parallel between sports and religion. In sports, "There is no substitute for victory" is a perversion of Grantland Rice's "For when the One Great Scorer comes to mark against your name, / He writes–not that you won or lost–but, how you played the Game" (144). In war, anything goes, as we all know.

Another who played for West Point was Robert Reese Neyland, famous coach of the University of Tennessee Volunteers. Whether Neyland was technically MacArthur's aide-de-camp at West Point in the early twenties may be questioned, but certainly he worked under MacArthur, serving as recreation officer, as commanding officer of the band, as prison officer, and as assistant football and baseball coach (Gilbert, *Neyland* 54). How one man could do all this and still serve as assistant adjutant and aide to the superintendent strains credulity, but the Neyland of legend was a superman. The record does reveal that MacArthur thought highly of him. In Neyland's final fitness report MacArthur wrote, "A most excellent young officer in every respect," "an extraordinary athlete." MacArthur rated him "superior" and claimed to have known him "very well" for "many years" (ibid., 55). The respect was mutual; Neyland, especially after retirement, often quoted MacArthur's credo on victory in sports and war recorded on the gymnasium at West Point.

Neyland deserves attention as a representative knight who had enormous influence upon the direction and character of modern football, especially in the South. Neyland's record spoke for itself: 173 wins, 31 losses, and 12 ties. (Rockne's record was 105–12–5.) What this success by two famous graduates of our most famous military academy and denominational school (Neyland in 1916 and

Rockne in 1914) means is difficult to say. No statistics measure the impact of their winning ways on education or on culture in general. Together they played major roles in institutionalizing knighthood in mid-America and made it so popular that only aging fools would dare to challenge its value.

Born in Texas in 1892, Neyland was appointed to the Military Academy by Sam Rayburn, at least according to Neyland, after attending a junior college and Texas A&M. A natural athlete, he was a teammate of Omar Bradley on Army's national championship football team of 1914 and also on the baseball team. (Neyland's pitching record was 35–5 with 20 straight wins.) In 1925 he came to the University of Tennessee as assistant coach and the next year became head coach, a position he held for twenty-one seasons over a twenty-six-year period, twice going on active duty. Once in charge at Tennessee, Neyland summoned two of his Army teammates, William H. Britton, who coached the ends, and Paul B. Parker, line coach. They were called the Three Musketeers, and all were imbued with a sense of destiny worthy of Templars on a crusade in a foreign land. When Neyland met his team on Labor Day, 1926–the date is telling–he greeted his squad as follows: "Men, we will practice two and one-half hours each day. That's all. Each practice will be organized. We will know what we want to accomplish each day, and we will work full speed." Neyland thereupon closed the practices to the public (Gilbert, *Neyland* 65). He was not the only advocate of secret knightly training, but he was perhaps its most celebrated exemplar until Paul Brown and George Allen.

Not just his record made Neyland a legend, but also his aggressive style of play and military manner of coaching. According to Gene McEver, Neyland's "greatest player," "Neyland ran his football team just like you'd run an Army. He was the first in command, and he didn't have much to do with the players." His method was precision and order, the same virtues admired by William Rainey Harper and Amos Alonzo Stagg. "If you saw Tennessee run a play from its balanced-line single wing, you knew that play had been rehearsed a minimum of 500 times" (Dolton 66).

All who knew Neyland felt that he brought his military background to the game of football. It would be more correct to say that

Neyland combined the language of religion and of war to come up with his thirty-eight maxims for winning. These included (1) "Thou shalt charge and block," (2) "Thou shalt charge and fight," (12) "Football is a battle. Go out to fight and keep it up all afternoon," (16) "You can't fight like a man with less than 100 percent loyalty and college spirit" (Gilbert, *Neyland* 66). His attitude could be summed up in this statement: "Pregame harangues, as a rule, do more harm than good. . . . Inspiration at zero hour is a poor thing to rely on. Good mental attitude the day of the game stems almost entirely from attitudes built up over a long period of time" (Bolton 68–69). Unlike Rockne, who was known for his pep talks, Neyland used the cool technique. Before the Florida game in 1928 he told his team, "If you go out there with tears in your eyes, you won't be able to see the ball. I want you to see it." The final score was Tennessee 13, Florida 12 (Gilbert, "Tall Man" 12).

Neyland's arrival in Tennessee was analogous to Stagg's coming to Chicago with Nathan W. Dougherty, Mr. Volunteer, playing the role of William Rainey Harper. Said Dougherty to the young army officer, "Even the score with Vanderbilt. Do something about the terrible series standings" (Bebb 126). The good soldier carried out the order by going on to compile a record of 16–3–2 against the Vanderbilt Commodores, coached by Dan McGugin, brother-in-law of Hurry-Up Yost. Thus McGugin at Vanderbilt and Neyland at Tennessee brought military football to Tennessee and the South. Just as Rockne had beaten the Military Academy at its own game, so Neyland defeated the aristocratic knightly order of the Old South. The advice of Tennessean Grantland Rice, who himself had been a Vanderbilt athlete, would become increasingly absurd in the growing military mind-set of the coaches of southern football.

As far as we know, Dougherty, a member of the National Football Hall of Fame from Tennessee (1909) and celebrated apologist for big-time sport in the Southeastern Conference, never made the same promises to Neyland that Harper made to Stagg; but he did everything but stand on his head to keep a regular army officer on full-time duty at Knoxville for twenty-one seasons. A folk tradition describes the athlete in American colleges who never graduates but stays on and on to play every season. Neyland's situation was similar but reversed: he was the army officer as coach who never left his post except for minor emergencies such as World War II. Dougherty, former dean of the School of Engineering, admits to the political string-pulling that speaks volumes of the inner workings of the old boy system behind the order of knighthood.

What happened is rather remarkable, since the U.S. taxpayers presumably paid in part for the University of Tennessee's rise to football prominence through Neyland's salary as an ROTC officer and later as engineer in southern offices. If they didn't–and we do not know for sure what the formal arrangements with the army were during those years–then the taxpayers were still short-changed by having Neyland continually on duty in Knoxville coaching football. In all the history of the armed forces I have never found another officer with such a sedentary assignment. There was, however, only one Neyland. Said Dougherty more than thirty years later, "By shenanigans of many kinds, we had kept Neyland here for 10 years" (170–71). Neyland, though, was in the view of both the army and the government a worthy investment, and no one in Tennessee questioned the arrangement.

In order to understand how an officer could be assigned to the same post for so long a period, it is necessary to understand the temper of the times, the twenties, and the military history that shaped them. The University of Tennessee, like other land grant colleges, was, because of the Morrill Act of 1862, a virtual replica of West Point until 1890. The Morrill Act, though, was only one step in the militarization of campus mentality at the University of Tennessee. From the outset the country was dotted with forts, first to protect settlers from the Indians and British and then, in the Civil War, from each other. As soon as the memory of the Civil War began to fade, the Spanish-American War arose, and the National Defense Acts of 1916 and 1920 added new impetus to military training in the land grant colleges (L.G. Anderson 45). One historian says that most turn-of-century university presidents welcomed military activities on campus, believing that such activities would have a positive effect upon student morality. The student army programs of World War I restored to the colleges the old Christian college religion. College presidents "tried to preserve moral education by promoting humanism, religion and football. When that failed they turned to military training." Eventually, however, the disciplined style both of the old religion and of the military alienated students and administrators, leaving the way free for the triumph in the twenties of electives, fraternities, and of course big-time football. The military features of college life remained, especially on the football field (Pearlman 51).

The conflict between styles of administration at the University of Tennessee is clear (see Folmsbee), and while the campus became increasingly civilian in the twenties, the legacy of the old discipline remained. Thus when Neyland made his appearance in 1926, the military heritage of the university was much in evidence. West Point officers were received with open arms, and the effort was still going strong to change Tennessee farm boys into knights in shining armor. In 1928, Neyland's third year at the University, 533 students, one-fourth of the male student body of 2,112, were enrolled in military science. In other states, such as Texas and Virginia, the percentage of enrollment was around 90 (Nash 29). If the young man cannot go to West Point, it is essential to bring West Point to him and to train him thoroughly in body and mind, teaching him, above all else, discipline, the key concept of both military training and football (ibid., chap. 4). It was precisely "discipline" that Neyland brought to Tennessee in 1926. He was on an assignment to an old "fort," more or less, and his goal was to demonstrate that the army way was the winning way.

Unlike Amos Alonzo Stagg and James Naismith, Neyland was not an overtly pious man. He did, though, allow locker-room prayers led by the captain, according to Len Coffman, star fullback on one of Neyland's strongest teams in the late thirties. Neyland's mission was not theological but military, and he apparently approached every assignment in the same way whether the enemy was Vanderbilt or the Japanese. When in 1942 Neyland was assigned to Kunming, China, and put in charge of supplying the American troops in China, Major General W.E.R. Covell said, "We've got the first team out there now." According to General Albert C. Wedemeyer, "Bob Neyland had to exercise tact and firmness in allocating the supplies to the ground forces, to the air forces, and to clandestine forces of OSS and Admiral Miles's Navy Group China. Neyland made a wonderful record" (Gilbert, "Tall Man" 13). Neyland presumably practiced the same lesson he had learned at West Point as an assistant football coach to then head coach John McEwan and as head coach at Tennessee. Neyland theorized that "football was akin to military engineering—a logistical problem of the appropriate use of personnel, moving at proper angles in relation to space" (ibid., 12).

During peacetime Neyland applied the principles of war to football, in wartime the principles of football to combat and logistics. At the theoretical level he, like Hurry-Up Yost, saw little difference (see Lawton 27–29). "The same Cardinal rules apply to both," Neyland said while in the China, Burma, and India Theater of operations. "Your men must be in good physical condition; they must have technical ability; and they must have high morale." The popular press blessed the association. As columnist Bob Considine reported at the time, Neyland turned the unloading of ships into a sporting event, his Indian laborers pushing to break the record of forty-four hours and five minutes to empty a liberty ship (quoted in *The General* 9). A brochure published by the University of Tennessee claims that "China would have become a conquered nation in 1943 without the campaign conducted by Neyland. He used the Calcutta docks and the Burma Road to provide those precious ingredients necessary to make warfare—guns, planes, tanks, food, cars, wheels, medicine, engines, needles, boots, men, and women. . . . In India, he had hundreds of teams engaged in baseball, basketball, softball, tennis, swimming, track, boxing, and just about every known sport. He erected 'Monsoon Square Garden' to permit sports during the rainy season" (ibid.). Neyland may or may not have been the savior of China, but to Tennessee football fans he was without a doubt a savior figure, an epic hero of the gridiron.

Upon his reassignment in Knoxville, he wanted, in addition to a winning record, a larger audience, which simply meant more seats in the stadium, and he wanted protégés, or new coaches. He succeeded in all endeavors. At the time of his death in 1962 scores of his former players were coaching, and seven were head coaches of major colleges. The stadium named in Neyland's honor would eventually seat over 95,000 fans, making it for a time the second-largest college stadium in the nation, behind Michigan Stadium

(101,001). For practically every home game it becomes in effect the fifth largest city in the state. It may be coincidence, but the two individuals most responsible for the erection of two of America's largest stadiums, Yost and Neyland, claimed to have learned important lessons of football from the study of war.

Dougherty, who hired Neyland and who pulled "shenanigans" to keep him in Knoxville, is also convinced that war and football are blood brothers. Dougherty was the engineering dean and chairman of the UT Athletic Board from 1917 to 1956, and he helped plan the monumental growth of Neyland Stadium. In *Educators and Athletes* Dougherty quotes other West Pointers, Dwight D. Eisenhower and Neyland's old boss, MacArthur. On the values of football, Eisenhower, as if reversing himself on his theory of the dangers of a military-industrial complex, said: "In football, in business, in the trades, the normal urge to excel provides one of the most hopeful assurances that our kind of society will continue to advance and to prosper. Morale—the will to win, the fighting heart—are the honored hallmarks of the football coach and player. This morale—this will, the heart—we need not only in athletic teams as individuals, but collectively" (156). MacArthur was in complete agreement, especially after being named recipient of the National Football Foundation's Gold Medal in 1959. On that occasion the general said: "The game has become a symbol of our country's best qualities: courage, stamina, coordinated efficiency. Many believe in these cynical days of doubt and indecision that through this sport we can best keep alive the spirit of reality and enterprise which has made us great. . . . Upon the fields of friendly strife are sown the seeds that upon other fields, on other days, will bear the fruit of victory" (ibid.). It should be noticed that MacArthur does not mention the values that I have called shepherd values, another dimension of the holy: compassion, restraint, and wisdom. Without them a society has no heart and probably no soul either. Nor does he mention the fruits of the spirit: "love, joy, peace, longsuffering, gentleness, goodness, faith, meekness, temperance." MacArthur would have argued no doubt that the fruit of victory should ensure the fruit of the spirit, which, to his credit, he helped to promote to some degree in postwar Japan.

As if to show civilian agreement with the military view of sports and war, Dean Dougherty cites a statement from the National Football Foundation on the values of football in all walks of life:

> Football is one great builder of man. It does more for a boy of school age than any other sport. It is not only, as indicated by President Whitney Griswold of Yale, a vital part of education and exercise, but it is, like other sports, a challenge to the spirit, a test of mettle, a way to educate youth to go far beyond the resources that are on the surface. For the boy, football builds stamina, courage, competitive fiber, self-reliance, teamwork, sportsmanship, and imbues him with the many qualities which help build our manhood and keep our country strong and our competitive spirit vibrant. [quoted in Nyquist and Hawes 156]

What is intriguing is that Dougherty (or the Foundation, or both) misrepresents the views of Whitney Griswold. Griswold did favor amateur athletics, but he strongly opposed athletic specialization, especially as represented by the athletic scholarship. In the same year that MacArthur received the Foundation Award–ten years before the publication of Dougherty's book–Griswold made it clear how he felt about the direction college football was taking in a speech at Johns Hopkins University. Instead of saying that football served noble aims, as Dougherty indicated, Griswold said that athletic scholarships are "one of the greatest educational swindles ever perpetuated on American youth." He went on to say that they undermine the structure of American education and even weaken the educational battle against the Soviet Union. "The Cold War continues," said Griswold, "and so does the athletic-scholarship racket, as if Russia did not exist" (quoted in Blaik and Cohane, "Abuses" 114). The cold war is over, but athletic scholarships are more of a paradox than ever.

Coach Earl H. "Red" Blaik of Army knew exactly what Griswold said and in an article for *Look* with Tim Cohane took Griswold to task for collating "the Cold War, Communism, and athletic scholarships" ("Abuses" 114). Blaik writes as one betrayed. In a sense he was, since Yale had always been the leader in the civilian wing of the Christian muscularity movement, though over the years, much like the YMCA, it dissociated itself from the phenomenon. Blaik points out how recent was Yale's and Harvard's dominance in football and argues that within three years Ivy League football could be restored to its former stature, "without a single academic compromise." This remark came, incidentally, from a man who lived through, with a great deal of knightly dignity, the West Point cribbing scandal of 1951. Blaik even indicates a certain hypocrisy on the part of the Ivy League in maintaining the level of competition they have chosen by grants and loans that are not as visible as the athletic scholarship. Blaik goes on to argue that football at West Point, just as MacArthur said, prepares athletes not only for battle but for life, because it is "the game most like war and . . . most like life" (ibid., 120). He concludes with three fundamental points:

1. Football should be secondary to the purpose of education

2. Championship football and good scholarship are entirely compatible

3. The purpose of the game of football is to win—and to dilute the will to win is to destroy the purpose of the game [ibid.]

Blaik's contentions, which no doubt were applauded by Dean Dougherty, are too simplistic. Of course, championship football and good scholarship are compatible, *if* the play could be maintained at some reasonable amateur level, *if* athletes really had time to do extended research in labs and libraries like other students, *if* they were not constantly exhausted physically and mentally from practice, strength work, and skill sessions (amounting to fifty or sixty hours per week), *if* they were not traveling (especially for basketball, baseball, and golf), and *if* they were not thinking about the mistakes of the last game (and feeling guilty about those mistakes) or the one to come. After leading Notre Dame to its eighth national championship, Lou Holtz, in contrast to Rockne, said he was "scared to death" of the next season's opening game with Rice, a team that did not win a game in 1988 and lost to Notre Dame 54–11. Does this type of mentality sound conducive to the sane coexistence of athletics and academics, regardless of what graduation rates may be? No, what really counts is victory. Coaches know that if they do not win they will be replaced by someone who can, for their mission has little relationship to the education of the athletes. At the same time that sports have been militarized and sanctified on the outside, they have been turned into enormous business enterprises on the inside. With knighthood it has always been that way, the drive for lucre under the twin banners of Christ and academic learning.

Blaik and Cohane also wrote a book about Blaik's career and football at West Point and Dartmouth called *You Have to Pay the Price.* The irony is that neither Blaik nor Cohane, even if they did understand the price of football in their own day, had a sense of inflation or knew what the knightly route they advocated would eventually cost the nation socially and culturally as well as financially and academically. As we come to terms with our national debt, it would be well if we also looked at the cost of college football, to see what shrines we have built in its honor and why. At least then we will know the identity of our gods, which may be stranger than we think.

In *Educators and Athletes* Dougherty does not mention that the official publication of the National Football Foundation and Hall of Fame advised young men not to attend universities with athletic dorms, which would include Dougherty's alma mater, the University of Tennessee. "Living in a separate dormitory for athletes," the Foundation tells young men, "would interfere with your friendships and life as a regular student" (Nyquist and Hawes 15). The athletic dorm "smacks of special privilege, and interferes with a real part of your education–the normal makings of friendship with a wide variety of other students. It sets you apart and tends to make you in law our '*employee.*' Football should not be so conducted that it requires segregation. Living in an athletes' dormitory would tend to develop a suspicious and hostile attitude on the part of other students toward you, and could lead you and your fellow athletes to take a poor attitude toward your main object–getting an education" (24).

The athletic dorm grew out of the ancient institution of the military barracks and was blessed in this country by West Point, which retains its military purity by having an all-military faculty. A source informs me that the West Point Geography Department intends to hire seven civilian faculty members by the year 2000 with the first hired for 1995-96. This is a small but encouraging step to remove the image of West Point, in the view of Colonel Anthony Herbert, decorated war hero, as "an institution that rests at the heart of the separation of the American Army from the American people" (Galloway and Johnson, dust jacket). Similarly, the athletic dorm stands as a symbol of the hired professional army, a group of mercenaries whose job is not to learn but to win ball games. The fact that the Fellowship of Christian Athletes regularly holds prayer meetings in the dorm at UT or elsewhere cannot disguise the real gods such segregated athletes of all races serve. Athletic dorms, by the way, are not necessary to success as Joe Paterno has demonstrated.

If we seek to discover the symptoms of our slide from the High Roman stage of empire into the Low Roman phase of domestic idolatry, we should look at athletic policies of the service academies and Notre Dame, the institutions with the strongest ties to military and religious traditions in the Old World. Cultural cracks are not alarming until they appear in the temples and shrines. Particular attention needs to be given to West Point, the mecca of knights. Similarly, Notre Dame may be called the Lourdes of college sports. At Oral Roberts University miracles are only expected and prayed for; at Notre Dame they occur regularly, especially in football. In spite of their chauvinistic warpings, each of the earlier phases of our sporting culture demonstrated certain virtues: the colonial or reformation period, bravery and courage; the revolutionary or national phase, a belief in the value of books and dedication to learning; the Hellenic or classic phase, all-round excellence and ideal balance between mind and body in individuals and society; and the High Roman phase, discipline and service to country. The fifth or Low Roman stage in which we now find ourselves retains the faults of the previous phases but has fewer of their virtues. Emphasis shifts from service, defined by Nathan Hale and John F. Kennedy, to the star syndrome: How do I get to the top? In spite of trappings proclaiming devotion to Christ and country, sport becomes a thing in itself, with its own gods, scribes, and temples, the endless halls of fame. To be sure, the spirit of Galahad, the acknowledged hero of the service academies, is celebrated at every opportunity, as at the Army-Navy game, but his knightly qualities seem increasingly anachronistic, as do, more unfortunately, the shepherd ones of Christ: patience, pity, and meditation.

A crack in the temple of knighthood occurred with the cribbing scandal at West Point in 1951, when Army was ranked number one in the nation. Some ninety cadets on the Army football team were expelled, becoming in effect scapegoats for the same type of institutional myopia that had plagued the YMCA for decades. Academy officials failed to realize the impossibility of maintaining the old standards of Thayer in military discipline and academics and also leading, not just participating in, the growing mania for competition in college football. Coach Earl Blaik, while not excusing the infractions, understood better than most. "The player at all service academies," he said, "carries a load no other undergraduate even begins to approximate" ("Red Blaik Speaks" 58). No doubt there are those who would challenge that claim but in any event the prevailing academy myopia, which failed to note the conflict between winning ball games and maintaining high academic standards, was transferred to the Air Force Academy where another cheating scandal occurred, involving, predictably, the football team (See Galloway and Johnson 113-25).

In the 1992 cheating scandal in electrical engineering at the U.S. Naval Academy, ten of the twenty-four midshipmen expelled were athletes (Brubaker Al). In all three service academies, the administrations compete in the modern football/education market and thus place inordinate demands upon their athletes, some of whom are ill prepared for academy curricula but still are admitted for their athletic ability. The honor concept is outdated and elitist, emphasizing education as initiation rather than exploration. "Duty, honor, country," the motto of all academies, could be changed with benefit to the nation to "duty, *honesty,* country." Knights would never agree, however, since "honesty" is not invested with martial dignity, as is the thunder-rolling word *honor.* In our universities the honor system originated at the University of Virginia in 1842, within an atmosphere of chivalry and Scottian romanticism, requiring that "the students should certify on their honor the receiving of no improper assistance" (Osterweis, *Romanticism* 88).

Wake Forest traces its honor code to 1838; Washington and Lee to 1865. Lore at the latter school has it that Robert E. Lee, upon becoming president, "tossed the school's thick book of student conduct out the window and announced a new code: Every student will conduct himself as a gentleman at all times" (Kelly 5).

Honor was a quality of a gentleman, something he possessed and defended, which no lesser person, certainly not a woman or a slave, could ever hope to own much less defend. Honesty, in contrast, is not a possession but a virtue we all should seek. In the ancient world *Parrhesia,* "honesty" or "unflinching frankness," was "an infinitely rare and precious commodity" reserved either for the philosopher or wife of a noble male figure (Brown, *Body and Society* 15), a quality in some ways at odds with, but certainly a check upon, honor. In *What Are People For?* Wendell Berry makes essentially the same point in our own time. "It is impossible not to notice how little the proponents of the ideal of competition have to say about honesty, which is the fundamental economic virtue, and how *very* little they have to say about community, compassion and mutual help" (135).

While the defenders of honor will claim that it subsumes honesty, which in one respect it does, honor also readily embraces secrecy and exclusivity. Honesty, on the other hand, seeks to break down barriers and to open up chambers of secrecy, so that all members of a democracy can judge and understand for themselves. Honor thus is aristocratic; honesty is democratic. The idea of honor to this day foolishly overclassifies documents of the primary government and is used to justify and disguise the covert activities and mistakes of "second governments" like the CIA. Similarly, in the service academies honor, as it applies to sports, is to some extent a ruse allowing those institutions to maintain the illusion that they are preserving a long and honorable renaissance ideal of versatility and at the same time attempting to compete with universities where sports have become a matter of specialization and even professionalization. The scandal is nationwide. Probably no myth has done as much damage to American education as that of "student-athlete" at the military academies and elsewhere (see Hochfield; Isaacs; Carter; Sperber, "College Sports," and Underwood, "Student-Athletes.").

Another crack in the temple of the old order reflects bowl and television policies, at first ambiguous and then blatant. In 1924 Navy played in the Rose Bowl, and Notre Dame played in the same bowl the following year. Neither returned to a bowl until the age of television, with Navy again leading the way in the Sugar Bowl in 1955 and Notre Dame in 1957 going to the Cotton Bowl, breaking Oklahoma's celebrated winning streak. The Air Force Academy, a child of our own times, adopted a bowl policy from the outset, playing in the Sugar Bowl in 1958, but the Military Academy did not accept a bowl offer until 1986, when it played in a postseason game in Michigan. How does one account for this reluctance and vacillation toward bowl play, reminiscent of the attitude of the church toward tournaments in the late Middle Ages?

For much of this century the bowls represented in the minds of leading academicians the rankest form of commercial exploitation of college football, totally unrelated to the educational benefits that a sensible, well-regulated football program should provide for participants. The only Ivy League schools ever to play in bowl games were Brown (Rose Bowl 1916) and Harvard (Rose Bowl 1920), twin blots as it were on the escutcheon of amateur athletics in the eastern colleges. The Military Academy saw nothing in the bowls that could serve the training of the warrior. This type of thinking prevailed at the Naval Academy as well. Even with a certain offer to play in the Sugar Bowl in 1955, Eddy Erdelatz, Navy coach, kept reminding his team that the biggest bowl of all was the Army-Navy game, that any other games would be anticlimactic, a point made by Earl Blaik of the Military Academy where for years the question of bowl play surfaced annually ("Red Blaik Speaks" 53). Similarly, for over three decades Notre Dame, holder of at least six national championships during its long break in bowl participation, remained morally aloof from such cold promotions, finding no connection between the New Year's tournaments and the traditional goals of education and religion. With the advent of television, however, even Notre Dame succumbed to temptation, abandoning the lessons of Yale in this regard as well as those of the Church Fathers. Modern priests rushed in where the liberal Ivys feared to retread. Now Notre Dame is in the national goldfish bowl with no way out, the envy of such aspirants to national power in football as Jerry Falwell.

In his lengthy and informative history of Notre Dame football, *Shake Down the Thunder*, Murray Sperber writes, "Notre Dame has long valued the mind as well as the body. Since the Greeks defined the dichotomy between the two, no institution has systematically achieved excellence in both. But the University of Notre Dame has engaged the conundrum more seriously than any other school in the world, and Notre Dame's struggle with its athletic culture and its academic aspirations will likely continue well into the next century" (501). In *Under the Tarnished Dome* Don Jaeger and Douglas S. Looney repeatedly point to examples of that struggle during the reign of Lou Holtz, who in restoring the winning tradition at Notre Dame, they claim, made the famous university indistinguishable from other "football factories," as seen in both the exploitation and special treatment of athletes, in spite of denials to the contrary. "What's most unsettling," they write, "is that Notre Dame is supposed to be . . . an academic and athletic utopia. Americans have always thought that in a sea of ugliness in college football, at least they could believe in the lagoon of beauty of Notre Dame. Time was, they could. Now they can't" (239). The book, as the jacket claims, "reveals the dark side of Holtz's methods: the physical and emotional abuse of his athletes; his callous and potentially dangerous treatment of players who are injured; his tacit acceptance of and outright failure to punish players for using steroids to build themselves up to his demanded levels."

While Jaeger and Looney deserve considerable credit for raising important questions about Holtz's antics and modus operandi in the most celebrated coaching position in the country, it should be understood that Holtz, whether or not he is guilty as they have charged, is carrying out university policy under the credo of our times: "Winning is the only thing." Yost pronounced it, while others—Heisman, Neyland, and even the sainted Stagg and Rockne—were so successful as to make any other goals implicitly secondary, no matter the lip service rendered to them, the education of the athlete included. Holtz's controversial methods of dealing with players is in fact not at all unusual but in the mainstream of the American coaching profession. John Heisman himself, the namesake for the trophy given annually to the best football player in the nation, said: "The coach should be masterful and commanding, even dictatorial. He has no time to say 'please' or 'mister.' At times he must be severe, arbitrary, and a little short of czar" (quoted in Bolton 212).

Whereas Holtz merely put a "stranglehold" on an official (160), Heisman, after the 1899 Auburn game, carried on an extended argument with an official in the Birmingham newspaper over disputed calls (see Givens 103–6). To be sure, many athletes were genuinely educated while playing for the coaches of earlier generations, but even then the seeds of greed were blowing in the wind, as reports of the Carnegie Commission attest. "The workings of commercialism," said the commission report of 1929, "have almost obliterated the nonmaterial aspects of athletics" (Savage et al. 310). It took a long time, but one famous American coach, Bear Bryant, finally admitted the truth: "I used to go along with the idea that football players on scholarship were 'student-athletes' which is what the NCAA calls them. Meaning a student first, an athlete second. We were kidding ourselves, trying to make it more palatable to the academicians. We don't have to say that and we shouldn't. At the level we play, the boy is an athlete first and a student second" (quoted in Michener 254). This is not to imply that Bryant did not have some academic standards as seen in Winston Groom's novel *Forrest Gump,* which in movie form became sentimental pabulum, losing much of its satiric edge. In the novel Forrest flunks out of Alabama for getting an F in Physical Education though making an A "in something called Intermediate Light." Since Forrest in his first and only season was the "Most Valuable College Back in the Southeastern Conference," Coach Bryant is understandably tearful when he tells his star that he has failed. "Then coach go over to a winder, an he say, 'Good luck, boy–now get your big dumb ass outta here' " ( 44). On his failing P.E., Forrest has this to say, " 'Why do I need to know the distance between goalposts on a soccer field anyway?' " (43). As Forrest departs, the team bids him farewell in front of the "Ape Dorm" or athletic dorm, also known on several campuses as "the animal house."

Jesse Jackson, who like Martin Luther King Jr. preaches a social gospel, understands what has happened in modern sports from a different perspective. A former college quarterback and sandlot baseball player, Jackson realizes that

> the basic values of sport have shifted. Athletes used to operate
> on the theory of enduring short pain for long-term pleasure. You
> endured the short-term pain of getting into shape, you studied

to get into college. You sacrificed early in life so you could prevail in the fourth quarter. All that has been replaced by the Quick-Six Generation that only wants the early score.

The great coaches were concerned about character. They taught quarterbacks, "if you can't control yourself, you can't control the team." When TV began to create more pressure on coaches to win, they began to make concessions. They put style ahead of substance. Kids were allowed to play when they should've been academically ineligible. That took away academic incentive. Kids were shot up with cortisone so they could play with injuries. Tutors were hired to keep the kids in school. The death of ethics is the sabotage of excellence. The concessions we've made lead the athlete to short-term pleasure and long-term pain. [quoted in Underwood, "Game Plan" 417]

As would anyone else at Notre Dame, Holtz has an impossible task, pretending that nothing essential has changed since the days of Rockne while knowing full well that at Notre Dame, Alabama, and elsewhere we are in what Allen Guttmann has called "a whole new ball game." Like all successful knights, Holtz is a brilliant field general, but we cannot look to him or to other famous knights, including Bobby at Indiana, pressurized as they are in their positions by boosters, to point to alternatives to the warped ideas we now serve. The dilemma faced by Notre Dame and the service academies is nothing less than a national crisis, for how it is resolved will affect athletics there and elsewhere for years to come.

In contrast to most universities, the past for Notre Dame is particularly burdensome. The "Touchdown Jesus" that watches over Notre Dame Stadium could not possibly mean that scoring is the only thing, that winning ball games is nonnegotiable. Further, the heavy emphasis on championship football contrasts sharply with the teachings of the saints. Ignatius Loyola's "spiritual exercises," while considerably different from the "exercises" of the American frontier, are not exactly equatable with gridiron drills deemed necessary for successful seasons. Francis Xavier, after taking the "spiritual exercises" for the first time, "repented of the vanity of his athleticism" (Broderick 43), a comment as troubling for Protestants as for Catholics. The swelling passion for victory at Notre Dame does not qualify it as an example of the *eutrapelia* (well-turningness) of Thomas

Aquinas. Its seduction by bowl committees betrays a lust for worldly power, praise, and money that Thomas More repeatedly indicted. In his *Utopia* chamber pots are made of gold, a startling reversal of values from those suggested even by the helmets of Notre Dame, and of Army and Navy as well. The archetypal lady served by the present system is not Mary, soul of wisdom (*Sophia*), so that anyone who honored her would be a philosopher first (*Philo-sophia*) and an athlete merely for fun or relaxation or even health. It is one much lower on the anima scale, the bitch-goddess of the knightly tournament, known everywhere for her love of winners and money and the unexamined life.

# 15

# Power in the Tube

Though differences exist between the attitudes of our contemporary heroes and those of earlier times, similarities are obvious. One could choose among many candidates, but a few will serve to make the point that not much has changed in our knightly ideals over the course of the twentieth century. Sportianity embraces the gospel of wealth and internationalism, exemplified by Ted Turner (the knight as media mogul); muscular Christianity and evangelism, typified by Jerry Falwell (the knight as priest); and chivalry and nationalism, illustrated by Oliver North (the knight as soldier-patriot). Mountainity, on the other hand, addresses stewardship, embodied in Loren Eiseley (the scientist as tracker).

The connections between the three sportsmen are obvious: Jerry Falwell petitioned for signatures for Oliver North's pardon over Ted Turner's "super station." Turner is a superman who, like Andrew Carnegie, is devoted to both competition and world peace. Turner is not free, though, of the problem that Carnegie had; for if Carnegie's wealth was based in part upon the exploitation of labor, Turner's in part is based upon the exploitation of sports and movies, some good and some semipornographic and sadistic, especially the late-night movies on TBS, where the blood runs freely. The managers of the networks apparently endorse the catharsis theory—that the more gore and games we see on the screen, the more peace we will have on the planet, leaving our violence and frustration on the couch before the tube.

The worldview of Turner the sportsman and "media-tor" is quite different from that of Thoreau the "inspector of snow storms," who advised us to read not the *Times* but the "eternities," the pages of nature. Thoreau's chase of the fox, Muir's walk to the Gulf, Loren Eiseley's celebrated circular romp with another fox, all suggest a playful philosophy contained in the Latin phrase *multum in parvo* (much in little). To what extent our around-the-clock entertainment (including news as entertainment) now suggests the opposite each reader can judge.

There are many examples of the contemporary connection of religion and sports. Protestant institutions of strong evangelical bent are notorious in their use of sports to gain converts. Jerry Falwell in one of his television shows said that "sports and music" are two chief means of getting young people into church. (Apparently he did not realize that he was using a pagan ideal that is in tension with the Christian heritage.) Falwell's goal, as he said on *60 Minutes*, is "to build champions for Christ." His goal was shared, at least before the big financial crunch, by Oral Roberts at the university named in his honor: "Athletics is part of our Christian witness. . . . Nearly every man in America reads the sports pages, and a Christian school cannot ignore these people. . . . Sports are becoming the No. 1 interest of people in America. For us to be relevant, we had to gain the attention of millions of people in a way they could understand" (quoted in Eitzen and Sage 123). Not surprisingly, the phrase "Expect a Miracle" is scrolled along the baseline at ORU. "Presumably," says one critic, "the Lord likes to see his favorite team win, and trouncing the heathens from the state college up the road proves, in its own inexplicable way, that the institution's position on theology was right all along" (Hoffman 66–67).

Just as play was linked to Christianity through the PTL Heritage Park, with such elements as the water slide and a tour of a biblical theme land, so sports, such as hunting and fishing, have also become areas of proselytism. Evangelist James Robinson chooses neither the athletic Christianity of Graham, Roberts, and Falwell nor the Disney approach of Jim Bakker. His focus is on the great outdoors and those who kill game therein. Robinson formed the Christian Outdoorsman Association, which encourages "Christian outdoorsmen . . . to become involved in witnessing to other outdoorsmen." He envisions "1,000,000 outdoorsmen joining together to proclaim Christ's message." He also publishes *The Christian Outdoorsman Magazine*, which is "a beautiful, full-color publication, filled with practical hunting and fishing information, interwoven with food for spiritual thought" (G. Miller 2).

Indoors with Falwell, Roberts, and Pat Robertson, in the stadium with Billy Graham, or in the Great Outdoors with James Robinson, we are covered on all fronts by modern evangelists who always have one hand out, whether a Bible, a rifle, or a fishing pole is in the other. And like the NFL on CBS—or rather ESPN—they come to us in living color, sponsoring a familiar knightly message.

On the night Billy Sunday died in 1935 "the boy who would become the most famous preacher of all time had just given his life to Jesus Christ" (Martin 52). The biographer speaks of course of Billy Graham. This might be called the "sportianic succession" of modern muscular Christianity, American-style. At long last someone brought Apollo and Christ together, a prophet *with* honor, as the title of William Martin's story declares. Or is something here out of balance or even reversed? One can point to dark spots in Graham's career, as his biographer does, but the effect is much the same one would note if the stars could be seen as dots in the noon dome of heaven. Graham's glory is orchestrated, even manipulated, to the point on occasion of self-idolatry. Even the spot where the certainty invaded Graham's soul, chasing out all doubt and inquiry, is made sacred. At a retreat center at Forest Home in California "a bronze tablet identifies the Stone of Witness where Billy Graham accepted, once and for all, the absolute authority of the Scriptures" (ibid., 112). As Tom Wicker observed in his review of Graham's biography for the *New York Times Book Review*, "Since no one else was present, Billy Graham himself must have given Martin his exact words," which are recorded as "I accept this Book by faith as the word of God." He must also have identified for plaque placers the spot where "the intellectual suicide," as Wicker calls it, occurred (9).

One of the trademarks of modern muscular Christianity is its anti-intellectualism. In contrast, the Victorian period in England boasted writers and thinkers of some stature, notably Charles Kingsley and Thomas Hughes. Americans have emphasized muscle rather than mind, hence Graham's attraction to and involvement with the movement from the outset. In July 1945 Graham joined the athlete-preacher Gil Dodds at Winona Lake, Indiana, to convene the first Youth for Christ conference. "In the next several years evangelists moved from the serendipitous rediscovery of what Youth for Christ called 'the sports appeal' to the deliberate use of sports and sports celebrities as a means to attract audiences, especially young males. When Graham left Youth for Christ to begin his own revivals in 1947, Dodds accompanied him to Charlotte and ran a pseudo-competitive six laps around the audience before Graham delivered the evening sermon" (Mathisen 12). Ever since, athletes have been a prominent feature of Graham's crusades; and if Christian athletes have supported his causes, he has in turn generously supported theirs. From 1971 to 1975, for instance, the Billy Graham Evangelistic Association provided seventy-two thousand dollars for the Fellowship of Christian Athletes (Martin 468).

If traditionally there has been in theology an understandable conflict between faith and works, Billy Graham has seen none between faith and sports, whether sports are viewed as work or play. His anti-intellectual stance proved enormously popular, endearing him to all who choose short views and quick action. If he is a man of God, he is also a man of numbers, as opposed to what has been called a man of letters, almost an extinct species in our culture. Morrow Graham, Billy's mother, believed that the door to hell ran through the campuses of state universities (ibid., 66). There is little evidence in the evangelist's life that he differs, making an exception only for the athletic departments, where godliness in his view has a better chance of surviving. At the height of the Vietnam War Graham proclaimed, "I think athletics turn the great energy of young people in the right direction. . . . People who are carrying the Viet Cong flag around the country are not athletes. If our people would spend more time in gymnasiums and on playing fields, we'd be a better nation!" (347, quoted). Graham has sanctified anti-intellectualism both by his praise of sports and his distrust of critical inquiry. "His view of humanity and its deepest need also remained essentially unchanged from the portrait he drew in the 1950s. The complexities of human nature plumbed by Shakespeare and Sartre, by Camus and Chekhov, by Bergman and, indeed, by the Bible itself need not occupy us unduly, he seemed to say, since virtually all human problems can be explained by reference to 'something that happened in the Garden of Eden long ago' " (575). For Graham this would be about four thousand years. His cosmology is medieval, if not ancient Egyptian. The costs to American culture of such simplistic attitudes are still being tallied.

Not surprisingly, Graham has been a close "spiritual adviser" of sports fans Dwight Eisenhower, Richard Nixon, Ronald Reagan, and George Bush. As Perry D. Young observes in *God's Bullies,* "God seems always to lead him among conservative Republicans, where the money—if not always the political power—is." Graham also tried to be friends with Harry Truman, but this did not work out: "Truman told Merle Miller years afterward that the big-time evangelist was no friend of his. 'He's one of those counterfeits. . . . All he wants to do is get his name in the newspapers.' Actually, Graham wanted to get his picture in the papers, too, and that's how he came to be declared persona non grata in the Truman White House" (Young 178).

In recent years Graham has professedly become more skeptical of "exercising political influence," though his support of the Gulf War would tend to negate such claims. After 1980 he began in press conferences and interviews to warn against "the mingling of spiritual and political goals" (Martin 472). What Graham never realized, even if he really intended to follow this change in philosophy, is that sports are the glue that joins spiritual and political goals. This was true in ancient Greece and Rome, in the Middle Ages and the Renaissance, and in the modern world. Graham, though, has never been one to look far for cultural connections or to wonder long if there might be interpretations of the Gospel other than his own.

Graham is typical of evangelists who see primarily a conflict between sensuality and beauty and rarely see one between beauty and ideology. Religion itself, they believe, is a source of physical power and beauty, and the personality at the center of Christianity is a supreme physical specimen himself, putting to shame the pentathletes of ancient Greece and Mr. America of the present day. Graham himself could not be more explicit on the matter. In a letter to a Dallas crusade convert, a former television actor and nightclub owner who was planning a film on the life of Christ, Graham wrote, "Please get a man with great strength in his face. I have seen so many pictures of Jesus as a weakling that I am sick of it. He was no sissie and he was no weakling. No sin or mar had come near his body. . . . He must have been straight, strong, big, handsome, tender, gracious, courteous" (quoted in Pollock, *Graham* 168). Biographer John Pollock says that "Graham was sure Christ must have been the most perfectly developed man physically in the history of the world," one whose eyes "could pierce the hypocrisy of a Pharisee yet had such tenderness that He could break a sinful woman's heart' " (ibid.). Here is the influence not of what the Bible has to say about the coming Christ, which Graham says he believes, but of the ideal of the knight who had two hearts. Graham's image of Jesus is about as different as any could be from the Christ prophesied by Isaiah: "Who hath believed our report? and to whom is the arm [that is, the power] of the Lord revealed? For he shall grow up before him as a tender plant, and as a root out of a dry ground: he hath no form nor comeliness; and when we shall see him, there is no beauty that we should desire him. He is despised and rejected of men; a man of sorrows, and acquainted with grief: and we hid as it were our faces from him; he was despised, and we esteemed him not" (Isaiah 53:1–3).

Admittedly Graham endowed his Jesus with tenderness, but physically he reminds one of Steve Reeves, Arnold Schwarzenegger, or even Max Headroom. Graham's Jesus is the one of Bruce Barton's *The Man Nobody Knows* and the object of worship of Sinclair Lewis's *Elmer Gantry*, a real two-fisted sort of guy, a go-getter, a man's man, as described in *Running with God: The New Christian Athletes:* "The painter's projection of the Man from Nazareth as a pale, anemic, kindly 'wax saint' with a haloed ring of light around his head is abhorrent to the Christian athletes. . . . 'Nobody like that could have walked through a "Lynching mob" without a hand touching Him or thrown over the tables of the money-changers in the temple without suffering immediate reprisal,' " Paul Dietzel believes. " 'I submit that Jesus of Nazareth was a strong, healthy, manly-appearing person whose body was firm muscled by honest toil and rigorous disciplines' "

(Hefley 119). Grace and pity are not the primary qualities sought in this savior, but rather guts and power.

Like most American evangelists before him, Graham has been essentially conservative, being careful not to rattle the establishment to espouse major social change. His Jesus is the Prince of Peace whose word is interpreted to allow for a "just war," according to Augustine, Aquinas, and Luther (see Pelikan 172–81). One Southern Baptist minister who took another view of Scripture was Martin Luther King Jr. King's Jesus is "the Liberator" who releases his people from bondage. Said King, "What was new about Gandhi's movement in India is that he mounted a revolution on hope and love, hope and non-violence" (ibid., 216–17, quoted).

Though King opposed the Vietnam War and did not promote the alliance of religion and sports, his message of nonviolent change has much in it about the struggle for freedom. In the six points outlining his strategy for nonviolence he makes clear, often using sporting metaphors, that the effort is only for the strong of heart, such as those who might enter any contest requiring courage and will. There is even a Nietzchean echo in the challenge:

> 1. Nonviolence is for the strong rather than the weak. It is a difficult discipline that eschews cowardice. It is not nonresistance but a particular method of resistance.
>
> 2. Nonviolence does not seek to "defeat or humiliate" the opponent, but to win him over. It is not employed for the purpose of scoring points but as a means of creating "the beloved community."
>
> 3. Nonviolence directs itself "against the forces of evil rather than against persons who happen to be doing evil." One may despise a particular form of evil, but one may not despise the doer of evil.
>
> 4. Without making suffering into something to be sought, nonviolence can bring home the truth that "unearned suffering is redemptive." It can be creatively enacted in ways that transform evil into a potential for good.
>
> 5. The attitude of nonviolence must be within the heart of the individual as well as in his outer actions. "The nonviolent

resistor not only refuses to shoot his opponent but he also refuses to hate him."

6. Nonviolence "is based on the conviction that the universe is on the side of justice." The practitioner can believe that he is not going against the grain of what is ultimate, but seeks rather to exemplify what is ultimate: redemptive suffering love. [R. Brown 81–82]

King was assassinated in 1968 in Memphis, Tennessee, while helping sanitation workers organize a strike for better working conditions. Just two years later Billy Graham came to Knoxville to carry on his work not of changing social conditions but of winning souls. His muscular Christianity has a leisure-class morality for the relatively affluent. Often accused of being a communist, King was no such thing. Instead he sought a middle way in his civil rights campaign. "Truth is found neither in traditional capitalism nor in classical communism. Each represents a partial truth. . . . Capitalism fails to realize that life is social. Communism fails to realize that life is personal. The good and just society is neither the thesis of capitalism nor the antithesis of Communism, but a socially conscious democracy which reconciles the truths of individualism with collectivism" (King 187). Both Southern Baptist ministers, Graham and King share common ground but differ profoundly in emphasis, Graham never deviating from a gospel of salvation and King giving his life for a gospel of social justice.

Perry Young points to the ancestry of Jerry Falwell as presented in a pamphlet prepared for a Founder's Day service in 1977. Entitled *Jerry Falwell, a Man in the People Business*–note the word *business*–the pamphlet begins with Adam, because "a man was needed to propagate and subdue" the world. Then the genealogy jumps to Washington and Lincoln and then to the evangelists Jonathan Edwards, Dwight L. Moody, Billy Sunday, and other great men of God. Then to Grand Central Station! "Today, when our nation, America, has reached the height of modern civilization and yet the depth of depravity, dangerously balancing on the brink of moral and spiritual destruction, God has again provided a man to meet the need and challenge of the hour. That man is Jerry Falwell. To God be the Glory for sending him to us" (quoted in Young 204–5). In muscular

Christianity Billy Sunday plays a role almost analogous to John the Baptist, pointing the way to the saviors of modern society, Billy Graham and Jerry Falwell.

Elsewhere in *God's Bullies* Young shows how deceitfully Falwell has exploited such subjects as Jimmy Carter and homosexuals for his own advancement. Falwell's "deception," Young claims, "masks" his "racist background and anti-Semitism" (199), which Falwell vehemently denies, stating that racism is "unscriptural" and pointing to his well-publicized relationship with Israel. Certainly Falwell's bragging on the accomplishments of his athletes, black and white, from the pulpit is not apparently racist no matter how questionable the practice might be otherwise. With Billy Graham, Falwell has been co-chaplain of Sportainity and perhaps its main cheerleader. Not only does Falwell sell the Gospel but patriotism too—in integrated packages as seen in his marketing of Jesus lapel pins, flag kits, and Christian's Bill of Rights from the pulpit (see D'Souza 125-26).

The one characteristic shared by televangelists in recent years, whether they be devotees of the play of the theme park (Jim and Tammy Bakker) or of the agon of the stadium or court of play (Jerry Falwell, Billy Graham, and Oral Roberts), is the constant need of money, in sharp contrast to those who first spread the Word without any money. Not one of the TV evangelists, judging from appeals or promises based on conversion, would agree with Thoreau's assertion that money never bought one necessity of the soul. Asked if he couldn't be just as happy living in an inexpensive house, Rex Humbard shot back, "No. It is an asset for me to have a nice house and an asset for my organization, because I entertain outstanding people." Humbard said that the poverty of his evangelist father "turned people off" and that members of his congregation were not offended by his Lincoln and his Cadillac (Plagenz, "Humbard" 10)

On one television program Roberts acknowledged that some people resented his houses, cars, and manner of dress and said he wanted to talk about it but he "never did" (ibid.). One who did talk about the need for money was Jim Bakker. In response to a comment about his and Tammy's air-conditioned dog house, brass giraffe, and Rolls-Royce, he asked angrily, "Why should God have junk? Have you been to the Vatican?" This remark was aired on 22 May 1987 on the *CBS Evening News*, and apparently even Jerry Falwell had had enough. In an interview published in the *Charlotte Observer*, Falwell declared that this "prosperity theology," what some call "health and wealth theology," is "the most damnable heresy being preached in the world today." Falwell went on to say that the new leaders of PTL were going to look carefully at "the personal lifestyle and quality of Christian Testimony" of PTL preachers and establish a new dress code at the water park, which would outlaw ultra-skimpy swimsuits ("PTL Scrutinizing" 10). On the same day as the publication of the interview, from the pulpit in Thomas Road Baptist Church Falwell gave clear notice in a sermon which I watched that while he might be tightening up on forms of play and display, agonic sports were as highly prized as ever. Called forth to testify was Kelvin Edwards, a leading scorer for Liberty Baptist who later played for the New Orleans Saints as well as for the Dallas Cowboys, "getting his brains knocked out," Falwell said. Falwell said Edwards planned later to teach school. Another of Falwell's graduates would be joining Tom Landry as a punter, Falwell said proudly, and a third had recently gone 4 for 5 for Pittsburgh with two home runs. One more time Falwell reminded his listeners that sports are a good means of recruiting young people.

What Falwell does not realize or acknowledge is that competitive sports, especially televised sports, are at the center of the health and wealth theology, as much as air-conditioned dog houses and brass giraffes. Indeed, the emphasis upon winning represents a corruption not only of religion but also of games, as Caillois points out in his study of play: "Transposed to reality, the only goal of *agon* is success. . . . Implacable competition becomes the rule. Winning even justifies foul blows" (54). Jerry Falwell is scarcely in a position to throw stones at anyone practicing a prosperity theology. His hand too is always out, not in supplication but in request, and it has been argued that you can never be sure which coffers the donations go into, in spite of appearances of the social gospel (see Frances Fitzgerald 151–52).

Like Billy Graham, Jerry Falwell avidly supported Ronald Reagan, with whom it was said he "shared strengths of charisma and oratory," both being "great communicators." Indeed Falwell may have been partly responsible for Reagan's triumph. In the 1970s Falwell even surpassed Graham as the most newsworthy Christian leader and became the leader of the Christian New Right, which included Pat Robertson, James Robinson, and others (Martin 472). Pollster Lou Harris believes that without Falwell's Moral Majority, Reagan would have lost by one percentage point to Jimmy Carter in the November 1980 election (see D'Souza 127). Falwell, also a Nixon man, believes "the nation would be better off if Watergate was never exposed" (ibid., after 112). Falwell thus was an ideal team player for Republicanism in the 1980s, with its emphasis upon power and sports, the new definition of *old-time religion.*

If Falwell pointed to athletic fields for moral metaphors, famous coaches returned the favor by quoting Scripture that inspired success. "Is Football the Most Important Thing in Tom Landry's Life?" asked a full-page ad in Family *Weekly* on 23 October 1983. The emphatic answer was no:

> You might think that football was the most important thing in Tom Landry's life. But it isn't. "The most important thing in my life," he says, "is my personal faith in God. I turn to Him for guidance and answers to my daily problems. In His word He has promised, 'I will instruct you and teach you in the way you should go' " (Psalms 32:8 New International Version). God's love and *power* are at work in Tom Landry's life. And you can enjoy God's love, and experience his wonderful guidance and *power*, in your own life. The Bible promises: "In everything you do, put God first, and He will direct you and crown your effort with success" (Proverbs 3:6 Living Bible).

The ad, like one that ran for months in the early 1980s on television, is for Jamie Buckingham's book called *Power for Living*, published in celebration of "the Year of the Bible as proclaimed by President Ronald Reagan and the Congress in February 1983." An ad citing Proverbs 3:16 (Living Bible) also appeared on a huge billboard overlooking much of the city of Nashville. The book shows how eight people, including Roger Staubach, Julius ("Dr. J.") Erving and Charles W. Colson, did not "allow worldly success to blind them from finding God's goal of success" (Buckingham 17). That last phrase, as much as any other, demonstrates the final absorption of sports into religion and religion into sports.

Many athletes, such as Roger Staubach and Dr. J., have become widely admired role models for the young, and I do not wish to imply that they or others are unworthy of such a demanding task. Would they be role models if they were Christian *and* poor? My criticism, then, is not with the superstars in *Power for Living* but with the superstructure of financial success and worldly fame that the book applauds. Throughout the Bible fame and money are eschewed, as well as titles and worldly achievement. In *Power for Living* the convenience with which the things of Caesar are reconciled with the things of God is amazing. Instead of reminding one of the obligation to others, the book becomes a sort of tool for personal advancement in the world.

The use of Proverbs 3:16 in the advertisement for *Power for Living* well illustrates what we have come to, paralleling quite clearly the sports dogma that winning is the only thing that matters. The Living Bible (with clear Pindaric echoes) promises "finding God's goal of success": "In everything you do, put God first, and he will direct you and crown your efforts with success." Note the world of difference between this rendering and that of the King James Bible: "In all thy ways acknowledge him, and he shall direct thy paths." *Paths*, a shepherd metaphor, suggests righteousness, whereas *success* suggests money and victory. Even if it is argued that *paths* does not bring righteousness to mind, the term certainly does not mean success in sports or business.

The epigraph for the book *Power for Living* comes from Isaiah 40:30, which in the Living Bible becomes: "Those who hope in the Lord will renew their strength. They will soar on wings like angels; they will run and not grow weary, they will walk and not be faint." Gone from the King James Version is the transcendent, promising "shall," and "wait upon the Lord" yields to "hope in the Lord." In our hyperactive age "wait upon" seems out of the question, and hope, after all, is one of the great virtues. In the movie *Chariots of Fire* this verse from Isaiah is a sort of epilogue as if in leaving this fine film we are asked to take the words literally and forget that they are metaphors just as are those of Isaiah 40:11: "He shall feed his flock like a shepherd: he shall gather the lambs with his arm, and carry *them* in his bosom, *and* shall gently lead those that are with young"(KJV). It is not so much the verses that get quoted that warp our times as those that rarely get attention, specifically those relating to a shepherd ethos.

In the next chapter of Isaiah there is in verse 41:10 in the Revised Standard Version an even more startling paraphrase, as quoted by W.J. Weatherby and Jim and Ann Ryun in *Chariots of Fire* and *A Christian Message for Today:*

> Fear not, for I am with you
> be not dismayed, for I am your God;
> I will strengthen you, I will help you.
> I will uphold you with my victorious right hand. [70]

In the King James Version the last line above is as follows: "I will uphold thee with the right hand of my righteousness." Thus "righteousness" gives way to "victorious right hand" just as in Proverbs 3:16 "paths" become "success." "Paths of righteousness" is a shepherd metaphor in contrast to "success" and "victory," which are goals of knights. In the twentieth century even God has become a knight, and the devil, of course, has always been one, bright and resplendent.

Admittedly some of the newer translations (as opposed to paraphrases, one of which the Living Bible is) retain some of the old language. In Proverbs 3:16, for example, the New International and the New Revised Standard retain the idea of "paths." Still a comparative look at three comprehensive concordances for three editions of the Bible will illustrate how the word "success" has blossomed in our age. In the King James Version there is one reference to "success" with five variants (Strong 984); in the Revised Standard Version, thirteen with thirty-seven variants (Whitaker 1060); and in the Living Bible thirty-six with one hundred variants (Speer 945). My count may not be accurate and there appear to be a few other uses unlisted by Strong. Nevertheless, it seems safe to say that in the modern paraphrase of scripture nothing succeeds like "success."

The cult of success reflects what now might be called a permanent drift away from Old Testament values with its never ending warnings against worship of idols and toward Hellenic way of thinking, which prized worldly achievement. In ancient Greece, where the athletic culture was based on shame as opposed to guilt, the idea of success was probably more prevalent than in Israel. This would help to explain the repeated appearance of the term or equivalents in the Lattimore translation of Pindar's odes, eighteen times in a text of approximately 150 pages. It may nevertheless be that for the Jews *success* meant a kind of power, though not imperial power but power of enablement or coping. And it may be that in some sense what we call "success" could mean "spiritual power for daily living." But even conceding all this, with its knightly confusion of the crucial difference between "aspiring for the good" and "doing good" insisted on by Thoreau, how is it that we need millionaire investors and millionaire athletes to remind us of the sage words of penniless prophets? What is stressed throughout the Bible and Greek literature is "excellence" (*arete*), which for the Greeks and Jews overlapped "success" but was not identical to it.

Power for Living is not an isolated example of the presumed relationship between the Holy Spirit and worldly success and power. Here are only a few others from recent years: *Move That Mountain* by Jim Bakker, *God's Voice to the Pro* by L. Fisher, *Running with God* by James C. Hefley, *Spirit Power: All You Need When You Need It!* by Larry Poland, and *Faith Made Them Champions* edited by Norman Vincent Peale.

Among these, the most intriguing is *God's Voice to the Pro*, centering on the efforts of "Doc" Ira Eshleman, "businessman, teacher, pastor, unofficial world sports Chaplain, founder of Bibletown in Boca Raton, Florida in 1950." The book outlines Eshleman's success in business and real estate and his ministry to professional athletes as an example of "Faith in Action." Published in 1969 by Sports World Chaplaincy, it proudly displays cover photographs of Eshleman presenting a Bible to President Richard Nixon and of Billy Graham hugging Eshleman in front of the 2,500-seat Bibletown auditorium. Most astonishing is Eshleman's essay called "A Pro's Look at the 23rd Psalm." Eshleman divided the psalm into phrases representing nine downs plus the touchdown. He describes his plan as follows: "Here is a Psalm called 'Everybody's Psalm' ... that speaks to everybody's need. We might think of this Psalm as a football field where play begins at the point when 'the Lord becomes our Shepherd' and ends at the goal line of our 'Dwelling in the house of the Lord forever' " (Fisher 105). The green pasture as gridiron may be the ultimate symbol of cultural transformation.

Power has long been the chief buzzword of American evangelism. In *Less Than Conquerors*, Douglas Frank provides a long list of "power books" that evangelicals used to boost themselves into the twentieth century. These include *Elijah and the Secret of His Power* by F.B. Meyer, *How to Obtain Fullness of Power* by R.A. Torrey, and *Power: "Received Ye the Holy Ghost?"* by J. Wilbur Chapman. Torrey, one of Moody's coworkers, observed that "from many earnest hearts there is rising a cry for more power in our personal conflict with the world, the flesh, and the devil, and more power in our work with others." Torrey lamented "the poverty and powerlessness of the average Christian" and characterized 99 percent of Christians as "mere weaklings" (Frank 251). The turn-of-the-century evangelicals, Frank notes, often used electrical or mechanical metaphors to describe the power of the spirit, A.C. Dixon emphasizing that "the measure of His power depends upon the wire of faith and consecration through which he may work the machinery of our lives and bring things to pass" (252–53). Today the powers of the Holy Spirit and the sporting spirit are often indistinguishable, both regularly conveyed to us by televised spectacle, either in the form of stadium crusade or the big game, usually without memorable metaphors such as the "wire of faith." Instead of metaphor, television is the medium, and all too often in our age of instant communication the message as well, the message of the advertisers of health, wealth, beauty, success, and power for living.

Martin Hengel in *Christ and Power* identifies the type of power to which the Scripture does refer, not the power for prosperity or power to be a hero or even healing or relief:

> Only when forced into it by his Corinthian opponents, and totally against his will, does Paul make reference to revelations he had received from the Lord. This same Lord denied his request for relief from a severe illness: "My grace is all you need; power comes to its full strength in weakness." The apostle confirms this by adding, "for when I am weak, then I am strong"

(2 Cor. 12:9–10). For this very reason the primitive community's apostolic message can never serve as the basis for a "theology of glory" but only for a "theology of the cross." The actual way of the community in this world has been traced out by the earthly, the crucified Christ, and not by the risen Christ in his glory. The risen Christ is not at our beck and call; he cannot be seen. Our only access to him is through a hope that has nothing to cling to except Jesus' own promise. [27–28]

From this crucified Christ, Hengel argues, comes the "power to produce change," as opposed to the power that gives riches and fame and overcomes pain. No one has expressed this "theology of the cross" better or more succinctly than the preacher Bevel in Flannery O'Connor's short story "The River." Standing in the river he speaks to the expectant,

> "If you ain't come for Jesus, you ain't come for me. If you just come to see can you leave your pain in the river, you ain't come for Jesus. You can't leave your pain in the river," he said. "I never told nobody that." He stopped and looked down at his knees.
>
> "I seen you cure a woman oncet!" a sudden high voice shouted from the hump of people. "Seen that woman get up and walk out straight where she limped in!"
>
> The preacher lifted one foot and then the other. He seemed almost but not quite to smile. "You might as well go home if that's what you come for," he said. [40]

Here is a traditional Christian doctrine that seems stranger now than at perhaps any other time in Western history, given as we are to a "theology of glory" and of "health and wealth" and of "finding God's goal of success." Meister Eckhart may have been charged for heresy, but it was not for his theology of the Cross: "It follows that to be a Son of God is to suffer" (65). Christ, he argues, does not remove pain but merely makes it meaningful through grace, a true power for living that neither health nor wealth can ever provide (see Eckhart 66–73). Like Eckhart, Paul sees in "the gospel the power to produce change, and this frees him from all autocratic and law-centered forces, frees him for a new life in which the 'fruit of the spirit—love, joy, peace, patience . . .' (Gal. 5:22)—takes over" (Hengel

27). This power "further shows itself in the overcoming of barriers that were especially grievous in the ancient world, those of nation and class: in Christ's community 'there is neither Jew nor Greek, there is neither slave nor free, there is neither male nor female; for you are one in Christ Jesus' (Gal. 3:28, cf. Col. 3:11)" (ibid., 41). Compared with success, the fruits of the spirit are "wimpy" values that cannot by endorsed by some until they have demonstrated their strength in athletics, war, or business.

In *Christ and Power* Hengel describes a social gospel based upon the teaching of the crucified Christ and a converted Paul, as opposed to a glorified risen Christ who is coming again and who is bent on retribution toward the hard-hearted and wicked. Note how often the fundamentalists speak of the Second Coming. Instead of God coming again, the social gospel emphasizes a God already here in the depths of our being and tries to awaken in us "the deepest springs of our social and historical existence," as Paul Tillich, a different kind of good-news messenger, has explained.

> The name of this infinite and inexhaustible ground of history is *God.* That is what the word means, and it is that to which the words *Kingdom of God* and *Divine Providence* point. And if these words do not have much meaning for you, translate them, and speak of the depth of history, of the ground and aim of our social life, and of what you take seriously without reservation in your moral and political activities. Perhaps you should call this depth *hope,* simply hope. For if you can find hope in the ground of history, you are united with the great prophets who were able to look into the depth of their times, who tried to escape it, because they could not stand the horror of their visions, and who yet had the strength to look to an even deeper level and there to discover hope. [quoted in Robinson 47]

Analysis suggests that what Tillich means by God is the "exact opposite of any *deus ex machina,* a supernatural being to whom one can turn away from the world and who can be relied upon to intervene from without." The God of the triumphalists is precisely a deus ex machina, a god from a machine who at the end of time will drop from the skies and separate the quick and dead into winners and losers. But this could hardly be the case if "God is not 'out there.'

He is in Bonhoeffer's words 'the "beyond" in the midst of life,' a depth of reality reached 'not on the borders of life but at its centre,' not by any flight of the alone to be alone, but, in Kierkegaard's fine phrase, by a 'deeper immersion in existence.' For the word 'God' denotes the ultimate depth of our being, the creative ground and meaning of all our existence" (ibid.).

Television triumphalists would have little patience with such intellectual theology, seeing hope not in the aims of social life and "moral and political activities," but in salvation through conversion, depending not so much on a god hidden in the depths of an experiencing and emergent attention but one who resides above and out there and who is coming again as promised, in which case life becomes not primarily a challenge for social change and moral development but an arena wherein is waged an unceasing battle of good and evil for the souls of the human race, where winning is the only thing.

Given their theological premises, it is uncanny how skillfully triumphalists preach both success and Armageddon at the same time, or rather alternately. The world is coming to an end soon, but send in your money anyway. God will repay many times over, if not in this world then in the next. Thus they keep the beleaguered public in a constant state of fear and hope, the technique mastered by Graham, who, like his contemporaries, presents a pessimistically eschatological view combined with a message of uplifting optimism. Christ is winning victories, the nation is awakening spiritually, but at the same time Armageddon, the ultimate victory for some, looms on the horizon (D. Cohen 182).

Like the Alger hero, the TV triumphalists worship success. Somewhat like the Merriwell hero, King and Eckhart sought quality. While success and quality share some features, the differences between them are considerable. Success is measured by quantity; quality is determined by style. Success is always intruding upon our field of vision; quality, as Robert Pirsig reminds us, must be seen out of the corner of the eye. Success glories—even wallows—in victory; quality rejoices in the harmony of motion, thus including play as well as sports, and in the harmony of experience, thus including justice. Success calls attention to the performer; quality, to the performance. Success points to records and past achievements; quality looks not to the outcome of games or crusades but challenges of skill within them, leaving victory as the mere residue of one's best efforts. Success is "worldly." So is quality, but it is also "divine." Success asks who won; quality, how the game was played or the life was lived. The real question is always this: How was the dance danced?

There are many types of knights; the more established varieties merely institutionalize the model. Members of the mafias, drug cartels, and urban gangs also follow the pattern, however much they seem in opposition to it. In fact they imitate it to the extreme. The eyes of youth especially, left without hope for harmonious tomorrows and social justice, have been focused on manly images of success on television, exemplifying strength and beauty. The principles of modern knighthood are unstated but obvious:

> 1. In the solutions to problems, books and ideas are not as important as games and power; education at best is, as college athletes are fond of saying, "something to fall back on," not something to climb with or for. (Heaven forbid that learning might be an end in itself.) The unthinkable bumper sticker imagined by one southern novelist is "No one is going to take my books from me." "Guns" is all too thinkable.

> 2. Accumulate stuff. It is enough to remember the wisdom of the another bumper sticker: "He who dies with the most toys wins."

> 3. Celebrate manliness, the fortification of sexuality. Form groups, cultivate exclusivity, defend the honor of your territory, wear insignia, go armed, swear brotherhood, and bond together. Think of winners and losers, "them versus us" rather than just us, the shepherds of the planet. Get even with history. Plan revenge like the Second Coming. The bloody ads for boxing over the "World's Most Important Station" provide the image.

The one hundred thousand policemen (blue knights) promised soon to be added on the city streets of the country (about six army divisions) and the rapidly expanding number of prisons are testimony, on the one hand, to our failure to educate and, on the other, to the only solution we know: the knightly one. In the history of our country we have had several systems of forts: those against Native Americans, those against the British, next against ourselves, and more recently against our youth–fort ghettos. Last is the archipelago of prisons. In time these might well surpass in number the political prisons in the Soviet Union under Stalin, offering final proof in the eyes of the knights of original sin, original sin being roughly analogous to failure.

For shepherds, the original sin would remain disobedience of what Thoreau called the Higher Laws. And the wisdom in these laws is the only alternative to our present predicament. To Thoreau this wisdom takes care of itself: "The moral law does not want any champion. Its asserters do not go to war" (*Journal* 1:334). In another passage Thoreau claims: "There are two ways to victory,–to strive bravely, or to yield. How much pain the last will save we have not yet learned" (1:147). Since for knights yielding or finding common ground (Thoreau's "community of love" [1:115]) is unthinkable, losing is the ultimate disgrace. This explains why some Christian groups were outraged when Jesus was called a loser.

Chronologically, the events or phases in the pincer movements leading to the Christianization, muscularization, and militarization–including internal armament–of American culture can be delineated as follows:

1. The passing of knighthood from the Old World to the New, as seen in John Smith and Miles Standish.

2. The glorification of home-grown military and athletic heroes such as Nathan Hale and Light Horse Harry Lee.

3. The spread of organized religion through the Second Great Awakening (1787–1805) and the evangelism it engendered.

4. The establishment of schools in the early nineteenth century under the auspices of such Ivy League Calvinist educators as Samuel Doak.

5. The championing of physical education, military training, and engineering in the second quarter of the nineteenth century by Ivy League educators such as Philip Lindsley.

6. The rise of the influence of West Point and the proliferation of military schools and seminaries throughout the land, includ-

ing the land grant colleges created by the Morrill Acts in the second half of the century.

7. The advent of the YMCA, especially in the colleges, and the spread of the "gridiron gospel," also in the second half of the nineteenth century.

8. The decline of the Y and the reemergence of bee-fighting frontier ministers such as Billy Sunday, who, ironically, was also undone by the media that made him.

9. The emergence of sporting television ministers such as Billy Graham and Jerry Falwell.

10. The reemergence of the old organizational spirit of the Y as seen in the scores of ministries using sports, especially televised sports, as a form of witnessing, with emphasis still upon salvation and success in contrast to a social gospel of justice.

The slick, televised, neatly packaged, and well-orchestrated programs of the modern crusaders such as Graham and Falwell seem at first glance to be of a different order than those of an earlier time, but the same characteristics are still evident:

1. The theory that sports build character (recapitulation).

2. The theory that sports provide a means of venting aggression (catharsis).

3. The confusion of spiritual grace with material success, of which the athlete is a visible symbol.

4. The cult of manliness and the principle of male bonding.

5. The segregation of the sexes and discrimination against women.

6. The certainty that Jesus was as perfect in body as in spirit.

7. An anti-intellectualism manifested in emphasis upon physical development, a skepticism of (or even hatred of) the arts and sciences, and a theology reduced to win-lose categories, salvation or damnation.

8. The equation of Christianity with Americanism or patriotism by means of athletics.

9. An almost passionate interest in statistics, win-loss records, power for living, and souls saved.

10. A self-righteousness that rejects alternatives to sports or religious belief.

The startling conservatism of evangelism in all periods of American history leads to this conclusion: "Organized mass evangelism is a powerful tool, but these mass techniques have really distorted the appeal to deep religious emotions that originally gave rise to religion. If there is indeed a real spiritual change coming, the revivalists, who represent the status quo, will not lead it, probably won't understand it, and will most certainly oppose it" (D. Cohen 209). The other feature of American life in addition to religion that evangelists have helped to distort is, of course, organized athletics. If it is time, as Bishop John Shelby Spong is brave enough to announce, that we should rescue the Bible from the fundamentalists, it is also time that we free sports as well. One of the sad commentaries on contemporary culture is that university athletic officials and televangelists have to be watched almost as carefully as parolees from prison to ensure compliance with rules and even laws. A code of ethics for evangelists is a telling paradox of our time. As one comedian has said, "I thought they had a code of ethics called the Bible!" As in television ministry, abuses in college sports (read televised sports) have reached epidemic proportions, and behind them all is the urge for more fans and money. As the revenue for television appearances increases, Allen Guttmann points out, coaches are driven to even greater lengths to produce championship "telegenic teams" that the networks will want to show. Recruiting and eligibility rules are shunted aside, and the players themselves are brought into the cycle of greed. This is not to say that television caused the problem, but it has certainly helped to perpetuate it (*Sports Spectators* 139–40).

Televised religion, like televised sports, has become show business and entertainment. I do not object so much to professional sports as business, since that is what they are by definition, but only to the attempt of professional players to serve as models of piety by praying on the sidelines or end zones and giving testimony of their beliefs, implying that God has approved fully of their violent profession and helped them attain success. The shift of professional sports toward religious ritual and the metamorphosis of evangelism and college sports toward televised entertainment have altered the faces of both religion and sport. This is puzzling, since neither sports nor religion originated in the commercial impulse, though it can be argued that both stem from the drive for power expressed early in the history of sports as the equivalent of money.

Finally, the perfect symbol of our televised predicament and the collective sins of our fathers is the much-bruited possibility of a fight between George Foreman and Mike Tyson for the heavyweight championship of the world. Supposedly each contestant would receive $50 million. In the view of many, it would be once again the battle between the Cross and the Crescent following Mike Tyson's celebrated conversion to Islam. We can be sure that Caesar's Palace will be a prime consideration as a site, though as of May 1995 Tyson has a contract with MGM Grand to hold six of his fights there.

# 16

# The Knight and the Shepherd

The institutionalization of American sports has comprised five discernible phases: colonization, nationalization, consecration, imperialization, and commercialization, all overlapping and connected. Essentially the rise of sports in America recapitulated the rise of both sports and Christianity in Europe. At the beginning both were strongly Hebraic. Then they were Hellenized, Romanized, nationalized, and finally in America televised. Our colonial period begins with Jamestown and Plymouth, with prayers offered up repeatedly to the stern God of the Old Testament, especially before battle. Indeed, he is even called "the God of Battle" by Samuel Doak in his prayer for the Overmountain Men. The Hellenistic phase flourished from around the 1850s until the turn of the century, with endless references to the Greeks, usually by educators or military apologists, and the High Roman phase began with the ascent of Theodore Roosevelt and the Spanish-American War. We are now in a Low Roman phase, one which, since the end of World War I and the golden age of sports, has been characterized by media and money. On the happy side, recent decades have also seen a democratization of American sports that helps to compensate for the abuses inflicted upon sports in the name of God, country, and money. Basically the pattern of evolution is a move from *paideia* to *ludus*, as described by Caillois. In one sense there is nothing very complex or surprising about the transformation. It is observable in every evolving culture and indeed in every life, from the frolicsome games of childhood to the super-serious struggle for power.

In the first phase of the evolution of American sports—colonization—knighthood, with its emphasis on martial arts as opposed to idle play, is established as the dominant cultural pattern in the new world by European immigrants, north and south. The second phase, nationalization, is evident in the deliberate connection of athleticism and sports with military heroism, as seen in the description of patriots such as Nathan Hale. Out of the struggle for independence come our own institutions of defense such as West Point, where physical fitness became virtually synonymous with military preparedness. In a prize-winning essay for the American Philosophical Society in 1797 Harrison Smith asserted that a program of military exercises fostered "national spirit" (Betts, "Mind and Body" 790). Sports, so closely related to drills and exercises—sports did, in fact, succeed them in the colleges—made an even greater contribution to the "national spirit."

Consecration did not begin until after the Civil War, with the commemoration of the war dead. By *consecration* I do not mean the elevation of sports into a separate religion but a dignification, the recognition of their vital role in remaking the country into one nation, under God, the best example of which is the dedication of Memorial Hall at Harvard on the fields of play, a "fit spot," in Charles W. Eliot's words, "to commemorate the manliness which there was nurtured" (*Turning Point* 29). In Eliot's view, manliness was not to be a quality of the past but the wave of the future, a trait to be instilled in the male youth of the nation. This message was explicitly stated even earlier, in 1865, on the other side of the country by John Swett, the educational reformer in San Francisco: "A four year's war taught the nation to place a higher value on physical manhood. . . . To lay a solid foundation for our own military strength as a nation, we must begin with three millions of boys in our public schools: and while we breathe into their hearts the spirit of patriotism, we must train them to muscular power which will give us fit soldiers to fight and win battles for the Republic" (Betts, "Home Front" 131).

With Theodore Roosevelt sports were taken beyond the idea

of defense and national unity and became a crucial feature of our High Roman or imperial phase. Games, after all, played a significant role in the advance of the Roman and British Empires, so why should the situation be any different for America, as it moved onto the world stage as a major power? In the international struggle first with Spain at the turn of the century and then with Germany a decade and a half later, the United States showed the old countries its own new versions of the old ideal of knighthood.

The last and final phase in the evolution of sports is commercialization or Low Roman, the one that still defines us. In many ways it is more decadent than imperialization, since it is devoid of the idea of sacrifice and service, and in this respect it is contrary to everything TR held dear about sports and American ideals. This does not mean, however, that what TR wanted to do with sports was right either, for the manliness that he, Henry Cabot Lodge, and others like Frederic Remington and Owen Wister valued was not essentially democratic and hence not a mode that we can look back to with great expectations for instruction in virtue. The contemporary commercialization of sports is exploitative, but so in different ways were the earlier uses, including the functions assigned to them by Eliot and Roosevelt, as different as the two were.

The transformation of sports into heresy occurred without our realizing what was happening. It engulfs our history and reaches back for over a thousand years of Western culture. Before we knew it, our treasured ideals celebrating the unity of mind and body, *mens sana in corpore sano, sapientia et fortitudo,* music and gymnastic, and strength and beauty were reduced to such simplistic proclamations as "Winning is the only thing," which for too many coaches, administrators, and alumni became "Winning ball games is the only thing." Just as religion has been warped to justify sports, so sports have been warped to assist in preparation for war and the waging of it, as a technique in the training of soldiers but mainly as a reinforcing symbol of manliness and knighthood.

Such a transformation is a perfect example of what Carl Jung called *enantiodromia,* the tendency of a virtue to become a vice. We did not reach our current predicament so much through private sin as through the excess of public virtue. We became narrow in proclaiming wholeness, closed our minds even while proclaiming freedom of thought. By incessant lip service to the unity of mind and body we forgot the meaning of moderation, an ideal common to Greeks and Jews that never equated with mediocrity.

We also lost another quality common to pagan philosophers and Old Testament prophets, that of skepticism, which means staying in the middle, as Emerson observes in his essay on Montaigne, for example. Among the prophets there was an almost predictable "overagainstness" directed toward the glorification of the ego and worldly fame and riches. The same was largely true of the Greek philosophers. Both groups greatly doubted that one could have too much of this world and a spiritual world as well. We need a revival of their critical or incredulous frame of mind when we hear announcements such as those of Charles Prebish, whose work convinces him that athletes encounter "ultimate reality" on a regular basis.

We can perhaps better understand the course that sports and religion have taken if we juxtapose the pervasive symbols of this study, the shepherd's staff and the sword of the knight, listing some qualities/symbols associated with each. Between them might be placed the Cross, as mediation and possibility. Analyzing such symbols is not the purpose here; the list merely partially suggests manifestation of their still-evolving differences. The main point, though, is obvious, I trust. The alliance of religion and sports in Christendom demonstrates a movement primarily toward the sword, so that what is conveyed even by the authority of the Cross is a sense that the shepherd world is inherently inferior, when in fact it is in many ways closer to what is most worthwhile in human life and belief. If anything, this world is closer to the spirit and letter of the Gospels than the knightly one. Indeed, the degree of transformation toward knighthood under the banner of the two-sword or two-heart theory is so pronounced and so sanctified as to be almost irreconcilable. The shepherd metaphor at least has Gospel authority, whereas the knight has little or none. The shepherd metaphor is used extensively in relation to the God of Israel and the prophesied savior (Psalm 77:20, 80:1; Isaiah 40:11; Ezekiel 34:23; Zechariah 13:7; John 10:14; Hebrews 13:20). Neither the salvation gospel, the stewardship

**Table 16.1  Symbols of the Shepherd and the Knight**

| Staff | Sword |
|---|---|
| Christ the Shepherd | Christ the Knight |
| Wisdom is the principal thing (Proverbs 4:7) | Winning is the only thing (Yost, Lombardi, Paul Bryant) |
| Vine | Sun |
| Prophet | Philosopher |
| Gospels | Letters |
| Becoming a child | Becoming a man |
| Humanness | Manliness |
| Amateur | Professional |
| Turning around | Overcoming |
| Citizen soldier | Standing army |
| New England town meeting | CIA |
| Consensus | Authority |
| Bios (God of nautre) | Mekos (God of machine) |
| Naturalist | Industrialist |
| Sierra Club | Boone and Crockett Club |
| Ducks Unlimited | NRA |
| Naturalness | Sophistication |
| Growing spiritually | Building character |
| Humorous | Serious |
| Humility | Pride |
| Curiosity | Adventure |
| Edenic | Agonic |
| *Paideia* (Caillois) | *Ludus* |
| Play | Sports |
| Being | Doing |
| Becoming | Being |
| Randomness | Organization |
| Having fun | Keeping score |
| Trust in experience | Belief in luck (Veblen) |
| Wonder | Magic |
| Taboo | Totem |
| Coonhound | German shepherd |
| Stories of the Desert Fathers | Lifestyles of the rich and famous |
| Picnic | Banquet |
| St. Francis | St. Michael |
| Paths | Super highway |
| Love | Duty |
| Ethics | Rules |
| General welfare | Special interests |
| Discovering gifts | Winning prizes |
| Gospel of nature | Gospel of wealth |
| Honesty | Honor |
| Green pastures | City of God |

Table 16.1  Symbols of the Shepherd and the Knight, cont'd

| Staff | Sword |
|---|---|
| Campground | Cathedral |
| Pasture | Stadium |
| Mountain | Fort |
| Dancing | Marching |
| Flute | Drum |
| Baseball | Football |
| Touch football | SuperBowl |
| Pickup basketball | March Madness |
| Earth as garden | World as stage |
| The commonplace | Sensationalism |
| Festival | Tournament |
| Teacher | Coach |
| Poet | Engineer |
| Thinking in pictures (symbolically) | Thinking mechanically (logically) |
| Gnosis (self knowledge) | Scientia (knowledge of the world) |
| Mythos (Pirsig) | Logos |
| Metaphors | Mathematics |
| Education | Training |
| Community | Tribe |
| Cooperation | Competition |
| Meditation | Action |
| Mysticism | Evangelism |
| Hidden God (*Deus absconditus*–Kung) | Revealed God (*Deus revelatus*) |
| Completion (Jung) | Perfection |
| Oceanic feeling | Ecstasy of victory |
| Social gospel | Salvation gospel |
| Personalism | Triumphalism |
| Crucifixion as tragedy | Second Coming |
| Grace | Glory |
| Praying in private | Praying in public |
| Praying without ceasing | Praying at events |
| Giving in secret | The United Way |
| *Multum in parvo* (much in little) | Monumentalism |
| Andrew Jackson | Sylvanus Thayer |
| Ralph Waldo Emerson | Andrew Jackson |
| Henry David Thoreau | Ralph Waldo Emerson |
| Charles W. Eliot | Walter Camp |
| Booker T. Washington | Charles W. Eliot |
| Dorothea L. Dix | Leonard Wood |
| Frank Merriwell | Frederic Remington |
| Mark Twain | Theodore Roosevelt |
| Emily Dickinson | Thomas W. Higginson |
| John Muir | Andrew Carnegie |
| Robert M. Hutchins | Amos Alonzo Stagg |

Table 16.1 Symbols of the Shepherd and the Knight, cont'd

| Staff | Sword |
|---|---|
| Jane Addams | Knute Rockne |
| Dwight Moody | Billy Sunday |
| Unknown Soldier | Douglas MacArthur |
| Martin Luther King Jr. | Billy Graham |
| Woody Guthrie | T.S. Eliot |
| Mother Teresa | Margaret Thatcher |
| Jackie Robinson | O.J. Simpson |
| Ralph Nader | Hugh Hefner |
| Will Rogers | Rush Limbaugh |
| Cottage | Castle |
| The Pietà | Venus de Milo |
| Joan Baez | Madonna |
| Truth | Beauty |
| The Muses | Apollo |
| Arts and sciences | Technology/professions |
| Participation | Success |
| Tending | Ruling |
| Conversation | Television |
| Huck Finn | Tom Sawyer |
| Ray Hicks | Ted Turner |
| Memories | Statistics |
| Ritual (Guttmann) | Record |
| Eternity (Arendt) | Immortality |
| Reading the eternities (Thoreau) | Reading the Times |
| Eternal now | Entropy time (clock time) |
| The past as present (Faulkner) | Nostalgia |
| Weather report | Sports report |
| 4-H | Boy Scouts |
| Ripeness is all (Shakespeare) | All is number (Pythagoreans) |
| Flowering | Exploding |
| Transformation | Sublimation (catharsis) |
| Overagainstness | Obedience |
| Sin | Crime |
| "Savior, Like a Shepherd Lead Us" | "Onward Christian Soldiers" |
| Family (Hearn) | Team |
| Enduring (Faulkner) | Prevailing |
| Right brain | Left brain |

gospel, or the social gospel can be envisioned without a deep appreciation of this central metaphor. Knighthood, in contrast, was imposed on Christian doctrine, not organic to it, the founders of chivalry misapplying a few athletic and martial metaphors in the Epistles and transforming the shepherd-warrior David into a companion knight of medieval Crusaders and even Caesar himself.

To be sure, there were false or foolish shepherds aplenty in ancient Israel (Isaiah 56:11; Jeremiah 50:6; Ezekiel 34:1–10; Zechariah 11:8, 15–17) and in Greece. Commenting on book 1 of Plato's *Republic*, Francis M. Cornford writes, "The ruler, from the Homeric king onwards, had been called the shepherd of the people. Thrasymachus truly remarks that these shepherds have commonly been less concerned with the good of their flock than with shearing and butchering them for their own profit and aggrandizement. This behaviour is called 'injustice' because it means getting more than one's fair share" (24). Ezekiel described such bad shepherds in this way: "The diseased have ye not strengthened, neither have ye healed *that which* was sick, neither have ye bound up that which was broken, neither have ye brought again that which was driven away, neither have ye sought that which was lost; but with force and with cruelty have ye ruled them" (34:4).

Ezekiel and other prophets wanted just shepherds instead of unjust ones, and this is precisely the intent of Socrates in *The Republic.* Says Cornford, "The shepherd *qua* shepherd cares for his flock; he receives wages in a different capacity, *qua* wage-earner" (24). Socrates expresses the function of the ideal in this way: "Surely the sole concern of the shepherd's art is to do the best for the charges put under its care; its own best interest is sufficiently provided for, so long as it does not fall short of all that shepherding should imply. On that principle it followed . . . that any kind of authority, in the state or in private life, must, in its character of authority, consider solely what is best for those under its care" (ibid., 27). There is little difference between the visions of the prophet and philosopher in regard to the basic features of a good and just society; only the language differs. In our society neither is valued. All honor goes to the celebrity, the movie star, war hero, politician, athlete, performer.

Ezekiel's words, as well as those of Socrates, proclaim in effect a law of cruelty: The bad shepherd paved the way for the emergence of the bad knight. Admittedly, the good shepherd has some things in common with the good knight, though crucial differences remain, so that the whole orientation of a culture is affected by the choice of models and the relationship between them. The world never needed knights; only better shepherds were required, as Ezekiel and Socrates realized. It could be argued that knights are not just soldiers but scientists as well, bringers of boons for the welfare of humankind, that Isaac Newton, for instance, was a knight. To this argument, if I must dignify it, I will merely say that Newton and others of his class of genius would have been just as great if orders had not been bestowed. The royal defenders of knighthood seek out the gifted not so much to honor genius as to honor themselves and the parasitic form of life they represent and help to inflict upon the rest of the world. Had I the money and influence to do so, I would consider an International Order of the Shepherd and present to genuine heroes of the good and just life garlands of greenery for their contributions to the sanity of the race and the salvation of the planet, to offset the effect of knightly awards by royalty and gold medals by the Olympic Committee. This is not to say that created knights and Olympic victors would automatically be disqualified for shepherd awards. It may be, of course, that to distinguish such heroism with external reward—even one of no public value-would invite corruption. (What would such a garland bring at public auction?) Perhaps virtue is, after all, its own reward.

I will acknowledge that in the adoration of the shepherd ideal it is just as easy to overlook vices as it is in the glorification of the knight, and this is a snare to be avoided. For example, it might be said that Hesiod's *Works and Days* (eighth century B.C.) starts the "shepherd" tradition in literature that stands in opposition to that of the knight represented by the *Iliad,* which glorifies fighting and competition. I use the term *shepherd* in a broad sense to include both the pastoral and Georgic literary traditions and the idea of the Good Shepherd in Judaic and Christian symbolism, all of which convey the idea of a way of life at odds with the life of invidious leisure and waste associated with chivalry and knighthood. The second part of *Works and Days,* according to one careful reader, "is a complete contrast to the culture of the nobility. . . . Instead it prizes the old moral code whose strength is in the slow, changeless wisdom of the farmer and his relentless daily toil" (W. Jaeger 1:62). Rural living, however, is no guarantee of justice, democracy, or utopia, as Hesiod's attitude toward women demonstrates, as argued by Marilyn French in *Beyond Power* (101-2).

One does not have to be a knight to be autocratic and mean, as rural violence amply proves. A routine of shepherd labor can degenerate into barbarism as quickly as the sports of knights. At some point both become mechanistic and deterministic and can only be saved by the common ground between them, the created world of freedom and play. There is no more lasting joy in endless competition to conquer than in incessant laboring to survive. Both brutalize and demean. Joy or meaning lies elsewhere, between the extremes of both. The proclamation of the ideal of the shepherd is no guarantee against abuses; my argument is simply that its virtues have been obscured by the popularization of the ideal of the knight, whose own virtues, as a result, become sordid.

To be sure, there is the problem of who determines the qualifications of shepherds and knights. After all, Stalin, who slaughtered millions of peasants, considered himself a shepherd. While I have referred to Jesus, Thoreau, Muir, and others as shepherds, the categories are not pure (purity is an essential knightly virtue, of course). I agree with Whitman, another of my shepherds, that we can only proceed by "faint clues and indirections" (10). And with Thoreau: "There is such an interval between my ideal and the actual in many instances that I may say I am unborn. . . . Life is not long enough for one success" (*Journal* 2:316).

Implicit in this study of the evolution of American knighthood is the two-heart or two-sword theory on which chivalry and knighthood rested, one heart hard as stone and one soft as wax. What fundamentally is wrong with this ideal? Wherever it has flourished it has symbolized combinations of nationalism, ethnocentrism, elitism, sexism, manliness, and racism. It is based on distrust, the love of arms, and self-righteousness. It needs an eternal enemy, which is why sports with its inherent competition is the natural ally and symbol of the combative posture that knighthood must maintain.

The ideal has its roots in the pagan world, as reflected in Plato's *Republic* in the metaphor of the watchdog who is loyal to his master but fierce toward strangers and enemies. The Christian ethic, based upon the ideal of the Good Shepherd and the Good Samaritan, is almost an opposite ideal, stressing love of neighbor as oneself instead of endless competition, forgiveness instead of revenge and rivalry.

Much closer to the shepherd ideal but not identical with it in matters of defense is that of the citizen-soldier. In 1947, when Harry Truman ordered the head on the American eagle turned around so that it faced the olive branches instead of the arrows, he was in theory at least trying to get the nation, and the world, to think of shepherding rather than fighting. What effect this symbolic reversal had on national policy and world events is open to endless debate. (The CIA was established in the same year.) Still, we must remember that the direction of the eagle's gaze is important. At West Point, the soul of knighthood, the eagle has arrows in both claws, as does the eagle symbolizing the Department of Defense. Knights are eternally suspicious of any talk of doves or olive branches.

If we can imagine for athletics another eagle facing a bunch of books in one direction and a bunch of balls in the other, there is no doubt where its gaze is turned, since "Winning ball games is the only thing," the first commandment of the new religion of sport. Ignored is the wisdom of the ages, but her retribution is subtle. As Faulkner's Ike McCaslin observed, we wreak on ourselves the very revenge nature would wish for us if she could speak in human tongue. Faulkner's Ike, Bayard Sartoris, and black community, as well as Thoreau and John Muir in a different manner, present us with alternative routes to living that are genuinely grounded in Scripture, as opposed to the code of chivalry of Bayard's father and the old southern aristocracy, which was grafted onto the Gospel message, distorting it in the process.

The fact that Christianity adopted chivalric, industrial, corporate, and sporting forms instead of abiding by the principles of social and stewardship gospels, the shepherd model, is perhaps the grand irony in Western Christendom and certainly is its most tragic dimension. It is as if the churches forgot their humble origins, a situation that also occurs in sports. We can be sure that all our stick-and-ball games, which account for most of our sports, originated in the wild with staff and stone. The sword, whether in tournament or war, was a latecomer to the world of competition. Knighthood not only took nature out of Christianity but also took play out of nature.

Knighthood did something else. It codified manners, defined taste and public virtue, and stratified society along aristocratic lines, with the knight himself being the symbolic figure for the young to imitate. In fact, history, in contrast to romance and legend, tells a different story. Near the end of her study, *The Knight in History*, Frances Gies writes this sobering conclusion: "Knights fought for profit and killed without mercy, robbed those whom they should have defended, and violated those they should have respected. Many medieval knights were Rolands, few were Galahads" (207). Barbara Tuchman agrees when in *A Distant Mirror* she writes, "Knights pursued war for glory and practiced it for gain" (84). Almost appropriately, the man who played such a major role in the creation of literary knights for us, Thomas Malory, was an ambivalent figure, purveyor of chivalric ideals on the one hand and quite possibly a thief and a rapist on the other, in prison at the time he created *Morte Darthur* (Altick 79). It is not necessarily a sin or crime to be in jail, as the lives of Saint Paul, Henry David Thoreau, and Martin Luther King Jr. remind us, but Malory may well have been in jail for different reasons. George Lyman Kittredge, the famous Harvard professor, came to Malory's defense but evidence against Malory is strong. "Kittredge was one of the greatest scholars of our time, but his refusal to believe that a man could rape the same woman twice reflects (to put it mildly!) a certain naiveté. The language of the indictment is so specific that the charge cannot possibly be dismissed as a mere legal formula" (82). We are left in the case of Malory, says Altick, "with the incredulous words of Sir Lancelot, in Malory's own version, haunting our ears: 'What,' said Sir Lancelot, 'is he a thief and a knight and a ravyssher of women?' " (ibid.) Say it ain't so, Sir Tom.

The problem pointed to throughout this study is chivalry's two-heart theory, one as hard as stone, the other soft as wax, both hearts constantly on public display. The truth is, however, that one does not easily leave the hard heart on the battlefield or ball field and turn lovingly to the muses, symbols of the arts and sciences.

Instead of leaving his emotions on the ball field or court of strife in a climate where winning is the only thing, the athlete all too often carries his rage and frustration with him wherever he goes. Thus, we have in our time the phenomenon of "Sexual Assault as Spectator Sport" as overwhelmingly documented in chapter 7 of *The Stronger Women Get, the More Men Love Football* (1994) by Maria Burton Nelson. Four studies cited by Nelson point to a higher rate of rape and sexual attacks by athletes than by nonathletes on college campus (129-30).

Nelson also argues that nonsexual assaults against women are common among athletes. In the wake of his celebrated murder trial, the most famous instance of a nonsexual assault is that of football star O.J. Simpson, who "pleaded no contest to beating his wife during a 1988 New Year's Day argument and was placed on two years' probation" (133). Instead of being an exception in this type of behavior, Simpson seems more like one of the guys. Other stars who admitted to nonsexual assaults of one kind or another against their wives include baseball player Darryl Strawberry, boxer Sugar Ray Leonard, and golfer John Daly (ibid.). While personal responsibility for such actions cannot be excused, our knightly system of glorified competition is also partly to blame for our general dilemma. In *The Hundred Yard Lie* Rick Telander writes, 'In my years in the locker room I have heard so much degrading talk of women by male athletes—particularly the use of women as objects to be conquered and dominated . . . that I feel certain the macho attitudes promoted by coaches contribute (perhaps unwittingly) to the athlete's problems in relating to women" (quoted in ibid., 134).

Super Sunday, our high holy day, has apparently for some males become super stimulation day in various parts of the country. Says Nelson, "Women are beaten daily, but Super Bowl Sunday seems particularly dangerous for American women. Though some battered women shelters report no correlation between football and wife beating, shelters in Philadelphia, Los Angeles, and Marian County, California have reported receiving more calls from distraught, bruised, and threatened women that day than on any other day of the year" (ibid., 134-35, see also Fraser and Ryan). It may not be frustration over loss that leads to violence but winning as *well*, as Garland F. White and others write in "The Impact of Professional

Football Games upon Violent Assaults on Women": "An explanation more consistent with the existence of patriarchy and the unequal power of men and women in society is that it is power itself and witnessing the *success of aggression* that triggers assaults on women. Winning reminds violence-prone viewers that power and aggression work and make them feel good. Like the winning team, they dominate over their surroundings and get the desired results with minimum costs" (167, italics added).

Let us consider our problems from this perspective. Adolf Hitler said that he wanted his youth to be "lithe and taut, swift as greyhounds, tough as leather and hard as Krupp steel" (Baynes 1:542). He wanted to see in the eyes of German youth "the gleam of pride and independence of the beast of prey" (Snyder 78). I doubt if there is a football coach in the United States who is an admirer of Hitler, yet who among them is not seeking to develop the same physical qualities in his youth that Hitler sought in German youth? Lean, mean, fast, and as fierce as the beasts of prey for which our teams are often named—these terms describe the types of players and teams coaches and fans long for—in other words, teams of knights with hearts hard as stone for the action at hand. It is a difficult matter indeed for the athlete to turn well from the environment of modern sport with its hype and hoke and will-o-the-wisp values and adopt at a moment's notice the soft heart needed for extended study, dialogue with the muses, and for civilized behavior in general. What is especially puzzling and worrisome today is the way that more and more ministers seem to find less and less difference between the ferocious spirit of sports and the tender fruits of the holy spirit.

The Greeks had a name for the abusive frame of mind growing out of an inflated sense of power. They called it "hubris" and wrote dramas it. In Israel it was known as the "sin of pride," of worshiping false idols, which prophets railed against. It doesn't seem possible that a television set with colorful, colliding images playing upon it could generate arrogance that would lead to physical harm of another, but just as incredulous is the fact that we have bestowed great fame and fortune upon the creators of those images for, in the case of Simpson, skillfully running with one piece of leather up and down a marked field and for running with another through airports as if we should all be in a bigger hurry than we already are. We have forgotten the vast difference between heroes and celebrities. Celebrities succeed but heroes sacrifice. Sacrifice, as Faulkner tried to tell us, is one of the old verities along with courage, honor, pity, and compassion—and honesty, too, we would hope. Old verities are eternal verities, deep and everlasting qualities that, as Emerson said of poetry, existed before time was. Success is cultural, temporal, varying from culture to culture, and often, upon honest reflection, shallow and absurd. That we have made heroes out of sports and film celebrities such as O.J. Simspson, regardless of the outcome of his celebrated trial, is a sure sign that we have lost sight of the painful and hard-earned lessons of our past, that our education is an abysmal failure regardless of the media marvels with which our technologists have provided us, such as the 100-inch television screen widely used in churches around the country for viewing Super Bowl 1995 and muscular testimony at halftime. It appears that bright and shining Zeus, patron God of the sports, has triumphed at last over old, cantankerous Jehovah who sometimes seems to be set over against just about everything, but maybe the battle isn't over yet. Owing to the colossal greed surrounding the major league baseball strike and the violence around the Simpson affair, again regardless of Simpson's guilt or innocence, more questions are being raised about the direction and values of modern sport as seen in this headline to an article by Andrew W. Miracle: "Simpson Case Challenges Faith in Religion of Sports." Amen.

Since antiquity the knight has been a celebrity, always dressed for a show either before or after the battle, quite unlike the shepherd, who shies away from public view. The shepherd plays; the knight displays. For the knight the whole world is a stage and the stadium is a perfect microcosm of that stage. For him, even war is a game with its "theaters of operations." The knight is invariably a performer since the prize he seeks as an athlete or earns as a warrior must receive public approbation commensurate with the deed performed. For the shepherd the earth is a garden not requiring any kind of audience but rather the presence of others in a community of mutual participation in work or play, whose end and process are joyful celebration. All that is needed is a sense of stewardship and a delight in being itself, as the examples of Samuel Johnson, Henry David Thoreau, and Loren Eiseley illustrate. The shepherd plays for the sake of play or re-creation; the knight, for the sake of success measured in money, fame, or glory.

As Robert Pirsig points out, quality depends upon caring (an essential shepherd virtue). On the other hand, the good beauty (*kalo kagathos)* of Greek heroes also appears virtually synonymous with quality, but the Judeo-Christian experience reminds us that the beautiful body may conceal, as well as reveal, a mean soul. This skeptical tradition argues that there is no automatic connection between performance (act) on the field and behavior off it (ethics). Flying into the face of the pagan idea of good beauty is the scriptural teaching of the shepherd, known not for beauty of person but for goodness and that of a kind not to be paraded before others. Good beauty is an urban ideal; the good shepherd a rural one. Both may partake of the divine, of quality, through caring or excellence or both. Good beauty emphasizes "striving for what lies ahead"; the good shepherd stresses enjoyment of what is already here, living peacefully with others and caring for the earth. It is true that Apollo, the god of games, may also turn out to be the god of flocks (Harrison 440). Once off Parnassus or Olympus, he is as apt to go into the countryside as into the city, as likely to dress like a shepherd as a knight or to wear no clothes at all. Apollo is also a magician, full of tricks, which means quite simply, as Jefferson said, that the price of freedom is eternal vigilance, that is, consciousness.

The feature of *arete* or of good beauty that the knight abandoned in the course of history was the mind, which the Greeks never tired of celebrating along with the body. The knight, however, is no philosopher. Whereas the philosopher quests after truth, the knight in history longs for adventure. Having no time for subtleties of thought, the knight thrives on action, playing games or watching them, reliving past wars and preparing for the next ones. The knowledge the knight most honors is technical or practical—how to make money, build an economy, and manufacture the most destructive weapon either for offensive or defensive action. The knight, though, always insists that his action is essentially defensive, even when he is far from home in the countries of other people, sacking cultures in the name of some noble cause, invariably connected to religion.

Because of the praise or money or both heaped upon him, the modern athlete has himself taken on the role of the knight, and modern theology has dutifully provided the justification, as seen, for example, in John T. McNeill's essay "The Christian Athlete in Philippians 3:7–14." The focal passage concludes with the much cited verse that has become the keystone of muscular Christianity: "I press toward the mark for the prize of the high calling of God in Christ Jesus." "What this chapter brings to emphasis," says McNeill, "is the sublimation in Christian experience of the athlete's intense all-out effort" (106). Paul, he says, would have been more excited about the resumption of the Olympic games in 1948 than many of us were, and "on a more spiritual level." Unlike other commentators trying to rationalize the link of modern sports and Christianity, such as Billy Graham, McNeill does understand that Paul is using metaphors. Like Graham, however, he draws the wrong inferences. Metaphors contrast as well as compare, and what Paul with his metaphor of seeking the prize is doing, especially in 1 Corinthians 9:24, is contrasting what one ought to pursue—an eternal, spiritual prize, hence a gift—with what the athlete pursues—a material, temporal prize that may well become a dumb idol. One wonders why promoters of muscular Christianity think these verses more relevant for the wisdom of the athlete than, say, the same numbered verses in the chapter of Philippians following the one quoted by McNeill. Philippians 4:5, for example, contains this: "Let your moderation be known unto all men." This is the philosophy of Benjamin Franklin, *moderation* meaning "forbearance" and "gentleness."

There is even a legitimate theological question as to whether or not the Christian's life or that of anyone else should be the "intense all-out effort" symbolized by the athlete, as McNeill seems to think. There is a language of "blessed assurance" throughout Scripture and Christian orthodoxy that is far less frenetic and fanatic, the injunctions to take no thought for the morrow, dear to John Muir, and to "take time to be holy," to enjoy creation, dear to Thoreau. That some theologians and ministers place an athletic construction upon texts stressing strain and effort tells more about them and their time than it does about scripture, which emphasizes far more a love of nature rather than physical exertion in contests.

"The moral and spiritual possibilities of sports," McNeill says with optimism, "ought not to be overlooked by the world's would-be peacemakers." Certainly the world's politicians, most of whom are knights rather than philosophers and hence ill equipped for the task of peacemaking, have often looked at sports in such a way, singing the praises of the Olympics, summer and winter, every two years, so that now the Olympics are viewed as prime time for religious proselytism. What we forget in discussing these possibilities is that sports are mere instruments or tools and not the generators of values. They reflect values and may perpetuate them, but they do not create them. As they always have, values arise in the human mind and heart, giving sure testimony of a society's attitudes toward learning and stewardship on the one hand and manly action and cultural prizes on the other.

Had I read McNeill's piece in 1948, when I was soaked in a world of high school sports and unexamined moral earnestness, though not of a proselytizing kind, I might have agreed with his observations. Possibly his own perspective has changed since that time. In any event, his theology is well established in schools, government offices, and churches. It is the ecclesiastical underpinning for sportianity and modern knighthood as well.

What do we do about the knight? The knight, especially the professional knight, is our problem. He enjoys neither the earth nor the lingering diversity of life upon it. Now, late in the war-ravaged twentieth century, the knight himself has a problem, as communism, the Russian version of knighthood, has collapsed upon itself, leaving the world with undreamed-of hopes for new possibilities of shepherding. The knight is ailing as never before, and Ted Hughes's poem "The Knight" of the late 1970s seems already prophetic. The knight, he says,

Has conquered. He has surrendered everything.

Now he kneels. He is offering up his victory
And unlacing his steel.

In front of him are the common wild stones of the earth—

The first and last altar
Onto which he lowers his spoils.

And that is right. He has conquered in earth's name.
Committing these trophies

To the small madness of roots, to the mineral stasis
And to rain.

An unearthly cry goes up.
The Universes squabble over him—

Here a bone, there a rag.
His sacrifice is perfect. He reserves nothing.

Skylines tug him apart, winds drink him,
Earth itself unravels him from beneath—

His submission is flawless.

Blueflies lift off his beauty.
Beetles and ants officiate

Pestering him with instructions.
His patience grows only more vast.

His eyes darken bolder in their vigil
As the chapel crumbles.

His spine survives its religion,
The texts molder—

The quaint courtly language
Of wingbones and talons.

And already
Nothing remains of the warrior but his weapons

And his gaze.
Blades, shafts, unstrung bows—and the skull's beauty

Wrapped in the rags of his banner.
He is himself his banner and its rags.

While hour by hour the sun
Strengthens its revelation.
[135–36]

In a poem by the same name, Adrienne Rich sees the knight as
still mounted in metal but in desperate straits, almost imploring,
without asking, for someone to relieve him of his miserable calling.

A knight rides into the noon,
and his helmet points to the sun,
and a thousand splintered suns
are the gaiety of his mail.
The soles of his feet glitter
and his palms flash in reply,
and under his crackling banner
he rides like a ship in sail.

A knight rides into the noon,
and only his eye is living,
a lump of bitter jelly
set in a metal mask,
betraying rags and tatters
that cling to the flesh beneath
and wear his nerves to ribbons
under the radiant casque.

Who will unhorse this rider
and free him from between
the walls of iron, the emblems
crushing his chest with their weight?
Will they defeat him gently,
or leave him hurled on the green,
his rags and wounds still hidden
under the great breastplate?
                    [32–33]

In Hughes's poem the knight disintegrates under the natural forces of wind and sun, but in Rich's he is still alive, though far from well, his "rags and wounds" hidden beneath his radiant armor. Both poems are marvels of insight, but Rich's is closer to our actual dilemma. The knight, though in agony himself, is still on some campaign that he himself does not in the least comprehend, still obsessed by some vague sense of conquest. Rich leads us to understand that just as we cannot ignore the knight, neither can we dispatch him. He may be unhorsed to walk the earth again like a shepherd, but even this must be done by the gentle word of the philosopher or poet. To take arms against him is merely to imitate his ways, and if we replace him in the saddle, we become what he always was, giving victory to all he represents.

It comes at last as a shock to realize that the warped knight is not the other as we would like to think but the wounded creature in each of us, ready to retaliate at a moment's notice and make the whole world pay for outrages against the soul. He is one of us, one of the "sons of God within," to use a phrase of Jung. He is also a type of scapegoat, having proved through glorious futility the deadly limits of agonic striving. Repeatedly the knight has experienced the worst life has to offer, for at his worst he himself is the agent of the hell he creates on earth. His wrath requires periodic explosions but only because it first requires the building up of fury and revenge, a fortifying against the other, like stacking artillery rounds in the magazine of the self. What the knight has not experienced and forever distrusts as an illusion of the devil are the original blessings of the shepherd's life.

Even the knight's grand defenders do the same. The end of history, that is, ideological struggle, says Francis Fukuyama, will be "a very sad time. The struggle for recognition, the willingness to run one's life for a purely abstract goal, the worldwide ideological struggle that called forth daring, courage, imagination, and idealism, will be replaced by economic calculation, the endless solving of technical problems, environmental concerns and the satisfaction of sophisticated consumer demands. In the post-historical period there will be neither art nor philosophy, just the perpetual caretaking of the museum of human history. I can feel in myself, and see in others around me, a powerful nostalgia for the time when history existed" (18). This lament is precisely that of Henry Adams, Frederic Remington, and Theodore Roosevelt at the turn of the last century for the passing of the warrior-artist, that is, the knight. *Götterdäm-merung,* the death of the gods, is always fashionable among elites, and one can never be sure if the knight really is dying or merely suffering a lingering malady.

As Fukuyama's comments imply, the demise of the knight does not necessarily mean the revival of the shepherd but possibly the triumph of the knight's first cousin, the administrator, the wizard of ennui. To die of boredom may be as bad finally as dying in battle, but perhaps there are other options, a life of growing like the vegetable kingdom instead of swelling like bureaucratic officialdom, becoming more conscious through inquiry and even private doubt rather than more unconscious through embrace of public dogma and televised faith, seeking the natural gift of play at least as much as the cultural prizes of sports.

What is required for such change is not annihilation of the other but a change of heart, a turning around. We cannot count on the knight's vaporization through self-immolation before the altar of nature, nor would anything be gained merely by toppling him from his steed or stripping him of his insignia and proclaiming victory. Our choices are not either/or as with traditional knights and evangelists. Even the classic examples are ambiguous and ironic. In the closing scene of *Don Quixote* the dying Don apologizes to friends for his former ways, himself having been unhorsed. "Good gentlemen, congratulate me and rejoice with me upon my no longer being Don Quixote de la Mancha but plain Alonso Quixano, surnamed the Good, on account of his innocence and simplicity of life. I am now an enemy of that whole tribe of heroes of tales of knight-errantry. Now I am aware of my own madness, into which I fell because of reading them, and now I abominate and abhor them" (Cervantes 516).

Quixote's friends are bereaved as much, and rightly so, by his conversion as by the approach of his death.

> "Dear Master," cried Sancho, blubbering, "do not die. Take my advice and live for many more years. The greatest madness a man can be guilty of in this life is to let himself die without being slain by anyone or destroyed by any other weapon than the hands of melancholy. Get up and let us go walking in the fields in shepherd's apparel . . . who knows that behind some bush we may find Lady Dulcinea, disenchanted and pretty to look at. . . .

> "If you take your defeat so much to heart put the blame on me. Say you were vanquished because of my carelessness in not tightening Rosinante's saddle girth. Besides, you must have read in your books of chivalry that it was common for one knight to unhorse another and for him who was beaten today to win tomorrow." [ibid.]

Don Quixote will have no more of such heroics, and after completing his repentance he "gave up the ghost." The notary observed that in "all books of the kind that he had read, no one had died quietly in bed, as a good Christian, like Don Quixote" (ibid., 517). To the reader as well as to his friends, Don Quixote is much more endearing as a foolish knight than he would be as a penitent recluse. Cervantes shows us that the sword of satire cuts two ways. We do not need to throw out everything about knighthood, provided we will at last have the opportunity, but only that which stultified us without our knowing it, a worldly glory that, even if attained, would not satisfy or last. The knight may, indeed must, keep a sense of adventure, but only if it becomes an adventure of growth, a quest for self-knowledge.

In his satire of chivalry Cervantes was not alone but reflected the spirit of genius of his age. If we would ask what are chief among the great contributions of chivalry, one legitimate response would be the ironic raison d'etre of perhaps the three most famous comic characters in history—Don Quixote, Falstaff, and Gargantua. Even the celebrated apologists for chivalry such as Johan Huizinga had finally to admit defeat, as Ernest Becker remarks in effect in *The Structure of Evil*:

> Cervantes could caricature chivalry because it was fair game—it was doomed to fail. It was a mere form that, as Huizinga so well said, constantly ran empty. It tried to realize itself in the world, and succeeded only in showing how utterly false it was. . . . Huizinga goes so far as to say that those who upheld the chivalric ideal were aware of its falsity. But falsity is relative to reality, and not to the dream. The recurrent renascence of ideals, like the bucolic and the chivalric, attests to man's groping for a better vision, an attempt to deprive life of its meanness. If the medieval synthesis was absent, if its fabled collectivism is an exaggeration, the social vision was not. With the decline of chivalry even the dream of the Middle Ages came to an end. Socially, it was succeeded by an epoch of decline, which we call the Renaissance. [216]

Becker is correct in speaking of the Renaissance as a decline, and the decline was moral as well as social. In science, art, and athletics, the Renaissance was a "success," reviving both the science of Greece and its athletic art. On the human side, the period represented the beginning of corporate barbarism and invidious distinction undreamed-of by ancient psychopaths. Its motto could well have been "Liberty for the few (that is, the oligarchy of knights), bondage for the many."

Becker goes on to say that "The Renaissance was less a 'revival' than it was a 'heightening' of currents already well under way–the development of uncontrolled forces: individualism, the complete undermining of any possibility of altruism and community, the fragmentation of art from a social into a personal joy, from a public into a private commodity" (217). "The Renaissance," says Huizinga in *Homo Ludens*, "roused . . . from their slumber" both "the pastoral life and the chivalrous life" to "a new life in literature and public festivity" (180). While, as he claims, the playful can be serious as in art, literature, and festival, it cannot be cruel as it was inevitably in the politics of the age, a chess game of power with peasants, slaves, and Indians as pawns.

Now, in our own times, in our own practices, in our own lives, we are realizing the costs of this "heightening." My only argument with Becker and with Huizinga is that the ideal of chivalry provided the ecclesiastical legitimacy for cruelties in *both* the Middle Ages and the Renaissance, as opposed to restraint, which had been adequately spelled out many times in Scripture, for instance in the First and Second Commandments. These require neither knight, tournament, nor vow, "the three most momentous elements of chivalric life" according to Huizinga (quoted in Becker 216), but incorporation of another set of symbols and attitudes, those related to the shepherd's staff.

The fundamental trouble with *mens sana in comore sano* and the two-sword and two-heart theories is that they have been mere code words for "manliness," meaning that knowledge is required not for the sake of the self but for the sake of adaptation to various forms of knightly nationalism. Hence the terrible debris of the human mind lies in the wake of knighthood, which disdains intellectual inquiry in favor of the drill approach to teaching as well as coaching. Among the flotsam and jetsam in the wake of the grand armada of these manly ideals are the academic majors of college athletes, an ongoing disgrace occurring not because athletes are dumb but because in our system of sports they are merely exploitable and expendable. A mind is a terrible thing to waste unless you are an athlete.

The muscularization of savior figures and religions leads inevitably to a form of tribalism, a "belligerent righteousness" in which "man-made ideals" substitute for "a transcendent reality which should challenge our prejudices" (Armstrong 391). In the case of Christianity, that transformation has a long history in the tradition of knighthood and even in western theology, which Albert Schweitzer tried to warn against in 1906 in The *Quest of the Historical Jesus*. "Jesus of Nazereth will not suffer himself to be modernised. As an historic figure he refuses to be detached from his own time. He has no answer for the question, 'Tell us Thy name in our speech and for our day!' " (312). Instead, Schweitzer concludes, "He comes to us as One unknown, without a name, as of old, by the lake-side." (403).

If there is one lesson this study offers, it is this—that to modernize Jesus is to muscularize Him and the culture of our time, and to muscularize is to militarize, as the long alliance of military drills, exercises, sports, and religion in the United States amply illustrates. Our culture as well as that of other so-called developed countries has become warped in the direction of the sword, so that the knight remains the most visible archetypal model in the world today, either as soldier, athlete, corporate executive, televangelist dressed for success, or all of these at once. Lowly shepherds everywhere are trying to clean up the mess that knights and true believers have made over the face of the planet, but we must remember that we are merely talking about ourselves or distorted sides of our collective self. What is needed is not a flip-flop of interest or values but a balancing that is natural and cultural and, above all, just, which means constant evaluation of the heroic and divine ideal, strength and wisdom, that both beckons and eludes forever.

# Works Cited

Adams, Henry. *The Education of Henry Adams.* Ed. Ernest Samuels. Boston: Houghton, 1973.

——. *Letters of Henry Adams, 1892-1918.* 2 vols. Ed. Worthington Chauncey Ford. 1938. Boston: Houghton, 1969.

——. "The United States in 1800." *Henry Adams: The Education of Henry Adams and Other Selected Writings.* Ed. Edward N. Saveth, 38-164. New York: Washington Square, 1963.

"Admiral Rickover 'Kicks' at Football as Military Aid." *Knoxville News Sentinel* 27 Nov. 1965:6.

Albertson, Ralph. *Fighting without a War: An Account of Military Intervention in North Russia.* New York: Harcourt, 1920.

Alderman, Pat. *The Overmountain Men: Battle of King's Mountain, Cumberland Decade, State of Franklin, Southwest Territory.* Johnson City, Tenn.: Overmountain Press, 1986.

Alexander, Chip. "Wake Forest's Hearn Points Way Toward Reform." *Charlotte News and Observer* 5 Dec. 1989:3C.

Allen, Frederick L. *Since Yesterday: The Nineteen-Thirties in America.* New York: Bantam, 1961.

Allen, Gay Wilson. *Waldo Emerson.* New York: Viking, 1981.

Altick, Richard D. *The Scholar Adventurers.* New York: Free Press, 1966.

Ambrose, Stephen E. *Duty, Honor, Country: A History of West Point.* Baltimore: Johns Hopkins UP, 1966.

Anderson, Charles R. "Thoreau Takes a Pot Shot at *Carolina Sports.*" *Georgia Review* 22 (Fall 1968): 289-99.

Anderson, Lester G., ed. *Land-Grant Universities and Their Continuing Challenge.* East Lansing: Michigan State UP, 1976.

"Are Sports Good for the Soul?" *Newsweek* 11 Jan. 1971: 51-52.

Arendt, Hannah. *The Human Condition.* Chicago: U of Chicago P, 1973.

Armstrong, Karen. *A History of God: The 4,000-Year Quest of Judaism, Christianity, and Islam.* New York: Knopf, 1994.

"Army-Navy Game Here, So Academies Decide." *New York Times* 9 Dec. 1905: 10.

Atkinson, Rick. *The Long Gray Line.* Boston: Houghton, 1989.

Ayers, Edward L. *Vengeance and Justice: Punishment in the Nineteenth-Century American South.* New York: Oxford UP, 1984.

Baker, Chester B. "Muir, John." *World Book Encyclopedia.* 1984 ed.

Baker, William J. *Sports in the Western World.* Urbana: U of Illinois P, 1988.

Baldwin, Alice M. *The New England Clergy and the American Revolution.* Durham, N.C.: Duke UP, 1928.

Ballowe, James, ed. *George Santayana's America: Essays on Literature and Culture.* Urbana: U of Illinois P, 1967.

Barbour, Philip L. *The Three Worlds of Captain John Smith.* Boston: Houghton, 1964.

Barker, Dianne P. *Billy Graham in Big Orange Country: The East Tennessee Crusade, 1970.* Knoxville: Crusade Executive Committee, 1970.

Baughman, Ernest W. *Type and Motif Index of the Folktales of England and North America.* Indiana University Folklore Series, no. 20. The Hague: Mouton, 1966.

Baynes, Norman H. *The Speeches of Adolf Hitler, April 1922-August 1929.* 2 vols. New York: H. Fertig, 1969.

Bebb, Russ. *The Big Orange: A Story of Tennessee Football.* Huntsville, Ala.: Strode, 1974.

Becker, Debbie. "Smiting Foes, Saving Souls at Liberty." *USA Today* 13 Sept. 1989: 1C.

Becker, Ernest. *The Structure of Evil: An Essay on the Unification of the Science of Man.* New York: Free Press, 1968.

Beers, Henry A. *Four Americans: Roosevelt, Hawthorne, Emerson, Whitman.* New Haven, Conn.: Yale UP, 1919.

Bellow, Saul. *Mr. Sammler's Planet.* New York: Knopf, 1970.

Bentley, Eric Russell. *A Century of Hero-Worship.* Philadelphia: Lippincott, 1944.

Bergin, Thomas G. *The Game: The Harvard-Yale Football Rivalry, 1875-1983.* New Haven, Conn.: Yale UP, 1984.

——. "To the Game: Happy Birthday." *Harvard Magazine* 86 (1983): 29-35.

Berkovitch, Sacvan. *The American Jeremiad.* Madison: U of Wisconsin P, 1978.

Berry, Wendell. *What Are People For?* San Francisco: North Point Press, 1966.

Bestic, Alan. *Praise the Lord and Pass the Contribution.* New York: Taplinger, 1971.

Betts, John R. *America's Sporting Heritage, 1850-1950.* Reading, Mass.: Addison-Wesley, 1974.

——. "Home Front, Battle Field, and Sport During the Civil War." *The Research Quarterly* 42, no. 2 (May 1971): 113-32.

——. "Mind and Body in Early American Thought." *Journal of American History* 54, no. 4 (1968): 787-805.

Binfield, Clyde. *George Williams and the Y.M.C.A.: A Study in Victorian Social Attitudes.* London: Heinemann, 1973.

Black, David. "Discipline and Pleasure; or, Sports and the Wild in the Writings of Thomas Wentworth Higginson." *Aethlon: The Journal of Sport Literature* 7, no. 2 (Spring 1991): 1-13.

Blaik, Earl H. "Red," and Tim Cohane. "College Football's Major Abuses." *Look* 24 Nov. 1959: 114-20.

——. "Red Blaik Speaks Out." *Look* 27 Oct. 1959:48-61.

——. *You Have to Pay the Price.* New York: Holt, 1960.

Blair, Walter, Theodore Hernberger, Randall Stewart, and James E. Miller Jr., eds. *The Literature of the United States.* 2 vols. Glenview, Ill.: Scott, Foresman, 1966.

Blay, John S. *The Civil War: A Pictorial Profile.* New York: Bonanza, 1958.

Boles, John B. *The Great Revival, 1787-1805.* Lexington: UP of Kentucky, 1972.

Bolton, Clyde. *Unforgettable Days in Southern Football.* Huntsville, Ala.: Strode, 1974.

Bone, Jamie. "Stand Up for the Right to Pray." *Lewisburg Tribune* 24 Oct. 1991: 4.

Bowers, John. *Stonewall Jackson: A Portrait of a Soldier.* New York: Morrow, 1989.

Boyd, Thomas. *Light-Horse Harry Lee*. New York: Scribner's, 1931.

Boyle, Robert. "The Unreal Ideal: Frank Merriwell." *Sport-Mirror of American Life*. Boston: Little, Brown, 1963.

Bracher, Karl D. *The German Dictatorship: The Origins, Structure, and Effects of National Socialism*. Trans. Jean Steinberg. New York: Praeger, 1970.

Bradford, Gamaliel. *Lee the American*. Boston: Houghton, 1940.

Broderick, James, S.J. *The Origin of the Jesuits*. 1940. Westport, Conn.: Greenwood, 1971.

Broun, Heywood Hale. *Tumultuous Merriment*. New York: Richard Marek, 1979.

Brown, Marion Marsh. *Young Nathan*. Philadelphia: Westminster, 1949.

Brown, Peter. *The Body and Society: Men, Women, and Sexual Renunciation in Early Christianity*. New York: Columbia UP, 1988.

Brown, Robert McAfee. *Religion and Violence: A Primer for White Americans*. Philadelphia: Westminster, 1973.

Brubaker, Bill. "At Navy, Conflicting Mission: School-Sports Rift Revealed by Scandal." *Washington Post* 22 May 1994: A1, 22.

Buckingham, Jamie. *Power for Living*. South Holland, Ill.: DeMoss Foundation, 1983.

Burman, Edward. *The Templars: Knights of God*. Wellingborough, Northamptonshire: Crucible, 1986.

Butler, Jack. *Jujitsu for Christ*. New York: Penguin, 1988.

Cady, Edwin H. *The Big Game: College Sports and American Life*. Knoxville: U of Tennessee P, 1978.

Caillois, Roger. *Man, Play, and Games*. Trans. Meyer Barash. New York: Free Press, 1961.

Calhoun, William Gunn. *Samuel Doak, 1749-1830*. Washington College Academy, Tenn.: Pioneer Printers, 1966.

Campbell, John C. *The Southern Highlander and His Home*. New York: Sage, 1921.

Cappon, Lester J., ed. *The Adams-Jefferson Letters: The Complete Correspondence between Thomas Jefferson and Abigail and John Adams*. Vol. 2. Chapel Hill: U of North Carolina P, 1959.

Carlyle, Thomas. *On Heroes, Hero-Worship, and the Heroic in History*. Ed. Carl Niemeyer. Lincoln: U of Nebraska P, 1966.

"Carnegie, Andrew." *The New Funk and Wagnells Encyclopedia*. 1952.

Carnegie, Andrew. *The Gospel of Wealth and Other Timely Essays*. Ed. Edward C. Kirkland. Cambridge, Mass.: Belknap, 1962.

Carter, Hodding, III. "College Sports Test: Define Oxymoron; Answer: Student-Athlete." *Wall Street Journal* 19 Apr. 1990: A15.

Cartwright, Peter. *Autobiography of Peter Cartwright, the Backwoods Preacher*. Ed. W.P. Strickland. New York, 1857.

Cash, W.J. *The Mind of the South*. New York: Vintage, 1941.

Cavallo, Dominick. *Muscles and Morals: Organized Playgrounds and Urban Reform, 1880-1920*. Philadelphia: U of Pennsylvania P, 1981.

Cawelti, John G. *Apostles of the Self-Made Man*. Chicago: U of Chicago P, 1965.

Cervantes, Miguel de. *Don Quixote*. Trans. Tobias Smollett. London, 1755. New York: Farrar, 1986. [Adapted translation from Karl F. Thompson, ed. *Classics of the Western World*. Vol. 4. New York: Harcourt, 1988.]

Chaudoin, Kimberly E. "Sports Ethics Issues Focus of [Russ] Gough Research, Book." *Lipscomb News* 17, no. 4 (April 1995): 2.

Clark, Thomas D. *The Rampaging Frontier: Manners and Humors of Pioneer Days in the South and the Middle West*. Bloomington: Indiana UP, 1939.

Cleaveland, Catherine. *The Great Revival in the West, 1797-1805*. Chicago: U of Chicago P, 1916.

Coffman, Len. Interview by the author on football and religion under Neyland, 16 Sept. 1987.

Cohen, Daniel. *The Spirit of the Lord: Revivalism in America*. New York: Four Winds, 1975.

Cohen, Ralph. "Part Two: 'Games and Growing Up: A Key to Understanding *Huckleberry Finn*.' " *The Adventures of Huckleberry Finn*, by Mark Twain. Ed. Ralph Cohen. New York: Bantam, 1965. 282-91.

Coleman, Kenneth, and Charles Stephen Gorr, eds. *Dictionary of Georgia Biography*. 2 vols. Athens: U of Georgia P, 1983.

Come, Donald Robert. "The Influence of Princeton on Higher Education in the South before 1825." *William and Mary Quarterly* 3 (Summer 1945): 359-96.

Cornford, Francis MacDonald, trans. *The Republic of Plato*. London: Oxford UP, 1978.

Cox, James M. *Mark Twain: The Fate of Humor*. Princeton, N.J.: Princeton UP, 1966.

Crane, John, and James F. Kielly. *West Point: The Key to America*. New York: Whittlesay House, 1947.

Cronin, Vincent. *Napoleon Bonaparte: An Intimate Biography*. New York: William Morrow, 1972.

Cunningham, Rodger. *Apples on the Flood: The Southern Mountain Experience*. Knoxville: U of Tennessee P, 1987.

d'Aulaire, Per Ola, and Emily. "*Now* What Are They Doing at that Crazy St. John the Divine?" Smithsonian 23, no. 9 (Dec. 1992): 32-45.

Davenport, Frederick Morgan. *Primitive Traits in Religious Revivals: A Study in Mental and Social Education*. New York: Macmillan, 1905.

Davies, John. "It's Baker! . . . Going for Another Touchdown!" *Esquire* 66 (Sept. 1966): 133-35, 171-76.

Davis, Richard B. *Intellectual Life in the Colonial South, 1585-1763*. 3 vols. Knoxville: U of Tennessee P, 1978.

Deford, Frank. "Endorsing Jesus." *Sports Illustrated* 26 Apr. 1976: 54-69.

Dougherty, Nathan W. *Educators and Athletes: The Southeastern Conference, 1894-1972*. Knoxville: U of Tennessee, Dept. of Athletics, 1976.

Doyle, Joseph B. *Frederick William von Steuben and the American Revolution*. 1913. New York: Burt Franklin, 1970.

*Drill and Ceremonies*. Field Manual 22-5. Washington, D.C.: Headquarters, Dept. of the Army, 8 Dec. 1986.

D'Souza, Dinesh. *Falwell Before the Millennium: A Critical Biography*. Chicago: Regnery Gateway, 1984.

Dulles, Foster Rhea. *American Learns to Play: A History of Popular Recreation, 1607-1940*. New York: Peter Smith, 1952.

Dupuy, R. Ernest. *Men of West Point: The First 150 Years of the United States Military Academy*. New York: Sloane, 1951.

Eckhart, Meister. *Meister Eckhart: A Modern Translation*. Ed. Raymond Bernard Blakney. New York: Harper, 1941.

Eddy, Edward Danforth, Jr. *Colleges for Our Land and Time: The Land-*

*Grant Idea in American Education.* 1956. Westport, Conn.: Greenwood, 1973.

Edwards, Harry. *Sociology of Sport.* Homewood, Ill.: Dorsey, 1973.

Eiseley, Loren. *The Unexpected Universe.* New York: Harcourt, 1969.

Eisen, George. "The Concept of Time, Play, and Leisure in Early Protestant Religious Ethic." *Play and Culture* 4, no. 3 (Aug. 1991): 223-36.

Eitzen, D. Stanley, and George H. Sage. *Sociology of North American Sport.* Dubuque, Iowa: William C. Brown, 1989.

Eliot, Ellsworth, Jr. *Yale in the Civil War.* New Haven, Conn.: Yale UP, 1932.

Eliot, Charles W. *Four American Leaders.* 1906. Folcraft, Pa.: Folcraft Library Editions, 1973.

———. *A Turning Point in Higher Education: The Inaugural Address of Charles William Eliot as President of Harvard College, October 19, 1869.* With an introduction by Nathan M. Pusey. Cambridge, Mass.: Harvard UP, 1969.

Ellis, Joseph, and Robert Moore. *School for Soldiers: West Point and the Profession of Arms.* New York: Oxford UP, 1974.

Emerson, Ralph Waldo. *Emerson's Complete Works.* 12 vols. Ed. J.E. Cabot. Boston: Houghton, 1883-93.

———. *Selections from Ralph Waldo Emerson.* Ed. Stephen E. Whicher. Boston: Houghton, 1960.

Erwin, John S. "Captain Myles Standish's Military Role at Plymouth." *Historical Journal of Massachusetts* 13, no. 1 (1985): 1-13.

Faris, John T. *Winning Their Way: Boys Who Learned Self-Help.* New York: Frederick A. Stokes, 1909.

Findlay, James F., Jr. *Dwight L. Moody: American Evangelist, 1837-1899.* Chicago: U of Chicago P, 1969.

Fischer, David Hackett. *Albion's Seed: Four British Folkways in America.* New York: Oxford UP, 1989.

Fisher, L. *God's Voice to the Pro.* Boca Raton, Fla.: Sports World Chaplaincy, 1969.

Fitzgerald, Frances. *Cities on a Hill: A Journey through Contemporary American Culture.* New York: Simon, 1986.

Fitzgerald, Ray. "It's Not Easy to Call Off the Dogs." *Sporting News* 192 (1981): 11.

Fleck, Richard F. "John Muir's Homage to Henry David Thoreau." *Pacific Historian* 29, nos. 2 and 3 (1985): 55-64.

Fleming, Thomas J. *West Point: The Men and the Times of the United States Military Academy.* New York: Morrow, 1969.

Flexner, James Thomas. *George Washington: Anguish and Farewell, 1793-1799.* Vol. 3. Boston: Little, Brown, 1970.

Folmsbee, Stanley J. "East Tennessee University, 1840-1879: Predecessor of the University of Tennessee." *University of Tennessee Record* 62, no. 3 (May 1959): 115-36.

Ford, Henry Jones. *The Scotch-Irish in America.* Princeton, N.J.: Princeton UP, 1915.

Fosdick, Harry Emerson. *The Manhood of the Master.* New York: Association Press, 1913.

Frank, Douglas. *Less Than Conquerors: How Evangelicals Entered the Twentieth Century.* Grand Rapids, Mich.: Eerdmans, 1986.

Fraser, Laura. "Super Bowl Violence Comes Home." *Mother Jones* 12 (Jan. 1987): 15.

French, Marilyn. *Beyond Power: Of Men, Women, and Morals.* New York: Ballantine Books, 1985.

Fuhrmann, Joseph T. *The Life and Times of Tusculum College.* Greeneville, Tenn.: Tusculum College, 1986.

Fukuyama, Francis. "The End of History." *National Interest* (Summer 1989): 3-18.

Galloway, K. Bruce, and Robert Bowie Johnson Jr. *West Point: America's Power Fraternity.* New York: Simon, 1973.

Gardiner, E. Norman. *Athletics of the Ancient World.* London: Oxford UP, 1930.

*The General: The Story of General Robert R. Neyland and the Neyland Scholars Program.* Knoxville: U of Tennessee, 1986. Brochure.

Gies, Frances. *The Knight in History.* New York: Harper and Row, 1984.

Gilbert, Robert W. *Neyland: The Gridiron General.* Savannah: Golden Coast, 1990.

——. "The Tall Man in the Grey Suit." *Tennessee Alumnus* (Summer 1983): 10-14.

Givens, Wendell. *Ninety-Nine Iron: The Season Sewanee Won 5 Games in 6 Days.* Birmingham, Ala.: Seacoast, 1992.

Goldstein, Jeffrey H., ed. *Sports Violence*. New York: Springer-Verlag, 1983.

Groom, Winston. *Forrest Gump*. New York: Berkley, 1988.

Guttman, Allen. *Sports Spectators*. New York: Columbia UP, 1986.

Halberstam, Michael J. "Stover at the Barricades." *American Scholar* 38 (Summer 1969): 470-80.

Hale, Edward E. *If Jesus Came to Boston*. Boston: Lawson and Wolffe, 1895.

Harding, Walter. *A Thoreau Handbook*. New York: New York UP, 1959.

Harrison, Jane Ellen. *Themis: A Study of the Social Origins of Greek Religion*. Cleveland: World, 1927.

Hartwell, Edward Mossey. *Physical Training in American Colleges and Universities*. Circulars of Information of the Bureau of Education, no. 5, 1885. Washington, D.C.: GPO, 1886.

Harvey, Matt. "Super Bowl Sunday Stokes Creative Fires of Clergy Nationwide." *Johnson City Press* 28 Jan. 1995: 7.

Hassrick, Peter H. *Frederic Remington: Paintings, Drawings, and Sculpture in the Amon Carter Museum and the Sid W. Richardson Foundation Collections*. New York: Harry N. Abrams, 1973.

Hawkins, Hugh. *Between Harvard and America: The Educational Leadership of Charles W. Eliot*. New York: Oxford UP, 1972.

Hawthorne, Nathaniel. *The Novels and Tales of Nathaniel Hawthorne*. Ed. Norman Holmes Pearson. New York: Random House, 1937.

Hearn, Thomas K., Jr. "Integrity in Intercollegiate Sports." *NCAA News* 21 July 1993: 4, 8.

Hefley, James C. *Running with God: The New Christian Athletes*. New York: Avon, 1975.

Henderson, Robert W. *Ball, Bat, and Bishop: The Origin of Ball Games*. New York: Rockport, 1947.

——. "*The King's Book of Sports* in England and America." *Bulletin of the New York Public Library* 52, no. 11 (Nov. 1948): 539-53.

Henderson, W.A. *King's Mountain and Its Campaign: An Address on Occasion of the Unveiling of a Monument to Its Heroes*. Greensboro, N.C.: Guilford Battleground Co., 1903.

Hengel, Martin. *Christ and Power*. Trans. Everette R. Kalin. Philadelphia: Fortress, 1973.

Henson, Pamela. "A Study of Children's Play in Appalachia." Georgetown U, 1973. Unpublished manuscript.

Hesiod. *Hesiod and Theognis.* Trans. Dorothy Wender. London: Penguin, 1976.

Heyen, William. "If Jesus Played Football." *America* 157 (24 Oct. 1987): 265.

Higginson, Henry Lee. *Addresses on the Occasion of Presenting the Soldiers' Field and the Harvard Union to Harvard University.* Boston: Merrymount, 1902.

Higginson, Thomas Wentworth. "Saints and Their Bodies." *Atlantic Monthly* 1 (Mar. 1858): 582-95.

Hinsdale, Burke A. *History of the University of Michigan . . . from 1837 to 1906.* Ed. Isaac N. Demmon. Ann Arbor: U of Michigan, 1906.

Hoagland, Edward. "In Praise of John Muir." *On Nature: Nature, Landscape, and Natural History.* Ed. Daniel Halpern, 46-58. San Francisco: North Point, 1987.

Hochfield, George. "The Incompatibility of Athletic and Academic Excellence." *Academe: Bulletin of Association of University Professors* 73, no. 4 (July-Aug. 1987): 39-44.

Hoffman, Shirl. "Evangelicalism and Religious Revival in Sport." *Arete: The Journal of Sport Literature* 2 (Spring 1985): 63-87.

Holmes, Oliver Wendell. "Autocrat of the Breakfast Table." *Atlantic Monthly* 1 no. 7 (May 1858): 871-82.

Hopkins, C. Howard. *History of the Y.M.C.A. in North America.* New York: Association Press, 1951.

Hovey, Kenneth. " 'A Psalm of Life' Reconsidered: The Dialogue of Western Literature and Monologue of Young America." *American Transcendental Quarterly* 1, no. 1 (1987): 3-19.

Hughes, Ted. *New Selected Poems.* New York: Harper, 1982.

Huizinga, Johan. *Homo Ludens: A Study of the Play Element in Culture.* 1944. London: Routledge and Keagan Paul, 1980.

——. *The Waning of the Middle Ages: A Study of the Forms of Life, Thought, and Art in France and the Netherlands in the XIVth and XVth Centuries.* Trans. F. Nopman. London: Arnold, 1939.

Hussey, Christopher. *R. Tait McKenzie: A Sculptor of Youth.* London: Country Life, 1929.

Hutchinson, D.S. *The Virtues of Aristotle.* London: Routledge and Kegan Paul, 1986.

Isaacs, Neil D. "The Losers in College Sports: Student-Athletes Are Pushed Aside by Hucksterism." *Washington Post* 16 Oct. 1977: Outlook section.

"Is Falwell a Cowboy Fan?" *Johnson City Press* 14 Oct. 1987: 37.

Jaeger, Don, and Douglas S. Looney. *Under the Tarnished Dome: How Notre Dame Betrayed Its Ideals for Football Glory.* New York: Simon and Schuster, 1993.

Jaeger, Werner. *Paideia: The Ideals of Greek Culture.* Trans. Gilbert Highet. 3 vols. New York: Oxford UP, 1945.

Jefferson, Thomas. *The Life and Selected Writings of Thomas Jefferson.* Ed. Adrienne Koch and William Peden. New York: Random House, 1944.

Jenkins, Dan. *Semi-Tough.* New York: Signet, 1972.

Johnson, Charles A. *The Frontier Camp Meeting: Religious Harvest Time.* Dallas: Southern Methodist UP, 1955.

Johnson, Owen. *Stover at Yale.* 1912. New York: Macmillan, 1968.

Katz, Fred. *The Glory of Notre Dame.* N.p.: Bartholomew House, 1971.

Kelley, Brooks Mather. *Yale: A History.* New Haven, Conn.: Yale UP, 1974.

Kelly, Pam. "College Honor Codes Remain Treasured, Student Bitterly Learns." *Charlotte Observer* 9 Dec. 1989: 1, 5.

Kershner, James William. "Sylvanus Thayer: A Biography." Ph.D. diss., West Virginia U, 1976.

King, Martin Luther, Jr. *Where Do We Go from Here: Chaos or Community?* Boston: Beacon, 1969.

Kinsolving, Lester. "Exploiting Athletes in Religion Questioned." *Johnson City Press* 12 Jan. 1971: 10.

Kitto, H.D.F. *The Greeks.* New York: Penguin, 1986.

Krout, John A. *Annals of American Sport.* Pageant of America, vol. 15. New Haven, Conn.: Yale UP, 1929.

Krutch, Joseph Wood. Introduction to *Thoreau: Walden and Other Writings.* Ed. Joseph Wood Krutch. New York: Bantam, 1962. 1-23.

Lang, Amy Schrager. " 'The Age of the First Person Singular': Emerson and Antinomianism." *ESQ: A Journal of the American Renaissance* 29 (1983): 171-83.

Laphick, Richard E., and John Brooks Slaughter. *The Rules of the Game: Ethics in College Sport*. New York, Macmillan, 1989.

Lardner, Ring W. "Sport and Play." *Civilization in the United States: An Inquiry by Thirty Americans*. Ed. Harold E. Stearns. New York: Harcourt, 1922. 457-61.

Larned, Charles W. *Education from a Military Viewpoint*. Manlius, N.Y.: St. Johns School, 1908.

Lawrence, Paul R. *Unsportsmanlike Conduct: The National Collegiate Athletic Association and the Business of College Football*. New York: Praeger, 1987.

Lawson, Hal A., and Alan G. Ingham. "Conflicting Ideologies Concerning the University and Intercollegiate Athletics: Harper and Hutchins at Chicago, 1892-1940." *Journal of Sport History* 7, no. 3 (Winter 1980): 37-67.

Lawton, J. Fred. *"Hurry Up" Yost in Story and Song*. Ann Arbor, Mich.: Edwards, 1947.

Leavy, Jane. "The Lord and the Locker Room." *Washington Post* 28 July 1988: D1, 8, 10.

Lenin, V.I. "Leo Tolstoy as a Mirror of the Russian Revolution." *War and Peace: The Maude Translation, Backgrounds and Sources, Essays and Criticism*. Ed. George Gibian, 1392-95. New York: Norton, 1966.

Leonard, George. *The Ultimate Athlete*. New York: Avon, 1977.

Lester, Robin. "Fielding H. Yost." *Biographical Dictionary of America,* Football suppl., 917-18. 1987.

——. "The Rise, Decline, and Fall of Intercollegiate Athletics at the University of Chicago, 1890-1940." Ph.D. diss., U of Chicago, 1974.

Leverenz, David. "The Politics of Emerson's Man-Making Words." *Speaking of Gender*. Ed. Elaine Showalter. New York: Routledge, 1989. 134-62.

Levin, Peter. *A.G. Spalding and the Rise of Baseball: The Promise of American Sport*. New York: Oxford UP, 1985.

Lewis, Sinclair. *Elmer Gantry*. New York: Harcourt, 1927.

——. *Gideon Planish*. New York: Harcourt, 1943.

Leyburn, James. *Folkways on the American Frontier?* New Haven, Conn.: Yale UP, 1936.

Limbaugh, Ronald H. "The Nature of John Muir's Religion." *Pacific Historian* 29, nos. 2 and 3 (1985): 16-27.

Lindsley, Philip. *An Address Delivered in Nashville, January 12, 1825, at the Inauguration of the President of Cumberland College.* Nashville: Joseph Norwell, 1825.

——. "The Cause of Education in Tennessee." Baccalaureate address at the University of Nashville, 4 Oct. 1826. *The Works of Philip Lindsley.* Ed. Le Roy J. Halsey Jr. Vol. 1. Philadelphia: Lippincott, 1866.

Link, Dave. "Rowe Refuses to Speculate on Outcome of Super Bowl." *Johnson City Press Chronicle* 19 Jan. 1985: 21.

Longfellow, Henry Wadsworth. *The Complete Poetical Works of Longfellow.* Boston: Houghton, 1922.

Lopez, Michael. "Transcendental Failure: 'The Palace of Spiritual Power.' " *Emerson: Prospect and Retrospect.* Ed. Joel Porte. Cambridge, Mass.: Harvard UP, 1982. 121-53.

Loud, Grover C. *Evangelized America.* 1928. Freeport, N.Y.: Books for Libraries, 1971.

Lovell, John P. *Neither Athens nor Sparta? The American Service Academies in Transition.* Bloomington: Indiana UP, 1979.

Lucas, John A. "A Prelude to the Rise of American Sport: Antebellum America, 1850-1860." *Quest,* monograph 11 (Dec. 1968): 50-57.

Lucia, Ellis. *Mr. Football: Amos Alonzo Stagg.* South Brunswick: Barnes, 1970.

Lynn, Kenneth S. *The Dream of Success: A Study of the Modern American Imagination.* Boston: Little, Brown, 1955.

Manchester, Herbert. *Four Centuries of American Sport, 1490-1890.* 1931. New York: Blom, 1968.

Mangan, J.A. "Play Up and Play the Game: The Rhetoric of Cohesion, Identity, Patriotism, and Morality." *Athleticism in the Victorian and Edwardian Public School: The Emergence and Consolidation of an Educational Ideology.* Cambridge, Eng.: Cambridge UP, 1981. 179-206.

Mangan, J.A., and James Walvin, eds. *Manliness and Morality: Middle-Class Masculinity in Britain and America, 1800-1940.* Manchester: Manchester UP, 1987.

Marble, Annie Russell. *The Women Who Came in the Mayflower.* Boston: Pilgrim, 1920.

Marburg-Cappel, Erich Geldbach. "The Beginning of German Gymnastics in America." *Journal of Sport History* 3 (Winter 1976): 236-72.

Marden, Orison Swett. *Little Visits with Great Americans*. New York: Success, 1903.

Martin, William. *A Prophet with Honor: The Billy Graham Story*. New York: Morrow, 1992.

Mathisen, James A. "From Muscular Christians to Jocks for Jesus." *Christian Century* 1-8 Jan. 1992: 11-15.

McCullum, John D., and Paul Castner. *We Remember Rockne*. Huntington, Ind.: Our Sunday Visitor, 1975.

McLoughlin, William G., Jr. *Billy Sunday Was His Real Name*. Chicago: U of Chicago P, 1955.

———. *Modern Revivalism: Charles Grandison Finney to Billy Graham*. New York: Ronald, 1959.

McNeill, John T. "The Christian Athlete in Philippians 3:7-14." *Christianity in Crisis: A Christian Journal of Opinion* 2 Aug. 1948: 106-7.

McNeill, William H. *Hutchins' University: A Memoir of the University of Chicago, 1929-1950*. Chicago: U of Chicago P, 1991.

Melville, Herman. *Poems of Herman Melville*. Ed. Douglas Robillard. New Haven, Conn.: College and UP, 1976.

Mencken, H.L. *The Vintage Mencken*. Ed. Alistair Cooke. New York: Vintage, 1955.

Merchant, Larry. *. . . And Every Day You Take Another Bite*. New York: Doubleday, 1971.

Messenger, Christian K. *Sport and the Spirit of Play in American Fiction*. New York: Columbia UP, 1981.

Michener, James. *Sports in America*. Greenwich, Conn.: Fawcett, 1976.

*Military Schools and Courses of Instruction in the Science and Art of War, in France, Prussia, Austria, Russia, Sweden, Switzerland, Sardinia, England, and the United States*. 1872. Ed. Henry Barnard. New York: Greenwood, 1969.

Miller, Greg. "Evangelist, Outdoorsman Brings Crusade to City." *Johnson City Star* 2 Nov. 1988: 2.

Miller, Henry K. "Some Relationships between Humor and Religion in Eighteenth-Century Britain." *Thalia: Studies in Literary Humor* 6 (Spring and Summer 1983): 48-59.

Miracle, Andrew W. "Simpson Case Challenges Faith in Religion of Sports." *Lexington Herald-Leader* 31 July 1994: E2.

Monaghan, Peter. "Religion in a State-College Locker Room: Coach's Fervor Raises Church-State Issue." *Chronicle of Higher Education* 18 Sept. 1985: 37-38.

Monjo, F.N. *A Namesake for Nathan: Being an Account of Captain Nathan Hale by his Twelve-Year-Old Sister, Joanna.* New York: Coward, McCann, and Geoghegan, 1977.

Montell, William Lynwood. *Killings: Folk Justice in the Upper South.* Lexington: The UP of Kentucky, 1986.

Moody, Dwight L. *The Way Home.* Chicago: Bible Institute Colportage Association, 1904.

Morison, Samuel Eliot. *Harvard College in the Seventeenth Century.* 2 vols. Cambridge, Mass.: Harvard UP, 1936.

——. *Three Centuries of Harvard, 1636-1936.* Cambridge, Mass.: Harvard UP, 1936.

Morris, Edward. *The Rise of Theodore Roosevelt.* New York: Coward, McCann, and Geoghegan, 1977.

Mowry, William A. and Arthur May Mowry. *American Heroes and Heroism.* New York: Silver, Burdett, 1903.

Mrozek, Donald J. "The Habit of Victory: The American Military and the Cult of Manliness." Mangan and Walvin .

——. *Sport and American Mentality, 1880-1910.* Knoxville: U of Tennessee P, 1983.

Nash, Willard L. *A Study of the Stated Aims and Purposes of the Departments of Military Sciences and Tactics and Physical Education in the Land-Grant Colleges of the United States.* Teachers College, Columbia University, Contributions to Education, no. 614. New York: Bureau of Publications, Teachers College, Columbia U, 1934.

Nelson, Maria Burton. *The Stronger Women Get, The More Men Love Football: Sexism and the American Culture of Sports.* New York: Harcourt, Brace, 1994.

Newsome, David. *Godliness and Good Learning: Four Studies on a Victorian Ideal.* London: Murray, 1961.

"North Graduation Address Optimistic about Legal Woes." AP story. *Johnson City Press* 3 May 1988: 8.

Nottingham, Elizabeth K. *Methodism and the Frontier: Indiana Proving Ground.* New York: Columbia UP, 1941.

Novak, Michael. *The Joy of Sports: End Zones, Bases, Baskets, Balls, and the Consecration of the American Spirit.* New York: Basic, 1976.

Nye, Russel B. "The Juvenile Approach to American Culture, 1870-1930." *New Voices in American Studies.* Ed. Ray B. Browne, Donald M. Winkleman, and Allen Hayman, 67-82. Lafayette, Ind.: Purdue Research Foundation, 1966.

Nyquist, Ewald B., and Gene R. Hawes. *Making College Count: A College Guide for High School Football Players.* New Brunswick, N.J.: National Football Foundation, 1964.

O'Connor, Flannery. *A Good Man Is Hard to Find and Other Stories.* New York: Harcourt, 1983.

Oriard, Michael. *Reading Football: How the Popular Press Created an American Spectacle.* Chapel Hill: U of North Carolina P, 1993.

——. *Sporting with the Gods: The Rhetoric of Play and Game in American Culture.* Cambridge, Eng.: Cambridge UP, 1991.

Osterweis, Rollin G. *The Myth of the Lost Cause, 1865-1900.* Hamden, Conn.: Shoestring, 1973.

——. *Romanticism and Nationalism in the Old South.* Baton Rouge: Louisiana State UP, 1949.

Otto, Rudolph. *The Idea of the Holy.* Trans. John W. Harvey. New York: Oxford UP, 1958.

Ownby, Ted. *Subduing Satan: Religion, Recreation, and Manhood in the Rural South, 1865-1920.* Chapel Hill: U of North Carolina P, 1990.

Palmer, John McAuley. *General von Steuben.* 1937. Port Washington, N.Y.: Kennikat, 1966.

Pappas, George S. *The Cadet Chapel: United States Military Academy.* Providence: Mowbray, 1987.

——. *The Cadet Chapel: United States Military Academy, West Point, New York.* West Point, N.Y.: Cadet Chapel Parish Council, 1987. Booklet.

Park, Roberta J. "Muscle, Mind, and *Agon:* Intercollegiate Debating and Athletics at Harvard and Yale, 1892-1909." *Journal of Sport History* 14 (Winter 1987): 263-85.

Parker, Dorothy. Review-Preface. *Mein Kampf.* New York: Reynold and Hitchcock, 1939.

Patten, Gilbert [pseud., Burt L. Standish]. *Frank Merriwell at Yale.* Philadelphia: McKay, 1903.

——. *Frank Merriwell's "Father": An Autobiography.* Ed. Harriet Hinsdale and Tony London. Norman: U of Oklahoma P, 1961.

Paxson, Frederick L. "The Rise of Sports." *Mississippi Valley Historical Review* 4 (Sept. 1917): 143-68.

Pearlman, M. "To Make a University Safe for Morality: Football and Military Training from the 1890s through the 1920s." *Canadian Review of American Studies* 12 (Spring 1981): 37-56.

Pelikan, Jaroslav. *Jesus through the Centuries: His Place in the History of Culture.* New Haven, Conn.: Yale UP, 1985.

Pellis, Ken. "Bodybuilders' Macho Ministry." *Charlotte News and Observer* 29 Oct. 1989: 4C.

Perry, Ralph Barton. "The Moral Athlete." Chapter 10 in *Puritanism and Democracy.* New York: Vanguard Press, 1944.

Peters, Samuel. *General History of Connecticut from Its First Settlement under George Fenwick to Its Latest Period of Amity with Great Britain prior to the Revolution.* Freeport, N.Y.: Books for Libraries, 1969.

Phillips, Scott Kershaw. "Primitive Methodist Confrontation with Popular Sports: Case Study of Early Nineteenth-Century Staffordshire." *Sport: Money, Morality, and the Media.* Ed. Richard Cashman and Michael McKernan, 289-303. Kensington: New South Wales UP, 1981.

Phinizy, Coles. "We Know of Knute, Yet Know Him Not." *Sports Illustrated* 10 Sept. 1979: 98-112.

Piehl, Mel. *Breaking Bread: The Catholic Worker and the Origin of Catholic Radicalism in America.* Philadelphia: Temple UP, 1982.

Pierson, George Wilson. *Yale College: An Educational History, 1871-1921.* New Haven, Conn.: Yale UP, 1952.

Pirsig, Robert M. *Zen and the Art of Motorcycle Maintenance: An Inquiry into Values.* New York: Morrow, 1974.

Plagenz, George R. "Rex Humbard Defends His Lifestyle." *Johnson City Press* 15 May 1987: 10.

——. "R-Rated Evangelists?: Father Outraged by Born-Again Proselytizing." *Johnson City Press* 23 Feb. 1984: 9.

Pollock, John. *Billy Graham: The Authorized Biography*. New York: McGraw-Hill, 1966.

——. *Crusades: 20 Years with Billy Graham*. Minneapolis: World Wide, 1964.

Porteus, Thomas C. *Captain Myles Standish: His Lost Lands and Lancashire Connections*. London: Longmans, 1920.

Posey, Walter Brownlow. *The Development of Methodism in the Old Southwest, 1783-1824*. Tuscaloosa, Ala.: Weatherford, 1933.

——. *Frontier Mission: A History of Religion West of the Southern Appalachians to 1861*. Lexington: UP of Kentucky, 1966.

——. *The Presbyterian Church in the Old Southwest, 1778-1838*. Richmond, Va.: John Knox, 1952.

——. *Religious Strife on the Southern Frontier*. Baton Rouge: Louisiana State UP, 1965.

Pound, Ezra. *Ezra Pound: Selected Poems, 1908-1959*. London: Faber and Faber, 1975.

Powel, Harford, Jr. *Walter Camp: The Father of American Football*. 1926. Freeport, NY: Books for Libraries, 1970.

Pratt, Richard Henry. *Battlefield and Classroom: Four Decades with the American Indian, 1867-1904*. Ed. Robert M. Utley. New Haven, Conn.: Yale UP, 1964.

Prebish, Charles S. *Religion and Sport: The Meeting of Sacred and Profane*. Westport, Conn.: Greenwood, 1993.

Prescott, William H. *History of the Conquest of Mexico with a Preliminary View of Ancient Mexican Civilization and the Life of the Conquerors*. 3 vols. Philadelphia: J.P. Lippincott, 1860.

Pridgen, Esther Pritchett. "The Influence of Doctor Samuel Doak upon Education in Early East Tennessee." M.A. thesis, East Tennessee State College, 1952.

"PTL Scrutinizing Preachers Who Buy Air Time on Network." *Johnson City Press* 25 May 1987: 10.

Pusey, Nathan M. Introduction to *A Turning Point in Higher Education: The Inaugural Address of Charles William Eliot as President of Harvard College, October 19, 1869*. Cambridge, Mass.: Harvard UP, 1969, v-xii.

Rader, Benjamin. "The Recapitulation Theory of Play: Motor Behaviour,

Moral Reflexes, and Manly Attitudes in Urban America, 1880-1920."
Mangan and Walvin, 123-34.

Raglan, Lord. *The Hero: A Study in Tradition, Myth, and Drama.* New York:
Vintage, 1956.

Rahner, Hugo. *Man at Play.* New York: Herder and Herder, 1972.

Ramsey, J.G.M. *The Annals of Tennessee to the End of the Eighteenth Century.*
1853. Knoxville: East Tennessee Historical Society, 1967.

Redfield, Robert. *Peasant Society and Culture.* Chicago: U of Chicago P,
1956.

*Reef Points, 1951-1952: The Annual Handbook of the Brigade of Midshipmen.* Ed.
E.B. Richter. Annapolis: U.S. Naval Academy, 1951.

Rice, Grantland. *Only the Brave and Other Poems.* A.S. Barnes, 1941.

Rich, Adrienne. *The Fact of a Doorframe: Poems Selected and New, 1950-1984.*
New York: Norton, 1984.

Roberts, W. Adolphe, and Lowell Brentano, eds. *The Book of the Navy.*
Garden City, N.Y.: Doubleday, 1944.

Robinson, John A.T. *Honest to God.* Philadelphia: Westminster, 1963.

Roosevelt, Theodore. *The Works of Theodore Roosevelt.* National ed. 20 vols.
New York: Scribner's, 1926.

Rourke, Constance. *American Humor: A Study of the National Character.* 1931.
Tallahassee: Florida State UP, 1986.

Royko, Mike. "An Impious Team." *Kingsport Times News* 22 Jan. 1988: 8A.

Ryan, Carmelita S. "The Carlisle Indian Industrial School." Ph.D. diss.,
Georgetown University, 1962.

Ryrie, Charles C., ed. *The Ryrie Study Bible* (King James Version). Chicago:
Moody Press, 1978.

Santayana, George. *George Santayana's America: Essays on Literature and
Culture.* Ed. James Ballowe. Urbana: U of Illinois P, 1967.

Sarano, Jacques. *The Meaning of the Body.* Trans. James H. Farley. Philadelphia: Westminster, 1966.

Savage, Howard S., John T. McGovern, Harold W. Bentley, and Dean F.
Smiley. *The Carnegie Foundation for the Advancement of Teaching: American
College Athletics.* Bulletin no. 23. New York: Carnegie Foundation,
1929.

Saveth, Edward N. Introduction to *Henry Adams: The Education of Henry Adams and Other Selected Writings*. New York: Washington Square, 1963, ix-xvii.

Schlereth, Thomas J. *The University of Notre Dame: A Portrait of Its History and Campus*. Notre Dame, Ind.: U of Notre Dame P, 1976.

Schofield, Edmund A. "John Muir's Yankee Friends and Mentors: The New England Connection." *Pacific Historian* 29, nos. 2 and 3 (1985): 65-89.

Schoor, Gene. *100 Years of Army-Navy Football: A Pictorial History of America's Most Colorful and Competitive Sports Rivalry*. New York: Henry Holt, 1989.

Schorer, Mark. *Sinclair Lewis: An American Life*. New York: McGraw-Hill, 1961.

Schulberg, Bud. "The Chinese Boxes of Muhammad Ali." *The Sporting Spirit: Athletes in Literature and Life*. Ed. Robert J. Higgs and Neil D. Isaacs, 191-200. New York: Harcourt, Brace, Jovanovich, 1977.

Schweitzer, Albert. *The Quest of the Historical Jesus: A Critical Study of Its Progress from Reimarus to Wrede*. 1906. New York: Macmillan, 1964.

Schweitzer, Ivy. *The Work of Self-Representation: Lyric Poetry in Colonial New England*. Chapel Hill: U of North Carolina P, 1991.

Sell, Henry Blackman, and Victor Weybright. *Buffalo Bill and the Wild West*. New York: Oxford UP, 1955.

Shaara, Michael. *The Killer Angels*. New York: Ballantine, 1974.

Shaw, Archer H. *The Lincoln Encyclopedia: The Spoken and Written Words of A. Lincoln Arranged for Ready Reference*. New York: Macmillan, 1950.

Sheehan, George A. *On Running*. New York: Bantam, 1978.

Sheldon, Charles M. *In His Steps: What Would Jesus Do?* Chicago: Advance, 1896.

Shi, David E. *In Search of the Simple Life: American Voices, Past and Present*. Salt Lake City: Peregrine Smith, 1986.

Shirer, Walter. *The Rise and Fall of the Third Reich*. New York: Simon and Schuster, 1960.

Shurter, Robert L. "The Camp Meeting in the Early Life and Literature of the Mid-West." *East Tennessee Historical Society Publications* 5 (1933): 142-49.

Smith, Ronald A. *Sports and Freedom: The Rise of Big-Time College Athletics.* New York: Oxford UP, 1988.

Snyder, Louis L. *Encyclopedia of the Third Reich.* New York: McGraw-Hill, 1976.

Sojka, Greg. "Going 'From Rags to Riches' with Baseball Joe; or, A Pitcher's Progress." *Onward and Upward: Essays on the Self-Made Man.* Ed. Thomas D. Clark, 113-21. Bowling Green, Ohio: Popular Press, 1979.

Speer, Jack Atkeson, ed. *Living Bible Concordance Complete.* Poolesville, Md.: Poolesville Presbyterian Church, 1973.

Sperber, Murray. "College Sports Inc.: The Athletic Department vs. the University." *Kappan Special Report* (Oct. 1990): K1-12.

——. *Shake Down the Thunder: The Creation of Notre Dame Football.* New York: Henry Holt, 1993.

Spong, John Shelby. *Rescuing the Bible from Fundamentalism: A Bishop Rethinks the Meaning of Scripture.* San Francisco: HarperCollins, 1991.

Stagg, Amos Alonzo. *Touchdown.* New York: Longman, Green, 1927.

Stead, William T. *If Christ Came to Chicago: A Plea for the Union of All Who Love in the Service of All Who Suffer!* Chicago, 1894.

Steckbeck, John S. *Fabulous Redmen: The Carlisle Indians and Their Famous Football Teams.* Harrisburg, Pa.: J.H. McFarland, 1951.

Stessel, Edward. "The Soldier and the Scholar: Emerson's Warring Heroes." *Journal of American Studies* 19 (1985): 165-97.

Stokes, Anson Phelps. *Memorials of Eminent Yale Men.* New Haven, Conn.: Yale UP, 1915.

Strong, James, ed. *The Exhaustive Concordance of the Bible.* New York: Abingdon Press, 1967.

Strutt, Joseph. *The Sports and Pastimes of the People of England.* 1801. Ed. J. Charles Cox. New York: Kelley, 1970.

Swan, Gary. "Religion's a Hit in Baseball Clubhouses." *Greeneville Sun* 25 Aug. 1990: B1, 2. AP story.

Sweet, William Warren. *Religion in the Development of American Culture, 1765-1840.* New York: Scribner's, 1952.

——. *Revivalism in America: Its Origin, Growth, and Decline.* New York: Scribner's, 1944.

Synnott, Marcia G. "The 'Big Three' and Harvard-Princeton Football Break, 1926-1934." *Journal of Sport History* 3 (Summer 1976): 188-202.

Taliaferro, H.E. *The Humor of H.E. Taliaferro.* Ed. Raymond C. Craig. Knoxville: The UP, 1987.

Tappan, Zua Marca. *American Hero Stories.* Boston: Houghton Mifflin, 1926.

Taylor, William R. *Cavalier and Yankee: The Old South and American National Character.* Garden City, N.Y.: Doubleday, 1961.

Telander, Rick. *The Hundred Yard Lie: The Corruption of College Football and What We Can Do to Stop It.* New York: Simon, 1989.

Tewksbury, Donald G. *The Founding of American Colleges and Universities before the Civil War.* 1932. New York: Archon, 1965.

Thoreau, Henry David. *The Journal of Henry David Thoreau.* 15 vols. Ed. Bradford Torrey and Francis H. Allen. Salt Lake City: Peregrine Smith, 1984.

——. *The Natural History Essays.* Salt Lake City: Peregrine Smith, 1980.

——. *Thoreau: Walden and Other Writings.* Ed. Joseph Wood Krutch. New York: Bantam, 1962.

Thorp, Willard, ed. *The Lives of Eighteen from Princeton.* 1946. Freeport, N.Y.: Books for Libraries, 1968.

Tillar, Thomas C., Jr., ed. *Tech Triumph: A Pictorial History of Virginia Tech.* Blacksburg: Virginia Tech Alumni Association, 1984.

Toynbee, Arnold. *The Breakdown of Civilization.* Vol. 4 of *A Study of History.* New York: Oxford UP, 1939.

——. "Scotland, Ulster, and Appalachia." *Voices from the Hills: Selected Readings of Southern Appalachia.* Ed. Robert J. Higgs and Ambrose N. Manning. New York: Ungar, 1978.

True, Alfred Charles. *A History of Agricultural Education in the United States.* U.S. Dept. of Agriculture, Miscellaneous Publication no. 36, July 1929. Washington, D.C.: GPO, 1929.

Tuchman, Barbara. *A Distant Mirror: The Calamitous 14th Century.* New York: Knopf, 1978.

Tucker, George. "Plan for NCAA Playoff May Require More Time." *Johnson City Press* 2 June 1994: 17.

Turner, Frederick Jackson. *The Significance of the Frontier in American History.* Ed. Harold P. Simonson. New York: Ungar, 1973.

Turner, Ralph L. "Citius, Altius, Fortius: The Spirit of the Third Reich." Masters thesis, East Tennessee State University, 1988.

Twain, Mark. *The Adventures of Huckleberry Finn.* Ed. Ralph Cohen. New York: Bantam, 1965.

——. *The Complete Short Stories of Mark Twain.* Ed. Charles Neider. New York: Bantam, 1957.

——. *A Connecticut Yankee in King Arthur's Court.* Vol. 9 of *The Works of Mark Twain.* Ed. Bernard L. Stein. Berkeley: U of California P, 1979.

——. *Mark Twain in Eruption: Hitherto Unpublished Pages about Men and Events.* Ed. Bernard Devoto. New York: Capricorn, 1968.

Twombly, Wells. *200 Years of Sport in America.* New York: McGraw-Hill, 1976.

Underwood, John. "A Game Plan for America." *Sport in Contemporary Society: An Anthology.* Ed. D. Stanley Eitzen, 416-30. New York: St. Martin's, 1984.

——. "Student Athletes: The Sham, the Shame." *Sports Illustrated* 19 May 1980: 36-72.

Vance, Scott. "Sport Is a Religion in America, Controversial Professor Argues." *Chronicle of Higher Education* 16 May 1984: 25-27.

Vertinsky, Patricia. "Escape from Freedom: G. Stanley Hall's Totalitarian Views on Female Health and Physical Education." *International Journal of the History of Sport* 5 (May 1988): 69-95.

Vorpahl, Ben Merchant. *My Dear Wister: The Frederic Remington-Owen Wister Letters.* Palo Alto, Calif.: American West, 1972.

Wagenknecht, Edward. *Henry Wadsworth Longfellow: His Poetry and Prose.* New York: Ungar, 1986.

Wagner, Peter. "Puritan Attitudes towards Physical Education in 17th Century New England." *Journal of Sport History* 3 (Summer 1976): 139-51.

Wall, Joseph Frazier. *Andrew Carnegie.* New York: Oxford UP, 1970.

Warren, Joyce W. *The American Narcissus: Individualism and Women in Nineteenth-Century American Fiction.* New Brunswick, N.J.: Rutgers UP, 1984.

Washington, Booker T. *Up from Slavery*. With an introduction by Louis R. Harlan. 1901. New York: Penguin, 1986.

Watson, Richie Devon, Jr. *Yeoman and Cavalier: The Old Southwest's Fictional Road to Rebellion*. Baton Rouge: Louisiana State UP, 1993.

Weatherby, W.J., Jim Ryun, and Anne Ryun. *Chariots of Fire* (based on a screenplay by Colin Weland) *and a Christian Message for Today*. San Francisco: Harper and Row, 1983.

Webb, Bernice Larson. *The Basketball Man: James Naismith*. Lawrence: UP of Kansas, 1973.

Weber, Max. *The Protestant Ethic and the Spirit of Capitalism*. Trans. Talcott Parson. New York: Scribner's, 1958.

Wecter, Dixon. *The Hero in America*. Ann Arbor: U of Michigan P, 1963.

Weeks, James. "Football as a Metaphor for War." *American Heritage* 39 (Sept.-Oct. 1988): 113.

Weisberger, Bernard A. *They Gathered at the River: The Story of the Great Revivalists and Their Impact upon Religion in America*. Boston: Little, Brown, 1958.

Weiss, Paul. *Sports: A Philosophic Inquiry*. Carbondale: Southern Illinois UP, 1969.

Wertenbaker, Thomas Jefferson. *Princeton, 1746-1896*. Princeton, N.J.: Princeton UP, 1946.

White, Garland F., Janet Katz, and Kathryn E. Scarborough. "The Impact of Professional Football Games upon Violent Assaults on Women." *Violence and Victims* 7, no. 2 (1992): 157-71.

White, G. Edward. *The Eastern Establishment and the Western Experience: The West of Frederic Remington, Theodore Roosevelt, and Owen Wister*. New Haven, Conn.: Yale UP, 1968.

White, Lynn, Jr. "The Historical Roots of Our Ecological Crisis." *Science* 155, no. 3767 (10 Mar. 1967): 1203-7.

Whitman, Walt. *Complete Poetry and Selected Prose*. Ed. James E. Miller Jr. Boston: Houghton, 1959.

Wicker, Tom. Review of *A Prophet with Honor: The Billy Graham Story*, by William Martin. *New York Times Book Review* 22 Dec. 1991: 9.

Wilkins, Clarence. *Clarence King: A Biography*. New York: Macmillan, 1958.

Wilkinson, Loren, ed. *Earth Keeping: Christian Stewardship of Natural Resources.* Grand Rapids, Mich.: Eerdmans, 1980.

Willis, Joe D., and Richard G. Wettan. "Religion and Sport in America: The Case for the Sports Bay in the Cathedral Church of Saint John the Divine." *Journal of Sport History* 4, no. 2 (Summer 1977): 189-207.

Wister, Owen. *The Virginian: A Horseman of the Plains.* New York: Harper, 1965.

Wolf, William J. *Thoreau: Mystic, Prophet, Ecologist.* Philadelphia: United Church Press, 1974.

Woolverton, John F. "Philip Lindsley and the Cause of Education in the Old Southwest." *Tennessee Historical Quarterly* 19 (Mar. 1960): 3-32.

Yardley, Jonathan. "Pitcher: The Real Frank Merriwell." *The Ultimate Baseball Book.* Ed. Daniel Okrent and Harris Lewine, 65-80. Boston: Houghton, 1988.

Young, David C. *The Olympic Myth of Greek Amateur Athletics.* Chicago: Ares Publishers, 1984.

Young, Perry Deanne. *God's Bullies: Native Reflections on Preachers and Politics.* New York: Holt, 1982.

Ziegel, Vic, and Lewis Grossberger. *The Non-Runner's Book.* New York: Collier, 1978.

Ziff, Larzer. *The American 1890s: Life and Times of a Lost Generation.* New York: Viking, 1966.

# INDEX

Yankee, 32, 58

Yellow Hand, Chief, 139

yeoman tradition, 58, 96 143

Young Men's Christian Association (YMCA), 53, 57, 71, 148, 189-207, 208, 212-13, 231, 246-50, 260-61, 275, 306; citizenship, 190; fourfold program, 189; manly thinking, 219-20; Moody, 247-50; Morrill Act, 212-13; social gospel, 260; Stagg, 191; Sunday, Billy, 253-54, 260; University of Tennessee, 208; West Point, 231;

World War I, 204-7. *See also* Williams, George

Yost, Fielding H. "Hurry -Up," 191, 196, 215, 239, 262, 263, 264, 270

Young Women's Christian Association (YWCA), 197, 253

Young, Brigham, 3, 263

Youth for Christ, 289

Zechariah, 316

Zeus, 323

Zingis Kan, 80